GEORGE III

MILITARY HISTORY
Wolfe at Quebec
The Destruction of Lord Raglan: A Tragedy of the Crimean War
Corunna
The Battle of Arnhem
Agincourt
Redcoats and Rebels: The War for America, 1770–1781
Cavaliers and Roundheads: The English at War, 1642–1649

HISTORY
King Mob: Lord George Gordon and the Riots of 1780
The Roots of Evil: A Social History of Crime and Punishment
The Court at Windsor: A Domestic History
The Grand Tour
London: The Biography of a City
The Dragon Wakes: China and the West, 1793–1911
The Rise and Fall of the House of Medici
The Great Mutiny: India 1857
The French Revolution
Rome: The Biography of a City
The English: A Social History 1066–1945
Venice: The Biography of a City
Florence: The Biography of a City

BIOGRAPHIES
Benito Mussolini: The Rise and Fall of Il Duce
Garibaldi and His Enemies: The Clash of Arms
and Personalities in the Making of Italy
The Making of Charles Dickens
Charles I
The Personal History of Samuel Johnson
George IV: Prince of Wales, 1762–1811
George IV: Regent and King, 1811–1830
Edward VII: A Portrait
Queen Victoria in Her Letters and Journals
The Virgin Queen: The Personal History of Elizabeth I
Nelson: A Personal History
Wellington: A Personal History

GEORGE III

A PERSONAL HISTORY

Christopher Hibbert

BASIC
BOOKS

A Member of the Perseus Books Group

This book was first published in Great Britain in 1998 by Viking of Penguin Books Ltd.
It is here reprinted by arrangement with Viking.

Copyright © 1998 by Christopher Hibbert.
Published by Basic Books,
A Member of the Perseus Books Group

FIRST U.S. EDITION

A CIP catalog record for this book is available from the Library of Congress.
ISBN 0-465-02723-7

98 99 00 01 02 /RRD 10 9 8 7 6 5 4 3 2 1

For Monica and Denis
with love

CONTENTS

LIST OF ILLUSTRATIONS

Colour

16. *The Apotheosis of Prince Octavius*, 1783, by Benjamin West. (The Royal Collection. © Her Majesty Queen Elizabeth II)

Black and White

17. *William Chambers*, c. 1760, by Sir Joshua Reynolds. (National Portrait Gallery, London)
18. *Design for a Corinthian Temple for Erection at Kew*, c. 1759, by George, Prince of Wales, later George III. (The Royal Collection. © Her Majesty Queen Elizabeth II)
19. *Composite Order*, c. 1759, by George, Prince of Wales, later George III. (The Royal Collection. © Her Majesty Queen Elizabeth II)
20. *Queen Charlotte with her Two Eldest Sons*, c. 1765, by Johann Zoffany. (The Royal Collection. © Her Majesty Queen Elizabeth II)
21. *Mrs Papendiek and Child*, engraving after a sketch by Sir Thomas Lawrence (1769–1830), from Mrs Papendiek's *Court and Private Life in the Time of Queen Charlotte: Being the Journals of Mrs Papendiek, Assistant Keeper of the Wardrobe and Reader to Her Majesty*, Vol. I, edited by her granddaughter Mrs Vernon Delves Broughton (Richard Bentley & Son, London, 1887)
22. *Lord Bute*, 1773, by Sir Joshua Reynolds. (National Portrait Gallery, London)
23. *The Scotch Colossus or the Beautys of ye Bagpipe*, etching, published by M. Darly, 1762. (© The British Museum, London)
24. George III and Family at the Royal Academy, 1789, engraved by Pietro Antonio Martini (1739–97) after Johann-Heinrich Ramberg (1763–1840). (Museum of London)
25. *Henry Fox*, later first Baron Holland, c. 1762, after Sir Joshua Reynolds. (National Portrait Gallery, London)
26. *William Pitt*, later first Earl of Chatham, c. 1754, by William Hoare (1707–99). (National Portrait Gallery, London)
27. Lord North addressing the House of Commons, etching, c. 1782, by an unknown artist. (Fotomas Index)
28. *John Wilkes Esq.*, etching, 1763, by William Hogarth (1697–1764). (Fotomas Index)
29. An equestrian statue of the King being pulled down in Bowling Green, New York, 9 July 1776, engraving by François Xavier Habermann (1721–96). (Fotomas Index)
30. *Lord Rockingham and his Secretary, Edmund Burke*, unfinished portrait, c. 1766, by Sir Joshua Reynolds, (Fitzwilliam Museum, Cambridge)
31. *Augustus Henry Fitzroy*, third Duke of Grafton, c. 1762, by Pompeo Batoni (1708–87). (National Portrait Gallery, London).
32. *George Grenville*, engraving by G. Walker after Sir Joshua Reynolds. (National Portrait Gallery, London)

Colour

55. *George III*, marble bust, 1773, by Joseph Nollekens (1737–1823). (President and Council of The Royal Society)

56. *A View of the Wilderness, with the Alhambra, the Pagoda and the Mosque in Kew Gardens*, oil on copper, c. 1763–5, by William Marlow (1740–1813). (Spink & Son Ltd)

57. *George III and Family at the Spa Well, Cheltenham*, hand-coloured engraving, 1789, by Peter La Cave. (Cheltenham Art Gallery and Museum, Gloucestershire/Bridgeman Art Library, London)

58. *The Republican Attack*, hand-coloured etching, 1795, by an unknown artist (New College, Oxford University/Bridgeman Art Library, London)

59. *The Bishop and his Clarke – or – A Peep into Paradise*, hand-coloured etching, 1809, by an unknown artist. (Bridgeman Art Library, London).

60. *William Pitt the Younger*, 1804–5, by studio of John Hoppner (1758–1810). (National Portrait Gallery, London)

61. *William Pitt Addressing the House of Commons on the French Declaration of War*, 1793, by Karl Anton Hickel (1745–98). (National Portrait Gallery, London)

62. *John Bull Humbugg'd, alias Both Ear'd*, hand-coloured etching, 1794, by Isaac Cruikshank (1756–1816). (© The British Museum, London)

63. *George III Returning from Hunting at Windsor*, hand-coloured etching by M. Dubourg after Robert Pollard (1755–1838). (The Royal Collection. © Her Majesty Queen Elizabeth II)

64. *Temperance Enjoying a Frugal Meal*, hand-coloured etching, 1792, by James Gillray. (© The British Museum, London)

65. *George IV when Prince of Wales*, c. 1798, by Sir William Beechey. (© Royal Academy of Arts, London)

66. *Queen Charlotte*, 1796, by Sir William Beechey. (The Royal Collection. © Her Majesty Queen Elizabeth II)

67. *George III*, engraving, c. 1820, by Charles Turner (1773–1857) after Joseph Lee (1780–1859). (The Royal Collection. © Her Majesty Queen Elizabeth II)

The illustration on page 1 is of George III, from a silhouette cut by his daughter Princess Elizabeth; and, on page 213, of George III, detail from *Church, King and Constitution*, a silhouette, c. 1793, by Charles Rosenberg (1745–1844) (Bridgeman Art Library, London)

The endpapers depict the illuminations at the Queen's House for George III's birthday, 4 June 1783, pen and watercolour on paper by Robert Adam (Agnew & Sons, London/Bridgeman Art Library, London)

AUTHOR'S NOTE

I wish to thank Her Majesty the Queen for gracious permission to make use of material in the Royal Archives, to quote from letters the copyright of which is hers, and to reproduce paintings, watercolours and drawings in the Royal Collection. I am also much indebted to Mr Oliver Everett, Assistant Keeper of the Royal Archives and Librarian at Windsor, for the kind assistance he has given me.

For their help in a variety of other ways I want also to thank Mr Christopher Lloyd, Surveyor of the Queen's Pictures; Professor Linda Colley; Professor Ian R. Christie; Jane Wess, Curator of the George III Collection in the Science Museum; Mary Nixon, Head of Fellowship and Information Services at the Royal Society; Jonathan Marsden, Deputy Surveyor of the Queen's Works of Art; Dr Francis Sheppard; Captain Gordon Fergusson; Margaret Lewendon, Richard Hough, Richard Way, Diana Cook, Bruce Hunter of David Higham Associates; Peter Carson and Eleo Gordon of Penguin UK; Bob Davenport who edited the book, and Lily Richards and Gráinne Kelly who helped me choose the illustrations; and the staffs of the Museum of London, the British Library, the Bodleian Library, the London Library and the Ravenscroft Library, Henley-on-Thames. Hamish Francis and Ursula Hibbert have been good enough to read the proofs; and my wife has made the comprehensive index.

I am grateful to Margaret Morris Cloake for permission to quote extracts from her translation of the journal of Mirza Abul Hassan Khan in *A Persian at the Court of King George*; to Aileen Sutherland Collins for permission to reproduce extracts from the diary of John Aspinwall first published in *Travels in Britain, 1794–1795*; and to Professor Colley for permission to quote from her *Britons: Forging the Nation, 1707–1837*.

Finally I must say how grateful I am to Professor Peter Thomas, biographer of Lord North and John Wilkes, for having read the book in typescript and for having given me much useful advice for its improvement.

CHRISTOPHER HIBBERT

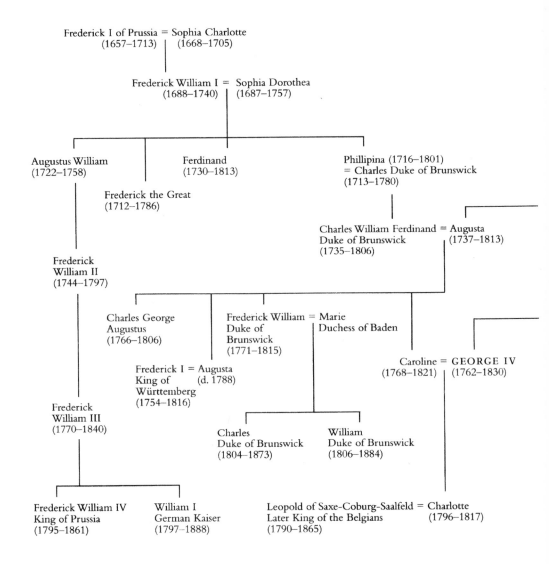

Frederick I of Prussia = Sophia Charlotte
(1657–1713) | (1668–1705)

Frederick William I = Sophia Dorothea
(1688–1740) | (1687–1757)

Augustus William
(1722–1758)

Ferdinand
(1730–1813)

Phillipina (1716–1801)
= Charles Duke of Brunswick
(1713–1780)

Frederick the Great
(1712–1786)

Charles William Ferdinand = Augusta
Duke of Brunswick   (1737–1813)
(1735–1806)

Frederick
William II
(1744–1797)

Charles George
Augustus
(1766–1806)

Frederick William = Marie
Duke of | Duchess of Baden
Brunswick
(1771–1815)

Caroline = GEORGE IV
(1768–1821) | (1762–1830)

Frederick I = Augusta
King of   (d. 1788)
Württemberg
(1754–1816)

Frederick
William III
(1770–1840)

Charles
Duke of Brunswick
(1804–1873)

William
Duke of Brunswick
(1806–1884)

Frederick William IV
King of Prussia
(1795–1861)

William I
German Kaiser
(1797–1888)

Leopold of Saxe-Coburg-Saalfeld = Charlotte
Later King of the Belgians   (1796–1817)
(1790–1865)

The Descendants of George I
(Son of Sophia, Electress of Hanover, granddaughter of James I)
continued overleaf

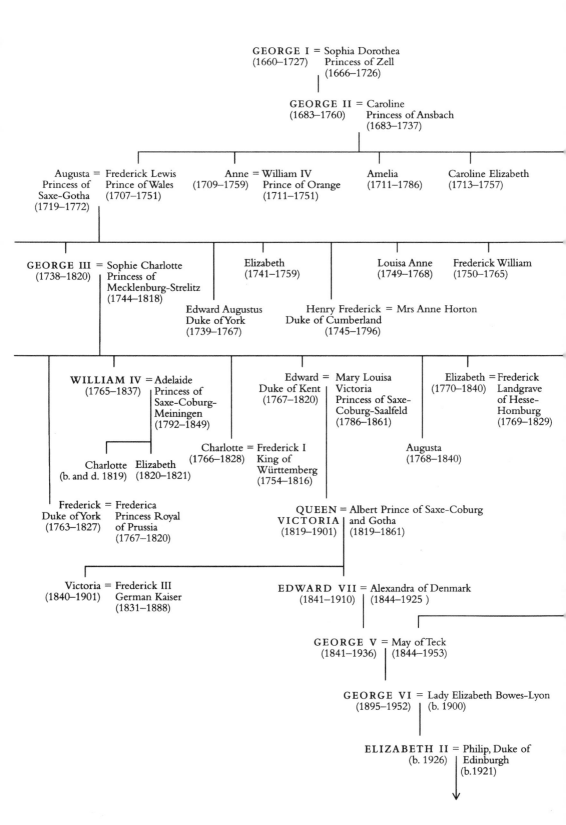

GEORGE I = Sophia Dorothea
(1660–1727)   Princess of Zell
(1666–1726)

GEORGE II = Caroline
(1683–1760)   Princess of Ansbach
(1683–1737)

Augusta = Frederick Lewis   Anne = William IV   Amelia   Caroline Elizabeth
Princess of   Prince of Wales   (1709–1759) Prince of Orange   (1711–1786)   (1713–1757)
Saxe-Gotha   (1707–1751)   (1711–1751)
(1719–1772)

GEORGE III = Sophie Charlotte   Elizabeth   Louisa Anne   Frederick William
(1738–1820)   Princess of   (1741–1759)   (1749–1768)   (1750–1765)
              Mecklenburg-Strelitz
              (1744–1818)
                          Edward Augustus   Henry Frederick = Mrs Anne Horton
                          Duke of York   Duke of Cumberland
                          (1739–1767)   (1745–1796)

WILLIAM IV = Adelaide   Edward = Mary Louisa   Elizabeth = Frederick
(1765–1837) Princess of   Duke of Kent   Victoria   (1770–1840) Landgrave
             Saxe-Coburg-   (1767–1820)   Princess of Saxe-   of Hesse-
             Meiningen   Coburg-Saalfeld   Homburg
             (1792–1849)   (1786–1861)   (1769–1829)

                 Charlotte = Frederick I   Augusta
        Charlotte   Elizabeth   (1766–1828) King of   (1768–1840)
(b. and d. 1819) (1820–1821)   Württemberg
                                          (1754–1816)

Frederick = Frederica   QUEEN = Albert Prince of Saxe-Coburg
Duke of York Princess Royal   VICTORIA   and Gotha
(1763–1827)   of Prussia   (1819–1901) (1819–1861)
              (1767–1820)

Victoria = Frederick III   EDWARD VII = Alexandra of Denmark
(1840–1901) German Kaiser   (1841–1910) (1844–1925)
             (1831–1888)

                          GEORGE V = May of Teck
                          (1841–1936) (1844–1953)

                          GEORGE VI = Lady Elizabeth Bowes-Lyon
                          (1895–1952) (b. 1900)

                          ELIZABETH II = Philip, Duke of
                          (b. 1926)   Edinburgh
                                       (b.1921)

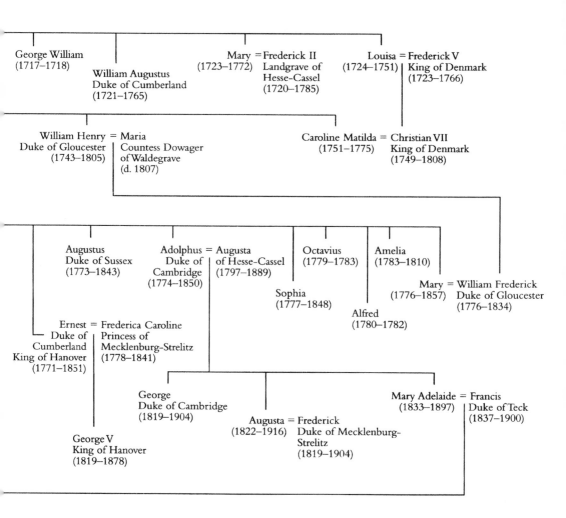

George William
(1717–1718)

William Augustus
Duke of Cumberland
(1721–1765)

Mary = Frederick II
(1723–1772) Landgrave of
Hesse-Cassel
(1720–1785)

Louisa = Frederick V
(1724–1751) King of Denmark
(1723–1766)

William Henry = Maria
Duke of Gloucester | Countess Dowager
(1743–1805) | of Waldegrave
(d. 1807)

Caroline Matilda = Christian VII
(1751–1775) King of Denmark
(1749–1808)

Augustus
Duke of Sussex
(1773–1843)

Adolphus = Augusta
Duke of | of Hesse-Cassel
Cambridge | (1797–1889)
(1774–1850)

Octavius
(1779–1783)

Amelia
(1783–1810)

Sophia
(1777–1848)

Mary = William Frederick
(1776–1857) Duke of Gloucester
(1776–1834)

Alfred
(1780–1782)

Ernest = Frederica Caroline
Duke of | Princess of
Cumberland | Mecklenburg-Strelitz
King of Hanover | (1778–1841)
(1771–1851)

George
Duke of Cambridge
(1819–1904)

Augusta = Frederick
(1822–1916) Duke of Mecklenburg-
Strelitz
(1819–1904)

Mary Adelaide = Francis
(1833–1897) | Duke of Teck
(1837–1900)

George V
King of Hanover
(1819–1878)

The Descendants of George I

PART ONE

'THE GREATEST BEAST IN THE WHOLE WORLD'

*I wish the ground would open this moment and sink
the monster to the lowest hole in hell.*

In the emphatic opinion of Sir Robert Walpole, King George II's First Minister, Frederick, Prince of Wales, was a 'poor, weak, irresolute, false, lying, dishonest, contemptible wretch that nobody loves, that nobody believes, that nobody will trust'. The judgement, harsh, bitter and prejudiced as it was, was widely shared at the King's court, the King himself having little time for his elder son, with whom he had been at odds almost ever since 1728, when the young man had come over to England following his education in Hanover. Indeed, he generally declined to speak to him, ostentatiously ignoring his presence, and referred to him as 'no true son of mine'. He must be 'what in German we call a *Wechselbald*', the King said. 'I do not know if you have a word for it in English – it is not what you call a foundling, but a child put in a cradle instead of another.'

As for Prince Frederick's mother, Queen Caroline, a sensible, intelligent though sarcastic and manipulative woman, the daughter of the Margrave of Brandenburg-Ansbach, she could not bear the sight of the 'avaricious, sordid monster'. He was 'the greatest ass and the greatest liar and the greatest *canaille* and the greatest beast in the whole world', and she heartily wished he were 'out of it'. One day, catching sight of the Prince from her dressing-room window, she exclaimed to Lord Hervey, Vice-Chamberlain of the Household, her face red with fury, 'Look, there he goes – that wretch! – that villain! – I wish the ground would open this moment and sink the monster to the lowest hole in hell.' None of the Prince's five sisters would have gone quite as far as this, but none of them much liked him, while one of them, Princess Amelia, said, 'He was the greatest liar that ever spoke and will put one arm round anybody's neck to kiss them, and then stab them with the other if he can.'

Lord Hervey also held him in the lowest esteem, and found it no irksome task to compose, at the Queen's request, a character sketch of her son which he was asked to read to her time and again. In it he wrote of the young man's 'silly pride', his extreme inconsistency, his avarice and his lewdness – a lewdness 'without vigour'.

Lord Hervey had reason to stress this last-mentioned fault. He was himself a spiteful, malicious, effeminate man with what the Duchess of Marlborough described as 'a painted face and not a tooth in his head'. But he was witty, charming, shrewd and amoral, the father of eight children, and 'a special favourite of women'. The Queen was deeply attached to him, as he was to her. He was, she said, 'her child, her pupil and her charge'. It was as well, she added, that she was so much older than he was, for otherwise she would be talked about 'for this creature'.

Lord Hervey had once been close to the Prince, but he had been replaced as his adviser by George Bubb Dodington, a rich, ingratiating politician of unreliable allegiances. This had rankled with Hervey; but what had annoyed him more was the Prince's having taken over his mistress, the Hon. Anne Vane, daughter of Lord Barnard, and having not only established her in Soho Square, at that time an extremely fashionable quarter, but also given her an allowance of £1,600 a year.

This was not the only woman whom the Prince had kept as a mistress. There was talk of an opera singer and of the daughters of an apothecary and of a man who played in a theatre orchestra. But, so the Prince's Privy Purse confided in Lord Egmont, he talked more 'of his feats in this way' than he actually performed them. Miss Vane told her previous lover, Lord Hervey, that the Prince was 'incredibly ignorant' in sexual matters; and Queen Caroline chose to believe that the baby to which Anne Vane gave birth and which was christened Cornwell Fitz-Frederick was certainly not the offspring of the supposed father, who, in her fixed opinion, was impotent. When the time came for the Prince to marry, his mother let it be known that she had no doubt that the poor bride would have a very thin time of it.

The bride had reason to fear so herself. The Prince had already been prevented by his father from marrying a Prussian cousin, and had subsequently declined to consider a Danish princess, who was reported to be both physically and mentally impaired, before causing consternation at Court by proposing to marry a commoner, Lady Diana Spencer – 'poor dear little Dye' as her father, the Earl of Sunderland, called her. Marriage to Lady Diana also forbidden, the Prince, with no great enthusiasm but with the hope of being granted a handsome settlement, agreed to marry a girl selected for him by his father: Princess Augusta, daughter of the Duke of Saxe-Gotha. She was rather taller than Prince Frederick, by then created Prince of Wales, would have wished, shy, reserved and a little awkward in her movements, by no means pretty, rather prim and rather boring; but it was generally agreed that she was good-natured and unaffected. Lord Waldegrave, a Lord of the Bedchamber and confidant of the King, decided that her behaviour was 'most decent and prudent', while the King himself, 'notwithstanding his aversion to his son, [behaved] to her not only with politeness but with the appearance of affection'.

According to Lord Hervey, the behaviour of the Prince of Wales was less seemly. He noted the Prince's nervous jocularity at dinner after the marriage ceremony in St James's Palace, his 'laughing and winking at some of the servants' as he ate several glasses of jelly, his appearance in the bedchamber after the Queen had undressed the Princess and 'everybody [had] passed through to see them', his absurd 'nightcap which was some inches higher than any grenadier's cap in the whole army'. 'There were various reports on what did and did not pass this night after the company retired,' Hervey added. 'The Queen and Lord Hervey agreed that the bride looked extremely tired with the fatigues of the day, and so well refreshed next morning, that they concluded she had slept very sound.'

When it was announced that the Princess was pregnant the Queen took leave to doubt the fact, or, if it were so, to doubt that the Prince was the father. 'Sir Robert,' she said to Walpole, 'we shall be catched. At her labour I positively will be [present] . . . I will be sure it is her child.'

Prompted by the Queen, the King had insisted that the birth should take place at Hampton Court in the presence of Their Majesties. The Prince was in no mood to obey them. He had hoped that, upon his marriage, at the age of twenty-nine, he would be granted an allowance commensurate with his expenses and his rank. As a bachelor he had received a mere £24,000 a year, with an additional £14,000 from the revenues of the Duchy of Cornwall, whereas his father as Prince of Wales had had £100,000 a year, almost three times as much.* On his marriage his allowance had been increased by a mere £12,000, to £50,000 – in his opinion a paltry sum which would certainly not enable him to settle his mounting debts. The Prince had therefore decided to defy his tight-fisted father by taking his grievance to Parliament. Supported by politicians eager to profit in the next reign, he contrived to have a motion introduced into the House of Commons for an address to the King on the subject of an increased allowance. The motion might well have been carried had not Sir Robert Walpole been so skilful a political manipulator. In the event Walpole ensured that his master, the King, had his way: the motion was defeated by thirty votes in the Commons and by 103 to 40 in the Lords.

Much annoyed by the number of votes in their son's favour, his parents were outraged by his next defiance of their authority, his disobedience of their order to arrange for the birth of the Princess's child to take place at Hampton Court. Determined to defy the King and Queen, the Prince decided to drive his wife away from Hampton Court as soon as the pains of childbirth came on. So, in the middle of the night of 31 July 1737, although no preparations had been made to receive them there, the Prince took his wife off to St James's Palace. The beds were damp, and the mother's only female companion, apart from two of her dressers, was Lady Archibald Hamilton, the mother of ten children, who was widely supposed to have succeeded Miss Vane as the Prince of Wales's mistress. At St James's,

* Because of the fluctuating rate of inflation and other reasons it is not really practicable to translate eighteenth-century sums into present-day equivalents. Multiplying the figures in this book by about sixty should give a very rough guide for the years before 1793. For the years of war between 1793 and 1815 the reader should multiply by about thirty, and thereafter by about forty.

where Lady Archibald rushed about in search of napkins and warm-ing-pans and tablecloths to serve as sheets, the baby, who was to be christened Augusta, was born within an hour of the mother's arrival, 'a little rat of a girl', in Lord Hervey's words, 'about the bigness of a good large toothpick case'. When the Queen was told how small and puny the baby was she seemed to be prepared to concede that it might be Frederick's after all. She drove to St James's to see for herself. 'God bless you, you poor little creature,' she said, looking down upon the child. 'You have come into a disagreeable world.'

Yet for his mother Prince Frederick's behaviour was unforgivable. It was clearly impossible for the family to remain under the same roof any longer. The Prince of Wales was told to vacate his apartments as soon as the Princess had recovered from her labour and not to presume to re-enter any part of the King's palaces. Copies of His Majesty's letter of reproof were sent to British embassies abroad as well as to foreign ambassadors in London, who were told that future visits by them to the Prince and his family would be 'disagreeable to His Majesty'.

The breach between father and son was thus complete; and was even further deepened when the people made it clear where their sympathies lay, the Prince, unlike his father, going out of his way to please them. Crowds cheered the Prince when he drove away from St James's Palace; and audiences rose to applaud him upon his subsequent appearance at the theatre. When it was suggested to the Queen that it might be as well, for the sake of their own standing and that of their Ministry, for Their Majesties to appear less antagonistic to their son and heir, she burst out angrily, 'My God! Popularity always makes me sick; but Fritz's popularity makes me vomit.'

FATHER AND SON

Convince the nation that you are not only an Englishman born and bred,
but that you are also this by inclination.

It was into this splintered family that the King's grandson, the future
King George III, was born on 4 June 1738 at a house in St James's
Square rented from the Duke of Norfolk.★ The child's grandfather,
whose wife had died a few months before, heard of the birth without
pleasure, commenting, with sardonic allusion to the Prince being
Governor of the Saddlers' City Livery Company, that the saddler's
wife had been brought to bed again.

The birth was two months premature, and the likelihood of the
baby's survival was considered so slender that he was baptized that
evening by the Rector of St James's, being given the names George
William Frederick. That he did survive was believed to be due to
his wet-nurse, Mary Smith, the 'fine, healthy, fresh-coloured wife
of a gardener', who was afterwards rewarded by her grateful charge
with the appointment of laundress at Windsor Castle, a position later
occupied by her daughter. Tended so dutifully and fed so well by
Mary Smith, the boy not only survived but prospered; and by the

---

★ Norfolk House, St James's Square, was reconstructed on a larger site by Matthew
Brettingham the Elder for the ninth Duke of Norfolk in 1748–52 at a cost of about
£19,000. Prince Frederick rented its predecessor furnished for four years at £1,200
a year.

Norfolk House was demolished in 1938 and the present house, No. 31, was built
on the site to the design of Messrs Gunton and Gunton. A plaque on the front of
the building records that it was there that General Eisenhower formed the first Allied
Force Headquarters, and planned the North African campaign of 1942 and the
invasion of north-west Europe in 1944. There is no plaque recording the birth of
King George III (*Survey of London*, vol. 29, ed. Francis Sheppard, Part 1 (London,
1960), 187–93).

time he was four years old he was described as contented and fat, 'a lovely child'.

He grew to be a dutiful one. His first tutor was the Rev. Francis Ayscough, a Fellow of Corpus Christi College, Oxford, and Doctor of Divinity, who had been tutor at the University to George Lyttelton, Prince Frederick's Private Secretary, whose sister he married.

Because Lyttelton was one of the Prince of Wales's supporters in the House of Commons who had voted for the motion in favour of an increased allowance, the appointment of his brother-in-law as Prince George's tutor was not welcomed by the widowed King. Nor was it a satisfactory appointment from his charge's point of view, since Ayscough was a rather dull, contentious man less suited to be a teacher than to be the Dean of Bristol, as he afterwards became. Yet Prince George and his brother, Edward, who was just a year younger, did not progress too slowly under his tutelage, learning their lessons well enough. By the time he was eight Prince George could read and write German as well as English, and three years later he was a fair master of both languages.

Prince Frederick took a conscientious interest in his sons' progress, writing to encourage them to enjoy reading, praising their letters in German, chiding them for not writing to him often enough. Unlike his own father, the Prince of Wales was in fact a good parent, encouraging his children – there were in all to be nine of them to survive their infancy: five sons and four daughters – to share his own interests in art and science, in gardening and astronomy, in music, and in amateur theatricals, in which, it was generally admitted, his eldest son did not shine, despite the advice given to him by the witty actor James Quin, who was introduced into the schoolroom to improve the boy's diction and deportment.★

For all his much talked-about frivolity, his visits to fortune-tellers and to bull-baiting at Hockley-in-the-Hole, his rowdy dinner parties

★ Quin did manage to improve Prince George's diction, for whereas his utterance was over-rapid in familiar conversation, he was to succeed in speaking well in public. When told years later how well his former pupil delivered his first speech from the throne, Quin exclaimed proudly, 'Aye, 'twas I that taught the boy to speak' (quoted in Melville, *Farmer George*, i, 223).

and late-night gambling, Prince Frederick's interest in science and the arts was neither superficial nor feigned to strike a contrast with his father, who, without going so far as to express his own father's supposed hatred of 'all bainters and boets', displayed no love for any art other than music. The Prince of Wales greatly admired and warmly commended the works of Jonathan Swift, of the Scottish poet James Thomson – whose ode 'Rule, Britannia', with music by Thomas Arne, was first performed at a fête given by the Prince – and of Alexander Pope, whom he went to see more than once at Twickenham, where, it has to be said, he was not always a welcome visitor: a tedious discourse on poetry once sent his host to sleep.

The Prince himself tried his hand at poetry and fiction; he wrote songs for masques and helped to write a play performed at Drury Lane; he was a patron of the architect and landscape gardener William Kent, who advised him both on the layout of the gardens of Carlton House in Pall Mall, which he had bought in 1732, and on the development of the botanical collection begun by his mother. He took great pleasure in music, playing the cello with some ability, patronizing Italian opera, and giving his encouragement to Giovanni Bononcini, the rival of King George's pensioner George Frideric Handel, and then, after Handel had composed an anthem for his wedding, to Handel himself. Above all, so far as his income allowed, he was a collector of pictures – two fine Van Dycks and two Rubens landscapes in the royal collection were chosen by him as well as paintings by Guido Reni, Jean Baptiste van Loo and Jan Brueghel – and a generous patron of living artists both English and French, earning the gratitude of, among others, Philippe Mercier, who painted him playing his cello with three of his sisters in the garden at Kew, of John Wootton, who portrayed him with a party of friends in Windsor Great Park, and of William Aikman, whose portrait of him with his brother, the Duke of Cumberland, and all five of his sisters is at Chatsworth. As well as pictures, the Prince collected furniture, china and silverware, maps and garden statuary.

Nor was the Prince a dilettante of the arts only. He enjoyed shooting and fishing; he hunted with zest and verve; he was one of the first Englishmen to play cricket, and was appointed Captain of Surrey; and, when at home, he joined in the children's games with enthusiasm.

He wrote to them with sincere affection and concern for their future well-being, expressing the hope that his 'dear children' would never forget their duty but 'always be a blessing to their family and country', and that when George in due course became King he would 'retrieve the glory of the Throne'. 'I shall have no regret never to have worn the Crown,' he told him, 'if you but fill it worthily. Convince the nation that you are not only an Englishman born and bred, but that you are also this by inclination.' It was an injunction that his son was not to forget.

His grandfather, the King, took little interest in Prince George's progress. He nominated him a Knight of the Garter soon after his eleventh birthday; but he did so only because he was advised that he would be harshly criticized by the Opposition for the neglect if he did not do so, and he seems not to have answered Prince George's respectful and dutiful letter of thanks for the honour, merely sending it on to one of his Secretaries of State.

Three months after this letter was written, a new and more satisfactory tutor for Prince George was appointed in place of Dr Ayscough, who remained for the moment in the Prince's Household but in a subordinate capacity, his duties largely limited to religious instruction. His successor was George Lewis Scott, a Fellow of the Royal Society, a barrister and a mathematician – in Lord Brougham's words, 'perhaps the most accomplished of all amateur mathematicians who never gave their works to the world'. He had been born in Hanover, where his father, a friend of the Elector, later King George I, was serving with a diplomatic mission. The statesman George Rose, who knew him well, said he was 'amiable, honourable, temperate' and had one of the sweetest dispositions he ever knew; while the novelist Fanny Burney later found him 'very sociable and facetious. He entertained [her] extremely with droll anecdotes and stories about the Great and about the Court.'

Despite Scott's admitted qualities, surprise was expressed in some quarters that Prince Frederick had placed the Princes in his care, because he was rumoured to have Jacobite sympathies; he had, so it was said, been recommended for the post by the elderly Lord Bolingbroke, now living in retirement at Battersea and working on a new edition of his *Idea of a Patriot King*, a work which was to have a profound effect upon Prince George's own views of his destiny. Certainly Bolingbroke had in the past intrigued with the supporters of the self-styled King James III, the Old Pretender, son of the Stuart King James II. He had been dismissed from his office of Secretary of State by King George I and, fearing impeachment, had fled to France to hold the same office for the Old Pretender. Bolingbroke had since been pardoned; but the protégé of a man with so compromising a Jacobite past was quite likely, it was suggested, to be tarred with a Jacobite brush.

Disregarding such accusations, with the assistance of Prince Frederick and the boys' recently appointed Governor, Lord North, later first Earl of Guilford – 'an amiable, worthy man of no great genius', in Horace Walpole's opinion – Scott set out a rigorous timetable for his two pupils. Had they been sent to Eton, as Lord Bolingbroke had been – even though, as the sons of wealthy parents, they would probably have been sent there with their own tutor – they would have spent hour after hour learning Latin and Greek to the exclusion of much else. Latin and Greek were certainly on the Princes' curriculum; but other subjects were given far more attention than they would have been at a boarding-school.

The boys' working day in the schoolroom was long, beginning at eight o'clock in the morning and ending at bedtime, which was never later than ten o'clock and sometimes nine. There was a break after morning school for an hour before dinner at three. After that lessons were continued until supper at eight. This was their daily round six days a week. On Sundays Dr Ayscough supervised their religious studies between attendances at church.

A later 'plan of instruction' required the boys to 'rise at seven o'clock and translate such parts of Caesar's Commentaries as they had before read till half past eight, at which hour breakfast, allowing until nine as a sufficient hour of time for that purpose'. Then came lessons in geometry, more Latin, 'at eleven, writing, arithmetic, dancing' and French. 'From twelve o'clock riding and other exercises &c. until dinner' at three. 'After dinner the Princes usually visit her Royal Highness the Princess', their mother, where they had lessons in German and history. The hours from seven to nine were spent in 'reading some useful and entertaining books such as Addison's works and particularly his political papers. Every Sunday after breakfast the Bishop of Norwich reads to their Royal Highnesses a practical explanation of the principles of the Christian religion.'

The Princes' routine was unvarying, but their surroundings were not. In 1742, when Prince George was four years old, the family had moved from Norfolk House, St James's Square, to a house, Leicester House, rented from the seventh Earl of Leicester, in Leicester Square, a fashionable development of the 1670s. There a Court was established in rivalry with the King's. Nine years later Prince George and Prince Edward – by then, so Horace Walpole said, 'a very plain boy with strange, loose eyes' – moved with their separate Household into the house next door to Leicester House, Savile House. Their father had houses in the country, too, apart from the White House at Kew. In 1737 he had rented Cliveden, a house which stood and still stands (though rebuilt in the nineteenth century) on a fine site overlooking the Thames near Maidenhead. Soon afterwards he bought another Thames-side property, Park Place at Henley-on-Thames; and, though his debts were still mounting apace, he rented Durdens at Epsom from Lord North for £300 a year.

While paying occasional visits to their father's country houses, Prince George and Prince Edward spent most of their time in London, bound to their regular routine until their lives were suddenly transformed by the death, in 1751, of Prince Frederick at the age of forty-four.

3

THE PUPIL AND HIS TUTORS

No boys were ever brought up in a greater ignorance of evil.

Prince Frederick's death was sudden and quite unexpected. Horace Walpole heard that, some time before, the Prince had been struck by a ball while playing tennis; other reports had it that he had been hit by a cricket ball. However caused, the injury had resulted in an abscess; the Prince had subsequently caught a cold, which may have developed into pleurisy; the abscess burst; and he began to cough painfully.

The cough continued [Walpole reported], the Prince laid his hands upon his stomach and said, *'Je sens le mort!'* The page who held him up felt him shiver, and cried out, 'The Prince is going.' The Princess was at the foot of the bed; she catched up a candle and ran to him, but before she got to the head of the bed, he was dead.

The next day the widow wrote to her father-in-law, the King:

The sorrow which overwhelms me does not make me the less sensible of the great goodness of Your Majesty . . . I throw myself together with my children at your feet. We commend ourselves, Sire, to your paternal love and royal protection.

The King did not pretend to be grieved by his son's death. On receiving the news he turned pale but merely announced *'Il est mort,'* without expressing any words of regret; and at the end of the year he commented bluntly, 'This has been a fatal year to my family. I have lost my eldest son but I was glad of it.' Nonetheless, he was prepared to be as kind as it was in his nature to be to the family his son had left behind. He sent the Princess a sympathetic reply to her letter, and went to see his grandsons, to whom he behaved so

14

benevolently that Prince George, then aged twelve, declared he 'should not be frightened any more with his grandpapa'.★

The Prince was, however, alarmed by the prospect of the future which had opened up for him so unexpectedly soon. When told of his father's death the colour had drained from his face. 'I feel some-thing here,' he had said, laying his hand on his heart, 'just as I did when I saw two workmen fall from the scaffold at Kew.'

Already by the death he had succeeded as Duke of Edinburgh, though not as Duke of Cornwall, as that was a title borne by the eldest son of the sovereign and the King did not care to part with the revenues of the estate which went with it. A month later Prince George was created Prince of Wales and Earl of Chester.

By then discussions had taken place as to the constitution of his Household, it being felt that, since most of its members had been appointed by Prince Frederick without reference to the King, it was necessary to make changes to ensure that the boy was surrounded by men sympathetic towards his grandfather's views and Government.

Lord North was dismissed and replaced as Governor by Lord Harcourt. This was not to prove a wise decision. After school at Westminster, Harcourt had gone on the Grand Tour and had afterwards served in the Army, in which he was to rise to the rank of lieutenant-general. A Lord of the Bedchamber in the King's Household, he had been present in June 1743 at the Battle of Dettingen, where his master, the last British sovereign to command an army in battle, had defeated a French and Bavarian force. Harcourt was later to serve as Ambassador in Paris and as Lord Lieutenant in Dublin before retiring to Nuneham Courtenay, where he was to die, having fallen down a well in an attempt to save the life of a favourite dog. He was very rich and very polite – too polite for the taste of Horace Walpole, no admirer of the 'civil and sheepish' fellow who was 'minute and strict in trifles', unlikely to teach his pupil 'other arts than what he knew himself, hunting and drinking', and 'in need of a governor himself'. Harcourt was, Walpole added,

---

★ Some time later, however, at Hampton Court, the King seems to have lost his temper with the boy and hit him, a blow which was said to have instilled in Prince George that dislike he felt for the place for ever afterwards (Jesse, *Memoirs*, i, 11).

perfectly satisfied that he had done his duty so long as he was unremitting in his exhortation to his royal pupil to turn out his toes.

Lord Harcourt's colleague, as the Prince's Preceptor, was Dr Thomas Hayter, considered to be a 'sensible well-bred man' who had progressed far and fast in the Church through the good offices of the Archbishop of York, whose private chaplain he had been and whose natural son he was widely supposed to be. Hayter had been appointed Sub-Dean of York before he was thirty through the influence of the Duke of Newcastle – the influential Secretary of State in his brother Henry Pelham's Administration – and Bishop of Norwich in 1749. A zealous Whig like Harcourt, he was expected to root out any Jacobite tendencies that might have been implanted in his pupil's mind.

His pupil did not much like him; his correctness verged on pedantry and his discipline on harshness. Prince George was eventually to decide that Dr Hayter was 'an intriguing unworthy man, more fitted to be a Jesuit than an English Bishop', while Prince George's mother 'supposed he was a mighty learned man, but he did not seem very proper to convey knowledge to children'. As for Lord Harcourt, he was to be described by the Prince equally dismissively as 'well-intentioned, but wholly unfit for the situation in which he was placed'.

Neither Harcourt nor Hayter was happy in his post. They had little to do with the Prince's lessons; but they did not get on well with those who had. Dr Ayscough had left; but George Scott was still a member of the Household as Sub-Preceptor; and one of the Duke of Newcastle's most intimate confidants, Andrew Stone, elder brother of the Archbishop of Armagh and a man of 'much reading, great knowledge, and exact memory', was Sub-Governor. Another member of the Prince's Household with close associations with the King's Ministers was James Cresset, the wily secretary of Prince George's mother.

None of these three men, in the shared opinion of Lord Harcourt and Dr Hayter, should have been appointed to their posts: they were inculcating in their pupil's mind most pernicious doctrines of arbitrary rule; they were pressing upon him ideas about the duties and powers of a monarch contained in the writings of that former Jacobite Lord

Bolingbroke; and they had encouraged him to read a book about the Revolution of 1688 written from a distinctly Jacobite viewpoint. Indeed, so Lord Harcourt went so far as to suggest, they were in touch with known Jacobites if not actually Jacobites themselves.

Ministers were not inclined to believe such stories; but they did think it as well to ask the Lord Chancellor and the Archbishop of Canterbury, Thomas Herring, a devoted supporter of the Hanoverian dynasty, to investigate the matter. No evidence to support the charges could be found; and it was generally supposed that they had been brought by the Governor and the Preceptor not so much because either of them believed in the improbable fact of a Jacobite conspiracy as because they considered that their authority in the education of the Prince was being usurped by subordinates who, by the very nature of their duties, saw far more of him than they themselves did and consequently exercised more influence over him.

Since the charges brought by Harcourt and Hayter were rejected by the King and his Ministers, both Governor and Preceptor felt obliged to resign; and there the matter might well have ended but for the appearance of an anonymous pamphlet which maintained that the 'misfortunes which this nation formerly suffered' were owing to princes of the House of Stuart being initiated from an early age 'in maxims of arbitrary power'. Now the nation was again in danger since the King's heir was being instructed not by 'noblemen of the most unblemished honour and prelates of the most distinguished virtue', but by 'low men' who were 'friends and pupils of the late Lord Bolingbroke'.

The author of this pamphlet was Horace Walpole, who not only much disliked Stone but also readily admitted to having 'a propensity to faction' and regarded the stirring up of trouble as 'a lively amusement'.

There were, however, those who took the accusations seriously: stories about Stone's having drunk to the Pretender's health were brought to the attention of Ministers, who advised the King to appoint a committee of the Privy Council to investigate the new charges. The committee concluded that they were all malicious inventions.

Even so there were those who hinted that the background of Lord

Harcourt's successor as Governor might lead to further accusations being made. For this successor, Lord Waldegrave, was the grandson of the Roman Catholic Henry Waldegrave, who had married Henrietta Fitzjames, natural daughter of King James II by Arabella Churchill. He had been raised to the peerage by King James, whose Christian name was bestowed upon his heir. His son, however, became a Protestant, a Lord of the Bedchamber to King George I and a much respected ambassador in Vienna; and there was, in fact, no reason to doubt that the grandson, the Prince's new Governor, was a sincere supporter of the Hanoverian succession. An urbane man about Court, he kept clear of politics. Indeed Henry Pelham told his brother the Duke of Newcastle that Waldegrave was 'totally surrendered to his pleasures'. Certainly he did not in the least wish to take up the appointment he was now offered, did his best to avoid accepting it, and was only too thankful to relinquish it when the time came.

From the beginning, while kindly received by the Household, Lord Waldegrave did not find his pupil as manageable as others had found him before his father's death.

I had been appointed Governor to the Prince of Wales towards the end of the year 1752 [Waldegrave recorded] . . . I found his Royal Highness uncommonly full of Princely Prejudices, contracted in the Nursery, and improved by the society of Bed Chamber women, and Pages of the Back Stairs.

As an entire change of the whole System of Education was impracticable, I soon perceived that the best which could be hoped for was to give him right notions of common things; to instruct him by Conversation, rather than by Books; and sometimes, under the Disguise of amusement, to entice him to the Pursuit of more laborious Studies.

The next Point I labour'd was to preserve Union and Harmony in the Royal Family . . . and [I] was a very useful Apologist whenever His Majesty was displeas'd with his grandson's Shyness or want of attention; and never fail'd to notify even the most minute Circumstance of the young Prince's behaviour which was likely to cause Satisfaction.

The Prince's awkward shyness was undeniably still marked. The King complained that his grandson 'lacked the desire to please'. His dislike of meeting people was exacerbated by his being denied experience of the world beyond his own little court and of people other than those who inhabited it or who were brought up to him when he was required to make appearances – awkward appearances as they turned out to be – at his mother's drawing-rooms. His brother Edward – his mother's favourite, as he had been his father's – was still his only companion of his own age. George Bubb Dodington, his father's former crony, who was now on friendly terms with his mother, considered that the young man ought to be allowed to widen his experience of the world and the manners of society beyond the gates of the royal residences. But the Princess, always ready to lament the manners of that society, remained convinced that this would prove his downfall, since 'young people of quality were so ill educated and so very vicious'. It was better that he should be kept away from such corrupt companions. One of his brothers, the Duke of Gloucester, later commented, 'No boys were ever brought up in a greater ignorance of evil than [George] and myself . . . We retained all our native innocence.'

So, the Prince of Wales continued lonely, 'silent, modest and easily abashed', in the words of Lady Louisa Stuart, a young lady about the Court who was to achieve some distinction as a writer. Yet Lady Louisa recognized that behind the 'awkward hesitation' were fine if only partially developed qualities, 'overlooked in his youth, and indeed not fully appreciated till a much later time'. These were an 'unspeakably kind heart, a genuine manliness of spirit' and 'an innate rectitude'. Lady Louisa might have added that the Prince was rather too priggishly conscious himself of this 'innate rectitude', which in later years he was prone to bring to the attention of occasionally exasperated Ministers.

As the months passed his tutors found that this kind heart and moral virtue were not accompanied by outstanding intelligence, though they did concede that their charge displayed a marked and encouraging curiosity as well as some taste, awakened and encouraged by his father, particularly in music and architecture.

He continued with his Latin studies – not, it seems, with any enthusiasm – as well as his French and German and now a little Greek. He had lessons in algebra and trigonometry as well as arithmetic, geometry and history, ancient and modern. He was taught some physics and chemistry, a little astronomy, 'natural and experimental philosophy', and the science of military fortification. He had a fencing master, as well as a dancing master, a riding master, a drawing master and a music master who taught him to play both the harpsichord and the flute with fair confidence. He also attended a series of lectures by Stephen Demainbray on electricity and astronomy, and demonstrations of electrical phenomena conducted by William Watson at his house in Aldersgate Street.

However, he did not prosper academically as well as his tutors hoped. He later confessed himself that he was 'conscious of [his] own indolence'. It was not so much that he was idle or stupid, however, as that he was lonely, insecure and unhappy, worried about the future, finding it difficult to concentrate, saying what he had to say, as he admitted, not with spirit but 'blushing and afraid'. Yet, inhibited as he was, it was noted that he was 'capable of great resentment where his dignity [was] trenched upon' and that, as Lord Waldegrave commented, his anger when displeased did not 'break out with Heat or violence but he became Sullen & Silent', and retired to his closet 'not to compose his Mind by Study or Contemplation, but merely to indulge the melancholy Enjoyment of his own ill Humour'. 'Even when the Fit is ended,' Waldegrave added, 'unfavorable Symptoms very frequently return, which indicate that on certain occasions his R:H: has too correct a Memory.'

He has a kind of unhappiness in his Temper, which, if it not be conquer'd before it has taken too deep a Root will be a damp to all his Pleasures and a Source of frequent Anxiety [this astute assessment continued] . . . He is strictly honest, but wants that frank and open Behaviour which makes Honesty appear amiable . . . His religion is free from all Hipocrisy but not of the most charitable sort: he has rather too much attention to the sins of his Neighbour. He has spirit but not of the active kind; and does not want Resolution, but it is mixed with too much obstinacy. He has great command of his Passions and will seldom do wrong, except when he mistakes wrong for right . . . Too great Attention to money seems to be his Capital Failing. However he is always just, and sometimes charitable . . .

Upon the whole, he has some Qualities of a great Prince, many of a good one, none which are essentially bad; and I am thoroughly convinc'd that hereafter when Time shall have worn away those Specks & Blemishes which sully the brightest Characters, & from which no man is totally exempt, He will be number'd amongst those patriot Kings, under whose Government, the People have enjoy'd the greatest Happiness.

The boy's mother, who was as ready as himself to condemn 'the sins of his Neighbour', while she showed him scant affection, took a close interest in his lessons and let it be known that she was none too satisfied with the progress her son was making. Not long before his fifteenth birthday, when she herself was no more than thirty-three, she said she wished the Prince of Wales was 'a little more forward and less childish for his age'. She had received a very scanty education herself; and since the death of her husband – to whom she had surrendered her own unremarkable personality to his belief that her main purpose in life was to bear his children – she had shown herself determined that her sons should not be so deprived. She was not at all sure that Lord Waldegrave was the right man to ensure that her sons were profiting as much from their admittedly wide-ranging education as they should. Governors, were, after all, 'a sort of pageant', men 'of quality for show'; and, while she had welcomed Waldegrave at first and made him feel 'almost a Favorite' – he was 'very well bred, very complaisant and attentive &c. and the children liked him extremely' – this early confidence in him did not last. Nor did the boys' initial respect. Indeed, the Prince of Wales, who had cause to believe that Waldegrave was responsible for spreading stories about his mother's sexual misbehaviour, was eventually to decide that his Governor was 'a depraved, worthless' man wholly unfitted for the post to which his grandfather had appointed him.

By the time this verdict was expressed the Prince of Wales had fallen under the influence of a man whom he was to regard in a very different light from that in which he had come to see his Governor, and to whom he was to become obsessively devoted.

4

THE 'DEAREST FRIEND'

I will with the greatest tenderness be yours till death separates us.

John Stuart, Earl of Bute, was the third Earl, having succeeded to the title at the age of nine on the death of his father in 1723. After leaving Eton he had occasionally attended debates in Parliament but did not speak there; and, having married Mary Wortley Montagu – daughter of a rich Yorkshire landowner, Edward Wortley Montagu, and of his wife, Lady Mary, the witty letter writer and erstwhile friend of Alexander Pope – Bute had spent most of the next nine years in Scotland, on the island of Bute, studying agriculture and botany and dabbling in architecture. On his return to London he had conceived a passion for amateur theatricals, unusual in a man of such pedantic learning, and had become an intimate friend of Prince Frederick, whom he had met at Egham races in the royal tent, to which he had been summoned for a game of whist during a rainstorm. Prince Frederick had appointed him one of his Lords of the Bed-chamber, and on the Prince's death he had been asked by the widowed Princess Augusta to remain at Court as Groom of the Stole.

He was a handsome man with 'the best legs in London', of wide-ranging interests, knowing a little about an astonishing variety of subjects, and more than most of his contemporaries about science and the classification of plants: he was the author of the nine-volume *Botanical Tables containing the Different Familys of British Plants* of which he had twelve copies printed at a total cost of £12,000. While his manner in society was inclined to be haughty and silent or pompously magisterial, he was polite and easy among his friends, though Lord Chesterfield said that 'he never looked at those he spoke to or who spoke to him'. Horace Walpole, who had been at Eton with him, regarded him as 'a man of taste and science' and believed 'his intentions were good'; he wished sincerely 'to blend and unite all parties'. William Warburton, the Bishop of Gloucester, also later commended his good intentions. 'Lord Bute,' Warburton was to say, 'is a very fit man to be Prime Minister of England. First he is a Scotchman; secondly he is the King's friend; and thirdly he is an honest man.'

Princess Augusta was said to be in love with him and, most improbably, to be his mistress. Indeed, Walpole, who had been led to believe this by his friend Lord Waldegrave, declared that he had no more doubt of their being lovers than if he had stumbled across them *in flagrante delicto* – and this despite the fact that Bute was perfectly content in his marriage to a fond and charming wife, the mother of his eleven children, and Princess Augusta, though certainly lonely and delighting in his company, was as renowned for her moral probity as she was for what Lord Shelburne called her propensity for 'dissimulation and intrigue'.* Yet Bute was the kind of man – didactic, humourless and moralizing – whom gossip-mongers delight in slandering, the more particularly in his case because, in a mistaken and unsuccessful attempt to 'keep tongues from wagging', he visited the Princess by way of the back stairs. He also aroused slanderous gossip when he took a house near the Princess's at Kew, where he played a large part in planning the gardens.

Lord Waldegrave, who, to be sure, would not have been expected or disposed to speak highly of Bute anyway, described the 'extraordinary appearance of wisdom, both in his look and manner of speaking: whether the subject be serious or trifling, he is equally pompous, slow and sententious'. He was 'not contented with being wise but

---

* Sir John Pringle, the distinguished Scottish physician who attended various members of the Royal Family from 1749 and was created a baronet by the King in 1766, told James Boswell in 1772 that, while the Princess Dowager of Wales 'would go down to posterity as having managed all the affairs of this nation till her death, and [as having] been concerned in a criminal intercourse with Lord Bute', he 'knew for certain' that, in fact, she had for these many years taken no share in politics and never had any 'improper connection with Lord Bute'. It would, he added, 'not be proper for him to mention them; but his situation about the Royal Family gave him an opportunity of knowing circumstances that made it certain that the Princess was altogether free of both these concerns' (G. Scott and F. A. Pottle, eds., *Private Papers of James Boswell from Malahide Castle*, vol. 9, 34–5; quoted in Waldegrave, *Memoirs*, 77–8).

would be thought a polite scholar and man of great erudition [but has] the misfortune never to succeed except with those exceeding ignorant . . . The late Prince of Wales used frequently to say that Bute was a fine showy man, who would make an excellent Embassador in a Court where there was no Business.'

Lord Shelburne, with whom Bute was to have close political relations, was equally caustic in his summation of his character:

He read a great deal but it was chiefly out of the way books of science and pompous poetry . . . [He had] a great deal of superficial knowledge . . . chiefly upon matters of natural philosophy, mines, fossils, a smattering of mechanics, a little metaphysics and a very false taste in everything . . . He was always upon stilts, never natural except now and then upon the subject of women . . . He was rash and timid, accustomed to ask advice of different persons, but had not sagacity to distinguish and digest, with a perpetual apprehension of being governed, which made him, when he followed any advice, always add something of his own . . . which sometimes took away the little good that was in it or changed the whole nature of it . . . He excelled as far as I could observe in managing the interior of a court, and had an abundant share of art and hypocrisy.

It was certainly true that Bute managed the Court with much artfulness. In the spring of 1756 the King proposed that a new establishment should be created for his grandson the Prince of Wales, who was to come of age that summer. In this new Household, which was to be set up at St James's Palace with an allowance of £40,000 a year, Lord Waldegrave, so it was suggested, should hold the most important office of Groom of the Stole. When this proposition was put to the Prince, he, so it was generally supposed, turned to Bute for advice and then wrote to object to leaving Savile House on the grounds that his mother, still living at Leicester House, would be grieved to lose him as a neighbour. At the same time Waldegrave was told it would save much embarrassment if he were to resign. With 'much hesitation and confusion' the Prince proposed that the head of his new establishment must be a man in whom he could confide and that, 'unless he was gratified in this particular, he should consider all those who were placed about him as his enemies'. Waldegrave did not trouble to hide the offence which this statement provoked; and the Prince, more embarrassed than ever, 'said little, and went immediately to his Mother, to give an Account of what had pass'd'. The Princess, having consulted Bute, summoned Waldegrave to apologize to him on her son's behalf.

[The Princess told Lord Waldegrave that her son] had said more than he really intended [according to Waldegrave's account given in his *Memoirs*]: that he had a great Regard for me, did not like new Faces, and was very desirous I should continue in his service. But that he had a very particular Esteem for the Earl of Bute, and had set his heart upon making him Groom of the Stole: that being Master of the Horse was equally honourable and if I would accept that Employment every thing might be made easy, and the King and her Son would both be satisfied. The Prince who was present assented to every thing she said, but enter'd no farther into the conversation.

Waldegrave declined the offer of being appointed Master of the Horse as well as a pension on the Irish establishment which was later offered him, though he later agreed to accept a profitable tellership in the Exchequer.

The King grumpily gave way, acceding to the appointment of Lord Bute as Groom of the Stole and to the Prince's Household remaining at Savile House. When the Prince was told of his grandfather's decision he was 'extremely pleased'. 'What! Has the King granted me both my requests?' he exclaimed. 'He has always been extremely good to me. If ever I have offended him I am extremely sorry for it. It was not my own act or my own doing . . .' He seemed on the point of saying more in his excitement; but checked himself in time and mentioned neither Bute's name nor that of his mother.

Everyone knew, though, that Bute and Princess Augusta had prompted him throughout the negotiations, and that Bute, with the Princess's warm approval and encouragement, was assuming the role of father to her son. He was kind to the young man, patient with his gaucheries, prepared to listen to his confidences, to encourage him in his lessons, to imbue him with Whig principles and a high regard for the Revolution of 1688 and the British constitution, to widen his interests, and to offer him that affection which had in the past been so fitfully shown him.

Lord Waldegrave had concluded that the Prince's 'parts, though not excellent, will be found very tolerable if they are properly exercised', and it was the intention of Bute, at once wily, ambitious and sincerely attached to the boy, to ensure that they were exercised to the full. He encouraged his pupil to study the histories and constitutions of his own and other countries and to draw what lessons from them he could, and to turn his mind to subjects which his contemporaries would certainly not have been required to study at Oxford or Cambridge – to agriculture, for instance, to international trade and, under the guidance of William Chambers, who was working for his mother at Kew, to the arts of drawing and architecture. Above all, the Prince was encouraged to write essays on the theme of regal power and constitutional monarchy, reflecting adversely upon the despotism of the Stuarts and, with Whiggish enthusiasm, praising the victory of William III over the Roman Catholic James II, and the triumphs of a people who would 'never refuse anything to a sovereign who they know will be the defender of their liberties'.

As the devoted pupil of Bute, whose 'holsome' guidance he sought in his every predicament and whose views and opinions he adopted as his own, the Prince strongly condemned his former 'incomprehensible indolence' and promised to do all he could to throw it off. As anxious to please Bute as any loving dutiful son might be to please his father, he assured him in letters at once self-critical, adulatory, even passionate and on occasions priggish, 'I will exactly follow your advice, without which I shall inevitably sink', 'What a pretty pickle I should be in on a future day if I had not your sagacious counsels', 'I am young and inexperienced and want advice. I trust in your friendship which will assist me in all difficulties', 'I will more and more show to the world the great friendship I have for [you]', 'I have often heard you say you don't think I shall have the same friendship for you when I am married as I now have. I shall never change in that, nor will I bear to be in the least deprived of your company', 'I daily find what a treasure you are to me', 'I will with the greatest tenderness be yours till death separates us.'

Constantly he confessed to his faults and inadequacies and promised to do all he could to reform and improve himself:

I am resolved in myself to take the resolute part, to act the man in everything, to repeat whatever I am to say with spirit and not blushing and afraid as I have hitherto . . . I will employ all my time upon business, and will be able for the future to give you an account of everything I read . . . You shall find me make such progress in the summer, that shall give you hopes, that with the continuation of your advice, I may turn out as you wish . . . I beg you will be persuaded that I will constantly reflect whether what I am doing is worthy of one who is to mount the Throne, and who owes everything to his friend. I will by my behaviour show that I know if I in the least deviate from what here I promise and declare, I shall lose the greatest of stakes, my Crown, and what I esteem far beyond that, my friend . . .

He assured his so greatly admired and beloved mentor that he considered his – Bute's – integrity and abilities greatly superior to those of any of the country's politicians and that, the longer he lived, the more he realized how little trust could be reposed in most other men in public life, who were 'intent on their own private interests instead of [those], of the public'. 'You are,' the Prince told him, 'the only man with whom one's reputation and honour can with safety be entrusted.' As for the King's present Ministers, they were, as Bute had encouraged him to believe, faithless scoundrels, almost to a man. The Duke of Newcastle, the fussy, nervous nominal head of the Government which William Pitt was so galvanically running, was a 'knave'; Pitt himself was 'a snake in the grass'; the 'old man' – the King, openly living with his German mistress after the Queen's death – made him ashamed of being his grandson.* It could not be denied that the Administration was prosecuting the war against the French which had broken out in 1756 with notable success, but at such an inordinate cost that the national debt was soaring. When he became King of his 'much loved country', he, with Lord Bute's help, would 'restore her to her ancient state of liberty', make her famous again 'for being the residence of true piety and virtue', and, not least, 'free her from her present load of debts'. In the meantime he could not fully share in the general pleasure occasioned by the British victories over the French in that *annus mirabilis*, 1759. A year later, when Montreal was captured following General Wolfe's daring assault upon Quebec, he wished his 'dearest friend joy of this success; but at the same time [he could not] help feeling that every such thing

---

* Commenting upon the worsening relations between the King and the Prince of Wales, and the customary hostility between Hanoverian rulers and their heirs, Lord Chesterfield observed, 'There is nothing new under the sun, nor under the grandson either' (Chesterfield, *Letters*, ii, 72).

raised those I have no reason to love'. For this was Pitt's war and these were Pitt's triumphs, and Pitt was no friend of his own dearest friend, Lord Bute; and, with Canada conquered, British troops would be sent into the continent of Europe to protect the King's beloved Hanover and the country would be drawn ever deeper into debt.

In November 1759, five months after his twenty-first birthday, the Prince of Wales took his seat in the House of Lords. Yet he was far from content to remain a mere member of that less than glorious assembly. His younger brother, Prince Edward, who had become a popular figure in London society, had been allowed to serve on an expedition to St Malo. Encouraged by Bute, who saw a means of causing difficulties for the Government, he wrote to the King seeking 'an opportunity of convincing the world that I am neither unworthy of my high situation nor of the blood that fills my veins'. He ardently requested a chance 'to support with dignity the post of danger', which he esteemed 'the post of honour'.

His letter remained unanswered for a week while the King, Newcastle and other Ministers considered how to respond to it. 'The King and those he has consulted have treated [me] with less regard than they would have dared to have done any Member of Parliament,' the Prince expostulated to Bute in his impatience. Bute went to see Pitt, who was understanding; but the non-committal reply which Pitt helped to compose for the King to send to his grandson was considered quite unacceptable by its recipient, who complained to Bute that its 'shuffling' evasions were 'unworthy of a British monarch'. As for Pitt, he had the 'blackest of hearts'; he was the most dishonourable of men; he would never be able to 'bear to see him in any future ministry'.

Bute once more called on Pitt, who did what he could to help, suggesting that the Prince might be allowed to act as a kind of apprentice aide-de-camp to the Commander-in-Chief, Lord Ligonier, who would be more than willing to act as his military instructor.

The King was at first extremely irritable when this proposition was hesitantly put to him by the Duke of Newcastle, then grudgingly

28

agreed to think about it – a concession which meant that nothing would be done. The Prince, exasperated that Edward had been allowed to serve abroad while he was kept at home 'like a girl', poured out his resentment in a letter of by now familiar complaint about the King to Lord Bute: 'He had long shown a want of regard both of you, my dearest friend, and consequently of myself.'

The Prince now decided to seek an audience of the King himself. This was not a success: he was embarrassed; his grandfather was dismissive; and, in his disappointment and frustration, the Prince became petulant and refractory. 'Slights and indignities are daily laid upon me from people from whom I might have expected a different conduct,' he complained. 'It is therefore impossible for me to bear them any longer. Some public mark must be given of my disapproving it.'

He thought he saw an opportunity to give this 'public mark' when Lord George Sackville, the youngest and favourite son of the Duke of Dorset, incurred the King's displeasure by failing to obey an order of his superior, Prince Ferdinand of Brunswick, at the Battle of Minden. He had been dismissed the service and 'adjudged to be unfit to serve his Majesty in any capacity whatever'. The Prince decided to take Sackville's part; and he would have invited him to one of his levees had not Bute persuaded him that this would do more harm than good to his cause, since Sackville's plight had not aroused much sympathy.

There was another reason for the Prince's discontent. 'You have often accused me of being grave and thoughtful,' he told Lord Bute:

It is entirely owing to a daily increasing admiration of the fair sex which I am attempting with all the philosophy and resolution I am capable of to keep under . . . How strong a tussle there is between the boiling youth of twenty-one years and prudence. The last I hope will ever keep the upper hand, indeed, if I can weather it out a few years, marriage will put a stop to this combat in my breast.★

★ There is a persistent legend that 'the boiling youth' had already had an affair with a young Quaker woman, Hannah Lightfoot. Mary Lucy Pendered in *The Fair Quaker, Hannah Lightfoot* accepted the story that the affair had resulted in three children. In a later book, *The Lovely Quaker*, John Lindsay asserted that a marriage had taken

Marriage was already in his mind. He had fallen in love with Lady Sarah Lennox, the extremely attractive eleventh child and youngest daughter of the second Duke of Richmond, a great-granddaughter of King Charles II, whom he had first seen at Court when she was not yet fifteen, some six years younger than himself. He had immediately been 'struck with admiration' for this beautiful creature. She was, he said, 'everything I can form to myself lovely'. She was 'the most charming of her sex'.

He was far from alone in his admiration. Henry Fox – that notoriously corrupt politician who had made a fortune as Paymaster General and had secretly married Lady Sarah's eldest sister, Lady Georgina Carolina – thought his sister-in-law 'different from & prettyer than any other girl [he] ever saw'. 'Her beauty is not easily described,' he wrote, 'otherwise than by saying she had the finest complexion, most beautiful hair, with a sprightly and fine air, a pretty mouth, remarkably fine teeth & excess of bloom in her cheeks.' Horace Walpole, who saw her act in a play, *Jane Shore*, at Holland House when she was seventeen, was equally captivated. She and Fox's niece, Lady Susan Fox-Strangways, 'were delightful and acted with so much nature that they appeared the very things they represented. Lady Sarah was more beautiful than you can conceive . . . [Dressed] in white with her hair about her ears, and on the ground, no Magdalen of Correggio was half so lovely and expressive.'

The Prince spoke of his love to Lord Bute. Developing a characteristic obsession, he could not sleep for thinking of her; he had heard

---

place and that one of the children of this marriage – and consequently the legitimate heir to the throne – was one George Rex, who became a wealthy and influential resident of the Cape of Good Hope and who, undoubtedly, bore a marked resemblance to King George III.

After studying parish registers, wills and records of land tenure, however, Professor Ian Christie has been able to trace back George Rex's authentic pedigree as far as his paternal grandfather and the parents of this grandfather's wife and to show that George Rex – his surname being a true family name, not a Latin pun – was the son of John Rex, a London distiller. The books linking him to George III and Hannah Lightfoot are, Professor Christie has written, 'based on evidence which is without exception hearsay or else suspicious in origin . . . There is no documentation for the most salient facts. This leads to wholly speculative assumptions that various records have been destroyed' (Christie, 'The Family Origins of George Rex of Knysna').

that the Duke of Marlborough 'had made up to her', and this intelligence so distressed him that, as he was still inclined to do in such moods, he retired to his chamber and remained there for 'several hours in the depth of despair'. She was very young, but he had hopes of 'one day raising her to a throne'; and, with great diffidence, he put this proposal to Lord Bute. It would break his heart, he said, if his dear friend were to advise him against it, yet, if that dear friend could hold out 'no hopes how to be happy', he would never trouble him again 'with this unhappy tale' and would have the 'happy reflexion in dying' that he had not been 'altogether unworthy of the best of friends though unfortunate in other things'.

Lord Bute, while assuring the Prince that he would give the matter due consideration, had no intention of giving him advice which they both might well have cause to regret; and, when he warned him against the match, the Prince accepted Bute's decision with resignation. 'The interest of my country shall ever be my first care,' he wrote, 'my own inclination shall ever submit to it. I am born for the happiness or misery of a great nation, and consequently must often act contrary to my passion.'

So the Prince turned his mind to thoughts of marrying a German princess, as his father had done after being persuaded to abandon ideas of marriage to Lady Diana Spencer. But for the moment all that need be done was 'by some method or other' to 'get some account' of these princesses for future reference. He would never agree to marry while 'this old man', his interfering and lubricious grandfather, was still alive. 'I will rather undergo anything ever so disagreeable,' he wrote, 'than put my trust in him for a single moment in an affair of such delicacy.'

The King – who declared that for the moment his grandson was 'fit for nothing but to read the Bible to his mother' – had already endeavoured to arrange a match between the Prince and Princess Sophie Caroline, second daughter of the Duke of Brunswick-Wolfenbüttel, a marriage to which the intended bridegroom was opposed, protesting that he would not be 'bewolfenbüttelled' – a word which Horace Walpole said that he did not 'pretend to understand, as it is not in Mr. Johnson's new dictionary'. The Prince was encouraged in his reluctance by his mother, who wanted to see him married to her niece, Frederica Louise of Saxe-Gotha, and who believed, in Lord Waldegrave's words, 'that the young Princess [of Brunswick] having merit and understanding, equal to her Beauty, must in a short time have the greatest influence' over her impressionable son.

DEATH OF 'THE OLD MAN'

*He appear'd grave and thoughtful, tho' it might be perceived by his
Countenance that he was not sorry to be a King.*

Early on the morning of 25 October 1760, the Prince of Wales,
accompanied by a small retinue, was riding down Gunnersbury Lane,
a country road which ran along the boundary of Gunnersbury Park,
the fine Palladian house soon to be occupied as her country residence
by his eccentric and crotchety aunt, Princess Amelia. He had not
long passed over Kew Bridge when a horseman came galloping down
the road towards him. The rider carried a message from Kensington
Palace: His Majesty the King had had a serious accident. Making the
excuse that his horse was lame, the Prince immediately rode back
to Kew, where he sent a letter to Lord Bute explaining what had
happened, that he had warned all the servants to be 'silent about
what had passed' if they valued their employment, and that he would
wait to hear from him 'to know further what must be done'. No
sooner had the letter been sent than a message for the Prince arrived
at Kew from Princess Amelia: her father, the King, was dead.

He had been called as usual at seven o'clock with a cup of chocolate
and, having drunk it, had gone into his water-closet. A few moments
later, in Horace Walpole's words, 'the German *valet de chambre* heard
a noise, listened, heard something like a groan, ran in, and found
the hero of Oudenarde and Dettingen on the floor, with a gash on
his right temple, caused by falling against the corner of a bureau. He
tried to speak, could not, and expired.'

The Prince's natural and immediate reaction on receipt of this
intelligence was to order his coach and drive to see Lord Bute, who,
together with William Pitt, had been summoned to Kensington.
Since it was a Saturday, all the senior Cabinet Ministers apart from

Pitt had left the previous evening for houses in the country, and Pitt himself had been ready to leave, having ordered his coach to the door of his house at 10 St James's Square. Instead, in response to a summons from the King's German mistress, Lady Yarmouth, he had driven immediately to Kensington Palace, where he was informed of His Majesty's death. Lord Waldegrave, who was also at Kensington, described the scene:

I found some Lords and Grooms of the Bedchamber, with other Attendants of his Majesty's Person, all looking decently grave, tho' I did not observe one sorrowful Countenance.

I also observed many Inhabitants of the Palace of Inferior Rank, earnestly soliciting Admittance into the Bedchamber, that they might gratify their Curiosity with the Sight of a Dead King ... The new King, George III, appear'd grave and thoughtful, tho' it might be perceived by his Countenance that he was not sorry to be a King.

He spoke little, except to [his uncle] the Duke of Cumberland, but his Looks and Manner were gracious to every one.

From Kensington, Pitt sent urgent messages to the Privy Councillors who lived near enough to London to attend an immediate meeting there; then he left for Kew, where he again saw Bute and, after that, the new King.

The Duke of Newcastle now appeared upon the scene, and he too was taken to see Bute before he saw His Majesty, who told him, none too truthfully, that he had always had 'a very good opinion' of him and that he knew that the Duke had displayed a 'constant zeal' for the late King and his family, then adding, 'My Lord Bute is your very good friend; he will tell you my thoughts at large.'

Lord Bute was, in fact, already preparing the speech which was to be made that evening at the meeting of the Privy Council after the Councillors had signed the proclamation of King George III's accession. When he had finished it he gave it to the King, who showed it to the Duke of Newcastle and to the two Secretaries of State, Pitt and the Earl of Holderness, a former ambassador in Venice who had been present with King George II at the Battle of Dettingen. King George III then asked the Duke of Newcastle to read the statement out.

The first few sentences were quite unexceptionable; but when he heard the final words – 'as I mount the throne in the midst of a bloody war, I shall endeavour to prosecute it in the manner most likely to bring an honourable and lasting peace' – Pitt, the driving force in the Government's prosecution of that war, now rose to protest. Claiming that he had not heard them distinctly, Pitt asked the Duke to repeat the words. After Newcastle had done so, Pitt proposed two amendments: 'bloody war' should be changed to 'an expensive but just and necessary war', and the reference to the bringing of peace should be qualified by the words 'in concert with our allies'. The King was reluctant to make these changes to the address which Lord Bute had written for him; but Bute himself, having at first claimed it was too late to make alterations at this stage, agreed that they might be made when the Lord Chief Justice, Lord Mansfield, supported Pitt and persuaded the King to give way on both points – which he did, so Waldegrave said, 'with great Unwillingness'.

It was clear to all by now that Lord Bute, although not yet a Privy Councillor, nor occupying a seat in the Cabinet, was assuming the authority of the King's First Minister. It was even noticed that the King pronounced certain words in Lord Bute's Scottish manner. Bute assured Pitt in private that he had no ambition to be appointed First Minister: he wished merely to advise and guide the twenty-two-year-old King in his apprenticeship. But, ignoring such protestations, Pitt told him that his 'advancement to the management of the affairs of the country' would not be in His Majesty's interest and that, if there were to be the least shadow of a change in the conduct of the war, he himself would resign from the Government. He was, in fact, determined to direct the policies of the Administration in the new reign as he had in the days of the late King, and declined to act with Bute in any kind of coalition.

He remained, however, as Secretary of State for the Southern Department, while Newcastle, now sixty-seven years old, retained his office at the head of the Administration as First Lord of the Treasury. Bute, created a Privy Councillor, was already Groom of the Stole; but, as he said to Lord Temple, the Lord Privy Seal, 'I suppose your Lordship does not mean to look upon me as a bare Groom of the Stole – the King will have it otherwise.'

The King did have it otherwise. Within three days of his accession he had insisted that Bute should be given a seat in the Cabinet, and in March 1761 he had him appointed Secretary of State for the Northern Department in place of Lord Holderness, who was dismissed with a pension of £4,000 a year. He consulted his 'dearest friend' on all matters, important and negligible, on political matters and on the trivialities of court procedure, even on the names of people to be invited to court festivities and on the seating arrangements for formal dinners. When it came to the choice of a bride he consulted Bute and no other member of the Cabinet.

Attempts to find a suitable bride being now resumed, Baron Philip Adolphus von Münchausen, the Hanoverian Minister in London, was asked to make discreet inquiries in Germany. He was told that the young King would not want a managing or clever young woman; nor one with political interests. But otherwise, provided she was amiable and reasonably intelligent and would not have difficulty in bearing children, almost any Protestant princess would do. She did not even have to be particularly good-looking, though a pretty face was, of course, to be preferred.

From Hanover the names of six possible young ladies were sent to London. None was considered suitable. Lord Bute pressed the claims of a princess from Brunswick; but the King did not want to marry into that family. Nor was it considered advisable for him to make an alliance with the house of Anhalt-Dessau, since its candidate's grandfather had married the daughter of an apothecary. The House of Brandenburg also had a skeleton in its cupboard in the shape of a princess who had had an affair with a ne'er-do-well. Another candidate suffered not only from the disfigurement of smallpox but also from a bodily deformity which, it was suspected, might inhibit pregnancy; yet another, after further inquiries, was described as obstinate; a fifth was too young; the sixth 'stubborn and ill-temper'd to the greatest degree'.

Baron Münchausen, told to supply more names, wrote to his brother in Hanover for further suggestions, adding that the 'King's longing and impatience increase daily'. Lord Bute told the Baron that until the King was safely married he could not be securely prevented from the indulgence of those desires against which he had contrived so far to protect him. There seemed to be, in particular, a danger that the King might yet succumb to the charms of Lady Sarah Lennox. Certainly Henry Fox, her brother-in-law, had not lost hope that, even if a marriage could not be arranged, the King might be induced to take the girl as his mistress and then he, Fox, might be in a position to supplant Lord Bute as His Majesty's intimate adviser, or at least to obtain the earldom after which he hankered. He proposed that Lady Sarah should appear regularly at Court and do her best to attract the King, even telling her, so Walpole said, to appear every morning dressed in fetching *déshabillé* in a field near Holland House through which the King was in the habit of riding. Fox was given grounds for hope that his scheme might succeed by a report he received from his niece, Lady Susan Fox-Strangways, an impressionable, rather flighty girl, of an ambiguous conversation at Court between the King and Lady Susan, who was an intimate friend of Lady Sarah:

'You are going into Somersetshire [where her father, Lord Ilchester, had a house at Redlynch]. When do you return?'
  'Not before winter, Sir; and I don't know how soon in winter.'
  'Is there nothing will bring you back to town before winter?'
  'I don't know of anything.'
  'Would you like to see a coronation?'
  'Yes, Sir. I hope I shall come to see that.'
  'Won't it be a much finer sight when there is a Queen?'
  'To be sure, Sir.'
  'I have had a great many applications from abroad but I don't like them.'

Lady Susan interpreted the King's words that followed as an intimation that he would prefer to marry an English girl: at first she supposed herself, and then that he must be referring to her friend Lady Sarah Lennox. Much encouraged by Lady Susan's report of this conversation, Fox was given further reason to hope that he might yet get Lady Sarah into the royal bed by accounts of the King's subsequent behaviour, his seeking out Lady Sarah at Court, his ambivalent remarks to her, his evident distress when she was said to be carrying on a flirtation with Lord Newbattle, son of the Earl of Ancram, a 'vain insignificant puppy' in the opinion of Fox but 'lively and not ugly'. It was agreed that Newbattle should seek his parents' consent to marry Lady Sarah, though she was still but seventeen.

The consent was not forthcoming, which was said to have 'hurt the lady's pride and surprised her'.

Then Lady Sarah fell from her horse and broke her leg while staying at Redlynch with her friend Lady Susan. Lord Newbattle airily dismissed the news as of no consequence. 'It will do no great harm,' he said, 'for her legs were ugly enough before.' Fox learned with satisfaction that the King, however, was most solicitous. 'He drew up his breath, wreath'd himself, and made the countenance of one feeling pain himself . . . He asked a hundred questions about her & was much concern'd she should be left in the care of a country surgeon.' When next the King saw her, after her return from Somerset, 'he colour'd & came up to her eager and in haste & talk'd much and graciously'. Four days later, so Fox learned, he saw her again at a birthday ball and 'had no eyes but for her, & hardly talked to any body else', while she 'returned the fondness of his eyes & gallantry of his discourse as much as ever he could wish'. Upon her next appearance at Court, with her aunt, Lady Kildare, the King once more showed himself

exceedingly fond and said loud enough for Lady Kildare to hear, 'I was told you were to go out of town. If you had I should have been miserable. For God's sake remember what I said to Lady Susan and believe that I have the strongest attachment.' The last words were spoken extremely loud & the whole with the greatest seriousness & fervour . . . On Sunday, June the 28th he fix'd his eyes & hardly took them off her all church time.

Years later Lady Sarah told one of her sons that the King now made a definite proposal of marriage, and that she accepted him. Both Fox and Lady Susan Fox-Strangways, who had begun, so she said, to think of herself as First Minister, were much disappointed when it gradually became clear that their family's ambitions were not to be realized and that the King was to marry a German after all. But Lady Sarah herself was quite philosophical about it. Indeed Fox believed that the sickness of her pet squirrel upset her more, and when 'in spite of her nursing' it died he thought 'it gave her more concern than H. M. ever did. That grief, however, soon gave way to the care of a little hedgehog that she sav'd from destruction in the field and is now her favourite.' 'I did not cry, I assure you,' she told Lady Susan:

I know you were more set upon it than I was . . . I have almost forgiven him; luckily for me I did not love him, and only liked him . . . The thing I am most angry at is looking so like a fool . . . but I don't much care. If he was to change his mind again . . . I should not have him for he is so weak as to be governed by everybody, [and I would] have but a bad time of it.

She was not prepared, however, to let him off lightly. When next she went to Court he 'looked frightened' upon catching sight of her and spoke to her 'in some confusion'. 'Our conversation was short,' she reported. 'Here it is: "I see riding is begun again, it's glorious weather for it now [it was 16 July]." Answer "Yes, it is very fine," – and add to that 'a very cross and angry look on my side, and his turning away immediately, and you know the whole.' She was determined, she said, always in future to be 'as high and grave as possible to him and his sisters'.

Yet it was not in her nature to be so. When asked to be a bridesmaid at the King's wedding she agreed without hesitation – much to the indignation of Henry Fox's wife, who considered her 'mean & dirty' to have accepted the invitation after all that had passed. But she was unrepentant: after all, being a bridesmaid was 'the best way of seeing the coronation'. Fox himself resignedly told her, 'Well, Sal, you are the first *vargin* in England . . . and the King shall behold your pretty face and repent.'

Before too long, happily married to her second husband – her first marriage, to Sir Thomas Charles Bunbury, having been dissolved in 1762 – she was speaking of the King affectionately as an 'old friend'. To be sure he had been in the wrong; but one did not love one's friends any the less 'for being in the wrong even towards oneself'; and she, after all, had been very young and 'thoughtless, wild and giddy'.★

★ Years later she decided to make use of the King's passion for her during this wild and giddy youth. She let it be known that, as an elderly, almost blind old lady with children unprovided for, she needed 'help very much'. The King granted her a handsome pension of £800 a year (Tillyard, *Aristocrats*, 134). Lady Susan Fox-Strangways, who eloped with an Irish actor, William O'Brien, voiced a common sentiment when she said that the King would have done better to 'give up his *favourite* than his *Berenice*. An English *beauty* as Queen wd have pleas'd his people as much as a Scotch Minister disgusted them. The talk of such a marriage was never unpopular & pretty generally expected' (Lennox, *Life and Letters*, Appendix A).

6

BRIDE AND BRIDEGROOM

Every hour more & more convinces me of the treasure I have got.

Among the new names of German princesses which had arrived in London was one that was offered without too much confidence: that of Princess Sophie Charlotte of Mecklenburg-Strelitz. She was a young woman, seventeen years old, of no particular talent or striking personality, certainly not pretty and of no greatly distinguished family, but of unblemished character, so it was believed, and of respectable lineage. She had had smallpox and not been marked by it.

Horace Walpole was to describe her in a letter to a friend:

She is not tall nor a beauty. Pale and very thin; but looks sensible and genteel. Her hair is darkish and fine [a lock was sent to the King, who confirmed that it was 'of a very fine dark colour and very soft']. Her forehead low, her nose very well except the nostrils spreading too wide. The mouth has the same fault, but her teeth are good. She talks a great deal, and French tolerably.

The King accepted the recommendation of the Princess without evident enthusiasm. 'I own 'tis not in every particular as I could wish,' he confessed to Lord Bute, having read the report upon her character and physical attributes, 'but yet I am resolved to fix here.' And, since he was resolved, he expressed a wish to have the marriage celebrated without delay and the bride dispatched to England 'as soon as possible', since 'she ought to be above a month here before . . . the august ceremony . . . so that she may have a little recovered [from] that bashfulness' to be expected in 'a young lady on her first appearance'.

He had been told that the Princess was in some ways gauche, since the court from which she came was far from fashionable; but he believed that 'a little [of] England's air [would] soon give her the deportment necessary for a British Queen'.

So, in June 1761, an agent proposed by Lord Bute made an informal approach to the Princess's widowed mother, the Duchess of Mecklenburg-Strelitz, who, delighted by the offer of a match so far more advantageous than her family could have reasonably expected, raised no objection to an official proposal being made to her by the King of England's mother, the Princess Dowager. The Duchess thought it as well to mention that her daughter had been brought up in the Lutheran faith; this, however, should prove no problem, since she was fully prepared to become a member of the Church of England.

So far the negotiations had been kept secret from the Cabinet. Even the Princess Dowager was not kept fully informed as to their progress, so that when, on 8 July 1761, messengers were dispatched to such members of the Privy Council as were in London that summer requesting them to attend a meeting at St James's Palace 'upon urgent and important business', only three men, apart from Lord Bute and the King himself – Newcastle, Pitt and Lord Hardwicke, Secretary of State for the Southern Department – knew what this business was. Most Councillors would conclude, so Newcastle supposed, that it was to acquaint them with the terms which it was proposed to offer to France for an ending of the war. But 'not at all', so Horace Walpole wrote to his friend Horace Mann, British Minister in Florence. 'To sanctify or to reject the pacification was not the question at issue.' The business to be discussed – *urgent*, perhaps, though Walpole could not see how it was *important* – was 'to declare a Queen'.

Lord Harcourt, the King's former Governor, was to be sent to the young lady's duchy ('if he can find it', Walpole added – for it was no larger than an English county of average size) to escort her to London. For this purpose he was appointed Master of her Horse – an honour he expected, so he said, as little as he 'did the Bishoprick of London just vacant'. The arrival of the bride could not, however, be arranged as quickly as the King hoped: first her mother died four days after the Privy Council had been told of the imminent wedding;

then the King fell ill with chickenpox. He felt much cast down, but wrote to his 'dearest friend' with sententious resignation, observing that man was 'ever liable to checks' and that he 'should be quite knocked down' were not the Princess's brother, the Duke of Mecklenburg-Strelitz, proving so amenable and declaring himself 'ready to do anything' that might be proposed.

Before his delayed departure with orders to bring back Princess Charlotte in time for her marriage on 8 September and the coronation on the 22nd, Lord Harcourt was given presents to take with him to hand to the Princess, including 'the finest bracelets ever seen', 'the finest pearl that can be' and the King of England's picture 'richly & most prettily set round with diamonds, & a diamond rose' – gifts sure to please the bride, whose love of jewellery was later to be described as 'inordinate'.

Lord Harcourt left home at the end of July, and on 7 August, his ship having anchored in the Elbe off Stade, he was on his way east towards Hamburg and across the plains to Neustrelitz.

Lord Bute's confidential agent, his friend and fellow Scotsman Colonel David Graeme, was already there and had, he said, formed a most favourable impression of the Princess. He was touched by her tears when talking about her mother, and by her having sent him a present of cherries for his breakfast with the request that, when eating each one, he would remember 'votre tres affectionée Amie Charlotte P. de M.' Her English, he discovered, was non-existent; she spoke French but 'midling well'. Yet she was evidently eager to make up for a rather inadequate education and was of a pliable disposition, 'capable of taking any impression or being moulded into any Form'. She was already quite an accomplished musician, having taught herself to play the glockenspiel as well as the harpsichord. Her singing voice was pleasant. All in all she had a 'Natural, Easy, and Composed Carriage, which, joined to her Mild temper, is more winning than a Politesse Faconnée'. Graeme had to agree with others that she was 'not a Beauty', that her figure was 'not quite that of a Woman fully formed . . . tho the Bosom [was] full enough for her age'. But, as his reports emphasized, she was above all 'Amiable' and, he concluded, even her 'Face was rather Agreeable than Otherwise'. The daughter of her German page thought so too: she had in this young woman's opinion an 'expressive and intelligent countenance'; she 'was not tall, but of slight, pretty figure; her eyes bright and sparkling with good humour and vivacity'.

All arrangements having been made for her departure from the homeland which she was never to see again – and her measurements having been sent to England for the guidance of London dressmakers – she set off for Stade, where she was taken in a rowing-boat towards the British yacht *Royal Charlotte*, which had been renamed and redecorated in her honour. Climbing on deck, she caught her first glimpse of the open sea which she was to find so unpleasant – an *'element terrible'*. The voyage to Harwich was an exceptionally rough one; and, although Lord Harcourt's son William (who had been appointed an equerry to the Princess) and the daughter of one of her attendants both later reported that she was 'gay & lively during the crossing, playing on her harpsichord . . . leaving the door of her cabin open so as to encourage her companions in their misery . . . singing or laughing all day long', this presented a far from faithful picture of her demeanour as the ship dipped and lurched through the waves.

The two ladies who had sailed out from England to accompany her across the North Sea were also 'very much out of order' during the crossing. These were the Duchess of Ancaster, her Mistress of the Robes, and the Duchess of Hamilton, First Lady of the Bedchamber, the discomfort of the first being exacerbated by her being pregnant and 'subject to hysteric fits', and of the other by concern for the lactation of the ass that she had insisted on taking aboard with her.

Also in attendance upon the Princess were a Prussian widow, Madame Coccei, 'a very Agreeable, Well bred Lady' who had fled to Strelitz when Berlin was threatened by the Russians; three of her late mother's ladies-in-waiting; and two younger *'Feme's de Chambres'*, Johanna Louisa Hagedorn and Juliana Elizabeth Schwellenberg, a tiresome, bossy woman who was to make life most burdensome for some of her English colleagues. The King had accepted these German attendants with some reluctance, having made it clear that he knew from his 'own experience' that women of this sort meddled 'much more than they ought to do'. He gave way, however, without undue protest when permission was sought to include the Princess's German page, who was also her hairdresser, Frederick Albert.

The King was anxiously and impatiently awaiting his bride's arrival, holding up a handkerchief at the end of his whip when he went riding each morning, to see which way the wind was blowing, and repeatedly glancing at a miniature portrait of his bride of which he seemed 'mighty fond' and which he would let no one else see. He had received most reassuring reports of the Princess's character and appearance in addition to those sent earlier by Colonel Graeme, who told Lord Bute that he would now 'Leave Her Good Qualities to be discovered by our Worthy Young Monarch Whose Domestick Happiness must so much depend upon what this young Plant shall Grow to'. The 'Tender Twigg', he could not doubt, would 'Easily and Readily bend to any Form'.

The King was notified of the Princess's safe arrival at Harwich in the care of the celebrated circumnavigator Admiral Lord Anson on the morning of Sunday 6 September. From Harwich she was driven to Witham near Chelmsford in Essex, the house of the rich and tactless bachelor the Earl of Abercorn, who, when the King later thanked him and said that he feared the visit of the Princess's entourage must have given him a good deal of trouble, replied bluntly, 'A good deal indeed.'

From Witham the Princess was driven on to Romford, the coach travelling slowly through the villages so that the crowds standing by the roadside could see their future Queen as she passed by. She was 'extremely courteous' to them, 'bowing to all who seemed desirous of seeing her', behaving, it was generally agreed, with surprising composure for a young woman in a strange country whose language she did not speak.

At Romford the King's coach was waiting to take her on to London after she had had a short rest and a cup of coffee. The King meanwhile thanked God for her safe arrival. 'I have now but one wish as a public man,' he said, 'and that is that God will make her fruitful.' As a private man he rendered the Almighty 'sincere and humble acknowledgements for this greatest blessing that He [had] been pleased to point out'.

As the coach drew up at the garden gate of St James's Palace, the Princess looked up, bowed, and clapped her fan together. Lord Anson jumped from the vehicle while it was still in motion, lost his balance, and fell over so that the 'wheell was near going over him'.

The King opened the gate as his brother, Edward, Duke of York, offered his arm to the Princess to help her down. It was noticed that her lip was trembling. She 'threw herself at his Majesty's feet', Lady Sarah Lennox's aunt Lady Kildare was told by Lady Harrington, whose house was next door to the Palace. 'He raised her up, embraced her and led her thro' the garden up the steps into the Palace.'

The guarded reports of her appearance which had been sent to the King had not fully prepared him for the reality. It was true that she looked, as Walpole said, 'sensible and genteel' and that she had a fine head of hair and good teeth, but she was undoubtedly a plain young girl with a large mouth, with a rather swarthy complexion and, her nostrils spreading wide, with something of the appearance of a mulatto. It was to be well known that in later years, when, as Horace Walpole said, her 'want of personal charms became less noticeable', her Chamberlain, Colonel Edward Disbrowe, observed that the '*bloom* of her ugliness [was] going off'.

Yet, if the King was disappointed by his bride's looks – as the daughter of her page said that he was – he did not show it. He presented her to his mother, his sisters and brothers, his uncle, the Duke of Cumberland, and his aunt, Princess Amelia, with apparent satisfaction.

She seemed slightly confused at first, rather nervous and uncertain, as though not yet recovered from her rough voyage, at the conclusion of which she had been 'much fatigued'. But at the Royal Family's dinner party later that afternoon she recovered her composure and spirits and ate, it was noticed, with a good appetite, even though she was to be married within an hour or two that very night, the hottest night of the year.

As the hour of the ceremony approached and she was dressed in her heavy, sumptuous bridal clothes, her velvet diamond-studded cap, her little bejewelled crown, her purple mantle laced with gold and lined with ermine, her necklace and earrings, her pearl-and-diamond aigrette, she became rather nervous again. And as she was led by the

Duke of York to the Great Drawing-Room, where the ladies of the Court were assembled, the Duke felt her fingers trembling in his hand. '*Courage*, Princess,' he said to her repeatedly, '*Courage*, Princess.'

In the Drawing-Room the peeresses who were gathered there came forward to be kissed on the cheek. This duty she performed without mishap; but when other ladies approached she appeared uncertain of what to do, until the King's older sister, Princess Augusta, took her hand in hers and held it out for them to kiss. At the sight of Lady Sarah Lennox and the other bridesmaids, nine of them, all in jewel-encrusted white silk gowns, she was heard to exclaim under her breath, '*Mon dieu! Il y en a tant! Il y en a tant!*'

Shortly before ten o'clock the bride and her numerous attendants moved off to the sound of trumpets and drumbeats. Between lines of Horse Guards they proceeded to the Chapel Royal, the ceiling of which had been painted to commemorate the marriage of King Henry VIII to Anne of Cleves over two hundred years before. Here were waiting the elderly, gouty Archbishop of Canterbury, Thomas Secker, who had baptized and confirmed the King, and John Thomas, Bishop of Winchester, who had been the King's Preceptor when Lord Waldegrave was his Governor.

When the congregation were all assembled, the King appeared and took his place beside his bride beneath a canopy which had been erected in front of the altar. The Archbishop, having been told that the Princess spoke no English, had already procured for her a copy of the office of matrimony translated into German as well as a prayer book in both French and German. But she had had no time to look into either. This did not matter, however, as she was required to say only two words at the appropriate moment – two words she uttered at the King's prompting: '*Ich will.*' The King himself declared his willingness to be her husband with his hand on his heart.

The next evening, at the ball which followed their first night together, he seemed delighted with his bride. He left her side for no longer than courtesy to his other guests required; and he was perfectly tolerant of her now revealed passion for snuff, even though, so Lady Northumberland noticed, it made him 'sneeze prodigiously'. At the drawing-room the next day, however, there was a slight embarrassment: among the guests was the old, short-sighted Earl of Westmorland, formerly a notorious Jacobite, who was believed never to have attended a Hanoverian drawing-room before. Catching blurred sight of a young lady whom he took to be the Queen, he dropped to his knees before her, took her hand in his, and was about to kiss it reverently when the astonished Lady Sarah Lennox exclaimed, 'Sir, I am not the Queen!'

It was the Queen's turn to be startled the day after that, when a large crowd of chattering people pressed round her carriage to get a glimpse of her as she was driven to the Theatre Royal, Drury Lane. Once inside the building, however, she recovered her composure and appeared greatly to enjoy the performance of David Garrick in *The Rehearsal*, a farcical comedy which George Villiers, second Duke of Buckingham, had had a hand in writing. It had been specially chosen for her by the King, who had seen it before and hoped that, although she would not understand the dialogue, she would be able to follow the plot and be amused by the antics of the performers. The evident pleasure she took in it seemed to make the King still more fond of his agreeable, amenable and affectionate Queen, with whom he was clearly so much taken. 'Every hour more & more convinces Me of the Treasure I have got,' he told Lord Bute, '& of my obligation to my Dearest Friend for the kind part he has taken in this affair which is the source of my happiness as a *Private Man*.'

There were those – Walpole among them – who thought that the pleasure he took in being a 'private man' was rather hard on the Queen, who was, years later, to speak of the 'dear King's great strictness, at [her] arrival in England, to prevent [her] making many acquaintances', to ensure that she ran no risk of becoming involved in the intrigues and tracasseries of the outside world. Prince William, his brother, thought that, having so 'bad an opinion of the world', the King carried this concern to shield the Queen from outside influences to excess, and he himself put a rather different interpretation upon his brother's motives. The King was, Prince William said, 'delighted with having entirely under his own training a young innocent Girl of 17 . . . & determined she shd be wholly devoted to him alone, and should have no other friend or society'.

Certainly the Queen was never allowed to forget the dangers of becoming involved in the 'Policies of the Country', since there 'never could be kept a Society without party which was always dangerous for any Woman to take part in, particularly so for the Royal Family'. So insistently did her husband instil into her the dangers of women becoming involved in the corrupt political world that the Queen was to declare in the future that she had a horror of 'medling in Politics': she abhorred it; it was *equal to sin*.

At St James's and at Richmond Lodge, their summer residence, she consequently led a carefully restricted life, seeing few people other than the ladies of the Court, the wardrobe women and bedchamber women who attended her closely and dutifully from the time of her rising until she retired to bed with the King at night. Indeed, Madame Schwellenberg, her Keeper of the Wardrobe, exercised a guardianship over her which even her husband found too strict. He protested at the possessive manner in which the woman denied access to her mistress to all those of whom she disapproved. He threatened to send her back to Neustrelitz, and talked to her so severely in the presence of his mother that the Queen was 'hurt very sensibly'.

It was a rare disagreement. The days and evenings of early marriage passed in quiet contentment. The Queen took English lessons both from Dr John Majendie, a canon of Windsor, and from her husband, and eventually she learned to speak the language quite fluently, with not too pronounced a German accent. She played her harpsichord; she was given singing lessons by Johann Christian Bach, son of Johann Sebastian; she sang to her husband, who played his violin for her as well as his flute and harpsichord. They had games of piquet and backgammon; they played with their dogs – the Queen's dog, Presto, being generally considered rather a nuisance, since it trotted after her and, being small, was liable to be overlooked and a hazard to the unwary. When the Queen was alone she took up her needle-work. In later years, on summer evenings she would sometimes go out to see her animals in their enclosures, a small menagerie which was to include a zebra and two elephants. Shortly before eleven o'clock, while Her Majesty's Necessary Woman was pushing a warming-pan between the linen sheets of their bed, she and her husband shared a modest snack of bread and milk and gruel.

7

FIRST IMPRESSIONS

His manner is graceful and obliging.

In those early days of his marriage the King was considered quite a handsome young man, though his heavy-lidded eyes were slightly protuberant in the Hanoverian manner; his lips were rather fleshy, and his nose a little too large, while his forehead receded. But none of these features was yet marked. He carried himself well and had a pleasing expression; and, at his wife's behest, he discarded his wig, allowing his own hair to grow, which, she thought, 'became him extreamly'.

Lady Susan O'Brien described him as 'a fine pleasant-looking young man – that is to say, a healthy complexion (not so white as his brothers were) fine teeth, a look of happiness & good humour that pleas'd everyone – me in particular'. Even Horace Walpole, always readier to find fault with his fellow men than to flatter them, described him as being 'good-natured', though 'full of dignity'. 'His person is tall,' Walpole wrote. 'His manner is graceful and obliging.' All in all he seemed to be 'the most amiable young man in the world'.

A fortnight after the royal wedding, on 22 September, the coronation took place. It was a splendid occasion, although before the service began the chaos of carriages struggling to reach Westminster Abbey 'created much confusion', in the words of William Hickey, then a boy at Westminster School, whose father had paid fifty guineas for a box high up in that part of the Abbey known as 'the nunneries'. 'Drivers and horses ran into each other whereby glasses and panels were demolished without number, the noise of which, accompanied by the screeches of terrified ladies, was at times truly terrific.'

When the confusion outside the Abbey had subsided, the ceremony inside was to be highly ritualistic – as custom dictated, though not as either the King or Queen desired, since, while both had a high regard for the traditional etiquette and customs of court life, neither had a taste for the kind of leading role in majestic pageantry which was to appeal so strongly to their eldest son. They arrived at Westminster Hall not in gilded coaches but in sedan chairs for what was to prove an exhausting day of twelve hours in the public eye.

Under the gaze of spectators some of whom had paid over £100 for rooms overlooking the route to the Abbey and others up to 1,000 guineas for a day's rent of a suitable house, the King marched from Westminster Hall to the Abbey under a canopy of cloth of gold, wearing crimson velvet robes, his 'coronation wig' and a jewelled cap of state. The Queen also walked under a canopy, silver bells at its corners, which was borne aloft by barons of the Cinque Ports, treading on the herbs, buds and petals cast along her path by attendants of the King's Herb Woman in a centuries-old custom dating from the days of plague.

At the door of the Abbey the King was greeted with the music of the organ, with fifes and kettledrums, and with chants of '*Vivat Georgius Rex*' by the King's Scholars of Westminster School. And at the moment in the long ceremony when the crown was placed on the King's head the boys raised their voices again in a loud cheer, accompanied by the acclamations of the large congregation, 'as if,' so a young gentleman down from Yorkshire observed, 'universal joy was in every body'.

William Hickey had 'a capital view of the whole ceremony'.

Their Majesties being crowned [he wrote], the Archbishop of Canterbury mounted the pulpit to deliver the sermon; and, as many thousands were out of the possibility of hearing a single syllable, they took that opportunity to eat their meal, when the general clattering of knives, forks, plates and glasses produced a most ridiculous effect, and a universal burst of laughter followed.★ The sermon being concluded, the anthem was sung by a numerous band of

---

★ Hickey's family and their friends enjoyed an excellent meal of 'cold fowls, ham, tongues, different meat pies, wines and liquors of various sorts' which had previously been sent to their box in the Abbey and which were handed round there by two servants (*Memoirs of William Hickey*, ed. Quennell, 18).

the first performers in the Kingdom, and it certainly was the finest thing I had ever heard.

On leaving the Abbey, Hickey made his way to watch the Coronation Banquet in Westminster Hall, where, through the kindness of some ladies who made room for him on their seats in the front row of the gallery, he was able to watch 'every particular' of the ceremony – the ushering in of the numerous dishes by the Lord Steward, the Lord High Constable and the Deputy Earl Marshal,★ all on horseback; the clattering appearance of the King's Champion, who rode into the Hall in full armour to throw down a gauntlet as a challenge to anyone who dared dispute the King's right to the throne; the baskets, handkerchiefs and garters let down by hungry onlookers in the galleries to friends at the tables below, who filled them with chicken legs and bottles of wine to be hauled aloft for eager consumption; the sight of the King and Queen, as hungry as anyone, helping themselves with relish to the food on their golden plates, both eating, as the poet Thomas Gray commented disapprovingly, 'like farmers'.

There was another fine meal to consume a few days later, on Lord Mayor's Day, when, at a banquet in Guildhall, the King and Queen and other guests sat down to a Lucullan feast comprising, among other delicacies, ortolans, quails, ducks' tongues, turtles, Westphalia hams, 'Knots of Eggs', 'Fine fat Livers' and thirty-two dishes of vegetables. In the preparation of these dishes, the cooks had required four gallons of both Jamaica rum and French brandy. In the accounts also appear the cost of twenty dozen bottles of champagne and fifty dozen of port.

Before enjoying this meal the King and Queen had watched the Lord Mayor's Procession from the balcony of a house in Cheapside where the King's grandfather and great-grandfather had watched earlier parades in their time. On this occasion the owner of the

★ The Deputy Earl Marshal was Lord Effingham, whom the King had occasion to rebuke for various inefficiencies in his arrangements. Effingham is said to have replied, none too tactfully, 'It is true, Sir, that there has been some neglect, but I have taken care that the next coronation shall be regulated in the exactest manner possible' (Jesse, *Memoirs*, i, 108).

house, an elderly linen merchant, David Barclay, had overcome the constraints normally imposed by his Quaker beliefs by having his façade and balcony adorned with brilliant crimson damask.

When the King and Queen had taken their places on the balcony, Mr Barclay's wife and daughters came into the adjoining drawing-room. 'His Majesty met us at the door,' one of the daughters reported, 'which was a condescencion we did not expect.' Nor did she expect the King to 'kiss all the female Friends present', which 'fluttered them and set their tuckers in agitation'. Miss Barclay was much struck by the behaviour of the Queen, whose dress, she noted, was 'as rich as gold, silver and silk' could make it. By contrast, her own and her sister's simple attire was like that of 'a parcel of nuns'. The Queen had 'not a fine face, to be sure' but a most 'agreeable countenance', and was 'vastly genteel'. She was provided with tea, which was passed to a lady-in-waiting who presented it to Her Majesty on bended knee, 'a form which Rachel and Rebecca [the two Quaker daughters of the house] would never have submitted to'. Did the young ladies speak French? the Queen asked of the lady-in-waiting who was acting as interpreter. It was regretted that they did not. So she asked that they should be told how much she regretted being unable to talk to them in English, a language she was doing her best to master but had not yet conquered.

On such occasions the King's pleasure in the agreeable manner of his wife was clear to see; and he showed himself as anxious to please her as she to please him, even going so far as to ask Lord Bute to find her some special variety of the snuff of which she was so unaccountably and unfortunately fond.

When, in the House of Lords, he gave his formal consent to a Bill providing generously for her maintenance should she be left a widow, it was remarked how low was her bow of acceptance and gratitude. She was to be allowed £100,000 a year (in modern times some £6 million) as well as the Lodge and its grounds in Richmond Old Park and Somerset House in the Strand, which was traditionally made over to Queen Consorts but had been little used by them of late. She was already receiving £40,000 a year for her personal expenses and the maintenance of her own Household.

This Household was for the moment established at St James's

Palace, where drawing-rooms were held on Thursdays and Sundays. At these drawing-rooms, while mindful of the King's injunction not to make unsuitable acquaintanceships, she obediently followed his advice to be 'civil to all'. He endeavoured always to be so himself, and to his wife he still displayed a devoted if sometimes oppressively possessive attention, dancing with her time after time at private balls, taking her to the theatre to see plays specially chosen by him for her, often to Shakespeare – much of whose works, he was later to confess, were not to his own taste – and to productions which she might more readily understand and appreciate, such as John Fletcher's comedy *Rule a Wife and Have a Wife* and John Gay's *Beggar's Opera*. The King also saw to it that she was served with the food she liked and, to make her feel at home, with German delicacies on her official birthday.

The King had no taste for rich food himself. He saw to it that court customs were observed – goose on Michaelmas Day, roast chine of pork with apple sauce and Shrewsbury brawn as well as turkey Périgueux on Christmas Day, wild boar's head in wine on New Year's Eve – but he ate little of such dishes himself, endeavouring, so he said, to curb a tendency to put on weight by 'the most vigorous exercise and the strictest attention to a simple diet'.

After breakfast, at which he preferred tea to coffee, he had nothing until dinner, which was served at four, though on court days he was often not free to have it by then. It was, in any case, by his request a very simple meal, usually consisting of soup, meat – he was particularly fond of mutton – and vegetables, followed by some sort of pudding. Sometimes, instead of mutton chops, there were cow-heels, pig's head, sauerkraut and a pudding known as 'Ribbon Pudding'. Advised that fruit was good for the health, he saw to it that there was always a good supply from the Windsor orchards on the table. He usually helped himself to an apple, a pear or a dish of strawberries at the end of a meal, and was once seen to scoop out the fruit from a tart and leave the pastry on his plate. Frequently his dinner was limited to cold meat, green salad and stewed pears. Only occasionally were there plovers' eggs or cherry tart. On Sundays he enjoyed a plate of roast beef. This, though, was a rare treat.

He ate all his meals quickly, even impatiently, and was sometimes to be seen pacing up and down as he swallowed a plateful of bread and butter before leaving London for the country. One of his equerries told Sir Nathaniel Wraxall how uncomfortably fast they all had to eat, since etiquette forbade them to continue with the meal once the King himself had finished:

We know so well how soon the King has finished, that after we sit down at table not a word is uttered. All our attention is devoted to expedition. Yet, with the best diligence we can exert, before we have half dined, his Majesty has already thrown himself back in his chair, and called for his *cup* with which he concludes his meal.

The italicization of the word 'cup' was well justified, since it was largely composed of a sort of lemonade and 'a monk of La Trappe might have drunk it without any infraction of his monastic vow'. The King would just as soon not have any wine at all, choosing to have barley-water instead. He never drank spirits. Before calling for his beverage, or before the meal began, if he was in no great hurry to get back to work or to go out riding he would relax the customary etiquette by telling his equerries, 'Don't regard me. Take your own time.'

Supper was served soon after ten o'clock, and this, too, was a simple meal at which guests were even more rarely seen than they were at dinner. Formal dinner parties were very rare events, held occasionally for foreign royalties or family celebrations, not for Ministers of the Crown, diplomats, or gentlemen and ladies of fashion. On the infrequent occasion when a banquet was given, however, the King took the trouble to ensure that his guests would not be disappointed: he would even go round the kitchens to see 'that all was going on right, not merely for the higher orders, but even for the soldiers in attendance'.

His own supper would often consist of no more than a cup of tea and a slice of bread and butter or a sandwich perhaps, mutton sandwiches first appearing in the Household Steward's accounts in 1784, not long after John Montagu, Earl of Sandwich, gave his name to the pieces of salt beef between two slices of toast which he ate to sustain himself either at the gaming table or, more likely, at his desk.

The bread at the King's table by the middle of the 1790s – when harvests were poor and prices were rising as a consequence of the war – was always potato bread or brown bread. He insisted on this in the hope that other households would follow his example.

Soon after the supper things had been cleared away the King retired, for he was sure to be up early in the morning: he once declared that seven hours' sleep was quite enough for a man, eight for a woman and nine for a fool. He was usually in bed with the Queen at eleven o'clock, and certainly no later than midnight, unless he had been obliged to stay up to attend to some pressing business or to put in an appearance at one of the rare court balls, at which he danced energetically, though not with notable grace; on one occasion, with Lady Mary Lowther as his partner, he joined enthusiastically in a dance known as the hempdresser for no less than two hours.

However late he was in getting to bed, the King invariably said his prayers before going to sleep, and usually looked into his Bible. Regular in attendance on weekdays at the eight o'clock morning service, he rarely missed matins on Sundays at either the Chapel Royal, St James's, or, in later years, St George's Chapel, Windsor. He took Holy Communion once a month, having no drawing-room that day and abjuring visits to the theatre during the previous week. The Sabbath was always observed with due reverence: there was no hunting that day; no cards were played in the evening; and after his daughters were born the Queen read them sermons when they grew old enough to understand them. Upon their sons the King was to impress the importance of recognizing the 'wisdom and goodness of the All Mighty', the duty incumbent upon them to 'obey His laws and to acknowledge their own humility in His sight': it was observed that he himself had removed his crown before receiving the Sacrament at his coronation.★

Although a devoted adherent of the Anglican Church – whose

★ He would have preferred not to take Communion at all on that occasion, since, as he said when asked if new Knights of the Garter were to do so before their installation, the Holy Sacrament was 'not to be profaned by our Gothic institutions'. He was told, however, that, at the coronation, the observance was 'indispensable' (Wraxall, *Historical Memoirs*, ii, 20–1).

services he attended with all possible regularity and exemplary reverence★ – he admired the zeal of the Nonconformists and the simple goodness of the Quakers, while the Methodists were, in his opinion, 'a quiet good kind of people who will disturb nobody'. He much admired the Countess of Huntingdon, who 'turned methodist' to the distress of her friends, bringing what she termed the 'new light' into aristocratic circles; and he expressed the wish that there could be a Lady Huntingdon in every diocese in the country. He was an admirer, too, of Lady Huntingdon's friend John Wesley, who in turn held the King in high regard. 'When will England,' Wesley asked, 'ever have a better prince?'

★ Fanny Burney observed this when she attended a service in St George's Chapel, Windsor, at the end of which the King made the traditional offering on behalf of the Knights of the Garter: 'The organ began a slow and solemn movement, and the King came down from his stall, and proceeded, with a grave and majestic walk, towards the communion table. When he had proceeded about a third of the way, he stopped, and bowed low to the altar: then he moved on, and again, at an equal distance, stopped for the same formality, which was a third and last time repeated as he reached the steps of the altar. Then he made his offering . . . He then knelt down, and made a silent prayer, after which, in the same measured steps, he returned to his stall.

'The air of piety, and the unaffected grace and dignity, with which the King performed this rite, surprised and moved me; Mr Smelt [Leonard Smelt, Sub-Governor to the Prince of Wales and Prince Frederick] even shed tears from emotion, in looking at him in this serious office. The King, I am told, always acquits himself with true majesty, when he is necessarily to appear in state as a monarch' (d'Arblay, *Diary and Letters*, ii, 27).

8

BUCKINGHAM HOUSE

A retreat not a palace . . .

The King and Queen had not been married long when His Majesty's eye fell upon a house in which the domesticity so much to his taste could be enjoyed far more easily than amid the formal and ancient splendours of St James's Palace. He had earlier considered the possibility of taking Wanstead House in Essex, a splendid place designed by Colen Campbell for Sir Richard Child in the early years of the century. But it had been decided that this was rather too far from London, and so it was agreed that they should buy Buckingham House, a house which the King felt he could make into a home, something he knew he could never do with either Hampton Court or Kensington Palace, both royal residences too painfully associated with unhappy days in the past.

Buckingham House was in an ideal situation at the west end of the Mall with views across St James's Park, conveniently situated for St James's Palace but secluded behind a courtyard surrounded by iron railings. A few weeks after its completion in 1705 it had been described as 'one of the great beauties of London, both by reason of its situation and its building . . . Behind it is a fine garden, a noble terrace (from whence, as well as from the apartments, you have a most delicious prospect) and a little park with a pretty canal.'

The red-brick house had been designed for John Sheffield, first Duke of Buckingham and Normanby, by William Winde, architect of the house in Lincoln's Inn Fields occupied by the Duke of Newcastle. It had been built on land part of which was owned by the Duke and part held on lease from the Crown. The leasehold land was known as the Mulberry Garden, being formerly a walled garden planted with thousands of mulberry trees which James I had created in the hope of promoting the culture of silk. The grounds had been designed by Henry Wise, gardener to William III, Queen Anne and George I.

The avenues to this House are along St James's Park, through rows of goodly elms on one hand, and gay flourishing limes on the other [the Duke of Buckingham and Normanby told a friend]; that for coaches, this for walking; with the Mall lying between them. This reaches to my iron pallisade that encompasses a square court, which has in the midst a great bason with statues and waterworks; and from its entrance rises all the way imperceptibly, 'till we mount to a Terrace in front of a large Hall, paved with square white Stones mixed with a dark coloured marble.

The Duke had died in 1721, and his widow, who claimed to be a natural daughter of James II by Catherine Sedley, had entered into negotiations for the disposal of the property first to the King's grandfather, then to the trustees of the newly founded British Museum. Nothing had come of these negotiations, and the property had come into the hands of the Duke's illegitimate son, Sir Charles Sheffield, who in the early 1760s agreed to sell it to the King for £28,000 – £2,000 less than the price asked of the British Museum trustees eight years before.

Much as he liked the house as it was, and anxious as he was to assure Lord Bute that it was to be 'a retreat not a palace', the King was intent on enlarging and improving it; and over the years he did so, providing it with no fewer than four separate libraries, the South and East Libraries, the Octagon and the Great Library, all of them approached only through the King's bedchamber on the ground floor and containing a remarkably eclectic collection of books.

Although he had shown an interest in buying books while Prince of Wales, the King's library really began with the purchase in 1762 of over 30,000 items from the collection of George Thomason, a seventeenth-century bookseller who had carried on his business at the sign of the Rose and Crown in St Paul's Churchyard. Formed over a period of some twenty years, this collection was largely composed of books, pamphlets, single sheets, tracts, sermons and newspapers which had poured from the presses, in both the Royalist and Parliamentarian interests, in the Civil War. One item, Thomason had been proud to say, had been given him by Mr Milton; another had been borrowed by King Charles I and returned 'speedily and safely'. Sent to Oxford for safe keeping, the collection had escaped destruction in the Great Fire of 1666, the year of Thomason's death; and it was eventually bought by the King for £300.

Three years after this the King's library was further extended by the purchase, for a far larger sum, of the collection of Joseph Smith, the British Consul in Venice, who had lived in that city since the age of eighteen and had made a fortune in commerce and dealing in works of art. Horace Walpole, who referred to him slightingly as 'the Merchant of Venice', said that Smith knew nothing of his books except their title-pages; but he was, in fact, a discerning collector, principally of books on Italian literature, which were listed in a catalogue printed in Venice in 1755 under the title *Biblioteca Smithiana, seu Catalogus Librorum D. Josephi Smithii Angli*. It was asserted in Venetian *saloni* that it was in order to get his hands upon the Consul's collection that John Murray, the unscrupulous English Resident in Venice, induced his sister to marry Smith when that by then 'curious old man' was over eighty. Murray's scheme did not bear fruit, however; and Smith's collection passed into the King's hands for £10,000.

Over the years, acting on the advice of his librarians and of such men as Stephen Demainbray, the astronomer, who had been the King's tutor in mathematics and natural history, Richard Dalton, the engraver and librarian, and Sir William Chambers, the architect, the King added more and more volumes to his collection, allowing £1,500 a year for this purpose – a sum often exceeded. From bookshops in England and abroad – in particular from Thomas Davies's bookshop in Russell Street, Covent Garden, where James Boswell first met Samuel Johnson – at sales in auction rooms and private houses, from dealers and from other collectors, books came to fill the shelves of the four libraries at the Queen's House, as Buckingham House was more generally known. John Adams, the future President of the United States, was to find these libraries 'in perfect order' in 1783, when he was American Minister in London, the books having been 'chosen with perfect taste and judgement'.

Although his agents were instructed never to bid 'against a scholar, a professor, or any person of moderate means who desired a particular book for his own use', the King's library eventually numbered some 65,000 books and 450 manuscripts. Among them could be found numerous editions of Boccaccio and of the Bible in different languages, (including a Gutenberg printing), over twenty volumes printed by Caxton, folios of Shakespeare, volumes of ancient classical authors, first editions, among them one of *Paradise Lost*, State papers, contemporary pamphlets, English and foreign periodicals, a collection of music books bought from the library of the composer William Boyce, and several of Handel's autograph scores, as well as the works of the King's contemporaries and near-contemporaries Sterne, Fielding, Smollett and Richardson, Gray and Scott, Frederick the Great, Rousseau and Voltaire, Gibbon, Burke, Boswell and Samuel Johnson, whose manuscript of *Irene* was also there.

It was in one of the King's libraries at the Queen's House in 1767 that the celebrated meeting of Johnson and the King took place. It was a meeting which much gratified Johnson's 'monarchical enthusiasm', and which he loved to relate with suitable embellishments and in great detail when requested by his friends.

Learning of Johnson's occasional visits to the library – which was readily opened by the Librarian to readers such as himself – the King asked to be informed when next he came there.* So one day when Johnson was sitting by the fire, deep in the study of a book, the Librarian went to tell the King of his opportunity. The King rose immediately, followed the Librarian, who lit the way with a candle, and came to a private door which he opened with his own key. Johnson was still in a profound study by the fire. The Librarian went up to him and whispered, 'Sir, here is the King.' 'Johnson started up, and stood still. His Majesty approached him, and at once was courteously easy.'

They spoke of Oxford and Cambridge, of Lord Lyttelton's *History*

---

* Permission to use the library was not denied to scholars of whose politics or religion the King disapproved, but His Majesty made it clear he had no wish to see them. When he heard that Dr Joseph Priestley, the chemist, a man of distasteful political and religious opinions, wanted to consult some volumes there he wrote, 'If Dr. Priestly applies to my librarian, he will have permission to see the library as other men of science have had; but I cannot think that the Doctor's character as a politician or divine deserves my appearing in it at all' (Dobrée, ed., *Letters of King George III*, 139).

60

of the Life of Henry the Second, which had just been published, and of the controversy between William Warburton, Bishop of Gloucester, and Robert Lowth, Bishop of St David's; they discussed literary journals, and the egregious Dr John Hill, a prolific writer on all manner of subjects, the fifth edition of whose *Old Man's Guide to Health and Longer Life* had appeared not long before. The King observed that he supposed Dr Johnson must have read a great deal; and Johnson replied that he thought more than he read now, but that he had read a great deal 'in the early part of his life'.

'His Majesty enquired if he was then writing any thing,' so Boswell related. 'He answered, he was not, for he had pretty well told the world what he knew, and must now read to acquire more knowledge. The King . . . then said, "I do not think you borrow much from any body." Johnson said, he thought he had already done his part as a writer. "I should have thought so too, (said the King,) if you had not written so well."'

No man could have paid a handsomer compliment than that, Johnson decided, 'and it was fit for a King to pay. It was decisive.' Later, 'His Majesty expressed a desire to have the literary biography of this country ably executed, and proposed to Dr. Johnson to undertake it. Johnson signified his readiness to comply with his Majesty's wishes.'

After the interview was over, and the King had left, Johnson turned to the Librarian and observed, 'Sir, they may talk of the King as they will; but he is the finest gentleman I have ever seen'; and he later added, 'Sir, his manners are those of as fine a gentleman as we may suppose Lewis the Fourteenth or Charles the Second.'

While Johnson was relating the details of the interview at Sir Joshua Reynolds's house, someone asked him if he had made any reply to the King's high compliment as to the merits of his work. 'No, Sir,' he replied. 'When the King had said it, it was to be so. It was not for me to bandy civilities with my Sovereign.'

It was generally agreed that Johnson had carried on the conversation very well. The Librarian reported that he had spoken to the King 'with profound respect, but still in his firm manly manner, with a sonorous voice, and never in that subdued tone which is commonly used at the levee and in the drawing-room'. Even Oliver Goldsmith was moved to overcome his envy and pay a rare compliment. He had listened to Johnson's account in silence, ruminating gloomily on a sofa at a distance from the others; but at length 'the simplicity of his natural character prevailed'. He sprang up from the sofa, walked across the room and 'in a kind of flutter, from imagining himself in the situation which he had just been hearing described, exclaimed, "Well, you acquitted yourself in this conversation better than I should have done; for I should have bowed and stammered through the whole of it." '

As he had shown in his conversation with Johnson, the King did not merely collect books, as Walpole said Consul Smith did: he looked into them, though some not as carefully as others, reading for instruction rather than pleasure, sometimes merely glancing through the index, once 'laughing heartily' as he confessed to Fanny Burney that, having looked up her name in the index to Boswell's *Life of Johnson*, he was disappointed to see that the book contained so few references to her.

Mostly, when he could spare the time from the inordinate amount of official papers which he had to attend to, he read newspapers, which often sent him to sleep within half an hour. Yet he knew his Shakespeare well, and of course his Bible. He was conversant with the works of Gibbon, David Hume and Bishop Burnet, and when he was impressed with a work, particularly one which confirmed him in his own opinions, he would take the trouble to make a précis of it. He was especially an admirer of Henry Fielding; and his compliment to Samuel Johnson on Johnson's own works was not an idle one. When an edition of Horace Walpole's works appeared in 1798 he read all five volumes and seemed to be 'very amused' by the letters, though he had to admit that Walpole's statements were 'not always quite strictly true'. He also read with enjoyment the articles by the Rev. Sydney Smith in the *Edinburgh Review*, commenting knowingly that Smith was 'a very clever fellow' but would never make a bishop.★

★ Although paid for from the Privy Purse at a total cost which has been estimated as being about £120,000, excluding the expenses of binding and the salaries of librarians, the King had always intended that his library should be a national institution not a private one, and in the next reign it was handed over to the British Museum by his son, King George IV, who told the First Minister that, as well as 'paying a just tribute' to the memory of his father, he had 'the satisfaction by this means of

The King was a keen collector not only of books but also of musical scores, coins, medals, clocks and watches, maps and model ships, which were displayed in galleries in the East Library in the Queen's House. He also collected drawings, and in 1762 he paid £20,000 to the heirs of Consul Smith for his fine art collection, which, as well as coins, antiques, gems and manuscripts, included Italian paintings – several by Canaletto, others by Zuccarelli, Rosalba Carriera, Giovanni Bellini and the Ricci, and genre scenes by Pietro Longhi.★ He also bought several fine drawings from the collection of Cardinal Alessandro Albani, a purchase negotiated for him by Robert Adam's brother James.

He did not pretend to be a connoisseur of art. He liked exact topographical scenes and pictures which told a story, pointed a moral, or celebrated some deed of heroism or self-sacrifice or some simple domestic scene such as Vermeer's *Lady at the Virginals*, one of his greatest acquisitions.

---

advancing the literature of the country'. In 1850 an article appeared in the *Quarterly Review* which suggested that the King had originally intended to sell the library to the highest bidder. Richard Heber, the book collector, hearing that the Tsar was interested in buying it, approached Lord Sidmouth, who arranged for the money which the King had hoped to receive from the Tsar to be paid to him out of the Droits of Admiralty (*Quarterly Review*, clxxv, 143). The Duke of York, who was very annoyed with his brother for having parted with their father's property, told Charles Greville that the King 'even had a design of selling the Library collected by the late King, but this he was obliged to abandon for the Ministers and the Royal Family must have interfered to oppose so scandalous a transaction' (*The Greville Memoirs*, i, 141). The Duke of Clarence was also 'much vexed' by his brother's action and would never visit the King's Library at the British Museum (Macaulay's Journal, Trinity College, Cambridge, entry for 29 November 1849). Peel, however, who was one of the trustees of the Museum and had much to do with the disposal of the King's Library, confirmed in his correspondence with W. R. Hamilton that it was King George IV's personal wish that it should go to Bloomsbury, as his father had always been so interested in the Museum (BM Peel MSS, quoted in Hibbert, *George IV: Regent and King*, 265).

★ Unlike his books, the King's art collection was not made available on application to strangers, since Buckingham House was 'treated as a private residence, accessible to only a few court officials and the occasional private guest. Nor did George normally permit artists to copy materials from the royal collection; he took the view that, once he gave one artist the privilege, he would be inundated with requests' (Brewer, *Pleasures of the Imagination*, 219).

He acknowledged the talent of Joshua Reynolds although he did not much like the man, finding him too self-assured, his pictures too expensive, and his dealings with the King's political opponents undesirable. He far preferred the less subtle American-born artists John Singleton Copley, who painted a charming portrait of three of his daughters, and Benjamin West, who was put to work on an immense representation of the Resurrection for the east window of St George's Chapel at Windsor as well as the decoration of St George's Hall with eight pictures depicting episodes in the life of Edward III. He also commissioned from West a painting of the departure of the Roman general Marcus Atilius Regulus from Rome; and to guide the artist in his work he took a copy of Livy from his library and read to him the story of this model of honour and endurance who suffered to be taken prisoner and tortured to death in Carthage rather than agree to an unjust peace. When the painting was finished, in 1769, the King was so taken with it that he asked West to provide him with six more paintings on related themes; and the year after his completion of the celebrated *Death of General Wolfe* – of which the King bought a replica to be set in the panelling of the Warm Room at Buckingham House – West was appointed Historical Painter to the King at a salary of £1,000 a year, while William Woollett, who made a print of this picture, was appointed Engraver to His Majesty.

Other distinguished artists employed by the Court were Thomas Gainsborough, whose pleasant, easy company the King and Queen both enjoyed,* Francis Cotes, George and Nathaniel Dance, Thomas Patch, Sir William Beechey, who became Portrait Painter to the Queen in 1793, and two artists of German descent: John Hoppner, whose mother was one of the Queen's attendants at Court, and John Zoffany, who was introduced by the King to the Grand Duke of Tuscany and commissioned by the Queen to paint the group of Grand Tourists in the *Tribuna of the Uffizi* in Florence which is one of the treasures of the Royal Collection. Zoffany was also

---

* At her death the Queen owned twenty-two of Gainsborough's drawings. When the artist took his *Woodman* to the Queen's House, the King pronounced it 'a masterpiece of the pencil' (Millar, *Later Georgian Pictures in the Collection of Her Majesty the Queen*, Text, xxi).

commissioned to paint a portrait of the King's two elder sons at the Queen's House, portraying them, presumably as requested, beneath a picture of the children of Charles I, a monarch whom the King greatly revered. In 1792 Thomas Lawrence became Principal Portrait Painter in Ordinary upon the death of Sir Joshua Reynolds, who had been appointed to that post without enthusiasm by the King in succession to Allan Ramsay, an artist recommended by Ramsay's fellow Scotsman Lord Bute, who took credit for helping to develop such taste as His Majesty possessed.

Yet if he was never a great judge of art, if his commissions after the purchase of Consul Smith's collection were largely limited to family portraits, and if his refusal to consider the merits of work he did not understand led him to reject such artists as Richard Wilson, the King served art well by warmly supporting the suggestion that a Royal Academy of Arts should be founded in London.*

For years there had been talk of establishing such an academy for the teaching and exhibition of works of art in London; and an invitation to 'throw upon paper some loose hints' on the subject had been extended to Sir William Chambers, who was in the habit of submitting works to the annual exhibitions of the Society of Artists, later to be known as the Incorporated Society of Artists of Great Britain, the treasurer of which was the King's Librarian, Richard Dalton.

Dalton was also a print dealer who had a warehouse in Pall Mall; but his business did not prosper, and he accordingly approached the King with a scheme to establish an academy of arts in this warehouse instead. 'His Majesty clearly saw the folly into which his librarian had precipitated himself,' wrote the author of *An Inquiry into the Rise and Establishment of the Royal Academy of Arts* in 1775; 'and therefore, from his natural humanity, as well as from a desire of promoting the fine arts, which he loved, he adopted the proposed plan . . . the label over the door containing the *Print Ware-house* was erazed, and another substituted in its place, viz. *The Royal Academy*'.

---

* There were reasons other than aesthetic for the King's rejection of Wilson, who lost favour at an early stage when he haggled over the price of a view of Syon House which had been commissioned by Bute for the King. Wilson caused particular irritation by offering to accept payment from the Crown in instalments (Langford, *A Polite and Commercial People*, 317.

At the same time the Incorporated Society of Artists was breaking up in acrimony, and several of its leading members, having resigned, approached the King with proposals for 'a well-regulated School or Academy of Design, for the use of students in the Arts, and an annual exhibition, open to all artists of distinguished merit'.

The King readily agreed to support this project with his patronage and financial support, and helped in the wording of an Instrument of Foundation, which he signed with the declaration that he would always be the Academy's 'patron, protector and supporter'. The Instrument was largely drawn up by Chambers, who let it be known that he would not be averse to becoming the new Academy's first President. It was held, however, that this office ought to be held by a painter, so Joshua Reynolds was approached – and much annoyed the King by hesitating before accepting the office, having consulted his friend Edmund Burke – while Chambers became Treasurer, a post which it was decided should be in the gift of the King, since, as His Majesty had been 'graciously pleased to pay all deficiencies' – and, indeed, had contributed £5,000 towards the Academy's initial costs – it was considered only proper that he should 'have a person on whom he places full confidence in an office where his interest is concerned'. The King was also granted the right to be consulted as to the nomination of the first Royal Academicians, and to nominate others for membership himself. Foundation members included Thomas Gainsborough, Angelica Kauffmann, Richard Wilson, Benjamin West (who succeeded Reynolds as President, much to the King's gratification) and the indefatigable Paul Sandby, brother of the Deputy Ranger of Windsor Great Park, several of whose charming coloured drawings of Windsor Castle were acquired for the Royal Collection.

Three years after the foundation of the Society of Artists, on 10 December 1768 the Academicians held their first meeting in Richard Dalton's former print house, where the new institution's name was already emblazoned over the door. In 1771 they moved to Somerset House, where the King also made rooms available for the Royal Society and the Society of Antiquaries and where he thereafter became a frequent visitor.

★

As well as libraries, the King supplied the Queen's House with a splendid Music Room, a Japan Room and a large Saloon Room, for which the seven Raphael cartoons painted for the Sistine Chapel tapestries were brought in from Hampton Court. Furniture, together with other pictures, was also brought from Kensington Palace and Windsor Castle; while new pieces, including a fine mahogany secretaire and 'a very handsome jewel cabinet', were specially made by the cabinetmakers of Long Acre, among them William Vile and John Cobb.★ The King also bought pieces at auction, once acquiring at an auction held near Marlow conducted by James Christie the Elder 'some very curious ivory chairs . . . 14½ guineas each . . . a couch 48 guineas and two small cabinets 45 guineas' which had been made in Madras for an employee of the East India Company.

In his hurry to move into the house, the King chivvied the tradesmen and servants, allowing the Housekeeper, Mrs Elizabeth Stainforth, only three weeks to make the house clean and tidy after crowds of sightseers had been allowed to troop round it by the servants of the previous owner. By 22 May 1762 it was deemed habitable, and on that night the King and Queen slept there together for the first time. The following year, on the night of his twenty-fifth birthday, the Queen gave a magnificent reception for her husband, who was taken up the grand staircase to her darkened apartments, where the shutters were suddenly thrown open to reveal the terrace and lawns and the long canal brilliantly illuminated in the light of four thousand lamps. The Queen's band played 'God Save the King'; then, as she and her husband went down to greet their guests and enjoy what the *Gentleman's Magazine* described as a 'supper of a hundred cold dishes followed by an illuminated dessert', the music of the King's beloved Handel filled the air.

By the time of this celebration the eighteen-year-old Queen had given birth to her first child. She had been obliged to leave chapel in a hurry one Sunday in the middle of February 1762. The Serjeant-

---

★ 'It is impossible to estimate the exact cost of the rebuilding and furnishing of Buckingham House, but enough details are provided in the Royal Accounts to indicate the vast scale of the expenditure. Apparently £13,885 14s. 6½d. was spent on rebuilding in the years 1762–3, and later additional sums of £10,197 and £9,757' (Healey, *The Queen's House*, 48–9).

Surgeon, Sir Caesar Hawkins, had been summoned and, on learning that she was feeling giddy and breathless, had had recourse to his favourite remedy of bleeding. The King had immediately written to his 'Dearest Friend', Lord Bute, to say that he would surely be 'too conversant not to guess what this is'. He himself would 'say nothing but deny nothing'. For the moment he could write no more than that, since the Queen was calling 'with impatience for Her dinner'. 'I desire,' the King ended his note, 'the whole of this may remain *entre nous.*'

Three months later the Queen's giddiness returned. Sir Caesar was again summoned and again ordered bleeding. The Queen did not approve of this treatment but patiently submitted to it. The experienced *accoucheur* William Hunter was now consulted, however; and, to the Queen's relief, he put an end to the blood-letting. Her Majesty thereafter had no more worrying symptoms, and continued towards her confinement with a healthy appetite.

It was the King who now fell ill, with a severe and feverish cold which incapacitated him for some days. When he was a little better, Bute suggested he should go into the country to escape the unhealthy London air. But the King did not think it would be safe for the Queen to go at such a time, and 'nothing in the World' would make him go without her. He knew 'the loss of Her now would break [his] Heart'.

Anxiously he awaited the time of her delivery. Sir Caesar Hawkins had fixed the date as 3 August; but that day passed with no signs of an imminent birth; so did the whole of the following week; and it was not until the early hours of the morning of 12 August that the Queen sent a message to her husband from St James's Palace to say that her labour had begun. He went immediately to fetch the dry-nurse.

Soon the rooms next to the bedroom in which the King's heir was to be born began to fill with doctors, attendants, nurses and members of the Royal Family. In the bedroom itself, the door of which stood open, was the midwife, Mrs Mary Draper, an elderly woman of many years' experience. In the adjoining rooms were the doctors, ready to answer a summons in case of complications but not otherwise required. Also here were the King's mother, the King himself, the Mistress of the Robes, various Ladies of the Bedchamber, dressers and servants, one or two members of the Cabinet, including the Lord Chancellor, and, reluctantly, the Archbishop of Canterbury.

It was a severe labour; but the midwife came out to assure the waiting throng that no complications were expected. The mother 'scarce cried out at all', the Duchess of Northumberland, a Lady of the Bedchamber, recorded; 'and at twenty-four minutes past seven she was delivered'.

Forestalling the Queen's Vice-Chamberlain, who had been told to hold himself ready to notify the King as soon as the baby was born, the incompetent and officious Groom of the Stole, Lord Huntingdon, hastened to His Majesty with the intelligence that he was the father of a baby girl. Protesting that he was 'but little anxious as to the sex of the child' so long as the Queen was safe, the King hurried to the bedroom, where he was shown 'as strong, large and pretty boy . . . as ever was seen'.

A fortnight later it was announced that, on the afternoons of drawing-room days, this pretty boy, already created Prince of Wales and, by right of birth, Duke of Cornwall, would be on display in his room at St James's Palace. Here, in his cradle behind a lattice screen, he was inspected by crowds of visitors, who were served in an ante-room with pieces of cake and a beverage known as caudle, a warm gruel spiced with wine.

Soon afterwards the baby, crying 'most lustily', was christened in the Queen's Drawing-Room by the Archbishop of Canterbury. As the names George Augustus Frederick were bestowed upon him, his father was seen to be deeply moved and to behave with the 'most affecting piety'.

The mother made a good recovery; and, although she had had her dinners alone for a fortnight after her confinement, husband and wife were eating together again by the end of the month. As if he expected the ordeal of giving birth to have weakened her, the King reported to Lord Bute that she was as 'nimble' as ever. Even so, he was most solicitous towards her, constantly urging her to sit down so that she did not tire herself unduly. As a husband he was 'really happy', he told Bute – assuring him, at the same time, that he was 'more sensible of his friendship than ever'. The letters he wrote to him from now on, however, were no longer the passionate outpourings of earlier years. He was slowly beginning to outgrow the devoted attachment of a prolonged adolescence.

9

DUTIES AND DIVERSIONS

*If the mind be not constantly in the habit of serious employment
it will lose its energy.*

The King's daily routine changed little throughout his reign. He always rose early, often before five o'clock, when, in winter, he would light the fire himself and climb back into bed until the clock struck the hour. He was very rarely still in bed at six; and he was to impress upon his children the value of the early morning hours, as being the best for work in the day, as well as the need to 'economise amusements'. When the day's work was done, there was 'no greater wisdom', he was to advise one of his sons, 'than so to economise amusements that they shall continue so during life, which, if too much sought after, naturally must sooner or later become irksome. Besides, if the mind be not constantly in the habit of serious employment it will lose its energy, and those powers a man may have been blessed with will entirely vanish.' He himself took care to ensure that he was absorbed in some activity or other all day long.

Having said his prayers, the King shaved, then settled down to deal with his correspondence and to read such dispatches and reports as might have been sent on to him by the various ministries. His comments on these papers, like his innumerable letters and his copies and summaries of important State papers, were written in his own hand, since he did not care to employ a private secretary for this purpose. He dated them carefully, giving not merely the day of the month, but the exact time of writing to the very minute. He was remarkably conscientious, as Lord Brougham was to observe:

The instructions to ambassadors, the orders to governors, the movements of forces, down to the marching of a single battalion, in the districts of this

71

country, the appointments to all offices in Church and State; not only the giving away of judgeships, bishoprics, regiments, but the subordinate promotions, lay and clerical; all these form the topics of his letters; on all, his opinion is pronounced decisively; on all his will is declared peremptorily. In one letter he decides the appointment of a Scotch puisne judge; in another the march of a troop from Buckinghamshire into Yorkshire; in a third the nomination to the Deanery of Worcester; in a fourth he says that if Adam, the architect, succeeds Worsley at the Board of Works, he shall think Chambers ill-used.

He gave careful attention, in fact, to almost all matters which were brought to his attention, trivial as well as important. He examined the detailed plans of fortified towns on the Continent; he carefully studied the uniforms of the regiments in his Army; he learned by heart the names of all the larger ships in his Navy; he went over, item by item, the figures in his accounts and, man by man, the voting record of Members of Parliament. He was once thrown into what he himself described as the 'greatest state of uneasiness he ever felt' when he had to come to a decision on the merits of Lady Beaulieu's complicated application for the earldom of Montagu.

He studied with the greatest care papers detailing the cases of malefactors sentenced to death, 'ever desirous to be perfectly con-vinced', as he once put it to one of his Secretaries of State, 'that there is no room for mitigating the rigour of the Law, before it takes its course'. Although he was usually content to be guided by the judges who had tried the cases brought to his attention, and was very rarely disposed to be lenient in cases of forgery, he was often moved to be merciful when struck by some pathetic or mitigating circum-stance in the malefactor's record.

Letters which most of his predecessors and successors might well have handed over to a secretary or left unanswered were given his personal and painstaking consideration. One day, for example, 'his Prescent Mayjesty King George ye third, London' received a barely literate letter from an English sailor who, while on shore near Bremen, had been pressed into the Prussian Army. He had written several times representing his case to 'his Mayjisty King of Prows in Berlien', but had received no reply. So, advised by a 'marchant from Ingland', he ventured to address 'tow or three lines' to his own sovereign. 'This letter,' the sailor concluded, 'must smugle away in toan Englishmans hands that none of the Offiscears catch me. iam 28 years of agge and 5 foot aleaven in hight and so no more at present, but remain, in prays to the Allmighty for your Mayjestys long rean and in peace with all men, James Richardson.' Long as the letter was, and difficult as it was to read, the King, having taken the trouble to decipher it, asked one of the Secretaries of State to make inquiries as to the truth of the man's statement, whereupon the Minister concerned wrote to the British Ambassador in Berlin to say that,

as the King's disposition inclines him to lend an ear to the complaints of the meanest of his subjects, he perused the letter with attention; and finding in it a remarkable air of truth and sincerity, he directed me to transmit it to you . . . and if the poor man's narrative be found conformable to fact . . . it is his Majesty's pleasure that you make application in his behalf to the King of Prussia and recover his liberty.

Four months later the man was discharged and sent home.

His stint of conscientious paperwork completed, the King would generally go for a ride before breakfast and then, after the most meagre of meals, have another ride accompanied by one or two members of his Household or family. In bad weather in London he rode in the manège which had been built in the grounds of the Queen's House. He would then return to his papers in the study before going to St James's for a levee, an audience, a Privy Council meeting, or a conference with one or more of his Ministers.

After returning for the four o'clock dinner, for which he was often late, the King went once again to his study to write more letters and memoranda, to consider applications for Church preferments or military promotions, or to read judicial reports. He then reappeared at about seven o'clock for tea and card games, usually commerce or 'whisk', while the royal band played in the background. On Sundays, when card games were forbidden, he might instead play a game of backgammon or chess with one of his equerries. There were occasional visits to the opera or the theatre, where the King displayed his love of farces by laughing so loudly, especially, as Thackeray put it, 'when a clown swallowed a carrot or a string of sausages', that the Queen was obliged on occasions to restrain him. He also relished the performances of Garrick's rival John Henderson, in Samuel Rogers's opinion 'a truly great actor', and of Sarah Siddons, who recalled:

The Royal Family very frequently honoured me with thier presence. The King was often moved to tears which he as often vainly endeavoured to conceal behind his eye-glass, and her Majesty the Queen, at one time told me in her gracious broken English that her only refuge from me was actually turning her back upon the stage at the same time protesting 'It is indeed too disagreeable.' In short all went on most gloriously at the Theatre.

So much did the King and Queen enjoy Mrs Siddons's performances that she was invited to give readings at the Queen's House, where she found 'Thier Majestys the most gratifying because the most unremittingly attentive of auditors'.

The King [she added] was a most judicious and tasteful critick both in acting and Dramatick composition. He told me he had endeavoured vainly to detect me in a false emphasis, and very humourously repeated many of Mr. Smith's [the Old Etonian, William Smith, known as 'Gentleman' Smith] who was then the principal Actor. He graciously commended the propriety of my action, particularly my total repose in certain situations. 'This is,' he said, 'a quality in which Garrick faild. He never could stand still; he was a great fidget.'

On one occasion when she arrived at the Queen's House Mrs Siddons was conducted into an antechamber where soon afterwards the King appeared 'in the aimiable occupation of drawing the Princess Amelia [his youngest child] then scarce three years old, in a little cane chair'.

He graciously said something to one of the ladies, and left the lovely baby to run about the room. She happened to be much pleased with some flowers in my bosom, and as I stoopd down, that she might take them if so disposd, I could not help exclaiming to a lady near us, 'What a beautiful baby! How I do long to kiss her!' When she instantly held her little Royal *hand* to my mouth to be kissed; so early had she learnd this lesson of Royalty. Her Majesty was extremely gracious and more than once during the reading desired me to take some refreshment in the next room. I declined the honour, however, altho' I had stood reading till I was ready to drop, rather than run the risk of falling down by walking backwards out of the room (a ceremony

not to be dispensed with), the floor, too, being rubbed bright. I therefore remained where I was, till Thier Majestys retired.

Once a month the King and Queen attended a Concert of Ancient Music, later known as a King's Concert, where no music less than twenty years old was performed and where no applause or call for encores was allowed except from the royal box. The directors, of whom the King was one, chose the programmes in turn. When the King's turn came round, the programme was almost certain to contain music by Handel, which he had loved far more than that of all other composers ever since he had been introduced to Handel himself as a boy.

Among his most prized possessions were a harpsichord which had once belonged to the great composer and the scores of some of his early and unpublished operas, which were copied for him by a man employed for this purpose. So great, indeed, was his admiration for Handel – a bust of whom by Roubiliac occupied a prominent position in the Japan Room at the Queen's House* – that he insisted that Charles Burney, author of *A General History of Music*, should revise some comments he had made upon the composer which the King considered did not do his hero justice. On occasions he was seen wearing a Handel medal on his coat.

The King also enjoyed the music of Johann Christian Bach, who settled in London in 1762 and soon afterwards became Music Master to Queen Charlotte. The year after his arrival in London, Johann Christian's opera *Orione* was produced at the King's Theatre, Haymarket, both the first and second performances being attended by the King and Queen, who in 1764 welcomed to London the eight-year-old Mozart, a fellow admirer of Bach. The King was as delighted by the boy as he was by his astonishingly precocious gifts, which Mozart demonstrated on both the harpsichord and the organ at the Queen's House, and, on coming across the prodigy and his father one day near St James's Palace, the King pulled down the window of his carriage to wave at them with cheerful bonhomie.

* This bust is now in the Queen's Presence Chamber at Windsor Castle.

10

A PROMISING START

There is a decency and dignity in his character that could not be expected at his years.

Despite his occasional late nights, regular early rising and days of hard work, the King seemed never tired in these early months of his reign.

He was determined to be and to be seen to be a conscientious monarch, bent, with Lord Bute's help, on playing a far more active role in public affairs than his grandfather had done in his last years, anxious, so he professed, to root out corruption, to end faction in politics, to ensure that the Crown was no longer in thrall to devious and self-seeking politicians, as he had been led to believe it had been in his grandfather's day. He also sought to put a stop to the practice of spending large sums of public money on subsidizing candidates at elections, though he was soon to accept that a certain proportion of his income and Secret Service money would have to be devoted to the payment of candidates prepared to support policies of which he himself approved, and that the first election of his reign (and subsequent ones) would have to be managed much as elections had been managed in the past, with the return of an appropriate number of men nominated or approved by the Court.

He was well aware that theoretically nothing in either the Bill of Rights of 1689 or the 1701 Act of Settlement stood in the way of his declaring war, nominating peers, appointing bishops and ambassadors as well as judges and army and naval officers, and summoning or dissolving Parliament. But in practice he was constrained from doing so, since the Civil List Act of 1698 was intended to give the monarchy finances enough only for the Court and the civil service. It was Parliament which voted money each year for the

Army and Navy and for servicing the national debt. The King, therefore, needed Parliament's approval of his Government, and he soon came to realize that his undoubted power of appointing Ministers was qualified by the necessity of gaining parliamentary support for their measures. That requirement was not, however, such a restriction as might have been expected, since there was a widespread belief that any King's Minister ought to be given a fair chance to prove himself and since the existence of a large 'court party' of office-holders in both Houses of Parliament ensured that the resignation of a First Minister was rarely brought about by parliamentary defeat.

As well as being set upon ending faction in politics, the King was also determined to demonstrate to his people that, while his immediate predecessors had cared more for Hanover than for the great country over which they had come to rule, he was, for all his German blood, a true-born Englishman – or rather, having regard to the country of Lord Bute's birth, a true-born Briton. 'Born and educated in this country,' he declared to the first Parliament of his reign, 'I glory in the name of Britain.'* Yet Britain, he frequently lamented, was passing through an age of depravity and profligacy, a 'selfish and unprincipled age'; and he was determined to do what he could to cleanse it. One of the first acts of his reign was to issue a proclamation for the 'Encouragement of Piety and Virtue':

We do hereby declare our royal purpose and resolution to discountenance and punish all manner of vice, profaneness and immorality . . . particularly in such as are employed near our royal person . . . and . . . we will, upon all occasions, distinguish persons of piety and virtue by marks of our royal favour . . . and we do hereby command and require . . . our loving subjects of what degree or quality soever . . . decently and reverently to attend the worship of God on every Lord's Day . . .

While there were those who regarded this proclamation with profound scepticism, even with derision, there could be no doubt

---

* The use of this word instead of 'England' or 'Englishman' was widely supposed to be Bute's responsibility. 'I suppose you will think *Briton* remarkable,' the Duke of Newcastle wrote to Lord Hardwicke. 'It denotes the author to all the world' (Harris, *Life of Lord Chancellor Hardwicke*, iii, 231).

that the King himself was both pious and virtuous and intent upon ensuring that the conduct he desired to inculcate in his 'loving subjects' would be observed at Court. It had to be said, though, that those who knew him best had observed in him an unfortunate lingering tendency to stress his own virtue when condemning the faults of others, as well as a disposition to harbour resentment. He endeavoured to be forgiving and to acknowledge the fact when he had been in the wrong. He once firmly maintained that 'no one should be above confessing when they have been mistaken'. 'In my opinion,' he also said, 'when a person has been perfectly in the wrong, the most just and honourable thing for him to do is to acknowledge it publicly.' It had, he declared years later, 'from his entrance into life been an invariable rule with him to store in his memory carefully every right and proper action of others and, as far as possible, to forget instances of a contrary conduct'. This was, however, a rule which he often found it impossible to obey.

Resolved to demonstrate his strict regard for economy as well as virtue, and to preside over a Court respected for its sobriety and the formality of its protocol, the young King, at Bute's behest, fulfilled a pledge of his father by announcing that he would accept a fixed Civil List of £800,000 in place of the larger if fluctuating traditional income enjoyed by his grandfather, King George II – a gesture which he was to have cause to regret, since the growth of a large family and the needs of his brothers and sisters were to oblige him to turn to Parliament for help in years to come.

At this time he was a popular figure. His grandfather had never been much liked and had had to bear the thought of that 'worthless' son of his, Prince Frederick, parading through the streets and standing on the steps of taverns to gain the favour of the people, while he himself was seen as a charmless, tight-fisted German curmudgeon. But in his later years even George II, a king living longer than any British monarch before him, had been quite kindly regarded by a people priding themselves on victories over foreign enemies and, for the most part, enjoying a gradually improving standard of living.

Inheriting this general feeling of goodwill, his grandson was welcomed to the throne with qualified enthusiasm. There were, of

course, those who expressed reservations and were cautious in their estimates of him. Lord Chesterfield wondered what might be expected of a young man who, 'like a new Sultan', had been 'lugged out of the seraglio by the Princess and Lord Bute and placed upon the throne'. Samuel Johnson spoke of his apprehension as to the future behaviour of a prince who had been so 'long in the hands of the Scotch'. Charles Townshend, the Secretary-at-War, gave his opinion of the King's character in four words: 'He is very obstinate.' Already there was gradually being created a myth that George III, with the encouragement of his mother and Bute, was bent on establishing a despotism on the Stuart model. In fact the King was, in general, to prove himself to be a model of constitutional propriety, anxious to have an influence upon the policies of his Government of the day but in no sense to decide or dictate them. He was certainly jealous of his power to appoint Ministers, but, having appointed them, he left them free to govern. 'The King will always leave his own sentiments and conform to his Ministers',' Lord Hillsborough, a future Secretary of State, was to say, 'though he will argue with them, and very sensibly. But, if they adhere to their own opinion, he will say, "Well. Do you choose it should be so? Then let it be."'

For the most part, opinions of the new King were most favourable. 'We are much pleased [with him],' Samuel Johnson eventually decided, and 'of him we are much inclined to hope great things.' Johnson's approbatory opinion was widely shared. Mary, Lady Hervey, said that everyone seemed to be pleased with the King's behaviour: 'So much unaffected good nature appears in all he does or says that it cannot but endear him to all.'

'There is a decency and dignity in his character,' wrote Mrs Montagu, 'that could not be expected at his years . . . religious sentiments and a moral conduct unblemished; application to business; affability to everyone; and an elevation of thought and tenderness of sentiment. There hardly passes a day in which one does not hear of something he has said, or done, which raises one's opinion of his understanding and heart.'

Fanny Burney praised his 'full and fine voice'. 'The King reads admirably,' she said, 'with ease, feeling, and force . . . I was very much surprised at its effect.' Horace Walpole remained well disposed towards him. 'His manner is graceful and obliging,' Walpole wrote. 'I don't say this like my dear Madame Sévigné,' he added, 'because he was civil to me, but the part is well acted . . . He has all the appearance of being amiable.'

The young King was, indeed, generally believed to be a moral and conscientious young man, and was certainly personable. Large, approving crowds gathered round his coach as he drove through the streets and cheered him as he alighted at the doors of Parliament. Doing his best to overcome his lack of confidence and social grace, he conducted his levees and drawing-rooms in a manner which met with the approval even of Horace Walpole: 'The levee room has lost so entirely the air of the lion's den. The young man don't stand in one spot with his eyes fixed royally upon the ground and dropping bits of German news. He walks about and speaks freely to everybody', although Sir Nathaniel Wraxall noticed that 'as he talks to one individual, he casts his regards, from time to time, on the person who stands next, thus anticipating and preparing himself before he begins a new dialogue'.

He strode briskly about the room, speaking quickly, asking questions, and, if not always listening too intently to the answers, giving an impression of lively curiosity. He was, for instance, much intrigued by the appearance at St James's one day of Omai, the first South Sea islander ever to be seen in England, who had been brought over from the Society Islands by Captain Tobias Furneaux in his ship *Adventure*. Although this young man, wearing a smart velvet suit, made a 'very good bow', he shocked the company by breezily greeting His Majesty with the words 'How do, King Tosh' – 'Tosh' evidently being 'a fair rendering of "George" into Tahitian'. Far from being offended, the King arranged for Omai to be inoculated, made him an allowance, and presented him with a sword, before Captain James Cook, on his third voyage, took him home to Tahiti.

The King had, however, not yet fully overcome his early shyness when confronted by people he did not know, often merely asking them when they had come to town and when they intended to leave, or inquiring – as he did of James Boswell at the biographer's first attendance at a levee after returning from a Continental tour –

1. Frederick, Prince of Wales, with three of his sisters in the grounds of the Dutch House at Kew in 1733. From a painting by Philippe Mercier.

2. Prince George, aged about eleven, with his brother, Edward, Duke of York, and their Preceptor, Dr Francis Ayscough. From a painting by Richard Wilson, *c.* 1749.

3. The thirteen-year-old Charles James Fox, son of Henry Fox, later first Baron Holland, standing beneath a window in the garden of Holland House next to his cousin, Lady Susan Fox-Strangways. Leaning out of the window is his young aunt, Lady Sarah Lennox, who married Sir Thomas Charles Bunbury while Sir Joshua Reynolds was painting this picture in 1762.

4. A miniature portrait, by the Swiss artist Jean-Étienne Liotard, of George, Prince of Wales, given to him on his fifteenth birthday, in 1753.

5. A miniature on ivory of Queen Charlotte painted by an unknown English artist, possibly Francis Sykes, *c.* 1763.

6. *The Marriage of George III*, a sketch by Sir Joshua Reynolds. The wedding took place in the Chapel Royal, St James's, on 8 September 1761. The Archbishop of Canterbury officiated, assisted by the Bishop of London. Lady Sarah Lennox and Lady Susan Fox-Strangways were among the ten bridesmaids standing behind the bride.

7. Queen Charlotte's coach being escorted back by the Royal Horse Guards
to the Queen's House in the snow. From a painting by Copley Fielding.
The King's Octagon Library can be seen on the left.

8. A watercolour by James Stephanoff of
the Octagon Library, the principal of four
libraries added to the Queen's House by
the King in the 1760s.

9. *A Lady at the Virginals with
a Gentleman* by Jan Vermeer.
One of the paintings in the
collection of Joseph Smith,
British Consul at Naples,
which was acquired by the
King in 1762 .

10. George, Prince of Wales, and Frederick, later Duke of York, depicted in the Second Drawing-Room or Warm Room in the Queen's House by Johann Zoffany, *c.* 1765. On the red damask-covered wall are Van Dyck's portraits of the children of Charles I and the Villiers family.

11. *George III, Queen Charlotte and their Six Eldest Children* by Johann Zoffany, *c.* 1770. The children are, from the left, Prince William, later William IV, holding a cockatoo, the Prince of Wales, later George IV, Prince Frederick, later Duke of York, Prince Edward, later Duke of Kent, with a spaniel, Princess Charlotte, and the infant Princess Augusta, clasping a teething coral.

12. John Opie's portrait of Mary Granville, Mrs Delany, the King's and Queen's dear friend, who was given a house and a pension when she came to live in Windsor.

13. Mrs Delany's friend Fanny Burney (Madame d'Arblay), the writer of novels including *Evelina*, who was appointed reader and Assistant Keeper of the Wardrobe to Queen Charlotte in 1786. The portrait is by her cousin, Edward Francis Burney.

14. *George III* by Benjamin West, painted in 1779 when Spain declared war on Britain and there was a threat of invasion by a Franco-Spanish fleet. In the background is a military camp; a groom leads the King's charger; behind him are the Marquess of Lothian and Lord Amherst, the acting Commander-in-Chief, who advised the King on the conduct of the American War.

15. The illuminations at the Queen's House for George III's twenty-fifth birthday on 4 June 1763 – one of Robert Adam's designs for the surprise celebrations ordered by the Queen.

16. *The Apotheosis of Prince Octavius* by Benjamin West (1783). The Prince, the eighth of King George's nine sons, is welcomed to heaven by Prince Alfred, his brother, who had died the year before. An angel supervises the meeting, which is watched by two cherubs on a cloud.

'Lately come over?' and then passing on.★ Sometimes he gave offence by a cheerfully tactless, ill-considered remark such as the one said to have been addressed to a Yorkshire squire: 'I suppose you are going back to Yorkshire, Mr Stanhope? A very ugly county Yorkshire.'

Similarly, when William Hamilton, Lady Archibald Hamilton's son, whose first wife had long since died, came to pay his respects upon his return as Envoy to Naples, the King asked the Queen to 'fish out' if he intended to get married again. After the Queen had phrased some far from subtle question which Hamilton evaded, answering by speaking of the happiness of his marriage to his late wife, the King joined the conversation and inquired whom Hamilton thought of making his heir. 'I suppose your nephew Mr Greville,' he added, without regard to the presence of Mr Greville standing immediately next to him.

As the years went by the King became adept at displaying favour and disfavour at these levees and drawing-rooms. When, for instance, Captain Horatio Nelson attended his first levee at St James's Palace upon returning from distinguished service in the Americas, the King received him with marked affability. Similarly, when next Nelson appeared at St James's, by then an admiral – 'this brave Admiral' as the King gratefully referred to him – his reception was as friendly as it had been on the earlier occasion. Peering at Nelson's empty sleeve, the King observed in his bluff way, 'You have lost your right arm!'

'But not my right hand,' Nelson responded with prompt assurance, indicating a brother officer whom he had brought to the Palace with him, 'as I have the honour of presenting Captain Berry.'

'Your country,' the King said, having acknowledged Captain

★ Boswell was not at all put out by this; and at subsequent levees the King proved far more communicative, asking after the progress of his life of Johnson, talking at some length about the Corsican patriot Pasquale di Paoli, and discussing how best to refer to Prince Charles Edward Stuart, the 'Young Pretender', in Boswell's *Journal of the Tour of the Hebrides*: the King thought 'grandson of the unfortunate James II' would be most appropriate. Boswell asked Paoli to hint to the King that he might be given some post about the Court where he could 'serve, defend, and worship the father of a whole people'. His veneration for the King, as his biographer said, 'was to grow almost oriental'. 'I felt,' Boswell himself said, 'an admiration and affection for my King such as a warm royalist alone can imagine' (Brady, *James Boswell*, 93, 291).

Berry, 'has a claim for a bit more of you.' Nelson was then formally invested with the Most Honourable Order of the Bath, the star of which he was so proud to have displayed on the portraits of him painted thereafter.

When he next attended a levee, however, his reception was very different, for by then Nelson was known to be conducting a passionate affair with Sir William Hamilton's second wife, the former Emma Hart, whom Queen Charlotte had made it clear she would on no account receive at Court.* The Admiral, accompanied by Sir William Hamilton, came to St James's wearing his usual glittering collection of medals and decorations, not only the star of the Order of the Bath and his battle medals but what a more tactful man might well have decided to leave at home on such an occasion, a brilliant spray of Turkish diamonds presented to him by the Sublime Porte as well as the King of Naples's Order of St Januarius. The King of England was not pleased to see his adulterous Admiral thus arrayed. His reception was 'not very flattering', a friend of Nelson's reported. 'His Majesty merely asked him if he had recovered his health', then turned away to talk to some obscure general and spoke to him 'near half an hour in great good humour. It could not have been about *his* success.'

In the earlier years of his reign, however, the King very rarely showed his displeasure in this kind of way. 'One hears nothing of the King but what gives one the best opinion of him imaginable,' wrote the poet Thomas Gray, confirming Horace Walpole's impression. The Paymaster General agreed with these verdicts: King George III was 'much admired'.

These levees at which people were given an opportunity of forming such opinions were held on Wednesdays and Fridays; and, until 1788, when Parliament was sitting, on Mondays also. Attendance

---

* Although he insisted that she could have no official position at Naples, the King had raised no objection to Sir William's marriage to Emma Hart when Hamilton returned from Italy to seek permission for it. Indeed, according to Sir William's niece, the King found the proposed match quite diverting and teased him about his pretty young friend: 'The King joked him about Em. and gave a hint that he thought he was not quite so religious as when he married the late Lady H.' (Fothergill, *Sir William Hamilton*, 251).

was restricted to men only, unlike drawing-rooms, which were for both men and women and at which both King and Queen appeared.

A drawing-room at St James's Palace was described by the Persian ambassador Mirza Abul Hassan Khan:

The guests were lined up on all sides and we tried in vain to make our way through the crowd. Then the Queen entered from another room, followed by ladies-in-waiting, beautiful as the Pleiades, and a young page, the son of a lord, who carried her long train so that it would not drag on the floor. There must have been 1,000 guests. The ladies wore 'hoop' skirts. Some wore Phoenix-like feathers in their hair; others wore jewels. The Queen mounted the dais and the loud acclaim of the crowd might have turned even Afrasiyab's [a King of Turan, legendary foe of Iran] heart to water from fear and trembling!

I found the ladies' dresses unattractive and I said so to my good friend [Sir Gore Ouseley, who was appointed Ambassador to the Persian Court] 'These strange costumes truly depress me – their everyday gowns are much more flattering to waists and bosoms than these tightly boned bodices!' As for English men's clothes, they are immodest and unflattering to the figure, especially their trousers which look just like under-drawers – could they be designed to appeal to the ladies? The ladies admire small feet – I have seen men wearing shoes so tight that their feet bulge over the sides! Both men and women consider small feet to be elegant and a sign of high birth.

The Queen stood on the Royal dais while the ladies brought their daughters forward to be presented . . .

At last the presentations were over and a young colonel made a passage for us into the Queen's presence . . . when she saw me and Sir Gore Ouseley she spoke to us with extreme condescension . . .

We left the dais and busied ourselves admiring the lovely ladies of London. I learned that young ladies are not presented to the Queen before the age of seventeen, and that, until they have had that honour, they do not go out in society or attend dinner parties and receptions. No member of a family touched by scandal is received at court.★

★ At an earlier levee, 'his Majesty . . . spoke to Sir Gore Ouseley about Persian books . . . and praised [Abul Hassan] with compliments worthy of a King: "Until today we have seen no ambassador from any monarch so young and so learned: it betokens the good fortune of the Government and the great glory of the Shah of Iran." The King praised Sir Gore Ouseley's Persian highly, and gave [him and Abul Hassan] leave to depart with eloquent instructions to [the] *mehmandar* [interpreter]' (Cloake, trans. and ed., *A Persian at the Court of King George*, 60, 137–8).

Unless some other time was notified, levees began at twelve o'clock. Invitations were not required; but those who attended were required to wear court dress or uniform, as were those whom they brought with them to present to the King. They were conducted to the Privy Chamber if their rank entitled them to the privilege, otherwise to the Presence Chamber, where members of the Household saw to it that they were arrayed in a circle around the room.

The King, having been dressed in his levee clothes by the Lord of the Bedchamber and the Groom of the Stole, proceeded to the Privy Chamber then into the Presence Chamber, all conversations ceasing at his approach. The King then went round the room, exchanging bows with each man in turn, addressing a few words to him, or entering into conversation, very occasionally passing by without a word as a token of his displeasure at some social or political misdemeanour. He had a good memory for faces, as well as for people's peculiarities and the details imparted to him about their private lives. The Duchess of Devonshire once observed that like his son, the future King George IV, he had 'a wonderful way of knowing what is going forward'. To those whom he knew and liked he would talk quite easily and make the occasional joke, often rather heavy-handed, occasionally quite witty. Once in conversation with the uxorious and philoprogenitive Charles Manners-Sutton, Archbishop of Canterbury, he observed, 'I believe your Grace has a large family – better than a dozen?' 'No, Sir,' replied the Archbishop, 'only eleven.' 'Well,' said the King, 'is not that better than a dozen?'

Ministers of the Crown, ambassadors, members of the Royal Family and leading supporters of the Government in the House of Lords and the House of Commons were expected to attend levees regularly or to send an apology if they were unable to do so. But it was accepted that, once they had been spoken to by the King, or at least had had their presence acknowledged by him, they were free to leave. Lesser people – a country gentleman, perhaps, waiting to be presented by his Member of Parliament, or the canon of a cathedral by the dean – might have to wait for as long as three hours, if the levee was well attended, before their turn came.

After or sometimes before a levee there might be a meeting of the Privy Council or the King might receive a Minister for a confidential talk in his Closet, a private room beyond the State Bedroom, upon entering which some Ministers, including Marquess Wellesley and the Earl of Chatham, went down on bended knee. Here, too, as the head of society as well as head of State, His Majesty would grant audiences to men and women of rank who had favours to request, grievances to lay before him or secrets to impart. On court days the King would also be called upon to receive senior officers on their appointment to new commands, clergymen on their elevation to bishoprics, diplomatists before their departure to foreign courts and after their return, baronets on their creation, noblemen on their steps upward in the peerage, as well as gentlemen who had come perhaps to present a future bride or an heir just come of age.

These court days were very tiring for the King, since he was on his feet commonly for five or six hours at a time, court etiquette requiring that during audiences not only all those shown into his Closet but he himself also should remain standing throughout the interview. It was not uncommon for the King and a member of his Cabinet to remain in conversation and on their feet for two hours and more. William Pitt the Younger was once to be kept standing for almost four.

Ministers were less inclined to share the good opinion of the King expressed by others. He was determined not to be trampled on, he told Lord Bute, otherwise his subjects would come in time to esteem him 'unworthy of the Crown'. Yet, for the moment he could not rid himself of Pitt, the Secretary of State – that man of 'pride and ambition' – because no one other than Pitt could command the support of the House of Commons; nor could he get rid of the cantankerous Duke of Newcastle, the First Lord of the Treasury, whose influence in the Lords and skills in management were equally indispensable. So, for the moment, he was reserved and uncommunicative with them both.

'I am the greatest cipher that ever appeared at Court,' Newcastle complained. 'The young King is hardly civil to me; talks to me of *nothing*, and scarce answers me upon my own Treasury affairs . . . Is this giving me the countenance and support which is necessary for me to carry on his Majesty's business, much less what is sufficient to make me happy and easy?' Newcastle supposed that he would have 'to submit' to the King's autocratic behaviour for the moment; but, he said, 'This method of proceeding can't last.'

Both Newcastle and Pitt had reason to suppose that neither of them would long remain in office and that Lord Bute was destined to take Newcastle's place. Upon his appointment as Secretary of State for the Northern Department in March 1761, Bute had written an unctuous, sententious and self-congratulatory letter to the King:

While they justly praise my King, some think I have a little merit in his education . . . I may want talent for business, faction may overwhelm me and court intrigues destroy me . . . but I know and feel in serving you I have done my duty to my God, my Country, and my King . . . To tread an unknown path I sacrifice peace, quiet and all my little happiness to your commands.

The first of the Ministers to be forced out of the Government was Pitt, who had been in disagreement with other members of the Cabinet over the peace negotiations between Britain and France, Pitt insisting in his lordly manner on a treaty which would both satisfy King Frederick the Great of Prussia and destroy the colonial power of France, others arguing for peace at almost any price before Britain was ruined. When negotiations collapsed and France entered into a secret alliance with Spain, Pitt proposed a declaration of war against the King of Spain, King Charles III, who much disliked Britain and longed to recover Gibraltar and Minorca from her. Most other members of the Cabinet opposed Pitt, who – to their relief, but to what Walpole described as the indignation and alarm of the nation – thereupon resigned in October 1761.

Pleased as he was to see Pitt go, the King had not been directly involved in the events that led up to his departure, and he succeeded in disguising his distaste for the man when Pitt came to surrender his seals. His Majesty granted him a pension of £3,000 a year for three lives and bestowed the title of Baroness Chatham upon his wife. In expressing his gratitude for these favours, which it was hoped would lessen his popularity, Pitt was at his most fulsome, 'sensibly touched', as the *Annual Register* put it, 'with the grandeur and condescension of this proceeding'. 'I confess, Sire, it overpowers – it oppresses me.' He was so proud to have received these 'gracious' and 'unmerited marks of approbation . . . from the best of sovereigns'. He then burst into tears.

There were those who condemned Pitt, maintaining that he demeaned himself by accepting such favours; but that he had lost little of his popularity with the people at large was demonstrated the next month when he provocatively accepted an invitation to a banquet at Guildhall on Lord Mayor's Day, when the King and Queen were also to be present. Their Majesties' coach was watched in silence; Lord Bute's coach was attacked by the mob, and Bute himself had to be rescued by the bodyguard of prizefighters whom he had now to employ to protect him from such assaults; while Pitt, the great war leader, was cheered to the echo. 'The streets, the balconies, the chimney tops, burst into a roar of delight as his chariot passed by,' wrote the daughter of one of the Queen's attendants. 'The ladies waved their handkerchiefs from the windows. The common people clung to the wheels, shook hands with the footmen, and even kissed the horses. Cries of "No Bute!" were mingled with the shouts of "Pitt for ever." ' When Pitt entered Guildhall he was welcomed 'by loud huzzas and clapping of hands, in which the very magistrates of the City joined'.

Pitt's friend the immensely rich William Beckford, soon to be Lord Mayor, had arranged that at the subsequent banquet the speeches dwelt at length upon Pitt's brilliant conduct of the war. The King and Queen were all but ignored.

DUKES AND MINISTERS

I care not one farthing for these men I now have to do with.

The war against Spain, which Pitt, in disagreement with most of his colleagues, had proposed, was considered to be inevitable after negotiations in Madrid broke down in December 1761; and the Duke of Newcastle's worries about the cost of such a war, which was declared on 4 January 1762, became more acute than ever. These worries were fully shared by the King, whose known desire for peace, in opposition to Pitt, contributed to his unpopularity. 'This fresh enemy makes my heart bleed for my poor country,' he told Bute. 'I think unless we can get rid of our expense *somewhere*, it will be impossible to bear up when a new power attacks us.' Although he was concerned for his subjects in Hanover, he decided that it was in Germany that these savings would have to be made. 'So superior is my love to this my native country over any private interest of my own,' he declared, 'that I cannot help wishing that an end was put to that enormous expense by ordering our troops home.' He also proposed putting an end to Britain's subsidy to Prussia; but he had no such scruples about this as he had about the withdrawal of troops from Hanover, since he had conceived a profound dislike for the 'proud, *overbearing*' King Frederick the Great. Besides, here was an opportunity to get rid of Newcastle, who advocated continuing the war in Germany despite the expense of it. 'The more I see of this fellow,' the King said, 'the more I wish to see him out of employment.' He had not long now to wait. On 26 May 1762 Newcastle was persuaded to resign. The King spoke to him in the kindly manner he had adopted when accepting the resignation of Pitt; and, like Pitt, Newcastle burst into tears.

The way was now clear for Bute; but Bute was hesitant. He had long wanted power, but was nervous of exercising it. He would have preferred to be a power behind the throne; he was not, he protested, sufficiently experienced in the business of politics, as both Pitt and Newcastle would have readily agreed. The King, though, was insistent: the successor to Newcastle he had had in mind for long, he wrote, was a man devoid of Newcastle's 'dirty arts', a man who would think of his country's good, not of jobs, not of rewards, peerages and pensions. If his dearest friend did not know the man by this description, he added archly, he would provide the further information that he lived in South Audley Street – where Bute lived at number 75. 'The thought of his not accepting the Treasury or of his retiring chills my blood,' he pressed Bute – who pleaded illness – in another letter. 'Is this a moment for despondency? No, for vigour and the day is ours. I know . . . my Dearest Friend's worth and therefore attribute his [reluctance to take office] to the dejection arising from his fever.'

Bute still hesitated. He was, he insisted, really not at all well: he was suffering from insomnia, and, as they often did at times of stress, his bowels were troubling him, and the rhubarb he was advised to take only served to make them worse. Moreover, as he was himself all too well aware, he remained an intensely unpopular figure in the country at large, despised as an incompetent Scotch interloper by the old English families, and detested and derided by the London mob, which met him with shouts of 'No Scotch rogues! No Butes!' as his carriage, always surrounded by his prizefighters, drove through the streets.

A frequent butt of pamphleteers and caricaturists, he was portrayed as 'a dreadful Scotch bison', while the King's mother, the Princess Dowager, still widely supposed to be Bute's mistress, was a tigress. Pitt was 'English Will' or 'honest Will': even the pension of £3,000 a year which had been granted to him on his resignation, and the peerage for his wife, escaped the censure which would certainly have been accorded a less respected figure.

'The press is with more vehemence than I ever knew set to work against Lord Bute,' commented Lady Sarah Lennox. 'The fire . . . is fed with great industry, & blown by a national prejudice which is inveterate and universal . . . He is most scurrilously accused . . . on being a Scotchman & a Favourite.'

In the prints which poured from the presses, Bute was attacked as a Scotchman who would bring other Scotchmen from their 'barren desert' in the north to batten on England's 'rich plains where milk with honey flows and plenty reigns'. He was shown as a he-goat riding a she-goat (the Princess Dowager) to hell; he was compared to Rizzio, the supposed lover of Mary, Queen of Scots, to Roger Mortimer, lover of Edward II's queen, Isabella, to Sejanus, administrator of the Roman Empire for the Emperor Tiberius and alleged murderer of Tiberius's son. The Princess Dowager, 'The Wanton Widow', was portrayed as the Queen in *Hamlet*, instructing Bute to pour poison into her sleeping son's ear. Nor did the King escape: he was shown with a Scotch petticoat hanging over his head, as a footman, holding a rattle and a fool's cap, and saying 'I am nobody', while being driven by Bute, accompanied by the Princess, roughshod over Magna Carta. He was portrayed as a stupid, selfish young squire responding to discontented tenants with the words 'You know, good people, I don't trouble myself about my Estate. I leave the management to my Stewards & Clerks. If they supply me with money that's sufficient.' He was also depicted as an ass, blindfolded, and as a lion drugged, or made ridiculous as he walks on his hind legs wearing a petticoat, jackboots and a Scottish cap topped by the fleur-de-lis while Bute leads him along by the nose and the Princess holds a thistle.* Nor yet did the King altogether escape the public insults which Bute had to endure in the streets. One day a mob surrounded his sedan chair when he was on his way to visit his mother at Carlton House, and a voice bawled out to ask him if he was 'going there to suck'.

It was the attacks on his mother which upset the King the most.

---

* Not all printsellers escaped prosecution by the authorities. In October 1762 the *Gentleman's Magazine* reported, 'A bill of indictment was found by the grand jury at the general quarter sessions held at *Westminster*, against a famous printseller, for vending in his shop divers wicked and obscene pictures, tending to the corruption of youth, and the common nuisance. There has of late been . . . a licentious use made of these wretched exhibitions . . . of which the offenders do not seem sufficiently apprized . . . Many of the representations that have lately appeared in the shops, are not only reproachful to government but offensive to common sense' (*Gentleman's Magazine*, Oct. 1962, quoted in Atherton, *Political Prints in the Age of Hogarth*, 82).

'They have also treated my Mother in a cruel manner (which I shall never forget nor forgive to the day of my death),' he protested to Bute. 'I do therefore here in the presence of Our Almighty Lord promise that I will remember the insults, and never will forgive anyone who shall venture to speak disrespectfully of her.'

Nor could the King forgive Henry Fox, not only for the way he had behaved in the matter of Lady Sarah Lennox but also because of all men in public life he was, in the King's opinion, the most corrupt, the most ready to put patronage and profit above service to his country, the most 'devoid of principles'. His memory was a good one, the King himself assured George Rose in later years, and what he 'did not *forget* he could not forgive'. Yet Fox was a clever man, uninhibited by scruples, with much experience of the House of Commons. He had been Secretary-at-War, Secretary of State and Leader of the House of Commons, as well as Paymaster General, and was an obvious candidate to fill the post of Leader of the Commons again. Indeed, Bute, having at last been persuaded to become the King's First Minister at the end of May 1762, decided in the autumn of that year that he could not very well carry on without Fox to support him as Leader of the Commons, since the criticism of the peace terms by George Grenville, the then Leader, made Grenville unsuitable in that office to carry the terms through the House. So the King reluctantly gave way; it was necessary sometimes, he concluded, to 'call in bad men to govern bad men'. And, after all, he decided in his censorious and still priggish way, there were few politicians who were not bad men. Henry Bilson Legge was 'obnoxious'; Charles Townshend, the Secretary-at-War, was 'vermin'; he had never yet met a man more 'doubtful or dilatory' than George Grenville; as for Pitt, that 'snake in the grass', he had 'the blackest of hearts'. Since the King entertained such low opinions of his Ministers, no one could be surprised that he had not yet mastered the art of conciliating them.

'It was very unpleasant for me' to have Fox in the Ministry, he complained, 'but I consented to it as that was the only means of getting my dear friend' to remain at the Treasury. He comforted himself with the reflection that it would be 'but for a time, the expedient of the moment only'.

He could never bring himself to like or trust Fox, though; and his being compelled to agree to his appointment to satisfy the needs of Bute was a painful necessity that cast an ever-darkening shadow over their friendship.

There were even darker shadows yet to come. Lord Bute was not only insulted and derided by the writers of pamphlets and the purveyors of prints, he was attacked with increasing violence by the mob. 'The new Administration begins tempestuously,' Horace Walpole observed. 'My father [Sir Robert Walpole] was not more abused after twenty years than Bute after twenty days.' On 25 November 1762, on his way to the opening of Parliament, Bute was hissed and spattered with rubbish and mud, and would no doubt have been seriously injured had not his bodyguard of prizefighters been there to save him from his adversaries. 'On his return in a Hackney-chair, the mob discovered him, followed him, broke the glasses of the chair and, in short, by threats and menaces, put him, very reasonably in great fear. If they had once overturned the chair, he might very soon have been demolished.'

That day, riding in his state coach to Westminster, the King, too, was greeted with catcalls. But His Majesty was not easily intimidated, and his courage was never in doubt: that evening he ignored advice not to attend the theatre. Bute was more easily frightened: he had had more than enough of these insults and physical assaults, which he believed were instigated and encouraged by his political enemies. A few days later he told the King that he wanted to resign.

The King was appalled. 'It overturns all the thoughts that alone have kept up my spirits in these bad times,' he replied to Bute's letter. 'I own I had flattered myself . . . that my d. friend would have assisted me in purging out corruption, and in those measures that no man but he that has the prince's real affection can go through. Then, when we were both dead, our memories would have been respected and esteemed to the end of time.'

His friend's proposed resignation had come at a time when, inexperienced, impatient and still lacking in self-confidence as he was, the King had most need of disinterested guidance. He had quarrelled with several influential men in public life whose good opinions he could ill afford to lose. He had deeply offended the

Duke of Devonshire, a former First Lord of the Treasury and now Lord Chamberlain of the Household, who had recently much displeased him by declining to attend a meeting of the Cabinet called to consider the terms of the peace treaty with Spain. Soon afterwards the King had encountered the Duke on his way from Kew to London in the company of the Duke of Newcastle. Believing that the two men were colluding in some measure of opposition to the Ministry, he told Bute that the next time he saw the Duke of Devonshire he would dismiss him from office. And so, when the Duke came to St James's Palace to pay his respects to the King before going home to Chatsworth, he was told by a page that the King declined to see him. The Duke then told the page to ask His Majesty with whom he should leave his wand of office; then, informed that he would be given his orders later, he left the Palace exclaiming, 'God bless you! It will be a very long time before you see me here again.' At the next meeting of the Privy Council, the King called for the list of members and, to quote from the Council Book, 'with his own hand struck the name of William Duke of Devonshire out of the List of Privy Councillors'.

The Duke's dismissal was immediately followed by the resignation of his brother, Lord George Cavendish, as Comptroller of the Household. When Cavendish came to hand back the staff of his office, the King was sullen and silent. 'At last he burst out,' so Cavendish said, '"If a person wants to resign his Staff, I don't desire he should keep it I am sure," gave his head a toss back, and retired towards the window to set the Staff down.'

'The sword is drawn,' the King declared three days later. 'Vigour and violence are the only means of ending this audacious faction.' When he heard that Newcastle, taking advantage of the feelings aroused by the King's dismissal of the Duke of Devonshire, had approached both Pitt and the Duke of Cumberland, the King's uncle, whom his nephew had never trusted, the King was more distressed than ever. 'It is hardly credible that the Duke of Cumberland will choose to take so offensive a step,' he wrote. 'If he does, he shall be treated as he deserves.' 'Courage, my d. friend,' he enjoined Bute, 'go on as you have begun and they will soon see that their disgrace is the sole fruit of [their] impious conduct.' These great dukes had

had their own way too long. They must be taught that to affront the King was no less than 'affronting Britain'.

Then there was fault to be found with the Duke of Bedford, who had been appointed Ambassador in Paris to treat for peace with France and, as a man eager for the conclusion of the war, had conceded more than the King approved, going beyond the limit of his instructions by agreeing that France should have a share in the fisheries of North America. 'It grieves me much he ever went [to Paris],' the King wrote. 'A man of more coolness and less jealousy in his temper would have done the business in half the time.'

Even so, he was deeply thankful that the war had come to an end at last and that the House of Commons had approved the preliminaries of the Peace of Paris by a very large majority in December 1762. It was all the more galling that Bute – still his 'd. friend', but with increasing reservations – was pressing to be allowed to abandon him just as the peace for which he had striven had been secured.

The King did all he could to keep Lord Bute in office. Believing, as Bute himself certainly believed, that the life of his friend was in danger, he was even prepared to recall Pitt to the Cabinet as a sop to the mob.

But Bute, who by now scarcely dared appear in the streets without being 'muffled in a large coat and with a hat and wig drawn over his eyes', did not want to be saved. 'The angel Gabriel,' he exclaimed, 'could not at present govern this country', which indeed, the King declared, was passing through 'the wickedest age that ever was seen'. Bute protested that his health could stand no more. He was 'heartily sick' of his situation, of the 'eternal unpleasant labour of the mind, and the impossibility of finding hours for exercise and proper medicine', not to mention sleep.

Towards the beginning of 1763 he protested that the only solution was for him to lay down his intolerable burden and for the King to appoint Henry Fox as his successor. The King could not have been more dismayed if Bute had proposed sending for the Devil: under Fox the whole country would be sunk in corruption. Yet, even so, if that were the only means of solving Bute's problem, he would have to agree to it, although from the very moment Fox became First Lord of the Treasury the King would no longer feel himself 'interested in public affairs' and would be happy only when there seemed 'a glimmering hope of getting quit of him'.

Fortunately, Fox did not want to be First Lord of the Treasury, making the excuse that strong objections to his taking the job had been raised by his wife, of whom he was exceptionally fond. Believing that he would be able to retain the profitable office of Paymaster General and given to understand that he would be created Baron Holland of Foxley, Wiltshire, he suggested George Grenville, Pitt's brother-in-law.

This proposal much distressed the King, who made his feelings only too plain when Grenville had an audience of His Majesty upon taking up office as First Lord of the Treasury on 10 April 1763. He was left in no doubt that he had been given the appointment only because Lord Bute did not wish to retain it, and that the principal seats in the Cabinet would be filled by Bute's nominees. Making it clear that he wished to have nothing to do with either Pitt or Newcastle, the King behaved in a decidedly cold manner; and, when Grenville made some reference to the support which Lord Bute was giving him, the King, in his own words, 'made him not the least compliment'.

In general, he protested after Lord Bute had gone to take a course of chalybeate waters at Harrogate, 'I care not one farthing for these men I have now to do with.' They were 'mean in their manners of thinking as well as their actions'; they forgot what they owed him, but they would suffer from it 'sooner or later'. Grenville was as tiresome and selfish as any of them. When he drafted the King's Speech, His Majesty told him to send it to Lord Bute for his approval. For, disappointed as he was in his friend's behaviour of late, he still relied upon him for advice and support and had not yet lost hope of persuading him to return as his First Minister in fact as well as in effect. The present Ministers were merely his 'tools': he would change them 'without regret'; he must uphold the constitution of his country, which, so he insisted, required that the Crown, not politicians, must direct its executive.

FAMILY LIFE

*I never saw more lovely children, nor a more pleasing sight
than the King's fondness for them.*

The King was happy to escape from political problems into the
domesticity of family life and the companionship of a wife who went
out of her way to please him. 'With her usual affection', she did not
press the claims of her brother, the Grand Duke of Mecklenburg-
Strelitz, when Lord Bute was offered a vacant Knight Companionship
in the Order of the Garter. Bute had offered to stand aside for the
Duke; but the King insisted he should not do so, and so the Queen
agreed that her brother should wait. It was a characteristic submission
to her husband's wishes. He for his part, however, indulged her in
many ways. He made no objection when she wished to acquire more
dogs; he tolerated her continuing addiction to snuff, and overlooked
her passion for jewellery; he paid over £100 a year for two Indian
mahouts, father and son, to supervise the pair of trumpeting elephants
which she kept with a zebra in a paddock at the Queen's House.

The Queen found much to do when the King was at work or
occupied with his many interests. She had her garden to look after;
she started taking Italian lessons; she studied books in both German
and French as well as English, and read treatises on health and the
care of children. She read books of sermons; she gave instructions
to John Bradburn, William Vile's former assistant and successor, on
the making of furniture both for her own rooms and for the royal
nursery. She received from the King a present of an organ, and no
doubt one of the three new harpsichords he bought in 1764 was also
a present for her. She had her various charities to attend to, and these
took up so much of her income as well as her time that she often
had to ask the King to lend her money to meet her payments to her

pensioners. He readily gave her the money, though he had more than enough charities of his own.

When the King was at home, the Queen still clearly enjoyed his company. She gave him little presents at intervals – once a wax model of the Prince of Wales. She held small parties for him – a particularly enjoyable entertainment one summer evening involved projections of 'Chinese shadows' as well as a concert and a fine supper provided by Frederick Kuhffe, the German confectioner. And she gave birth to his children with a regularity that could not fail to please him, his approval of large families being well known. When told that the Countess of Aylesford was about to give birth to her twentieth child, he said that he hoped she would have twins – 'the more the merrier'.

In fulfilling the King's hopes for a large family of his own, the Queen suffered comparatively little in her labour after the pain of her first experience of it. Her second child, Frederick, the future Duke of York, was born on 16 August 1763 so quickly that the King – who had asked to be given information 'when the Labour seemed to be near' – was first given notice of the birth by the screaming of the child. The third son, William, later Duke of Clarence and William IV, was born on 21 August 1765 after labour had progressed in 'the most kindly way'. Just over a year later, on 15 September 1766, appeared Charlotte Augusta Matilda, the Princess Royal. Then, on 2 November 1767, came the biggest baby the Queen had yet delivered, Edward, later Duke of Kent and father of the princess who was to become Queen Victoria. Within a year the Queen was expecting her sixth child in a few days' time.

The King on this occasion was hoping for another daughter – so keenly indeed that, when Dr William Hunter made some remark about the Queen perhaps having another son like 'those lovely Princes above stairs', he burst out crossly, 'Dr Hunter, I did not think I could have been angry with you, but I am; and I say whoever sees that lovely child, the Princess Royal, above stairs must wish to have a fellow to her.'

The King's wish was granted. Princess Augusta Sophia was born after a short labour on 8 November 1768. Another daughter, Princess Elizabeth, followed, after the Queen's longest period yet free from pregnancy, on 22 May 1770. The year after that came a fifth son, Ernest, the future Duke of Cumberland, who was followed by two more sons: Augustus, Duke of Sussex, and Adolphus, Duke of Cambridge. There were five children yet to come: three girls – Mary, Sophia and Amelia – and two boys – Octavius and Alfred.

Their parents moved regularly with varying numbers of these fifteen children from one of their houses to another. In the earlier years of their marriage they left the Queen's House for Richmond Lodge from the beginning of June to the end of September, returning to London on drawing-room days and when the King was called there by the demands of public affairs. He always went back unwillingly, for, as he said, he saw 'as little of London as possible', never being 'a volunteer there' and considering St James's Palace 'a dust heap'.

He and his wife lived what was described as a 'very retired' life at Richmond Lodge, disturbed only on Sundays, when the gardens, landscaped by Lancelot Brown and Michael Milliken, were opened to the public and curious visitors swarmed across the lawns, tried to peer in at the windows, and left behind such a mess of paper and other detritus that the King complained he always much disliked the look of the place on a Monday morning before the gardeners had cleared it up.

At Richmond the King showed himself to be a loving and, some thought, even rather too indulgent father to his children when they were small, giving them presents and, whenever he could, attending their birthday parties and the treats that were arranged for them, boat races on the river and fancy-dress parades in the garden. At one of these parties a friend of the family saw the King 'carrying about in his arms by turns Princess Sophia and the last prince, Octavius'; on another, more domestic, occasion she described him playing with his youngest daughter 'on the carpet beneath a large table on which [were spread] books, work, pencils and paper'. 'In the next room,' she added, 'is the band of music which plays from eight o'clock to ten. The King generally directs them what pieces of music to play, generally Handel's.' 'I never saw more lovely children,' she wrote, 'nor a more pleasing sight than the King's fondness for them.'

The King and Queen 'have their Children always playing about them the whole time', wrote another observer; and most evenings, when their father had finished work, they were brought down again between six and seven o'clock 'to play in the room with [their parents] till about 8'.

At an early age the children were introduced to the pleasures of the theatre, and special performances were arranged for them. The King asked to be sent reports of their progress in the schoolroom, and in return sent them letters with love from their Papa. The Queen would tell him how well Octavius was learning to count or how Mary – who had asked to be lifted up to see Papa coming and had been told he was not coming just yet but that her mother would give him a message when he did – answered 'Minny say *Goody Papa, poor Papa*'. 'Dear little Minny remains quite uneasy about not finding you anywhere in the House,' the Queen told him the following week. 'Every coach she sees is Papa coming, and nothing satisfies her hardly but sitting at the window to look for you.'

When Prince Alfred died before he was three years old, the first of the two of his children who were to die in infancy, the King was deeply distressed, and when Prince Octavius, of whom he had been especially fond, died the following year he was heartbroken. 'There will be no Heaven for me,' he said, 'if Octavius is not there.' He told the Earl of Dartmouth that every hour, 'encreases the chasm I do feel for want of that beloved object'.

Mrs Scott, the wife of Edward Scott of Scots Hall, Kent, and mother of his numerous children, who had been the Prince of Wales's wet-nurse, reported that His Majesty 'at times would shed the dignity of the monarch and crawl about on the floor on his hands and knees with the children; but on the approach of the Queen (at all times dignified and strict, especially with the Duke of York) His Majesty would assume a royal demeanour'.

He also assumed a stricter manner with the elder boys when the time approached for them to leave the nursery. He continued to attend their birthday parties; he allowed them to appear at the celebrations on his birthday on 4 June and the fireworks parties given by the Queen at Richmond. He often put in an appearance at the Princes' drawing-rooms held on their mother's official birthday, and was also to be seen in the audience at the plays they performed in such elaborate costumes as Prince George and Prince Frederick can be seen wearing in Zoffany's portrait of them with their mother at the Queen's House – the Prince of Wales as Telemachus, Prince Frederick as a turbaned Turk.

His father took Prince George to the theatre to see a children's play, *The Jovial Crew, or the Merry Beggar*. He allowed him to accompany his parents to a military review on Wimbledon Common and to Cranbourne Lodge for the races at Ascot. Yet the King was distressed by accounts of quarrels and storms in the noisy nursery, where one day a nursemaid lost her temper with Prince William and banged his head violently against a wall, while the Sub-Governess was so exasperated by her charges that she took to drink. So, when the Prince of Wales was eleven and Prince Frederick ten, it was decided that they must be placed under stricter discipline with tutors at the Dutch House, now known as Kew Palace, a house built in 1631 by a rich London merchant of Dutch descent, which stood just to the north of the White House on the other side of the road which led from Kew Green to the Thames towpath. A substantial, gabled red-brick house, it was one of several properties at Kew which were leased or owned by the Royal Family, or by various members of the Court, whose numerous liveried servants could be seen on summer evenings strolling amid the cattle grazing on the Green.

Kew now became quite gay [recalled Mrs Papendiek, daughter of the German page, Frederick Albert], the public being admitted to the Richmond Gardens on Sundays and to Kew Gardens on Thursdays. The Green on those days was covered with carriages, more than 300 *l.* being taken at the bridge on Sundays. Their Majesties were to be seen at the windows speaking to their friends, and the royal children amusing themselves in their own gardens. Parties came up the water too, with bands of music . . . The whole was a scene of enchantment and delight.

For the elder Princes weekdays were not so delightful. They had to be up at six o'clock and in the schoolroom by seven, in accordance with a regime supervised by Dr William Markham, Bishop of Chester and a former Head Master of Westminster, a tall and portly man, inclined to be both pompous and short-tempered, whose 'business', so one of his former pupils at Westminster said, 'was rather in courting the great than in attending to the school'. Yet the Prince of Wales was fond of Markham, who was not an unkindly man, and was sorry when the King, deciding he was too easy-going, replaced him with Dr Richard Hurd, Bishop of Lichfield and Coventry, 'a stiff and cold, but correct gentleman' with a most decorous manner which 'endeared him highly to devout old ladies' and, indeed, to the King, who grew extremely fond of him. Hurd's chaplain, the Rev. William Arnold, was appointed Sub-Preceptor in place of Cyril Jackson, much to the Princes' relief, since Jackson, so Prince Frederick said, 'used to have a silver pencil-case in his hand while we were at our lessons, and he has frequently given us such knocks with it on our foreheads that the blood followed them'.

Under the watchful eye of their tutors, the Princes were kept hard at work, or at some form of supervised recreation, from early in the morning until eight o'clock at night, to meet the strict demands of the King, who frequently expressed the firm belief that no change for the better could be expected in the 'unprincipled days' in which they lived except by 'an early attention to the education of the rising generation'. 'I have no wish concerning my sons,' he once said, 'but to make them by a good education enabled to [develop] any talents they may possess, and as such become a credit to their family and of utility to their country.' So the Princes received constant moral guidance and regular exhortations from their father. In one of these he warned them that 'little dependence can be placed on any thing in this world and the best method of continually pursuing your duty is the continually placing before your eyes that the Supreme Being has put you in an exalted situation; and that you are therefore accountable to him for your conduct'.

My dear sons [the King wrote in another letter], place ever your chief care on obeying the commands of your Creator. Every hour will shew you that no comfort can be obtained without that. Act uprightly and shew the anxious care I have had of you has not been misspent and you will ever find me not only an affectionate father but a sincere friend. May heaven shower the choicest blessings on you both and on the rest of my children.

His mother, though she seemed more concerned that his bodily constitution should remain unimpaired, gave the Prince of Wales similar advice, urging him 'to disdain all flattery' and 'abhor all vice', to 'fear God', to do 'justice unto everybody and avoid partiality', and, above all, to display 'the highest love, affection and duty towards the King'.

Increasingly the Prince found it difficult to obey his mother's last injunction. The King, who had loved him when he was a baby, had now, in his concern that he should develop those characteristics which would be so essential to him when he inherited the throne, become his severest critic, complaining to the boy's Governor that the child was 'duplicitous' and had 'a bad habit of not speaking the truth'. The older the Prince grew, the further he felt removed from his father's affections.

As the King had been, the Prince was denied the close companionship of other children, apart from his brother Frederick, just as he was constantly and carefully sheltered from any adult who might fill his mind with thoughts about the wonders, excitements and evils of the outside world. That vicious world must be veiled from him, his father insisted, by those who 'cirrounded' him, just as it had been veiled from himself. Already showing signs of becoming excessively fond of food and clothes and flattery, the boy must be taught the virtues of rigorous simplicity, hard work, punctuality and regularity, and at the first signs of laziness, laxness or untruthfulness he must be beaten. And beaten he was. One of his sisters later recalled how she had seen him and Prince Frederick 'held by their tutors to be flogged like dogs with a long whip'. They responded by behaving to their parents not in a rebellious way but in a manner which the Duchess of Northumberland described as 'rather too formal'.

The Queen does not seem to have protested; but the establishment of her two elder sons in a Household of their own marked a turning point in her marriage, which gradually became less perfectly contented than it had been in earlier days. She now saw the boys only on Fridays and Saturdays. Also, her husband was more often away from home than in the past, dealing with increasingly time-consuming official matters, and when at home he was frequently preoccupied, no longer quite so attentive to her wishes as once he had been. It seemed a sad indication of a slowly changing relationship that he had shaved the hair from his head and had once more taken to wearing the wig that she had persuaded him to discard, assuring him he looked so much better without it. And he was always in such a hurry: when they drove back to Kew from London the coachman was told to waste no time on the journey.

It is remarked of Their Majesties that when they travel on the road they go with the greatest speed imaginable [it was reported]. A gentleman on horseback accompanies them . . . from Kew Bridge to Hyde Park Corner, and he says that the horses in their chaise galloped every step of the way, and they could not have gone at a less rate than 14 miles per hour. This is the usual pace at which they go . . . Several persons at different times have been thrown down and hurt, not being able to get out of the way soon enough.

After the birth of her ninth child, Prince Augustus, when she was still not yet thirty years old, the Queen suffered from post-natal depression, exacerbated by bouts of homesickness. She told her brother of her '*douleurs extreme*', and complained of the monotony of her life. The King spoke of paying a visit to Hanover, and she longed for the day when they could make the journey and she could see her family once more. But time and again the visit was postponed.

Essentially, however, theirs was still a happy marriage, and was to remain so for several years to come. As John Wesley said, the King 'believes the Bible . . . he fears God and he loves the Queen'. 'Their behaviour to each other speaks the most cordial confidence and happiness,' one of the Queen's attendants was to write in the 1780s. 'The King seems to admire as much as he enjoys her conversation . . . The Queen appears to feel the most grateful regard for him.'

I cannot here help mentioning a very interesting little scene at which I was present, about this time [wrote Fanny Burney]. The Queen had nobody but myself with her, one morning, when the King hastily entered the room, with some letters in his hand, and addressing her in German, which he spoke very fast, and with much apparent interest in what he said, he brought the letters up to her, and put them into her hands. She received them with much agitation, but evidently of a much pleased sort, and endeavoured to kiss his hand as he held them. He would not let her, but made an effort, with a countenance of the highest satisfaction, to kiss her. I saw instantly in her eyes a forgetfulness, at the moment, that any one was present, while, drawing away her hand, she presented him her cheek. He accepted her kindness with the same frank affection that she offered it; and the next moment they both spoke English, and talked upon common and general subjects.

13

A TURBULENT MINISTRY

Every day I meet with some insult from these people.

At the beginning of August 1763 George Grenville bluntly informed the King that he must choose between supporting his Administration and forming another one. An approach was accordingly made to the Duke of Bedford, who agreed to take office provided William Pitt, Grenville's brother-in-law, joined the Government and Bute withdrew from politics altogether. But Pitt declined to serve with Bedford, or, indeed, with anyone responsible for the Peace of Paris, the treaty which had ended the Seven Years War in February that year. The King accordingly, and with evident reluctance, told Grenville that he would agree to the present Administration remaining in office. On 21 August, however, the Secretary of State for the Southern Department, Lord Egremont, was 'struck down with apoplexy'. His sudden death had long been expected, since, as Horace Walpole said, 'he used no exercise and could not be kept from eating': he himself had said shortly before he died, 'Well, if I have but three turtle dinners to come, and if I survive them, I shall be immortal.'

On hearing the news of Egremont's death the King immediately consulted Lord Bute and agreed with him that it had now unfortunately become necessary to approach William Pitt, who was accordingly summoned to the Queen's House for a lengthy audience. George Grenville was summoned too, and kept waiting for two hours. When at last he was admitted to His Majesty's presence he was treated with scant civility. Nothing was said about Pitt having been there before him, although Grenville knew he had been, having noticed at the entrance his sedan chair, a conveyance made so conspicuous by a leather protuberance constructed for his gouty foot that Pitt himself remarked that it was as familiar to the public as if his name had been painted on it. After little more than a quarter of an hour the King bowed in dismissal of his second visitor, said it was getting late, and withdrew from the room with the words 'Good morrow, Mr Grenville', which were repeated at the door.

The next day Grenville was again summoned to the Queen's House, this time at the unusual hour of eight o'clock in the evening. The King was in 'the greatest agitation', having been presented by Pitt with quite unacceptable demands, including, so Grenville said, the exclusion from office of 'all that had any hand in the Peace, which he represented as dishonourable, dangerous, and criminal', and the introduction of 'all those who had engaged in the Opposition'. The King accordingly asked Grenville to remain in office, not troubling to hide his reluctance in doing so, though assuring him that he would give him his support.

Grenville accepted the offer on condition that he would not have to contend with any confidential advisers not in his Cabinet. The King assured him that Lord Bute wished to retire and had, in any event, gone away for a time, so the question would not arise.

No sooner had the matter been settled, however, than fresh disagreements arose between the King and his First Lord of the Treasury, who was determined that Lord Bute, on his return to London, would not exercise that influence over the King which had led to such trouble in the past. He strongly objected, therefore, when the King proposed to appoint a friend of Bute's, Sir William Breton, to the post of Keeper of the Privy Purse, a position previously occupied by Bute himself. Grenville insisted that the appointment must be given to a Member of Parliament, so that his own position might be strengthened in the House. The King grew angry, insisting that he and not his Minister had 'the right of disposing of an office so immediately about his own person'. Eventually Grenville conceded the point; but he did so with an ill grace and that character-istic verbosity which so irritated the King and which Grenville himself remarked 'agitated and disturbed him to such an extent that on at least one occasion his Majesty changed countenance and flushed so much that the water stood in his eyes from the excessive heat of his face'. 'When he has wearied me for two hours,' the King said, 'he looks at his watch to see if he may not tire me for an hour more.' 'That gentleman's opinions,' he added, 'are seldom formed from any motives than such as may be expected to originate in the mind of a clerk in a counting-house.' Eventually he decided that he would rather have the Devil as a visitor than be forced to listen to George Grenville.

The King's exasperation with Grenville was by no means peculiar to himself. Others – political friends and opponents alike – found the man 'to a proverb tedious'. His favourite occupation was talking, Walpole said, and 'brevity was not his failing'. Formal, exact and obstinate, his one pleasure in life, according to Edmund Burke, was to be found in the conduct of public affairs: he seemed to have 'no delight except in such things as in some way related to the business that was to be conducted within the House of Commons'. Men found it difficult to believe that he had nine children, or even that he had a home life at all. Once, when he fainted in the House and there were loud calls for ammonia to bring him round, George Selwyn, the Member for Gloucester, who was usually asleep but celebrated for his wit when awake, remarked that the only method of returning him to his senses would be to hold a copy of the Commons's Journals under his nose.

Yet, sanctimonious as was his manner, he was not above feathering his family's nest at public expense; and it was this that played a large part in turning the King's irritation with him into positive detestation. As an untiring and pious advocate of economy in all matters – while eager to make money for himself whenever opportunities occurred – Grenville had declined, as a Lord of the Treasury, to sanction a grant of £20,000 for the purchase of land so that the garden of the Queen's House could be extended to the south-west. The land was consequently sold to speculative builders, and a row of tall houses was built in what became known as Grosvenor Place – a development overlooking 'the King in his private walks . . . to his great annoyance'.

Nor did Grenville scruple to interfere in what the King considered his own rights in the matter of patronage, going so far as to protest, when the office of Court Painter fell vacant on the death of Hogarth, that anyone who spoke to His Majesty on patronage business without

Grenville's consent could expect to be dismissed within the hour — a protest which the King described as 'insolent'.

On 7 April 1765 the King invited his uncle, the Duke of Cumberland, to the Queen's House to help him solve his problems. The Duke, whom the King had so much disliked and distrusted in the past, was then forty-three years old but looked much older. He had suffered a stroke five years before, soon after his return from an unsuccessful campaign on the Continent, and had grown immensely fat. He was quite blind in one eye and could see but imperfectly with the other. He was sorely troubled with asthma and with abscesses in his leg after having been wounded at Fontenoy in 1745; and he had had to undergo a painful operation, which he endured with stoical bravery, insisting on holding a candle for the surgeon to work by.

He was then living in retirement in a house in Upper Grosvenor Street, by now a much respected and well-liked figure, his reputation as the so-called 'Butcher of Culloden' all but forgotten. His nephew treated him with much respect, and, since there was no one else in the family to whom he felt able to turn for political advice, and since he had undertaken not to consult Bute, the King had sent for him to help him change his Ministers, even though the Duke had shared Pitt's hostility to the Administration of Lord Bute and to the Peace of Paris.

The Duke was understanding and sympathetic, fully in agreement with his nephew's concern for the honour of the Crown and ready to do all he could to bring into being a 'strong and lasting ministry'. He entered into negotiations with Pitt and Newcastle and with the Duke of Northumberland, until recently Lord Lieutenant of Ireland, whose son Hugh was married to Lord Bute's daughter, Lady Anne Stuart.

The negotiators were instructed to observe the 'utmost secrecy and celerity'; but soon their discussions were the subject of eager talk in London drawing-rooms, and both Grenville and the Duke of Bedford, Lord President of the Council, approached the King about them. To Grenville's questions the King gave flurried answers: 'Mr Grenville, I will speak to you another time about that. I promise you I will speak to you. You may depend upon it I will speak to you.'

The negotiations did not progress with the 'celerity' which the King had hoped they might. Pitt was not forthcoming. He had gone home to Hayes Place in Kent, and remained there, complaining that his health was not up to a return to office and pretending to suppose that Bute's influence over the King was still a consideration that must be taken into account. In an effort to persuade Pitt to join his new Administration, the King took the highly unusual step of asking the Duke of Cumberland himself to go down to Hayes Place. The Duke remained with Pitt for over five hours, making all manner of concessions on his nephew's behalf. But Pitt remained immovable; and the King, having recognized his error in exasperating his present Ministers while uncertain of those he hoped would replace them, had to make demeaning gestures to Grenville in order to persuade him to remain in office. Grenville, having complained of the King's treatment of him at what was even for him extravagant length, and having yet again brought up the spectre of Bute as *éminence grise*, said that before coming to any decision he would have to talk to his colleagues in the Cabinet and, having consulted them, he would then return to the Queen's House.

These colleagues met that evening after dinner at the Duke of Bedford's handsome home on the north side of Bloomsbury Square. They had not been long in conversation when a messenger arrived with a peremptory note from the King, who had been clearly nettled by Grenville's long lecture on the impropriety of his behaviour. 'I am surprised that you are not yet come, when you knew it was my orders to be attended this evening. I expect you therefore to come the moment you receive this.'

Evidently concerned by the sharp tone of this note, Grenville hurried back to the Queen's House, where, at about ten o'clock, the King received him with the impatiently spoken words 'What conditions do you mean to ask?'

Grenville replied that the Cabinet was still in consultation; but he could say immediately that his colleagues would require an undertaking that Lord Bute would never again interfere in the business of government, that there must be a clear understanding of exactly what was to be the Duke of Cumberland's future role, and that Bute's brother, James Stuart Mackenzie, would have to leave his post as Lord Privy Seal in Scotland, this last condition causing the King to 'fall into great agitation', since it would mean breaking his word to Mackenzie, who had been promised security in that appointment.

Further conditions were presented to the King the following morning, after the Duke of Cumberland had informed his nephew that all manner of persuasion had failed to move Pitt to come to their rescue and that Newcastle and his former colleagues would do nothing without him. These additional conditions included a demand that the well-liked Marquess of Granby, the dashing cavalry leader who had become, in Walpole's words, 'the mob's hero', should be appointed Commander-in-Chief (a post vacant since the departure from it of the ancient Lord Ligonier), that Henry Fox, now Lord Holland, should be dismissed as Paymaster General, and that no successor to the Earl of Northumberland should be appointed as Lord Lieutenant of Ireland without the full approval of the Cabinet.

Throughout the course of the day and long into the night the King discussed these conditions with a succession of advisers, including the Lord Chancellor, the Earl of Northington and the Duke of Cumberland.

At the Queen's drawing-room that Thursday the King made it plain how deeply disturbed he was. Lord Egmont described him as being 'in great agitation' as he told him of the conditions which had been laid down. He had submitted to them all, however, except that of giving the command of the Army to Granby. But the requirement that Mackenzie must be dismissed filled him with 'great indignation'. He 'saw evidently that they were not satisfied with his parting with his power, but that nothing wd. content [Grenville] but parting with his honour too'.

The following day, 24 May, the King remained 'very gloomy, with an air of great dissatisfaction'. When Grenville told him that one of the men given a new appointment wished to express his thanks for His Majesty's 'goodness', he replied sharply, 'It's your goodness, Mr Grenville, not mine.'

I wish sometimes I were a private man [he wrote to Bute] that I might with my own arm defend my honour and freedom against men whose families have formerly acted with more duty to the Crown than these wretches, their successors . . . Every day I meet with some insult from these people; I have been for near a week as it were in a feaver. My very sleep is not free from thinking of the men I daily see . . . Lord Granby is so weak that the last man that sees him has him . . . Excuse the incoherency of my letter; but a mind ulcer'd by the treatment it meets from all around is the true cause of it.

For the most of that summer the King was impatient and discontented, complaining bitterly of the behaviour of his Ministers, of the failure of the Lord President of the Council to turn up for Cabinet meetings, of the 'hurry and precipitancy' with which Lord Halifax, Secretary of State, discharged his duties, and of the general incompetence of the Earl of Sandwich, the other Secretary of State. He declined to speak to Grenville unless direct questions were asked him; to others, Ministers or would-be Ministers, he was either dismissive or, if they were not in Grenville's good books, ostentatiously friendly. 'He shows his Ministers all the public dislike possible,' Lord Chesterfield commented, 'and at his Levee hardly speaks to any of them, but speaks by the hour to anybody else.'

The King wrote of the Government being composed of 'insolent' men lacking 'weight, ability and dutiful deportment'. It was intolerable that the sovereign should be dictated to by 'low men' and that the world might well suppose that England was at such a low ebb that 'no administration [could] be formed without the Grenville family'. If only, he lamented gloomily, it were possible to 'dissolve all factions and to see the best of all partys in employment'.

He had not been well for several weeks. His health had not much troubled him in the past: he had soon recovered from his attack of chickenpox in 1761, and the next year, although he had complained of pains in the chest and a racking cough, this illness, too, had been thrown off within a few days, after doses of laxative and potions of asses' milk. At the beginning of 1765, however, the pains in the chest had returned with a feverish cold, and his doctor had thought it as well to bleed him several times and to keep him in bed. In February and again in March the fever and pains had recurred, and he was bled twice more. His countenance and manner were described as being 'a good deal estranged'. Now, in May, he once again felt thoroughly out of sorts; he was unable to sleep for more than two hours a night, so he told his doctors, and, in a pathetic act of submission, he asked Grenville if it would be all right for him to go into the country for a few days.

At Richmond on Sunday 26 May he did not feel up to taking Holy Communion, and the drawing-room that week had to be cancelled. Three days later, however, he was well enough to appear in public again, and had sufficiently recovered his spirits to be able to resist some of the further demands which Grenville and his Ministers now importunately made of him: the appointment of a friend of the Duke of Bedford, for example, to the office of Master of the Horse to the Queen – an office which had always been recognized as in the gift of the Crown and not of the Government.

The manner in which the demands were made were quite as provocative as the demands themselves. The irascible Duke of Bedford was particularly offensive when he called at the Queen's House before going down to Woburn on 12 June, bringing with him a paper, approved by his Cabinet colleagues, which accused the King of failing to give them the support they had a right to expect from him and of continuing to allow the Earl of Bute to interfere 'at least indirectly in public counsels'.

Bedford, opinionated and tactless, insisted upon reading aloud the document, which ended with the words 'Does not this favourite, by interfering in this manner, and not daring to take a responsible employment, risk the hazard to himself and, which is of more consequence, risk the King's quiet and the safety of the public?' The King made no answer, merely bowing as a signal for the Duke to retire. Yet he was so angered by the man's impertinence that if, so he said, he had not broken out into a 'most profuse perspiration, his indignation would have suffocated him'.

'You will, my dear Lord, easily conceive what indignation I felt at so very offensive a declaration,' the King told the Lord Chancellor, 'but I mastered my temper and we parted with cool civility.'

Intended to force the King to submit to the Cabinet's authority, the paper prepared by Grenville, Bedford and their colleagues helped to persuade him to dismiss Grenville from office and turn once more to the Duke of Cumberland, who was asked to approach Pitt yet again to discover if there was any way in which he could be persuaded to form a government. But since the office came to him by way of the Duke of Cumberland, to whom he had no wish to be beholden, and since he could not come to satisfactory arrangements with his brother-in-law Lord Temple, Pitt repeated his unwillingness to return to office. So Cumberland was obliged to try to form an administration himself; yet, as so many of those whom he would have liked to have had in it declined to be considered, either out of loyalty to Pitt or out of a continued and unjustified suspicion of Bute, he was reduced to the necessity of appealing to friends who had no previous experience of ministerial work.

The man chosen to take Grenville's place as First Lord of the Treasury was a member of the Jockey Club, the thirty-five-year-old Marquess of Rockingham, a former Lord of the Bedchamber, who had served in the Duke of Cumberland's army at the age of fifteen in 1745 and was now head of the former Newcastle party. A staunch supporter of the Hanoverian succession and defender of the dignity of the Crown, he was an honest and extremely rich young man who had not so far distinguished himself in the House of Lords, where he was known as a dull and hesitant speaker.

Secretary of State for the Northern Department was the thirty-year-old Duke of Grafton, a man who had at least made a reputation for himself as a speaker in the House of Lords but one who, like the Marquess of Rockingham, was much occupied with the affairs of the Jockey Club and with women.*

---

* The Duke lived with a celebrated courtesan, a Bond Street tailor's daughter, Mrs Horton – 'the Duke of Grafton's Mrs Horton, the Duke of Dorset's Mrs Horton, everybody's Mrs Horton'. Three days after a scandalously collusive divorce, his wife, the mother of his three children, ran off with her lover, the Earl of Upper Ossory, while the Duke, having pensioned off Mrs Horton, married as his second wife a daughter of the Rev. Sir Richard Wrottesley, Dean of Windsor, by whom he had twelve children.

In the year of the Grafton divorce, Lord Bolingbroke also divorced his wife by a similarly collusive arrangement, which prompted the King to write to the Lord Chancellor to do something 'that might be likely to prevent the very bad conduct among the ladies of which there have been so many instances lately' (Coke, *Letters and Journals*, iii, 52–3; Stone, *Road to Divorce*, 336–7).

The Secretary of State for the Southern Department was Lieutenant-General Henry Seymour Conway, who had served bravely under the Duke of Cumberland at Fontenoy and had also fought at Culloden. An enterprising, cultured and inventive man, he had, unlike Rockingham and Grafton, had some experience of office, as Lord Lieutenant of Ireland. But the Government which Cumberland had contrived to form – and in which the now aged Duke of Newcastle was Lord Privy Seal and the equally aged Lord Winchilsea was Lord President of the Council – was not a Ministry which was expected to survive for long. Certainly it was not well qualified to weather the storm which might be expected should John Wilkes, who had caused such trouble to the previous Government, decide to return to London from his Continental exile.

14

JOHN WILKES

Like Satan preaching against sin . . .

John Wilkes had come to prominence in the summer of 1762 with the appearance of a weekly periodical, the *North Briton*, which he had helped to found. It was a periodical in which he scurrilously abused Lord Bute, whose Scottish blood had helped to lead Wilkes to choose the name in allusion to the *True Briton*, a publication edited by Tobias Smollett and called into existence to support the Government. In the issue of the *North Briton* numbered 45 and dated 23 April 1763, following innuendoes in earlier issues about Bute's relations with the Princess Dowager, there had appeared not only an attack upon the Government but also a suggestion that the King's Speech contained a downright lie. This was considered to be an allegation which went a step too far and, in consequence of it, proceedings were instituted against Wilkes, who was arrested and imprisoned in the Tower, where, with typical insouciance, he asked not to be put in a cell previously occupied by a Scotchman, for fear of catching the pox. But it was easier to put Wilkes in prison than to keep him there, for he was a Member of Parliament and, as such, enjoyed certain privileges.

Wilkes — exceptionally ugly, with a pronounced squint — was a man of insinuating charm who claimed without much exaggeration that it took him 'only half an hour to talk away his face'. He had been born in October 1725 in St John's Square, London, the son of a wealthy malt distiller, and at the age of twenty-one had married a Buckinghamshire heiress of strong Nonconformist beliefs, from whom he was soon separated by mutual consent after she had given birth to a daughter to whom her father became devotedly attached. Although profligate and sensual — an enthusiastic participant in the libidinous festivities of the 'Medmenham Monks' until expelled because of his attacks in the *North Briton* on certain fellow members of the society – he had strong political ambitions and, having failed to get elected to Parliament for Berwick-upon-Tweed – despite his bribery of the captain of a boat bringing opposition voters to Berwick, who were, so it was said, landed instead on the Norwegian coast – he succeeded in bribing sufficient voters at a later election to become Member for Aylesbury, where he was also appointed Colonel of the Buckinghamshire Militia.

In London, although not a distinguished speaker in the House, he became celebrated for his quick wit in private company and for his ability to charm those whom he had thoughtlessly or intentionally offended. One of these was Samuel Johnson, who not only disapproved of Wilkes's demagogic escapades and blasphemies but also resented his having questioned in print Johnson's reckless assertion in his dictionary that the letter 'H seldom, perhaps never, begins any but the first syllable'. Wilkes had observed 'the author of this observation must be a man of quick *apprehension* and a most *comprehensive* genius'. This had rankled with Johnson; but Wilkes had made amends by using his influence at the Admiralty to procure the release from the Navy of Johnson's black servant, who had run away to sea and much regretted having done so. Later, James Boswell contrived a meeting between Johnson and Wilkes at a dinner party. When told who was to be his fellow guest, Boswell had expected Johnson to exclaim, 'Jack Wilkes, Sir! I'd as soon dine with Jack Ketch!' But, in the event, Wilkes was so polite, his manner so ingratiating, his conversation so entertaining and instructive that Johnson was completely won over and eventually decided, after sharing with him several jokes at the expense of Scotland and the Scottish people, that Wilkes was a most agreeable fellow after all. It was a verdict which Edward Gibbon endorsed. 'I scarcely ever met with a better companion,' wrote Gibbon, while acknowledging that Wilkes was 'a thorough-going profligate in principle as in practice, his life stained with every vice and his conversation full of blasphemy and indecency . . . He has inexhaustible spirits, infinite wit and humour, and a great deal of knowledge.'

The King, who had never met Wilkes, could not be expected to agree with Gibbon and Johnson about a man of such dubious morals who claimed that, given a grain of truth, he would mix it up with 'a great mass of falsehood so that no chemist [would] ever be able to separate them'. The insults to his mother, the allegations of his mendacity, the sarcastic wit of the rogue were too gross for the King to bear. It was characteristic of Wilkes that, having been asked to make up a table at cards, he should have declined the offer on the grounds that he was so ignorant he could not tell the difference between a knave and a king. So, while not having instigated the proceedings against him, the King was understandably much gratified by the decision of his Ministers to have Wilkes arrested and imprisoned and, in a search for evidence against him, to take into custody also – by authority of a general warrant which did not name them – 'the authors, printers and publishers of the North Briton, No. 45'.

The King was, also understandably, much annoyed when, the following week, Wilkes, by then the hero of the mob, was released by the Chief Justice of the Court of Common Pleas, Charles Pratt, later Lord Camden, on the grounds that his imprisonment was a breach of parliamentary privilege.

This being considered so, Ministers decided that the sooner Wilkes were to be expelled from Parliament the better. A means of getting him expelled occurred to a man acquainted with him as a member of the 'Medmenham Monks' and who had been a victim of Wilkes's maliciously witty pen. This was Lord Sandwich, Secretary of State for the Northern Department, and allegedly the butt of one of the most famous sallies of Wilkes, who, upon Sandwich's telling him he would die either of the pox or on the gallows, immediately responded, 'That depends, my Lord, upon whether I embrace your mistress or your principles.' Sandwich knew that Wilkes was responsible for an obscene and blasphemous parody of Alexander Pope's *Essay on Man*. So, at the beginning of the parliamentary session in November 1763, Sandwich, having obtained proof sheets of this profane parody, entitled *Essay on Woman*, from Wilkes's private press, read out part of it in the House of Lords, making pious comments upon it which Lord Despenser commented was 'like Satan preaching against sin'. It was voted a libel and a breach of privilege.

Meanwhile in the Commons, on a Government motion, issue number 45 of the *North Briton* was also voted a seditious libel. It was ordered to be burned by the common hangman before the Royal Exchange. There, however, the crowd that had gathered assaulted the Sheriff and his constables and, to shouts of support for Wilkes and execration of his opponents, snatched away the condemned paper and burned instead a boot and a petticoat, universally recognized by now as symbols representing respectively, Lord Bute and Augusta, Princess Dowager of Wales.

The King was described as being both 'disturbed' and 'exasperated' by this riot. He had been following the course of the Wilkes affair with the closest attention, noting with extreme annoyance the large sums awarded by sympathetic London juries to Wilkes's printers and their compositors, who had sought damages for wrongful arrest, asking for detailed reports of the debates in Parliament, and making note of the names of Members who voted against the Government. One of these was Horace Walpole's friend Henry Seymour Conway, who was at that time not only in command of the First or Royal Regiment of Dragoons but also a Groom of the Bedchamber and thus a man who, having both a position in the Royal Household and an army command, ought, the King felt, to support his Ministers' measures. He therefore required the dismissal of Conway from 'both his civil and military commissions', just as he had already insisted upon the dismissal of Lord Temple from the Lord-Lieutenancy of Buckinghamshire for having expressed sympathy for Wilkes when required to replace him as Colonel of the Buckinghamshire Militia.

It was consequently with profound relief that towards the end of November 1763 the King was informed that the House of Commons had resolved that seditious libel was not covered by parliamentary privilege; and the King was even more pleased to learn that, having been badly wounded in the groin in a duel with an unpleasant Member of Parliament whom he had described in the *North Briton* as a 'mean, abject, low-lived, dirty fellow' and who had returned the insult by calling his adversary 'a cowardly rascal, villain and scoundrel', Wilkes had thought it as well during the Christmas vacation to leave London for the Continent. In his absence Ministers carried a motion to have him expelled from the Commons, and succeeded in having him declared an outlaw. Soon afterwards the King was said by Grenville to be continuing 'more than usually cheerful' and 'pleased with the success and conduct of his affairs'.

There had been occasions during the Wilkes affair when it was feared that his supporters would provoke serious riots in London in protest against the hounding of a man whom they saw as an upholder of liberty and as a champion of the people prepared to cock a snook at established authority.

The possibility of such riots was rarely far from people's minds. Benjamin Franklin, who came to London as Agent for Pennsylvania in 1764, wrote that within a single year in that decade he had 'seen riots in the country about corn; riots about elections; riots about work-houses; riots of colliers; riots of weavers; riots of coal-heavers; riots of sawyers; riots of chairmen; riots of smugglers in which custom-house officers and excisemen have been murdered and the King's armed vessels and troops fired at'. He might well have added that during earlier years he had been in England there had also been riots against turnpikes and toll collectors, and against press-gangs and schoolmasters, French footmen and Irish labourers, the prices of London theatres, and bawdy houses.

Not long after Wilkes's arrest the rejection in the House of Lords of a Bill for raising the duties on the importation of Italian silks led to riots of weavers in Spitalfields, many of whom were unemployed. Some four thousand of them, so it was estimated, marched to Kew to deliver a petition to the King. Although there were no disturbances upon that occasion, the Queen was very frightened; and the King, while never easily alarmed himself, was deeply concerned on her behalf. The next day he consulted the First Lord of the Treasury to see what could be done for the protection of his family and his Ministers, and also for the relief of the weavers, whom he had undertaken to help when they had presented their petition. Later that day, on his way to the House of Lords, his coach was chased by a threatening mob; while the Duke of Bedford, who had spoken in the House against the proposed legislation on imported silks, was jeered, pelted with rubbish, and hurt by a heavy stone which cut his hand as he raised it to protect his forehead. The windows of houses of merchants believed to be dealing in foreign silks were smashed; and gunsmiths' shops were broken into and arms carried away. Order was not restored until the Riot Act had been read and a cavalry charge had cleared the mob out of Bedford Square.

Three days later the rioters in what Walpole called 'prodigious numbers' attacked the Duke's Bloomsbury Square house and started to pull down the wall which surrounded the courtyard. They were still at work when the gates were thrown open.

A party of horse appeared, and sallying out while the Riot Act was read, rode round Bloomsbury Square, slashing and trampling on the mob, and dispersing them . . . In the mean time a party of the rioters had passed to the back of the house, and were forcing their way through the garden, when fortunately, fifty more horse arriving in the very critical instant, the house was saved, and perhaps the lives of all that were in it.

The next day another large mob gathered outside the house, but they appeared to be more interested in inspecting the damage that had been done to the wall than in making another assault upon it.

The Square was crowded, but chiefly by persons led by curiosity [Walpole commented]. As my chariot had no coronets I was received with huzzas; but when the horses turned to enter the Court, dirt and stones were thrown at it. When the gates opened, I was surprised with the most martial appearance. The Horse Guards were drawn up in the Court, and many officers and gentlemen were walking about as on the platform of a regular citadel.

Although the worst of the rioting was by then over, the Government and the King were still concerned: there were reports that further attacks were to be made on Bedford House, and on the houses of all other opponents of the imported-silk Bill, and that every shop in London which sold Italian silk was to be knocked to the ground. The Secretary of State, Lord Halifax, suggested that the Marquess of Granby should be appointed to fill the vacant post of Commander-in-Chief, on the grounds that he 'might save the lives of these deluded wretches, which may be exposed and sacrificed by another commander equally well-intentioned but less a favourite of the people'. Since the other commander Halifax referred to was clearly the Duke of Cumberland, the King retaliated by offering his uncle the appointment of Captain-General, a post which the Duke declined on the grounds that the danger from the 'poor wretches' was exaggerated. The Duke wished to God that His Majesty had no more formidable enemies than these.

This was on 20 May 1765, when the Duke was involved in those difficult and protracted discussions which, in July, resulted in the formation of that most strange of administrations ostensibly presided over by the Marquess of Rockingham. The Duke had never fully recovered from the illness that had assailed him in March, when it had been supposed he was past hope of recovery. After dinner on 31 October, at the age of forty-four, he died at home from a clot of blood on the brain.

The Duke's death threw the newly formed Administration into turmoil. It seemed to several of its members that the only hope of their survival was to bring in Pitt. But the King was concerned that taking in Pitt might involve having to accept Pitt's brother-in-law, that *bête noire* George Grenville, not to mention Grenville's brother, Lord Temple, a dreaded trio known as 'the family'. 'I constantly told them [the Ministers],' the King wrote, 'that I had three times in vain [authorized approaches to be made to Pitt], that it could never again arise from me: that Mr Pitt had declared the last time he was with me that he must for ever retire.'

Even so, the Marquess of Rockingham pleaded that Pitt's advice and assistance were more than ever necessary now, since there were disturbances in America that threatened the very foundations of the relationship between Britain and her overseas colonies.

15

TROUBLES IN AMERICA

A mighty continent increasing daily in numbers and strength . . .

The Seven Years War with France had established Britain as the world's leading colonial power and had left her with vastly increased territories to administer in North America. The problem the Government now had to face was to pay not only for the war's victories but also for the cost of defending and administering the territories which had been secured. When George Grenville was in office he had decided that it was only proper that at least part of the high cost of maintaining a force of ten thousand men in America, as a safeguard against French revenge and Indian depredations, should be met by the American colonists themselves, who, in his opinion, had contributed very little to the war effort. After all – even though Americans complained that the British army was really intended to keep them in subjection – it was their homelands which were to be protected; moreover, their taxes were so relatively slight that an American paid no more than sixpence a year, against the average English taxpayer's twenty-five shillings. Also, smuggling must be stopped and an end be put to the disgraceful mismanagement whereby it cost £8,000 to collect £2,000 worth of customs duties in American ports.

Grenville had accordingly proposed first a new Revenue Act, or, as it came to be known, Sugar Act, which imposed a duty of threepence per gallon on imported molasses, then a Stamp Act which decreed that all manner of legal and other documents, from insurance policies to liquor licences, would be invalid unless they bore stamps of varying denominations.

Since stamp duties had long been imposed in England, the King was presumed to agree that there was no reason at all why Parliament, in the proper exercise of its duties as the supreme constitutional authority in the Empire, should not impose such duties in America also, particularly since the money raised from the sale of stamps was to be used expressly for the pay of troops in the American colonies. Nor was there anything in the Stamp Act which could be said to be contrary to the Bill of Rights of 1689, the constitutional outcome of the Glorious Revolution which had ensured the Protestant succession to the English throne and had established the principle of parliamentary supremacy. So unexceptionable, indeed, did this perfectly legal piece of legislation appear to be that it had not even been mentioned in the lengthy correspondence that passed between the King and George Grenville. English public opinion and English newspapers, when they took notice of it at all, were quite as satisfied as was the King as to its fairness and propriety.

It was, however, seen in quite a different light in America; there, early in the morning of a hot August day in 1765, a large crowd of Bostonians marched on Hanover Square, where, on a branch of an elm tree, hung an effigy of the wealthy merchant who had accepted the office of Distributor of Stamps for Massachusetts Bay. Throughout the day all passers-by were stopped and required to go through a mock ceremony of buying a stamp as a means of showing them just how irksome and burdensome the new imposition would be. The effigy was then carried up to Tower Hill and thrown on a huge bonfire; a building believed to be the Distributor's intended stamp office was pulled down; his house was attacked, its windows were smashed and its furniture was thrown into the street. A few days later the house of the Lieutenant-Governor of Massachusetts was also attacked; his furniture, too, was smashed, and, like that of the Distributor, who was intimidated into resigning his office, was hurled out of the broken windows, together with family portraits. He was considered lucky to have escaped with his life.

Opposition to the Stamp Act was not confined to the colonies. William Pitt, who said that he rejoiced in America's resistance, was opposed to it, as were Edmund Burke, at that time the Marquess of Rockingham's private secretary, Isaac Barré, the massive and swarthy Member for Chipping Wycombe, and several other lesser-known men in the Commons, as well as Pitt's friend Lord Camden, who said that it was impossible for one 'petty island in Europe' to presume to hold in dependence a 'mighty continent increasing daily in numbers and strength'. Even those who approved of the Stamp Act in principle suggested it was impracticable. British merchants were losing business, because one of the most effective responses to the Act was to impose an embargo on trade with Britain. Besides, the only way to enforce obedience was to send out more British troops. But where were these to be found? And how were they to be paid?

Rockingham advised repeal of the Act. Grenville, whose legislation it had been, insisted that it must be enforced. The King, who continued to support the common view that Parliament had as unquestionable a right to tax American colonies as it had to tax British citizens, yet who appreciated the difficulties of enforcement, favoured a compromise by which the Act might be modified.

In this dilemma Rockingham, without the King's authority, sent a Member of Parliament as messenger to Bath, where Pitt was still nursing his gout, to make yet another vain approach to him, while the King unwisely turned once again to Lord Bute, who was scarcely more accommodating than Pitt. Eventually Rockingham decided that the issue must be made one of confidence. If he lost the vote he would resign. Contemplating the unpalatable prospect of having to take back George Grenville, the King made no further objections to repeal of the contentious Act. Questioned on the point by the Duke of Newcastle, he replied, 'Yes I am [for repeal] now. I was not at first, but now I am convinced and think that it is necessary.' So it was that in February 1766, the King's views on the matter being generally known and after a powerful speech by Pitt, who protested that England should not take money out of the Americans' pockets without their consent, a motion by Grenville to enforce the Stamp Act was lost – much to the gratification of the colonists, who erected statues to both Pitt and George III in New York City, and greatly to the annoyance of Grenville, who peevishly declared that it was now 'clear that both England and America were governed by the mob'. Yet while this particular Act was to be repealed, the King supported the ministerial policy that the Americans must not be allowed to suppose that Parliament had abandoned its right to tax the colonies in future. Accordingly, before repeal, a Declaratory Act was passed confirming Parliament's power 'to make laws and statutes . . . to bind the colonies and people of America . . . in all cases whatsoever'.

The lead that he had given in the repeal of the Stamp Act showed that William Pitt, now fifty-eight years old, was far from being a spent force; and the King, who had recently told Rockingham that it was quite right that the First Minister 'should have put an end to the idea of writing to Mr. Pitt', was reluctantly coming to believe that he would have to call him to the direction of affairs, if only he could do so without having to call upon the other members of 'the family' as well. There was 'nothing', he said, that he 'would not rather submit to' than turn to them; but there was no doubt that the present situation could not continue much longer, the Ministry being so feeble. He complained to Bute of his 'many grievances': he could neither eat nor sleep, he said; nothing pleased him but musing on his 'cruel situation'. But Bute could offer little comfort, while the Government grew weaker and more exasperating by the week. The Duke of Grafton resigned as Secretary of State and, much to the annoyance of the King, who did not like him, the young and inexperienced Duke of Richmond, Lady Sarah Lennox's brother, was brought into the Cabinet in his place. Then there was trouble over the King's having promised his three younger brothers that most of the Duke of Cumberland's allowance of £25,000 a year would be divided between them – a promise which the Marquess of Rockingham alleged could not at present be fulfilled because the time taken up by American affairs had made it impossible to consider the matter until the following year. 'Rockingham wants me to break my word, which I cannot do,' the King complained in one of his recurrent moods of self-commiseration. 'I mean to stand by [my brothers] . . . See what treatment I receive from every set of Ministers . . . Because a few weak boys are unwilling this session to pass the provision for my brothers my word is to be set at naught. My prudence is now exhausted and I am enclin'd to take any step that will preserve my honour.'

Almost any government, the King decided, would be better than

Rockingham's, composed as it was of these 'incompetents'; and once he had been persuaded that if he called upon Pitt he would definitely not have to put up with 'the family' – and that Pitt would form a government without regard to party distinctions – he was eager for an immediate change, for the creation of an administration which would satisfy his longing 'to extricate this country out of faction' and to establish a principled government prepared to submit to his own firm guidance.

Pitt himself was not to be the ostensible leader of the new Administration. Pleading that his health could no longer stand the strain of the House of Commons and clearly unwilling to join the Government on any terms other than his own, he desired to be created Earl of Chatham – much to the dismay of his friends – and took office as Lord Privy Seal at the end of July 1766.

The Duke of Grafton became First Lord of the Treasury; General Conway became Leader of the House of Commons; and the Hon. Charles Townshend, a clever young man, witty and energetic, possessed of a marvellous talent for mimicry and repartee, with a loud voice, an even louder laugh, and a taste for high living which earned him the nickname 'Champagne Charlie', was appointed Chancellor of the Exchequer. No places were found for either Newcastle or Rockingham, while Lord Bute, disgruntled by the offhand, not to say dismissive, manner in which he was treated by the newly ennobled Earl of Chatham, complained to the King that his heart was 'half broke' and his health ruined by the 'unmerited, barbarous treatment' he had received.

It appears that Bute went to grumble about his treatment to the Princess Dowager of Wales one day when the King had gone to her house for breakfast. His mother – so the King himself told the Duke of York, who in turn told Charles Greville – took the King aside and said to him, 'There is someone here who wishes very much to speak to you.'

'Who is it?'

'Lord Bute.'

'Good God, Mamma! How could you bring him here? It is impossible for me to hold any communication with Lord Bute in this manner.'

He did see him, however; and Bute 'made a violent attack upon him for having abandoned and neglected him'. The King replied that 'in justice to his Ministers he could not hold any communication with him unknown to them'. Lord Bute then angrily declared that he 'would never see the King again', whereupon the King, angry now in his turn, replied 'Then, my Lord, be it so, and remember from henceforth we never meet again.' 'And from that day he never beheld Lord Bute or had any communication with him.'*

For some time now the King had, in any case, been more inclined to confide in and seek advice from the second Earl of Egmont, a gifted, ambitious man who was 'never known to laugh, though indeed to smile and that was at chess', and the first Earl of Northington, a handsome, upright, conscientious lawyer, Lord Chancellor for several years, who was, like Egmont, a rather gloomy man much troubled by gout and known as 'Surly Bob'.

With Bute dismissed from royal favour, the King was anxious to give Lord Chatham his almost unqualified support: he readily agreed to his suggestions as to ennoblement and patronage, approving the creation of three new dukedoms, though he had formerly been reluctant to sanction any increase in the peerage, had firmly told Rockingham 'on many occasions' that he had no intention of doing so for the moment, and thereafter created no more dukes outside the Royal Family. He even consented to Chatham's proposal of an alliance with Prussia. When Chatham's gout began to trouble him again and he was obliged to take to his bed, the King wrote of his concern and sent assurances of his most sincere sympathy, even though he did not like the man any better now than he had done in the past, considered he made too much of a fuss about his complaint, and, a plain-speaking man himself, was exasperated by Chatham's letters, which, even allowing for the writer's fervent regard for the concept of monarchy, were ludicrously effusive. In one, characteristic of others, he asked 'to be permitted to lay himself with all duty and

---

* In Charles Greville's account the Duke of York said that the King told him that this altercation with Lord Bute took place in a pavilion at Kew in 1764 (*The Greville Memoirs*, i, 161–2). Bute himself, however, told Louis Dutens, the diplomatist and man of letters, that he last saw the King in 1766, and this date is probably correct (Dutens, *Memoirs*, iv, 1821).

submission' at the King's feet, and 'to pour out a heart overflowing with the most reverential and warm sense of His Majesty's infinite condescension . . . and royal magnanimity'.★

While Chatham remained unable to 'attend His Majesty's most gracious presence', the Government floundered and fumbled, its members at cross purposes and contradicting each other in their speeches. 'The Earl of Chatham is at Bath,' a member of the Opposition wrote, 'and consequently the King's Administration has also got the gout and hobbles terribly.' The King did all he could to keep up his Ministers' spirits, declaring encouragingly, for example, that 'these things will happen' when they were defeated in the House of Commons on a motion to reduce the land tax, and urging his brothers, the Dukes of Gloucester and Cumberland, to attend and vote for the Administration in the House of Lords.

But he was growing increasingly impatient with his Ministers, and particularly with Chatham, whose illness he believed to be not as severe as the invalid claimed at Bath, where he was reported to be ensconced with 'more equipage, household and retinue than most of the old patriarchs used to travel with in ancient days'. 'He comes nowhere but to the Pump Room,' George Selwyn was told. 'Then he makes a short essay and retires.' The Duke of Grafton was doing his best in Chatham's absence; but he was not the man to face up to an Opposition which now comprised not only Grenville, Rockingham and the Duke of Bedford and their supporters, but even, in one division, the King's own brother, the Duke of York. Yet, when Grafton sought Chatham's advice on ways in which the Government could be strengthened, Chatham replied that he was too ill to discuss the matter. Having returned home from Bath, he was sunk in gloom in a darkened room into which servants pushed his meals through a hatch. Rarely speaking to his wife, he was described by his solicitor as 'miserable beyond description' and 'so much confused he scarcely knew what subject he was speaking on'.

The King pleaded with him 'to make an effort' and give Grafton some encouragement, otherwise he would throw in the sponge.

★ It was said that 'at the levée, Lord Chatham used to bow so low, you could see the tip of his hooked nose between his legs' (Albemarle, *Memoirs*, 78).

'Five minutes conversation with you would raise his spirits for his heart is good,' the King wrote to him. 'Mine, I thank Heaven, want no rousing,' he added in characteristic self-congratulation, 'my love to my country, as well as what I owe to my own character and to my family, prompt me not to yield to faction. Be firm, and you will find me amply ready to take as active a part as the hour seems to require.'

This letter, reminding Chatham of his 'duty' and 'honour', achieved its purpose. Feeling rather better, he agreed to see Grafton and approved of his approaching the Opposition parties to see what could be done to prop up the Government. The negotiations, protracted and at times acrimonious, eventually resulted in a mélange which fully satisfied no one and prompted Chatham to resign in October 1768, much to the King's astonishment. 'Tho I have within these eight years met with enough to prevent my being much surprized at anything that may happen,' he wrote to Grafton, who now became the actual rather than the ostensible head of the Administration, 'yet I cannot conceal the not having expected the letter you received the last evening from Lord Chatham.' He wrote also to Chatham himself, endeavouring to change his mind, protesting that he had 'a right to insist' on his remaining in his service, and relying upon his 'assistance in resisting the torrent of factions' the country so much laboured under. Even though confined to his house, Chatham's very name would be sufficient for his 'administration to proceed'.

But Chatham was deaf to entreaties; and replied in a letter in that convoluted and affected style by now only too familiar:

Penetrated with the high honour of Your Majesty's gracious commands, my affliction is infinite to be constrained by absolute necessity from illness to lay myself again at Your Majesty's feet for compassion . . . Should it please God to restore me to health, every moment of my life will be at Your Majesty's devotion, in the mean time the most gracious thought Your Majesty deigns to express of my recovery is my best consolation. I am, Sir, with all submission and profound veneration Your Majesty's most dutiful and devoted servant.

In the event Chatham was never to hold office again. Without his help, the Duke of Grafton had to deal as best he could with the troubles consequent upon the return of John Wilkes to England.

16

JOHN WILKES RETURNS

Wilkes and no King! God save great Wilkes, our King!

John Wilkes had made the most of his days in exile. He had gone first to Paris, where he was 'received by Diderot as a brother in arms . . . was also countenanced by the French court and made a figure in the salons'. He lived in the rue St-Nicaise with an Italian dancer, Gertrude Corradini, with whom he travelled to Italy, where he was conducted round the ruins by Johann Winckelmann, Chief Supervisor of Antiquities, 'a gentleman of exquisite taste' in the opinion of Wilkes, who was all the more taken with him on his pretending not to notice their absence when, overcome by lust, he and Corradini disappeared for a few moments to make love behind a convenient monument. 'This was all the more obliging,' Wilkes commented, 'because he must necessarily pass such an interval with the mother of Corradini who had as little conversation as beauty.'

On his return to Paris, having spent three months in Naples, Wilkes was forced to conclude that his extravagance had rendered further residence on the Continent impossible. His money was nearly all gone, and, in anticipation of his outlawry, he had disposed of his remaining property with the intention of benefiting his beloved daughter, for whose expensive education he was still paying. So it was that, although outlawed and found guilty of blasphemy in his absence, he came home by way of Holland, arriving in London on 6 February 1768.

Ignored by the Ministry, he wrote a letter asking for pardon and sent his servant with it to the Queen's House for the attention of the King, who, affronted by the man's not having submitted a formal petition in the usual way, ignored it. A few days later Wilkes announced that he was to stand as a candidate for the City of London at the general election. He had support enough among the general populace, but few of those had a vote – when told that one of his supporters was a turncoat, he cheerfully replied, 'Impossible! Not one of them has a coat to turn' – and, while also supported by many of the 'middling sort', it was not expected that he would be elected. Nor was he.

Undeterred by having come bottom of the poll of seven candidates, he immediately afterwards stood for Middlesex. On this occasion steps were taken to ensure his election. When James Boswell – who had enjoyed Wilkes's company on the Continent but now avoided him, disapproving of his politics – passed through Brentford on his way from Oxford, he found the whole road in possession of the mob, who were roaring, 'Wilkes and Liberty!', chalking 'No. 45' on every coach that passed, and threatening to knock down pedestrians who did not shout for Jack Wilkes with them. Returned with a large majority, the duly elected Member of Parliament then surrendered to a charge of outlawry and was committed by the Lord Chief Justice of the King's Bench, Lord Mansfield, to the King's Bench Prison in St George's Fields, Southwark, for twenty-two months and fined £1,000 – a punishment he accepted with nonchalance, picking his teeth.

The rules of the King's Bench were not strict, prisoners, mostly debtors, being permitted to buy the right to move freely within the three square miles surrounding the prison; and Wilkes made full use of the privileges allowed him, writing letters to his constituents, composing inflammatory articles for newspapers, accepting money towards the payment of his £20,000 worth of debts as well as presents from supporters – including all manner of delicacies and forty-five hogsheads of tobacco from America – and enjoying the favours of several female admirers, who were welcomed with open arms.

His supporters crowded round the prison in increasing numbers, threatening violence. As many as 40,000 handbills were issued by the authorities, urging them to keep the peace and 'to convince the world that liberty is not joined with licentiousness'.

The King was naturally outraged that a man condemned as an outlaw and guilty of blasphemy should be allowed to sit as a Member of the House of Commons, and he told the Chancellor of the

Exchequer that it was 'highly proper', indeed 'very essential', that he should be expelled. 'I think his speech in the court of King's Bench on Wednesday last reason for to go as far as possible to expel him; for he declared number 45 [of the *North Briton*] a paper that the author ought to *glory in* and the blasphemous poem a mere *ludicrous production*.'

While the Government discussed their dilemma, Wilkes's champions and the unruly populace of London in general – discontented weavers, coal-heavers, sailors, hundreds of unemployed protesting at the cost of bread and beer, as well as unruly apprentices and unskilled labourers – demanded Wilkes's release and Government action to relieve their distress. On the evening of his election for Middlesex, on 28 March, the mob had rampaged through the streets, smashing windows, including those of Lord Bute, Lord Egmont, the Duke of Newcastle and 'even that of the Lady Mayoress's bed-chamber' in the Mansion House and demanding illuminations as a sign of support for Wilkes wherever houses remained in darkness. The Duke of Northumberland saved most of his windows by getting his servants to provide the mob with ale; the Duchess of Hamilton's, despite a battering which lasted for three hours, were saved by the stoutness of her shutters. The precise and dignified Austrian Ambassador was dragged out of his coach to have the number 45 chalked on the soles of his shoes – an outrage which he made the subject of a strong complaint to Ministers, who found it, so Walpole said, 'as difficult to help laughing as to give him redress'.

That night the King, 'full of indignation', did not go to bed and authorized the use of troops if necessary. 'I shall not stir from my house,' he wrote to Lord Barrington, the Secretary-at-War, 'so that you may come or send to me if any thing arises that requires my immediate decision.'

The next night demands for candles and lamps in windows were repeated; and so bright did these make the streets that Benjamin Franklin thought the consequent illuminations exceeded the 'greatest occasions of rejoicing' ever seen in London. Carriages were again chalked with the number 45, and so were the doors of houses. A new cry was heard: 'Wilkes and no King!' Before the troubles were over, Franklin voiced the opinion that, if the King had had a bad character and Wilkes a good one, George III would have lost his throne. The King himself considered that 'almost [his crown] depended upon' a satisfactory outcome of the crisis.

In anticipation of further disturbances the Southwark magistrates had received instructions from the Secretary of State, Lord Weymouth, not to delay calling up troops, since a military force could 'never be employed to a more constitutional purpose than in support of the authority and dignity of the magistracy'. Encouraged by this, on 10 May one of the magistrates read the Riot Act and ordered a company of soldiers to shoot when a demonstration outside the King's Bench Prison threatened to get out of hand. At least six people were killed and many more were wounded in the subsequent musket fire, several of them spectators of the riot rather than rioters themselves, one of them being 'a valuable and well-disposed young creature' who was mistaken for an agitator wearing a similar red waistcoat.

Informed that the uproar, later to be known as 'the Massacre of St George's Fields', had been subdued by the Army, but not that the subjugation had been brutally clumsy, the King expressed his approval of the vigour displayed by the Southwark magistrates. He had been at Kew on the day of the bloodshed in Southwark and had written to Lord Weymouth to assure him that he was ready to leave for London immediately if his presence there were required. The next day he did leave, having written to Weymouth to express his belief that, though he 'did not delight in it', bloodshed had been the 'only way of restoring due obedience to the laws'. He also wrote to Lord Barrington, to congratulate him on the behaviour of the Foot Guards.

His belief that bloodshed would restore order proved too optimistic, however: there were further riots in the days that followed. The houses of two magistrates, who had ordered the removal of a poster proclaiming Wilkes as a champion of liberty, were assaulted, and raucous shouts of 'Wilkes and Liberty' were heard outside the House of Lords, together with cries of 'It's as well to be hanged as starved!' The Mansion House was attacked again; and a boot and a petticoat were paraded about on a gibbet through cheering crowds on Cornhill.

Further bloodshed was to come when seamen from the docks went on strike for higher wages and prevented all ships leaving the

Pool of London, coming into furious conflict with coal-heavers and lumpers, whose livelihood was threatened by the seamen's strike.

The King clung to the belief that in 'these very licentious days' the Government must stand firm against the threatened anarchy and authorize the use of troops whenever necessary, while he himself did everything that could be done to overcome the difficulty of providing sufficient troops to answer the calls which magistrates were continually making upon them. In the meantime, the King urged, Ministers must see to it that the dissolute and insolent troublemaker largely responsible for the unrest should be expelled from the House of Commons.

While there were those in the Government who thought it might be as well to leave the man where he was and not provoke further unrest by taking action against him, the Cabinet obediently decided to bring in a motion for Wilkes's expulsion after he had given further provocation by issuing a 'scandalous and seditious' libel against Lord Weymouth, who, so Wilkes alleged, had planned to use force against demonstrators well before the riots in St George's Fields. The motion was carried by a satisfactory majority on 3 February 1769.

Less than a fortnight later, however, on 16 February, Wilkes was again elected Member for Middlesex. Again he was expelled from the House and again he was elected, no other candidate being prepared to stand against him. He was promptly once more expelled.

The next month a large group of aldermen set out to drive to St James's Palace from the City to deliver a loyal address to the King; but few of their carriages managed to reach it, their way being blocked by a riotous mob which hurled rubbish at them and smashed their windows, shouting 'Wilkes and no King! God save great Wilkes, our King!' The Riot Act was read to no avail; several arrests were made, but there were very few subsequent prosecutions.

'This seems to me so extraordinary,' the King wrote to the First Lord of the Treasury, 'that I hope you will enquire into it and send me a full account of what passed . . . If there is no means by law to quell riots, and if juries forget they are on their oath to be guided by fact not faction, this constitution must be overthrown and anarchy (the most terrible of all evils) must ensue. It therefore behoves every honest man with vigour to stand forth.'

There now came forward a man whose dislike of Wilkes induced him to agree to a suggestion that he should stand as a candidate for Middlesex at the next election. This was Lieutenant-Colonel the Hon. Henry Lawes Luttrell, a sardonic Irishman who already sat as Member for the borough of Bossiney in Cornwall and who had once reportedly declined to accept a challenge to a duel from his own father on the grounds that it had not been given by a gentleman.

When it was known that he had agreed to vacate his Cornish seat to stand against Wilkes in Middlesex, bets were placed on the duration of his life; and when, following his defeat at the polls by 1,143 to 296, he was nevertheless declared duly elected by vote of the Commons, his opponent being pronounced unfit to sit in Parliament, he 'did not dare to appear in the streets or scarce quit his lodging' for several weeks.

The Commons's action in declaring Colonel Luttrell elected led to the King's being sent a flood of petitions complaining of the corruption of Parliament and the complaisant attitude of a venal Government. The authors of most of these petitions took care not to attack the King himself. Yet, as their 'gracious monarch', the 'father of his people', His Majesty was urged to examine and redress the petitioners' complaints. There were other petitions, however, in which the King was either implicitly or openly accused of condoning or even encouraging his Administration's malpractices.

A particularly outspoken petition was presented by the City of London, whose Lord Mayor, Chatham's friend the rich William Beckford, was ostentatiously snubbed by the King when next he attended a levee at St James's. A second petition followed it, then a third, which was presented by Beckford himself, who was accompanied to the Palace by a crowd of noisy supporters and who, when the petition was rejected as being 'dangerous to the constitution of the Kingdom', had the temerity to register an objection personally to the King, an unheard-of breach of etiquette which shocked His Majesty into silence.

More unsettling still to the King's peace of mind was an attack upon him in a published letter by the astute, acerbic and influential political writer who signed himself 'Junius' and who is now known to have been Philip Francis, assistant to Lord Barrington. 'Junius' did not hesitate to attack the King personally, nor to hint at the possibility of revolution. In an open letter addressed to His Majesty, praising Wilkes and condemning the Government, whose 'sole object for many years' was 'the destruction of one man', 'Junius' told the King that it was 'not too late to correct the errors of his education'.

You have still an honourable part to act ['Junius' continued]. The affections of your subjects may still be recovered. But before you subdue their hearts, you must gain a noble victory over your own. Discard those little, personal resentments, which have too long directed your public conduct . . . Pardon this man [Wilkes]. Let it appear to your people that you can determine and act for yourself. Come forward to your people. Lay aside the wretched formalities of a King, and speak to your subjects with the spirit of a man and in the language of a gentleman. Tell them you have been fatally deceived . . . Remember that [the security of your title to the crown] was acquired by one revolution [in 1688]; it may be lost by another.

Once again the canard that the King was under the malign influence of his mother and Bute was spread about the town, even though his mother was dying of cancer of the throat and Bute was travelling on the Continent incognito under the name Sir John Stuart. It would be 'happy for this country', 'Junius' wrote, if the Princess Dowager were dead. On 1 April 1771 an effigy of her and one of Bute were drawn in carts to Tower Hill, the execution ground for traitors, where they were decapitated by chimney-sweeps before a large crowd and then thrown on to a bonfire. The King was hissed on his way to the House of Lords, and an apple was thrown at his head.

In calmer times, before cancer had weakened her, the Princess Dowager was often to be seen at Richmond and Kew, inspecting progress on the botanical garden she had created with the help of Lord Bute and the head gardener, William Aiton, and looking round the temples and other buildings under construction in the grounds to the designs of William Chambers, whose orangery and pagoda had been completed in the early 1760s. On these days she would frequently have breakfast with her son and daughter-in-law, who were in turn regular guests at her own table. But of late the dutiful visits paid to the Princess had become both irksome and depressing, since, in her painful illness, she had become mournful and crotchety.

Suspected even now of still being an evil influence behind the throne and of attempting to undermine the King's Ministers, she was accused of all manner of underhand activities; and, to the angry annoyance of the King, a Member of Parliament went so far as to demand an inquiry into her conduct when she was already mortally ill.

She was visibly losing ground, the King told his brother the Duke of Gloucester in November 1770; and a week later her speech, so he reported, was growing 'less intelligible'. 'She hourly emaciated,' he wrote, 'and has dreadful faintings towards night, which must soon put an end to a situation that it is almost cruel to wish to see her long continue in.'

Weak and ill as she was, however, with 'risings of the viscera', she insisted on getting out of bed and being dressed when her son and daughter-in-law went to see her on 7 February 1772, though by then she could not speak. She died that night; but even in death her enemies declined to leave her in peace. At her funeral service in Westminster Abbey, so Horace Walpole said, the mob outside 'huzzaed for joy'. They surged forward to the Abbey doors and stripped the black cloth from the wooden platform.

17

'A MAN OF ADMIRABLE PARTS'

You will never meet with that proper obedience to the laws of this country until you have destroyed that nest of locusts.

Throughout the troublesome months in which the later stages of the Wilkes affair had plagued the Court and Cabinet, the King had been able to rely upon the support of the Leader of the House of Commons, a man he had known since boyhood and one to whom he bore so close a resemblance that it was rumoured they must be intimately related. This was Frederick North, only son of Lord North, later first Earl of Guilford, who had been the King's Governor. Frederick North was a clumsy, awkward man with what Walpole described as 'two large prominent eyes that rolled about to no purpose (for he was utterly short-sighted). A wide mouth, thick lips and inflated visage gave him the air of a blind trumpeter.'*

---

* Lord North's father had joined Prince Frederick's Household as a Gentleman of the Bedchamber in 1730, two years after having married Lady Lucy Montagu, daughter of the second Earl of Halifax, an allegedly rather flighty young woman. Rumours that the physical resemblance between the King and the younger Lord North was due to a shared paternity were first aired in print by Sir Nathaniel Wraxall, who commented upon the fact that both men went blind (*Historical Memoirs*, i, 310). The well-informed Horace Walpole did not believe the rumours, and on a pamphlet issued in 1787 referring to North's relationship to the King he wrote against North's name, 'falsely supposed son of the late Pr. of Wales' (C. D. Smith, *The Early Career of Lord North*, 41).

Lord North's most recent biographer observes that it is difficult to find anyone who took the story seriously. 'Charles Townshend, North's predecessor at the Exchequer, once referred to him as a "seeming changeling", but it is difficult to regard that as important evidence . . . It has been argued nevertheless that even if the story is untrue its very existence affected public interpretation of North's apparent reluctance to gainsay George III . . . If this was the case it would surely have been a popular topic with political satirists. Yet of the 550 or so cartoons in the British Library for which the catalogue entry gives North as the main or subsidiary subject

Educated at Eton and Trinity College, Oxford, North had spent three years on the Grand Tour, and at the age of twenty-two had entered the House of Commons as Member for the family borough of Banbury, which he represented until succeeding his father as second Earl of Guilford. Never a commanding orator, though skilled and often amusing in debate, he soon became one of the best liked and most respected men in Parliament. Easy-going, cultivated, something of a Latin scholar, the fond father of seven children, consistently good-natured, if on occasions obstinate, he was well described by Edward Gibbon as 'one of the best companions in the Kingdom', by Nathaniel Wraxall as a man in whose company it was impossible to be bored, and by Edmund Burke as 'a man of admirable parts, of general knowledge, of a versatile understanding, fitted for every sort of business, of infinite wit and pleasantry, of a delightful temper, and with a mind most perfectly disinterested'.

He had certainly proved himself to be an astute manager and manipulator of the House of Commons, and was to be a shrewd leader of a coalition whose members were drawn together by a common desire for office. He was ostensibly a Whig, but he came from a Tory family and his instincts were those of a Tory. He never associated himself with the great Whig families, and he shared the King's strong dislike of faction.

His Majesty found him refreshingly congenial and could talk to him with an ease he had rarely felt with his other Ministers apart from Lord Bute; for Lord North was never condescending, never disrespectful, never devious or dishonourable, content to appear far less able than he was. Often during debates in the House of Commons he would seem to be asleep, slumped in his seat with his feet lolling on the Treasury Bench, when he would interpose an astute comment to disconcert, though rarely to offend, the Opposition spokesman.* The King enjoyed his company and his conversation, amusing yet

only two of them, published in 1773 and 1782 respectively, appear to allude to a blood relationship with the King' (Whiteley, *Lord North*, 6).

* His son-in-law, Lord Glenbervie, told the story of how Lord North fell asleep one day in the House during a long and boring speech by George Grenville. When Grenville seemed to be approaching the end of his speech, North was woken up by John Robinson, his political manager, the Member for Westmorland, to hear Grenville still droning on . . . 'I shall now draw the attention of the House to the revenues

free of malice, as much as everyone did. He could think of no one whom he would like better as head of a new administration; and in January 1770 he was able to gratify his wish as the Duke of Grafton's Ministry slowly disintegrated. Lord Camden, the Lord Chancellor, supported a motion of censure on his own Government over the Luttrell-versus-Wilkes affair and spoke of its 'arbitrary measures' which had made him hang his head in shame. His office was then offered to Charles Yorke, a former Attorney-General, who hesitantly accepted it, then, almost immediately, died. The Duke of Grafton, who for some months had been spending less time at his desk than on the racecourse or in the arms of his mistress, Mrs Horton, resigned his office. So did the Commander-in-Chief, the Marquess of Granby, who, like Camden, declared in the House that he repented of his vote in favour of Colonel Luttrell's admission as Member for Middlesex.

When the names of Lord Rockingham and Chatham were suggested as replacements for the Duke of Grafton, the King spoke of abdication. He told General Conway, however, that he would try to go on 'if Lord North would put himself at the head of the Treasury'. Lord North, who had already been sounded out, was then offered the premiership, and, having satisfied himself that the Opposition was not strong enough to push him out, he accepted the offer. By the end of March 1770 his authority in Parliament was unquestioned.

Lord North had not been long in office when news reached London from America of a series of clashes between British soldiers and the people of Boston. On 2 March 1770 a group of British soldiers, redcoats of the 29th Regiment, had gone to a ropewalk in the town to obtain some spare-time work to augment their meagre pay. The

---

and expenditure of the country in 1689.' 'Upon which Lord North said to the person who had jogged him, "Zounds, you have wakened me near one hundred years too soon"' (Glenbervie, *Diaries*, i, 237). On another occasion, when an Opposition Member, who was attacking him in a long and tedious speech, declared, 'Even now the noble Lord is slumbering over the ruin of his country!', North slowly opened his eyes and murmured, 'I wish to Heaven that I was' (Fox, *Memorials and Correspondence*, i, 121).

soldiers had already made themselves unpopular in Boston because of their taking on occasional jobs for less than the going rate of pay, as well as their rough and rude behaviour when off duty in the streets, their drunkenness, their chasing after women, and various other misdemeanours reported, exaggerated and sometimes invented by local newspapers. A worker at the ropewalk told one of the soldiers that if he wanted work he 'could go and clean [his] shit house'. The soldier lost his temper, dashed forward, and was knocked down. Three days later there was a more serious affray in which five Bostonians were killed and others were wounded – a 'massacre' that was for years annually commemorated on 5 March in Massachusetts as a day worthy of the most solemn remembrance, until 4 July became a day of national celebration instead.

As the months passed, tempers cooled in America and the colonies enjoyed a period of prosperity and quiet; but resentment against the British Parliament continued to fester and was exacerbated by a decision taken in London that, while the other custom duties which had been imposed by Charles Townshend as Chancellor of the Exchequer would be withdrawn, that on tea must be retained 'as a mark of the supremacy of Parliament'. 'There must always,' the King agreed, 'be one tax to keep up the right. And as such I approve of the tea duty.' Consequently foreign tea continued to be smuggled into Atlantic ports; customs officers and other officials found the law as difficult to enforce as ever; and there were still violent disturbances whenever a conscientious official or naval officer insisted upon carrying out his instructions to the letter.

Smuggled tea was consumed in enormous quantities, while officially imported tea was ostentatiously declined by patriotic Americans, who termed it the 'beverage of traitors'; and when in November 1773 the British ship *Dartmouth* entered Boston harbour with a cargo of tea from India, to be sold in America by agents of the East India Company, there were loud demands that the ship and her cargo must sail away forthwith. Orders given by the rich Governor of Massachusetts, a member of one of the colony's oldest families, that the tea must be unloaded were ignored; and a party of men disguised as Mohawks, with faces darkened by soot and representing themselves as symbols of oppressed America, marched down to Griffin's Wharf in the moonlight, clambered aboard the *Dartmouth* and two other ships carrying cargoes of Indian tea which had followed her into Boston, broke open the tea chests with tomahawks, and hurled their contents into the water. Afterwards an officious customs official, who had already been tarred and feathered in Maine, was dragged out of his house, tarred and feathered again, and paraded through the streets in a cart which was halted from time to time so that he could be beaten.

When reports of these disturbances reached England there was general agreement that the colonists had now overstepped the limits of tolerable misbehaviour and there could be no further concessions to their revolutionary leaders.

The King had initially been less inclined to believe that the 'mother country' should be severe with the recalcitrant Americans than some of his more belligerent Ministers. He spoke of 'firmness' but also of 'moderation'; and when in 1769 the hawkish Lord Hillsborough had proposed the withdrawal of their charter from the people of Massachusetts the King had objected that so provocative a gesture seemed more likely to 'increase the unhappy feudes than to asswage them'. Slowly, however, he had come to the view that a firm stand was essential, agreeing with Lord North that once the Americans were quiet and showed 'respect for the mother country', then would be the time for the mother country to be good-natured to them.

In the meantime he had no patience with the so-called British 'patriots' who supported the Americans' rebellious stand, which was, in fact, at this time supported by probably less than half the Americans themselves. Charles James Fox, the son of Henry Fox, now Lord Holland, was a prominent example of these 'patriots' and, in the King's opinion, 'as contemptible as he is odious'. Lord Chatham, who had declared that the country should withdraw from the dispute with the Americans 'while we can, not when we must', was another 'trumpet of sedition'. Edmund Burke, who – while conceding that Parliament had a right to control 'all inferior legislatures' – consistently opposed various aspects of the Government's American policy, was 'a pest'. 'Perhaps no one period of our history,' the King said, 'can produce so strange a circumstance as the gentlemen who pretend to be patriots, instead of acting agreeable to such sentiments, avowing the unnatural doctrine of encouraging the American colonies in their disputes with their mother country.'

Although Thomas Paine, the future author of *The Rights of Man*, was to challenge 'the warmest advocate for reconciliation to show a single advantage [America could] reap by being associated with Great Britain' and declared that 'the Authority of Great Britain over this continent' was 'a form of government which sooner or later *must* have an end', the inhabitants of the mother country were largely in agreement with the King, the 'violent destruction of the tea', in the words of Benjamin Franklin, having 'united all parties'. 'The popular current both within doors and without,' Burke regretfully confirmed, ran 'strongly against the Americans'. Some time later over 150 addresses were sent to the King condemning the Americans' rebellion and their so-called 'tea parties', which had taken place in New York as well as in Boston and which even the Earl of Chatham, who had roundly condemned the Stamp Act, described as 'certainly criminal'.

Edward Gibbon, a former officer in the Hampshire Militia and Member of Parliament for Liskeard, who had just started work on his *Decline and Fall of the Roman Empire*, spoke for many when he declared, 'I am more and more convinced that we have both the right and the power on our side, and that though the effort may be accompanied with some melancholy circumstances, we are now arrived at the decisive moment of persevering or of losing for ever both our trade and Empire.'

Samuel Johnson, who was occasionally seen in Gibbon's company at the Turk's Head, was even more forthright, stating the Ministry's case in the most uncompromising terms. 'He who accepts protection, stipulates obedience,' Johnson wrote in his 1775 pamphlet *Taxation no Tyranny, An Answer to the Resolution and Address of the American Congress*; and he went on to say that since 'we have always protected the Americans, we, may, therefore, subject them to government'. Members of the English Parliament had a perfect right to impose taxes on the English colonies, since they were payments 'exacted by authority from part of the community for the benefit of the whole'. As the American rebels refused to agree to these incontrovertible and unexceptionable propositions, they must be forced to accept them, with, however, 'the least injury possible to their persons and possessions'. If they remained obdurate, Johnson contentiously proposed, the American Indians should be given arms; so should black slaves, who should be encouraged to plunder the plantations of the slave owners.

Johnson was violently upbraided for his vituperative words, condemned as a 'mercenary reptile' and, in allusion to the pension which had been granted him, damned as a court hireling.* Yet there were many who agreed with him. John Wesley, the first religious leader of importance to protest against slavery, approved of Johnson's pamphlet; so did Robert Orme, the historian of India, who said that Johnson deserved his pension of £300 a year for this work alone. One Member of Parliament, Charles Van, actually proposed that Boston should be destroyed like Carthage. 'I am of the opinion,' he said in the House, 'you will never meet with that proper obedience to the laws of this country until you have destroyed that nest of locusts.' Johnson, in one of those outbursts of extravagant overstatement which occasionally overcame him in moods of excitement, went even further than this when he declared that the Americans as a whole were 'a race of convicts' and should be content with anything allowed them 'short of hanging'.

Lieutenant-General the Hon. Thomas Gage, who was married to an American and who had seen much service in America, was of the opinion that so long as the British behaved like lambs the colonists would play the part of lions, but that if the Government were resolute the Americans 'would undoubtedly prove very meek'. Gage said as much to the King when he was summoned to an audience before returning to America as Commander-in-Chief.

---

* Samuel Johnson had been granted his pension in 1762, soon after 'the accession of George the Third to the throne . . . opened a new and brighter prospect to men of literary merit, who had been honoured with no mark of royal favour in the preceding reign', wrote James Boswell. 'His present Majesty's education in this country, as well as his taste and beneficence, prompted him to be the patron of science and the arts; and . . . Johnson having been presented to him as a very learned and good man, without any certain provision, his Majesty was pleased to grant him a pension of three hundred pounds a year . . . Lord Loughborough [later Lord Chancellor] told me, that the pension was granted to Johnson solely as the reward of his literary merit, without any stipulation whatever, or even tacit understanding that he should write for administration' (Boswell, Life of Johnson, 264).

The same sentiments were expressed by Thomas Hutchinson, who had resigned as Governor of Massachusetts and had come to England to give advice to the Government on American affairs. He assured the King that firm legislation would result in 'speedy submission'. Army officers who had served in America supported this view. One suggested that the colonists' talk of taking up arms would go 'no further than words'; another agreed that they would do nothing when the time came for action. 'To hear them talk you might imagine they would attack us,' he said. 'Yet whenever we appear they are frightened out of their wits.'

Encouraged by such opinions, by the strength of public opinion and by the mood of a supportive Parliament, the Government brought in a series of Acts mostly directed at the rebels of Massachusetts, in the expectation that other colonists would come to heel once they realized what might be their lot if they continued recalcitrant. 'The dye is now cast,' the King wrote, determined to protect the rights of Parliament and to defend his view of the constitution:

The colonies must either submit or triumph. I do not wish to come to severer measures, but we must not retreat. By coolness and unremitted pursuit of the measures that have been adopted I trust they will come to submit . . . I own, though a thorough friend to holding out the olive branch, I have not the smallest doubt that, if it does not succeed, once vigorous measures appear to be the only means left of bringing the Americans to a due submission to the mother country the colonies will submit . . . I know I am doing my duty and can never wish to retract.

'I cannot help being of opinion,' he added later 'that with firmness and perseverance America will be brought to submission. If not, old England will . . . perhaps not appear so formidable in the eyes of Europe.'

Yet even now, as other ports declined to take advantage of Boston's predicament, and, one by one, other colonies expressed their sympathy for Massachusetts, the Americans were to be given every encouragement to give way peaceably. General Gage was instructed by Lord Dartmouth, who had been appointed to the recently created office of Secretary of State for the American Colonies, to 'use every endeavour to quiet the minds of the people', and 'by mild and gentle persuasion to induce submission'. The troops must, of course, be ready to meet any opposition, but the King hoped that 'such necessity [would] not occur'.★

When General Gage landed in America he was deeply alarmed by the growing unrest he found there. 'Affairs here are worse than even at the time of the Stamp Act,' he reported. 'I don't mean in Boston but throughout the country . . . If you think ten thousand men enough send twenty, if a million [pounds] is thought enough, give two; you will save both blood and treasure in the end.'

The Cabinet did not oblige Gage by sending as many men as he had hoped for; but, having decided that he was not capable of dealing with the deepening crisis, they did dispatch to America three generals, all of them, like Gage himself, with aristocratic connections. The oldest of them, at fifty-two, was John Burgoyne, widely supposed to be an illegitimate son of Lord Bingley, a former Chancellor of the Exchequer. 'A vain, very ambitious man', in the opinion of Horace Walpole, who called him Julius Caesar Burgonius, Burgoyne had sailed for America with reluctance, pressed to do so by Lord Barrington, who assured him that the King had specially asked for his services there. He was of the opinion that even now the Americans might be persuaded to return to their old loyalties by peaceful means, and he had vainly hoped to be sent to New York rather than to Boston to reopen negotiations.

The senior of these three generals, the Hon. William Howe, son of the second Viscount Howe, also had sympathetic feelings for the Americans and, as a Whig Member of Parliament for Nottingham, had opposed the Government's colonial policy – an attitude indulgently considered by the King as an excusable aberration, since Howe was a member of a family well regarded at Court, his mother being widely believed to be a natural daughter of King George I.

★ 'To portray the King as a hardliner is evidently misleading,' Professor Peter Thomas has written. 'His involvement in the making and implementation of policy had been at the behest or request of his ministers, not on his own initiative . . . At each moment of crisis, right up until the outbreak of war, his hopes were centred on a political solution, and he always bowed to his cabinet's opinions even when sceptical of their success. The detailed evidence of the years from 1763 to 1775 tends to exonerate George III from any real responsibility for the American Revolution' (Thomas, 'George III and the American Revolution').

The third general to arrive in Boston Harbour towards the end of May 1775 was Henry Clinton, a grandson of the sixth Earl of Clinton and cousin of the Duke of Newcastle, a competent officer but a difficult, tactless man, lonely, aloof and, in his own words, 'a shy bitch'.

Whether or not he and his two colleagues were any more capable of dealing with the crisis than General Gage was a subject much debated in London. 'I don't know what the Americans will think of them,' Lord North was quoted as saying. 'But I know that they make me tremble.'

Immediately upon landing, all three generals were disturbed to find what Clinton described as 'nothing but dismay amongst the troops'. For weeks thousands of colonists had been assembling in camps around Boston, most of them still wearing the homespun clothes in which they had left their farms but all of them armed and most of them expert shots. In the subsequent battle fought on Bunker Hill to the north of the town on 17 June 1775 over 400 Americans were killed or wounded; but the British losses were far more severe, no fewer than sixty-three officers being wounded and twenty-seven killed, as well as over 1,000 of their men. Since he held the battlefield, General Howe claimed the victory, yet it was not a victory to celebrate. Most of his men had fought bravely, marching with determination against the Americans' position after being twice repulsed. But the day's fighting had witnessed much 'disgraceful disorder' in the British ranks; and the army had suffered too many casualties and was too exhausted to pursue the Americans far. 'All was confusion,' General Clinton commented. 'Officers told me they could not command their men and I never saw so great a want of order.' The Americans had shown themselves to be far from being 'very unfit for war', as it had been suggested they were.

They had eventually been driven off Bunker Hill; but the British were still surrounded in Boston; and, as one English officer asked, who could tell how long they would be able to hold it before the rebels built forts which would make the harbour unsafe for shipping? Besides, untrained in tactics though they were, the Americans were ready and quick to learn; and a fortnight after the fighting on Bunker

Hill a general of experience and great talent arrived to give them the instruction and discipline they needed. This man, appointed by Congress as Commander-in-Chief of their Continental Army, was George Washington.

18

'AN UGLY JOB'

A prince whose character is marked by every act
which may define a tyrant . . .

The first reports of the fighting in America to be received in England had come from rebel sources, which had suggested that the British troops had behaved with appalling brutality – a 'cruelty not less brutal than the Americans' venerable ancestors had received from the vilest savages of the wilderness'. While the *London Gazette* officially informed its readers that no reliable information had been received from America, one of the rebels' agents in London circulated all newspaper offices with a note to the effect that the horrifying reports so far received were perfectly reliable and that the affidavits of eyewitnesses were available at the office of the Lord Mayor of London.

The Lord Mayor was John Wilkes, who, thanks largely to contributions from supporters on both sides of the Atlantic, had emerged from the King's Bench Prison a reasonably wealthy man as well as a popular hero whose portrait was exhibited in shop windows, painted on tavern signs, and displayed on all manner of objects from pot lids to bell handles. He had been elected Alderman for the Ward of Farringdon Without, and in October 1774 had taken up his duties at the Mansion House, where, not long before, the windows and chandeliers had been smashed by the stones of rioters because the building had not been lit to celebrate his election as Member for Middlesex.

Wilkes was one of the most vociferous advocates of the American rebels. He was also one of the warmest supporters of those London merchants who opposed the war as damaging to their trade and who were among the principal subscribers to the Constitutional Society, which, at a meeting at the King's Arms tavern on Cornhill, inaugurated a fund for 'the relief of widows [and] orphans . . . of our beloved American fellow subjects . . . inhumanely murdered by the King's troops'.

While Wilkes and his friends in the City, and such of their supporters in Parliament as Isaac Barré, heatedly condemned the King and his Ministry for having taken up arms against the colonists, the country at large remained of the opinion that the war would have to be continued. 'The sword alone can decide the dispute,' the *Morning Chronicle* declared; and 'the ruin of the British Empire would inevitably take place' were the King's troops to be defeated. How such a defeat could be averted was a question of constant debate.

It was, of course, conceded that a war fought against an entire continent 3,500 miles distant would not be easily won. General Harvey, the Adjutant-General, who told General Howe that America was 'an ugly job, a damned affair indeed', argued that it would be quite impossible to subdue the whole continent. With the British Army in its present state, this was 'as wild an idea as ever controverted common sense'. The King thought so too, and spent much time pondering the problems that the Army faced. Indeed, throughout the course of the war, he spent hours considering how best to wage it, writing memoranda and papers on all manner of subjects from the deployment of troops and their enlistment to the role of the Navy, the supply of equipment, the state of dockyards and the stock of timber, often offering advice more sensible and realistic than that of his senior officers, yet as anxious to learn as to advise. 'I give you infinite trouble,' he wrote to the First Lord of the Admiralty, the Earl of Sandwich, after arrangements had been made for the Surveyor of the Navy to attend at St James's to instruct him on the essentials of ship design, 'but it is from a desire of being a little au fait of ship building.'★

★ 'The climax of the royal interest came in the summer of 1773 [when Sandwich suggested a visit] to Portsmouth to view the dockyard and the fleet. Nothing like this had happened in England for nearly a century, and this very public demonstration of royal interest and approval served several purposes . . . It advanced the King's own knowledge; "I do not mean a visit of empty parade, but to come back au fait of the mode of conducting so complicated an affair as the fitting out a ship." It provided

The strength of the Army on paper was no more than 48,647 men scattered about the globe. About 16,000 were in England and Scotland, 12,000 in Ireland, 9,000 in various garrisons in India, Africa, Minorca, Gibraltar and the West Indies, and some 8,000 in America. And, since the pay that they received was a mere pittance, recruiting was a very difficult process. From the beginning of the fighting in America, the Government had endeavoured to attract more recruits by shortening the terms of enlistment and by offering bounties to volunteers and pardon to malefactors. It had also been decided to lower the standards of physical fitness – which had, in any event, never been high – and to impress convicted smugglers as well as 'all disorderly Persons who could not, upon Examination, prove themselves to exercise and industriously follow some lawful Trade or Employment' and 'incorrigible rogues . . . convicted of running away from and leaving their Families chargeable upon the Parish'. At the same time bounties were increased and promises of exemption from future parish service were given to volunteers.

In his anxiety to bring in more suitable recruits than the existing measures could supply, the King had suggested 'sending beating orders to Ireland'; but this had been objected to in Cabinet. He had also proposed that 'nobility and gentry of property [should] be persuaded separately in their parishes to give half a guinea in addition to the levy money for the encouragement of each of their parishioners enlisting in the Army'.

Despite all the inducements offered, however, and all the expedients which were resorted to, recruitment into existing regiments was disappointingly slow, since, so Lord North said, the 'ardour of the nation' had not yet 'arisen to the pitch one could wish'.

The alternative of raising new regiments was not favoured by the King, who shrank from being pestered with requests for the granting of commissions and promotions to unsuitable candidates and who knew only too well that, when the new regiments were disbanded

---

a public demonstration of royal interest in and support for the Navy . . . It also showed off the reality of British naval power and the speed with which it could be mobilized to foreigners like the French ambassador, who was invited to see the assembled fleet' (Rodger, *The Insatiable Earl*, 200).

at the end of the war, all officers who had served in them would add to the general expense by demanding half-pay.

The Cabinet decided, therefore, that they would have to look to Germany for the men they could not find in Britain. So, in 1775, five regiments of Hanoverians became mercenaries for the British, four of them being sent to Minorca and Gibraltar to release British troops from the garrisons there. The Landgrave of Hesse-Cassel, the King's uncle, was persuaded to part with some of his soldiers; other regiments came from the ruling families of Mecklenburg-Strelitz and Brunswick-Wolfenbüttel. An approach to Russia, however, was quickly rebuffed by Catherine the Great, who did not have 'the civility to answer in her own hand' but, as the King complained tartly, threw out 'some expressions that may be civil to a Russian ear but certainly not to more civilized ones'.

The Opposition were soon strongly protesting against this use of mercenaries and the proposed enlistment of American Indians against the colonists; and when the Government made clear its intention of prohibiting all trade with America so long as the rebellion continued, the attacks became more biting than ever. In the House of Commons, the King's brilliant bugbear Charles James Fox accused the Cabinet of 'want of policy, of folly and madness'. They were utterly unfit to govern America. Lord North was condemned as a 'blundering pilot who had brought the nation into its present difficulties'. Violent assaults were also made upon the capable Lord Sandwich, the First Lord of the Admiralty, and upon the Duke of Dorset's son, Lord George Germain, who, as Secretary of State for the American Department from November 1775, was largely responsible for the conduct of the war in America and for defending that conduct in the House.

Germain had 'all the requisites of a great minister', wrote his Under-Secretary, 'unless popularity and good luck are to be numbered amongst them'. Although companionable enough in the company of his family and friends, his manner was haughty, sometimes overbearing, at other times distant and coldly polite. In his office he was brisk, energetic and forthright; and in the House of Commons, though liable to lose his temper when goaded, he was skilled in debate and nearly always spoke well. In his first speech as a Minister he had declared that he had always held to the view that Parliament had the right to tax the colonies, and what he had so consistently believed he now stood in office to maintain.

The Cabinet, with the King's approval, had been anxious to bring Germain into office in place of Lord Hillsborough's successor, the less forthright Lord Dartmouth, because of his views thus expressed; and they had taken great trouble to satisfy Dartmouth's pride and pique by arranging for him to become Lord Privy Seal. In his early months as a Minister, Lord George Germain and the King worked well together and drew comfort from each other's stand in the face of worrying reports from America about the progress of operations there.

The battle on Bunker Hill had been followed by the evacuation of Boston; and on 4 July 1776 the American rebel leaders had issued their Declaration of Independence, in which King George was accused of all kinds of 'injuries and usurpations', of refusing his consent to 'wholesome and necessary laws', and of obstructing the administration of justice. 'He has plundered our seas,' the Declaration continued, 'ravaged our coasts, burned our towns' and 'excited domestic insurrections among us'. In the original draft, drawn up by Thomas Jefferson, the King was also accused of having encouraged slavery in America in defiance of the wishes of the American people – an accusation that some thought rather hard to substantiate, since Jefferson himself, like many other members of Congress, owned slaves and had no intention of relinquishing them. So this charge, as well as several other passages, were deleted from the final text. But King George remained 'a prince whose character is marked by every act which may define a tyrant' and one 'unfit to be the ruler of a free people'.

The Declaration of Independence had been followed by fighting in and around New York which ended in the rebels retreating into Pennsylvania and a general feeling that the uprising in the colonies was as good as suppressed. But then came Washington's dashing victory at Princeton, which encouraged a fresh revolutionary spirit in his army; and at Germantown outside Philadelphia on 4 October 1777 General Howe lost so many men, and, despite two battles won and the capture of Philadelphia, was so dispirited by the limited progress he had so far made in the war, and by a growing awareness that he was unequal to his task, that he wrote to London to say that his orders were impossible to execute without reinforcements and that, if more troops were not forthcoming, he wished to resign his command. Less than a fortnight later General Burgoyne surrendered at Saratoga; and in the following year France, followed in 1779 by Spain, came into the war on the Americans' side.

19

SURRENDER AT YORKTOWN

I have always said . . . that I would be the first to meet the friendship of the United States as an independent power.

When reports of Burgoyne's surrender at Saratoga on 17 October 1777 reached London, the King's Ministers, so one of Lord George Germain's secretaries told Edmund Burke, were 'in a state of great distraction', not knowing what to do or which way to turn. Writing hurriedly, 'over his chop', Burke passed the news to the Marquess of Rockingham, who he knew would be delighted to hear of their anxiety and who, indeed, confessed that his heart was now 'at ease'.

The Opposition had been given just the ammunition they required to mount a devastating attack upon the Government's conduct of the war; and Charles James Fox made the most of his opportunity, declaring in the House of Commons that all those who had supported the war were as criminally responsible as the King's Ministers. In the Lords, Lord Chatham, despite his age and infirmities, stood up to deliver a passionate speech:

No man thinks more highly than I of the virtue and valour of British troops; I know they can achieve anything except impossibilities; and the conquest of English America is an impossibility . . . *You cannot conquer America . . .* You may swell every expense and every effort still more extravagantly . . . traffic and barter with every pitiful German prince that sells his subjects to the shambles of a foreign power; your efforts are forever vain and impotent, doubly so from this mercenary aid on which you rely, for it irritates to an incurable resentment the minds of your enemies . . . If I were an American, as I am an Englishman, while a foreign troop was landed in my country, I would never lay down my arms, never – never – never!

Following such speeches in the Lords and the Commons, a debate on the state of the nation was set down for 2 February 1778. On that day, after a noisy crowd had stampeded through the doors into the galleries, Members settled down in silence to listen once more to Fox. In his rapid yet lucid way he spoke for two hours and forty minutes, taking care not to affront patriotic feeling in the country by exulting in British defeats, yet, with careful and telling effect, demonstrating what the *London Chronicle* described as the 'most striking proofs of judgement, sound reasoning and astonishing memory'. He surveyed the whole course of Britain's dispute with America, demonstrated how the war had been mismanaged, and suggested that to recognize an independent America was not necessarily to harm British interests, since independent America could prove a powerful friend. He ended by proposing a motion that no more regiments of the Old Corps – that was to say of the existing Army – should be allowed to sail across the Atlantic.

This motion posed a serious problem for the Government. It was well known that the establishment of the Old Corps was well under strength, that the King himself had warned against the folly 'of sending in our present Weak State another Old Corps out of Great Britain'. Yet events had already shown that the present strength of the army in America, as General Howe had protested, was not enough to defeat the rebels.

At the end of Fox's highly effective speech, Members waited for a Government spokesman to reply; but none rose to do so. Ministers looked at each other and glanced away. Fox had reduced the Government to silence. 'Not one of the Ministers knew what to say,' Walpole commented, 'and so said nothing.'

Fox's motion was, in the event, defeated; but Ministers could draw little comfort from this success. They were still 'greatly alarmed' in the words of the *Gazetteer*; while other papers condemned them for declining to 'answer a single syllable' in refutation of a speech of such 'good sense'.

No Minister was more alarmed than Lord North, who knew only too well how eager were the country's European enemies to see Britain humbled, and how ready was France to spend large sums in support of a democratic revolution which in other circumstances would have been condemned as abhorrent. Never a resolute man and not in good health, North wrote to the King to emphasize how unsuitable he himself was to hold his high office at such a critical time. 'Your Majesty's service,' he said, 'requires a man of great abilities, who can choose decisively, and carry his determination authoritatively into execution . . . I am certainly not such a man.'

This defeatist attitude was certainly not one which the King was prepared to tolerate. He himself refused to be cast down: the surrender at Saratoga was 'very serious' to be sure, but 'not without remedy'. There were, he insisted, thousands of American loyalists who, with proper support, would turn against the rebels. As for the intervention of France and Spain in the struggle, this was unquestionably a 'very unhappy event', but it was one which his mind was 'perfectly prepared to meet'. And, if it were the case that Britain could not raise sufficient forces to win the war on land in America, then a war at sea was the 'only wise plan'.

The Cabinet, however, could not agree: a naval blockade might take years before it was effective; a victory on land had been promised, and that was what must be achieved. So Ministers advised the King that three more battalions should be sent to America, one of them from the Old Corps. The King hesitated to agree to this: his views on keeping the well-trained and well-disciplined Old Corps at home were well known. Yet he felt that he must accept his Cabinet's advice and so replied that he would 'not object on this occasion'.

Meanwhile, Lord North persisted in his protestations of inadequacy. His 'spirits, strength, memory, judgement and abilities' were, he said, all 'sensibly and considerably impair'd'. The King continued to bolster his confidence and persuade him to stay. 'You are my sheet anchor,' he told him on one occasion; on another he appealed to his 'sense of honour' and his 'personal affection' for the King: he must not allow thoughts of resignation to take hold in his mind. 'I love you as a man of worth,' he assured him, 'and I esteem you as a Minister.'

But North was not to be cajoled or comforted. He fully recognized his inability to lead a country at war as Chatham had done, his failure to 'oblige every department of government to act under his direction', in Germain's words. He was becoming panic-stricken. 'The present Ministry can not continue a fortnight as it is,' he wrote to the King on 15 March 1778, 'and there is nothing that seems so likely to stem the first violence of the torrent as sending to Lord Chatham. If His Majesty can not consent to that . . . [Lord North] is afraid the whole system will break up.'

This proposal the King rejected with horror. Nothing, the King protested, could ever induce him to approach Lord Chatham 'or any other branch of the Opposition'. 'Honestly,' he continued, 'I would rather lose the crown I now wear than bear the ignominy of possessing it under their shackles. I might write volumes . . . No consideration in life will make me stoop to Opposition . . . [to that] set of men who certainly would make me a slave for the remainder of my days . . . It is impossible that the nation will not stand by me . . . If they will not, they shall have another King.'

Lord North persisted: he would rather be executed than face the 'constant anguish of mind' attendant upon his remaining in office. 'His former incapacity' was 'so much aggravated by his present distress of mind' that he would 'soon be totally unfit for the performance of any ministerial duty'. In one of those moods of black despair that occasionally overwhelmed him, he confessed that his mind was 'ten times weaker than it was'. 'Let me not go to the grave,' he begged, 'with the guilt of having been the ruin of my King and country.'

The King endeavoured to brace and hearten the man both by his own encouragement and by pressing two of his informants in the Government, John Robinson, the Treasury Secretary, and Charles Jenkinson, Secretary-at-War, to do all they could to stiffen North's resolve. 'Mr Robinson,' he wrote in one characteristic letter, 'must to-day attempt his irksome part of rouzing Lord North.'

At length the King partially relented: he would agree 'to accept any description of person' who would 'come devotedly' to the support of North's Government, provided North still remained at the head of it. He would even have Chatham and Fox, provided he did not have to negotiate with either of them personally and it was fully understood that they were to be colleagues in the existing Administration, not leaders of a new one. North knew, however, that Chatham could never be persuaded to agree to this. Although he was seventy years old, and in most indifferent health, he would insist upon being head of any administration in which he served.

But then at the beginning of April 1778 Chatham had a seizure in the House of Lords.

A pale, thin, wasted figure, he had hobbled into the House leaning on crutches and supported by his son, set upon opposing the Duke of Richmond, who was to propose the withdrawal of British forces from America. While strongly advocating conciliation, Chatham was just as firmly opposed to complete capitulation. He had argued against acceptance of the Americans' Declaration of Independence and the dismemberment of an empire which he himself had done so much to create. He now protested that it would be preferable to fight the whole of Europe rather than to agree to the rebels' demands under duress from foreign powers. Suddenly he fell back in a fit. He was taken home and died a few weeks later.

By then the King had reluctantly agreed to release North at the end of the parliamentary session; but it appeared that North was not now after all so set upon going. He had recovered from the dark depression which had recently overwhelmed him and was ready to face his responsibilities with less gloomy apprehension. Weary as he was, he said, if the King 'really found it necessary to detain him' he would continue beyond the end of the session and until such time as His Majesty was able 'to arrange his servants in the manner most agreeable to himself and the most advantageous to the public'.

It was evident that, once the King appeared to be ready to offer him the comforts of retirement, North began to regard with dismay the loss of the pleasures of office. When all was going well, it was very enjoyable to be the King's First Minister. Besides, His Majesty had been extremely generous to him: he had appointed him Ranger of Bushey Park; he had made him a Knight of the Garter, a most unusual honour for a member of the House of Commons; he had arranged for him to receive £20,000 from the Secret Service to pay off the pressing debts which some believed were responsible for his moods of deep depression; he had appointed him Lord Warden of the Cinque Ports, worth £4,000 a year; and he had promised him another sinecure worth £10,000 a year. 'I am anxious to give that to your family,' the King had assured him kindly, 'whether or not you remain in your present situation.' Lord North was not a rich man in comparison with several of his colleagues. His father, although well able to do so, would never make him an adequate allowance; his estates brought in no more than £2,500 a year; and he had his seven children to consider. The King's offer was bound to touch him. On 23 May he wrote, 'Lord North thinks it his duty to repeat that, though his earnest wish certainly is to retire, yet he is ready to continue in his present office as long as His Majesty deems it for his service that he should continue there.'

As a means of encouraging North, of giving a lead to the Government in general, and of emphasizing his supreme position in the executive, the King broke with his own precedent by personally presiding at a meeting of the Cabinet held at the Queen's House, where, in an hour-long address, he spoke of his confidence in Lord North, condemned the inefficiency of certain ministerial departments – expressly excepting from his strictures the Admiralty under Lord Sandwich – justified his own conduct, as he was so often inclined to do, and protested that he would rather lose his life than see his dominions dismembered.

The problem that now faced the King and North was how best to deal with the threat of renewed war with the French, who would certainly try to seize the West Indian sugar islands. The King had already expressed the sensible opinion that, should a war against France become inevitable, 'the only means of making it successful' would be to withdraw most of the troops from America and employ them against the French and Spanish settlements, for, as he said, 'if we are to be carrying on a land war against the rebels and against those two powers it must be feeble in all parts and consequently unsuccessful'.

Before making a more limited deployment of troops in America, however, the Cabinet proposed making one more effort to come to a tolerable settlement with the rebels. Plenipotentiaries were accordingly instructed to approach rebel leaders with an offer to recognize Congress, to suspend all objectionable Acts of Parliament, to give up the right of taxation, even to consider admitting American representatives to the House of Commons – in effect to grant America virtual internal home rule – provided that the many Americans who had remained loyal to the King were restored to their property, that debts due to British citizens were honoured, that military commands in America were held as from the King, that the British Parliament regulated trade, and, above all, that the Declaration of Independence was withdrawn.

There had never been much likelihood of this overture being considered by the rebels. Nor was it. The British diplomats sent to America to discuss it with them, affronted by the unyielding attitude of Congress, sailed for home, leaving the Commander-in-Chief in America, Howe's successor, Sir Henry Clinton, with advice to stop treating the rebels as subjects whose loyalty might be regained but as enemies who must be fought with ruthless animosity.

Six months before, the British and German troops in America, led by capable officers, might have decisively defeated the rebel army, ill disciplined and ill supplied as it had been, in the dreary, almost deserted landscape of Valley Forge. But since then Washington's patience and determination and the efficient training methods of the Prussian soldier of fortune Baron Friedrich Wilhelm von Steuben had transformed a collection of discouraged and disintegrating regiments into an efficient fighting force. Besides, the King and his Ministers had now to consider not only the threat from Washington's army but also the threat from France.

The King clung to the belief that 'a majority of the people of America' still wished to be his subjects, that the rebels must sooner or later sue for peace, and that he would then be able to show that the 'parent's heart [was] still affectionate to the penitent child'.

In the meantime he concurred with the Cabinet that the main fight against the rebels should be transferred to the south of America. Here, it was believed, there was a greater proportion of loyalists in a sparser population than in the north, and these loyalist sympathizers were thought to include thousands of black slaves for whom the cause of the revolutionaries held no appeal and of whom the white population in America was always more or less in fear. But the British were no more successful in the south than they had been in the north; and at the beginning of October 1781, in Virginia, George Washington amazed his companions by throwing off all his normal restraints, jumping up and down, and wildly waving his arms in the air, a handkerchief in one hand, his hat in the other. A French fleet had arrived in Chesapeake Bay with three thousand troops: the southern British army was trapped in Yorktown. On 19 October, in a field encircled by mounted French troops and watched by silent Americans, the British threw down their arms to the mournful tap of drums and the sound of fifes. The War of Independence was over.

The King put a brave face upon his army's defeat. He contended that the loss of his forces in the province of Virginia was merely a setback; and he encouraged Government speakers in the House of Commons who assured their fellow Members that the unfortunate events at Yorktown had been brought about by the interference of the French and that better news could soon be expected. 'A good end may yet be made to this war,' he declared, 'but if we despond certain ruin ensues.' Lord North, too, spoke with verve and confidence, although when the news from Yorktown had first been brought to him the effect, so Lord George Germain said, was like that of a musket ball to the breast. He had paced up and down the room, exclaiming in mingled horror and relief, 'O God! It is all over!'

He soon recovered himself, speaking in the House with apparent confidence against the proposition that 'all further attempts to reduce the revolted colonies to obedience are contrary to the true interests of this Kingdom'.

Fox, who squarely laid the blame for the country's plight on 'the influence of the Crown', treated the Government's stand with scorn. So did Lord Chatham's twenty-two-year-old son, William Pitt, who condemned the 'most accursed, wicked, barbarous, cruel, unjust and diabolical war'. 'The expense of it has been enormous,' Pitt added, 'far beyond any former experience, and yet what has the British nation received in return? Nothing but a series of ineffective victories or severe defeats.'

There could, indeed, be no doubt that the mood of the country had changed since the 1770s. Then there had been widespread support of the war and for the King's Ministers; now that support was waning fast. It was conceded that the British and German soldiers who had been sent to America had no doubt, for the most part, fought bravely. But neither the generals commanding them nor the Ministers directing them had been fully equal to their tasks. Even Members who were predisposed in favour of the King and Lord North and who, like Edward Gibbon, considered the colonists to be in the wrong were forced to conclude, as Gibbon himself concluded, that it was 'easier to defend the justice than the policy of the [Government's] measures'. 'I shall never give my consent,' Gibbon said, 'to exhaust still further the finest country in the world in this prosecution of a war from whence no reasonable man entertains any hope of success. It is better to be humbled than ruined.'

On 22 February 1782 Horace Walpole's friend General Conway rose in the House and, in a forceful speech, proposed that offensive war be abandoned. The Government survived by a single vote. Five days later, however, when the motion was brought forward again, it was carried by nineteen votes. At two o'clock the next morning, Lord North wrote to the King to propose that a new administration should be formed.

The King was most reluctant to agree, protesting once more that he would rather lose his crown than call in a set of men who would make him a slave, that no consideration on earth would make him 'in the smallest degree an instrument in a measure that would annihilate the rank in which the British Empire stood among the European States'. So the Government, which had publicly declined to accept defeat but had privately conceded that the war was lost, tottered along for a month; and when Lord North again tendered his resignation, His Majesty, his mind, as he put it, 'truely tore to pieces', crossly replied, 'If you resign before I have decided what I will do, you will certainly for ever forfeit my regard.'

It was, therefore, not known for certain whether or not Lord North was to remain as First Lord of the Treasury when the House of Commons met on 20 March to debate a proposal that the King's Ministers should be removed from office. His fellow Members entered the Chamber that Wednesday afternoon in their bag wigs and flowered waistcoats, swords at their sides, taking their seats on the benches, looking up as each new arrival came through the door, anxious not to miss the appearance of Lord North. Four hundred Members had arrived in the Chamber before the clock struck four.

The hum of their talk could be heard in the snow-covered street outside. At last Lord North appeared, uncommonly well dressed in what appeared to be a new suit, a ribbon over his coat.

Lord Surrey then rose to put forward the proposal which had been advertised; but, before he could speak, Lord North also stood up and declared, 'I rise to speak to that motion.' He opposed the motion, he said, for the good reason that he had already handed in his resignation, and that his Administration was, in any case, dissolved. A man of greater abilities, he conceded, might well succeed to his office, but 'a successor more zealous for the interests of his country, more anxious to promote those interests, more loyal to his Sovereign, and more desirous of preserving the constitution whole and entire' would not so easily be found.

It could not be denied, however, that, in his time as the King's First Minister, the Crown, the old aristocratic society and the Army which between them they controlled had suffered a defeat from which they never fully recovered and a loss of confidence which was never fully restored.

Only too conscious of this loss of prestige, the disgruntled King, annoyed with North for having announced his resignation despite his pleading, was not prepared to be gracious. On North's formally resigning his post, His Majesty is said to have 'parted with him rudely without thanking him', adding, 'Remember, my Lord, that it is you who desert me, not I you.'

For months the defeat in America rankled bitterly in the King's mind. Constantly he referred to it with profound sadness and resentful anger, casting wide the blame for his country's humiliation, and involving in his condemnation his generals, Lord North and his other Ministers, as well as the inhabitants of that 'revolted State', though never himself. As late as November 1782 he could write to the First Lord of the Treasury:

I cannot conclude without mentioning how sensibly I feel the dismember-ment of America, and that I should be miserable indeed if I did not feel that no blame on that account can be laid at my door, and did I not know that knavery seems to be so much the striking feature of its inhabitants that it may not in the end be an evil that they become aliens to this kingdom.

As the years passed, however, he came to take a more benign and forgiving view both of Lord North and the United States. When John Adams, who was to become Washington's successor as President, was appointed the first American Minister to the Court of St James's, in 1785, he 'made the three reverences' upon his being shown into His Majesty's Closet, so he recorded: 'one at the door, another about half-way and the third before the presence, according to the usage established at this, and all the Northern Courts of Europe'. The King, later acknowledging Mr Adams's manner as 'very proper', said to him, 'I will be very free with you. I was the last to consent to the separation; but the separation having been made and having become inevitable, I have always said, as I say now, that I would be the first to meet the friendship of the United States as an independent power.'

The King then changed the subject. Smiling, or rather laughing, he said, 'There is an opinion among some people that you are not the most attached of all your countrymen to the manners of France.'

'I must avow to your Majesty,' replied Adams, rather embarrassed by this observation, 'I have no attachment but to my own country.'

'An honest man,' the King said approvingly, 'will never have any other.'

He then bowed to indicate that the audience was at an end. 'I retreated,' Adams wrote, 'stepping backwards, as is the etiquette; and, making my last reverence at the door of the chamber, I went my way. The Master of the Ceremonies joined me the moment of my coming out of the King's closet, and accompanied me through the apartments down to my carriage; several stages of servants, gentlemen-porters, and under porters, roaring out like thunder as I went along, "Mr Adams's servants, Mr Adams's carriage, &c."' The King, Adams concluded, 'is, I really think, the most accomplished courtier in his dominions. With all the affability of Charles the Second, he has all the domestic virtues and regularity of Charles the First.'

20

THE KING'S BROTHERS

A disgrace to the whole family . . .

The King's brothers caused him as much anxiety as his political problems and international affairs. Edward, Duke of York, the eldest of them, was, in Lady Louisa Stuart's harsh words, 'silly, frivolous and heartless, void alike of steadiness and principle; a libertine in his practice, and in society one of those incessant chatterers who must by necessity utter a vast deal of nonsense'. Certainly the Duke was a rather foolish man who enjoyed raffish company and crude practical jokes. He shared none of his brother's interests, and frequently annoyed him by interfering in politics, voting from time to time with the Opposition. Fond of each other as they had been as children, their friendship had been uneasy ever since the King had declined to appoint the Duke to the bishopric of Osnabrück, an office, founded by Charlemagne and worth some £20,000 a year, which was held alternately by a Protestant and a Roman Catholic bishop, who did not necessarily have to be in holy orders. The right to appoint the Protestant bishop was held by the House of Hanover; and, since King George I had appointed his brother bishop in 1715, it was expected that when next a Protestant was to be appointed the King would likewise nominate his eldest brother. King George III, however, had not done so, delaying the appointment until his second son was born and then nominating him. By way of recompense he gave the Duke of York £16,000 with which to buy a house. But the relationship between the two men never returned to the happy intimacy of their childhood days, so that the King was all the more grieved to receive a penitent letter dictated by the Duke as he lay mortally ill at Monaco during a tour of the Continent in 1767. In this pathetic letter the Duke paid his 'last weak duties to the King' and hoped that the generosity of his brother's temper would 'make him forgive his unheeded past conduct'.

Relations between the Duke of Gloucester, to whom this letter was dictated, and the King, five years his senior, were far more cordial, at least partly because Gloucester had no wish to interfere in politics. He was of a quiet, retiring disposition, weak in health, and spent much of his time abroad in the hope of improving it. When, on one of these prolonged Continental tours, the Duke fell ill, his brother, the King, sent out no fewer than three doctors to attend him and, hearing of his recovery, wrote to tell him how profoundly relieved he was, how his fear that he might lose him had caused him the 'greatest grief', and how he could scarcely relate what he had suffered without tears. But this, he added, had only taught him how much he loved him.

He also trusted him and confided in him as his favourite brother, and was persuaded to disbelieve or at least to ignore persistent rumours that the Duke had secretly married Maria, Dowager Lady Waldegrave, the widow of the King's former Governor, Earl Walde-grave, a woman nearly eight years older than the Duke and the mother of three daughters. The marriage, however, was a fact: it had taken place clandestinely on 6 September 1766 in Lady Waldegrave's house in Pall Mall, where it had been solemnized by her chaplain. For six years the King was induced to suppose that his brother remained a bachelor, though he could not but suspect that Lady Waldegrave was his mistress. 'The report of the week,' wrote Lady Sarah Bunbury, formerly Lady Sarah Lennox, shortly before the secret wedding, 'is that the King has forbid the Duke of Gloucester to speak to his pretty widow . . . He has given her five pearl bracelets that cost £500 − that's not for nothing surely.'

One day in September 1772, his wife being pregnant, the Duke wrote to the King to confess what he had done, adding that 'the world being so much acquainted with his marriage' it was 'neither decent nor right' that His Majesty should be 'supposed to be ignorant of it'.

The King was deeply grieved, as much by the fact of the marriage as by his brother's deception and the unpalatable knowledge that his new sister-in-law, the illegitimate daughter of Horace Walpole's elder brother by a fashionable milliner, was the granddaughter of his grandfather's Whig First Minister. He felt that he had no alternative but to inform his brother that he might either continue to appear at Court without his wife, as though the marriage had never occurred, or be banished from it if the marriage were to be openly acknowledged. The Duke refused to conceal his marriage; so he was forbidden access to the Court and it was made known in society that visiting the Duke and Duchess would be frowned upon by Their Majesties.

The Duchess was much offended. She was a proud, vain woman as well as a beautiful one, haughty and managing. She held court, despite the King's proscription, as though her marriage had been a perfectly open one. She encouraged her husband to share her resentment at being excluded from the Royal Family and to meddle in politics in a manner he had never done before, giving countenance to politicians in opposition to the Ministry and voting on occasions with them in the House of Lords. His behaviour was not likely to make the King look with favour upon his application for provision to be made for the children which the Duchess bore him, particularly when the Duke intimated that, if nothing were done in this regard, he would get one of his friends in the Opposition to bring the matter up in Parliament.

'My heart is wounded,' the King wrote to Lord North on receipt of his brother's letter:

I have ever loved him with the fondness one bears more to a child than a brother. His whole conduct from the time of his publishing what I must ever think a highly disgraceful step has tended to make the breach wider. I cannot therefore, on a repetition of this application, give him hopes of a future establishment for his children, which would only bring on a fresh altercation with his wife whom I can never think of placing in a situation to answer her extreme pride and vanity . . . It is natural the King should not apply to Parliament for provision for the children of a younger branch of his family when he has not as yet done it for his own numerous offspring . . . But I am certain you know my way of thinking too well to doubt that, should any accident happen to the Duke, I shall certainly take care of his children.

This letter was written in 1775. Two years later Parliament voted satisfactory provision for both the King's and the Duke of Gloucester's children. The King's younger sons were voted £10,000 a year each, his daughters £6,000 a year; the Duke's son was to receive £8,000 a year, his daughter, Sophia Matilda, £4,000 (a third child had died in infancy). The Duke was allowed a further £4,000 a year when his son, William Frederick, later second Duke of Gloucester of the latest creation, went up to Trinity College, Cambridge.

Thankful that his children were thus well provided for, the Duke – who had suffered a nearly fatal illness in the year in which the settlement was made – was glad to be reconciled with his brother, who, according to Horace Walpole, the Duchess's uncle, wept when the Duke went to see him 'and told him he had ever loved him the best of his family, and hoped to see him often'. The King, however, was certainly not reconciled to the Duchess, with whom, indeed, the Duke himself was becoming increasingly exasperated, openly regretting his 'juvenile indiscretion' in having married the tiresome woman, and beginning an affair with one of her Ladies of the Bedchamber, Lady Almeria Carpenter.

The Duchess was told by her disillusioned husband that she might continue to live in his house provided she behaved 'more respectfully' towards him 'before the world'. Perhaps she did so, since she did remain in the house and was there when, much to the distress of his brother the King, her husband died in 1805. Thereafter, for the two years she herself had left to live, the King treated the widow kindly for the sake of her children, of whom he was fond.

There could be no such reconciliation with the King's youngest brother, Henry, Duke of Cumberland, as there had been with the Duke of Gloucester, for Cumberland, who had been brought up by his mother within the confines of her Household, was, in the King's opinion, 'incorrigible'. He had been a notorious womanizer since his early youth, carrying his mistress of the day about with him in his carriage in Hyde Park, displaying a simultaneous penchant for other young women, most of them married, and becoming involved in an action for what was then known as criminal conversation brought against him by Lord Grosvenor, the future first Marquess of Westminster's father, whose wife's letters from the Duke of Cumberland were read out in court and played a large part in damages being estimated at £10,000, a sum which, with the addition of £3,000 in costs, the Civil List was hard pressed to pay. The Duke was subsequently rumoured to have married his mistress for the time being, and he certainly did marry a pretty young widow, 'very well made with the most amorous eyes in the world and eyelashes a yard long'. This was the Hon. Anne Horton, widow of Andrew Horton of Catton in Derbyshire, sister of the widely disliked Henry Lawes Luttrell – who had stood unsuccessfully against John Wilkes in the Middlesex election of 1769 – and daughter of Simon Luttrell, Lord Irnham, afterwards Earl of Carhampton, who was condemned by Lady Louisa Stuart as 'the greatest reprobate in England'. Mrs Horton's marriage to the Duke was conducted clandestinely in her house in Mayfair in 1771.

The Duke informed the King of the marriage when he made one of his rare visits to see his brother at Richmond Lodge on 1 November that year. They were walking in the woods around the house when the Duke pulled a paper from his pocket and held it out to the King, who took it and read of the 'disgraceful step' his brother had taken. The King walked on 'for some minutes to smother [his] feelings'. He then said he could not believe that what the Duke had written was true. Assured that it was, he asked his brother not to tell their mother what he had done: in her 'bad state of health' it would be better if the King broke the news to her himself, having thought about what he was to say, being, as he had told Lord North earlier, not fond of talking about 'delicate matters unprepared'. He added that the Duke had 'irretrievably ruined himself' and that, having been guilty of such 'disgraceful conduct', it would be better if the Duke and his wife went to live abroad: 'any country was preferable to his own'.

In any country [the King wrote] marrying a subject is looked upon as dishonourable, nay in Germany the children of such a marriage cannot succeed to any territories; but here, where the Crown is but too little respected, it must be big with the greatest mischiefs . . . I must therefore on this occasion show my resentment. I have children who must know what they have to expect if they should follow so infamous an example.

Apart from the disrespect shown to the King in a country where even the son of a country gentleman would be expected to have the blessing of the head of his family before proposing marriage, there were political objections to the Duke of Cumberland's marrying a woman no fewer than four of whose brothers, as well as her Irish father, sat in the House of Commons, not to mention the fact that, on his income of about £15,000 a year, Cumberland could not hope to maintain a household suitable to his rank as a senior member of the Royal Family and in line of succession to the throne.

The more he thought about it, the more the King considered the marriage 'a disgrace to the whole family'. If the Duke agreed never to mention the step he had taken, nor to allow 'Mrs Horton', as the King still called her, 'publickly to take his name', he would be prepared to receive him again at Court. But if he would not agree to this the King would never have any further communication with him, nor receive those who paid their respects to him and 'Mrs Horton', whom, as Sir Nathaniel Wraxall delicately put it, 'he held in great alienation because he believed that she lent herself to facilitate or gratify the Prince of Wales's inclinations on some points beyond the limits of propriety'.

The Duke and Duchess defied the King, 'laughing forms and etiquette to scorn' at Cumberland House, as Lady Louisa Stuart put it, and receiving 'tag, rag and bobtail (pardon the vulgar phrase) rather than allow numbers to be wanting'. The Duchess's racy sister, Elizabeth Luttrell, 'marshalled the gaming table' there.

She also gathered round her the men, and led the way in ridiculing the King and Queen . . . A mighty scope for satire was afforded by the Queen's wide mouth, and occasionally imperfect English, as well as by the King's trick of saying What! What! his ill-made coats, and general antipathy to the fashion. But the marks preferably aimed at were his *virtues*; his freedom from vice as a man; his discouragement of it as a sovereign . . . his sincere piety and humble reliance upon God.

The breach between the King and Cumberland was never healed, though the Duke was allowed to retain his profitable office of Ranger of Windsor Park. In May 1780 the King wrote, 'The whole political sentiments and conduct of the Duke of Cumberland are so adverse to what I think right that any intercourse between us could only be of a cold and distant kind and consequently very unpleasant.' Before her death their mother had tried to bring them together without success; and if subsequently they sometimes appeared in each other's company this was largely because the King, anxious to break the influence the Duke had over the impressionable Prince of Wales, his nephew, wished to keep an eye on them. One day in 1781 he went hunting with them both; but on his return he told the Duke of Gloucester that neither of them had addressed a single word to him.

Fortunately the Duke's finances were in such a poor state that he spent much of his time abroad, well away from the temptation to dabble in politics – a propensity from which the Duchess, to give her her due, endeavoured to divert him.

When the Duke died, at Cumberland House in September 1790, he and the King remained unreconciled; but the King was reported to be 'much hurt'. He still refused to receive the widowed Duchess as a member of the Royal Family; but he allowed her to continue in possession of Cumberland Lodge in Windsor Park and he offered her a pension of £4,000 a year, on which she was able to live in modest comfort on the Continent until her death in 1803.

To ensure that none of his sons formed such *mésalliances* as two of his brothers had done, the King decided to forbid them by law. His decision resulted in the Royal Marriages Act of 1772, which, still in force today, not only made it illegal for any member of the Royal Family to marry without the sovereign's consent but also rendered invalid marriages thereafter contracted without such consent. Should the consent of the sovereign be withheld to someone over twenty-five, however, a year's notice could be given to the Privy Council and then the marriage could take place despite the sovereign's refusal, provided that neither House of Parliament raised an objection. The sons and daughters of those royal princesses who married into foreign families were exempt from the Act, but, apart from them, it applied to all descendants of King George III.

The Act did not pass into law without much trouble and opposition. Edward Gibbon did not remember 'so general a concurrence of all ranks, parties and professions of men' in deploring what he himself termed a 'most odious law'. Yet, he supposed that, as the

Bill was 'universally considered' to represent the King's wishes, it would become law.

The King was in no doubt that it certainly ought to do so; and he wrote to Lord North to say that he expected 'every nerve to be strained to carry the Bill through both Houses with a becoming firmness', since it was a question that immediately related not to the Government but personally to himself.

Even though he threatened to 'remember defaulters', however, and to remove from their places those who held offices in his gift, there was widespread opposition in the House of Commons to a Bill which would in effect make it virtually impossible for the King's sons officially to marry women other than Protestant princesses and for his daughters to marry almost anyone at all who was not a Protestant prince.

The Bill passed its second reading in the Commons but narrowly, by 200 votes to 164. The King asked Lord North to let him have a list of its opponents – on which he would have seen with annoyance the name of Charles James Fox – telling North the list would be 'a rule for [his] conduct in the Drawing-Room tomorrow'. 'Every engine' must be employed to secure the passage of the Bill, which eventually was passed by 168 votes to 115, thanks to the skill of Lord North. In his gratitude and relief at seeing the Bill pass into law, however, the King quietly dropped all threats against those who had opposed it, and greeted such of them as attended his levees quite without the obvious displeasure which he had warned Lord North he would display.

THE KING'S SISTERS

Perverted by a wicked and contemptible Court . . .

Both his married sisters, Augusta and Caroline Matilda, had, like their brothers, caused the King worry and unhappiness.★ Princess Augusta had been married in 1764 to Charles William, the Hereditary Prince, later Duke, of Brunswick, with whom she pretended, in letters to her brother, to be highly satisfied. 'May I say, though he is my husband,' she had written of him five years after her marriage, 'that I never knew anybody with a more real good heart. You know he is sensible and clever. In short, he is monstrously fond of me and I am a happy woman.'

Her brother had much doubted that this was so; and when she came to England to comfort their dying mother he found her 'much graver than formerly'. He rather thought from her 'whole manner' that it went on 'but coldly between her and the Hereditary Prince', though she had not 'dropped the most distant hint of it'.

She did, however, drop a hint to her younger sister, Caroline, to whom she confided that her husband's humour grew 'every day worse' and that she had lately found 'a great alteration in him towards her'. She did everything in her power, however, to ensure that her discontent should not become public knowledge; while the Duke, for his part, tried to hide from the world that they were 'not well together'.

Although the King had been much offended when Augusta had paid a visit to England with her husband soon after her marriage and had allowed herself to be courted by the Opposition, he had always been kind to her; and she was grateful for the affection which he

---

★ There were two other sisters, Louisa and Elizabeth, both of whom died before they were twenty years old.

showed her. His 'old, faithful and attached sister' would have been 'a sad creature', she told him, had she not felt the 'truest gratitude and the most sincere affection for all the kindness that neither time nor absence could eradicate'.

The unhappiness of his sister Caroline Matilda caused the King even more distress than that of Augusta. She, too, had suffered an unhappy marriage, which she had contracted at the age of fifteen with her cousin King Christian VII of Denmark and Norway, son of Frederick V and his first wife, Louisa, daughter of King George II. Joshua Reynolds had said that the prospect of this marriage had so distressed the poor girl that she could not stop crying for long enough for him to do justice to her wedding portrait, since her husband-to-be was a tiresome, conceited little man whom King George III much disliked. Terrorized in his youth by a brutal Governor and debauched by corrupt pages, King Christian had become mentally unstable and had fallen under the influence of Johann Friedrich Struensee, a clever court doctor of insinuating charm who became the young Queen Caroline's lover and virtual ruler of the kingdom. When the Queen had given birth to a child in the summer of 1771, the baby girl was so widely believed to be Struensee's that the congregations at Te Deums ordered to be said in churches throughout Denmark had risen and departed *en masse*.

A conspiracy against Struensee had culminated in the arrest of both him and the Queen. He was beheaded after his right hand had been cut off; she, having been held in the fortress of Kronborg, had been permitted to depart as an exile to Celle, a small town on the banks of the Aller in her brother's Hanoverian electorate. The King, who had expressed the hope that 'by mildness' his sister would be brought back to 'the amiable character' she had had before being 'perverted by a wicked and contemptible Court', had given instructions that no effort should be spared to make her life as content as possible at Celle. He had advised her to 'continue that circumspection' in her behaviour that had 'gained great credit' during her misfortunes, for this was the 'most effectual means' of showing what a blessing she might have been to Denmark had the Danish court 'possessed any principle of honour and integrity'.

The exiled Queen had not been inclined to take such advice. Although strongly advised by her brother to have nothing to do with those now in power in Denmark, nor with anyone who might plot to overthrow them, she had dreamed of being united with her children after a revolution had brought a new government to power in the country. She had not, however, lived to become involved in any such plot. She had died suddenly in May 1775, and had been interred in the burial vault of the Dukes of Celle, next to the remains of Sophia Dorothea, her great-grandmother, the wife of King George I. She was not yet twenty-five years old.

17. William Chambers, the King's tutor in architecture and subsequently Architect to the King. From a portrait by Sir Joshua Reynolds, *c.* 1760, when Chambers was about thirty-four.

18. A design by George III, when Prince of Wales, for a *Corinthian Temple for Erection at Kew*. The many compass points suggest that Chambers's twenty-one-year-old pupil took great care in the execution of this drawing.

19. Another design, *Composite Order*, by the then Prince of Wales, executed at about the same age.

20. Johann Zoffany's portrait of Queen Charlotte with her two eldest sons, the Prince of Wales and Frederick, later Duke of York, in fancy dress as Telemachus and a Turk.

21. *Mrs Papendiek and Child*, from a sketch by her friend Sir Thomas Lawrence. Daughter of Frederick Albert, Queen Charlotte's German page, she wrote her memoirs of court as an old lady in the 1830s.

22. Lord Bute, one of the Lords of the Bedchamber in the Household of Frederick, Prince of Wales, who became George III's 'dearest friend' and trusted mentor.

23. *The Scotch Colossus or the Beautys of ye Bagpipe.* This print of 1762 is one of numerous rude caricatures insulting Lord Bute and the Dowager Princess of Wales, who is shown beneath Bute's phallic bagpipe and looking up his kilt.

24. With the King's encouragement and support, the Royal Academy was founded in 1768, with Joshua Reynolds as its first President. The King is shown visiting an exhibition at Somerset House with the Prince of Wales and several of his other children.

25. Henry Fox, later first Baron Holland, from the portrait by Sir Joshua Reynolds. The father of Charles James Fox and brother-in-law of Lady Sarah Lennox, Fox made a fortune as Paymaster General.

26. William Pitt, later first Earl of Chatham, from the portrait by William Hoare, *c.* 1754. Pitt the Elder, 'the first Great Commoner', became the King's most influential minister in 1756.

27. Lord North, the King's friend and First Minister during the American War of Independence, addresses the House of Commons.

28. *John Wilkes Esq.* by William Hogarth. Wilkes and his supporters lampooned Hogarth, whose work was much admired by the King. Hogarth replied with this cruel caricature of the squint-eyed demagogue to whom the King referred as 'that Devil Wilkes'.

29. On 9 July 1776 the statue of George III in Bowling Green, New York was pulled down and destroyed. Those responsible were white militiamen and civilians, not black slaves as shown in this engraving by François Xavier Habermann.

30. The second Marquess of Rockingham and his Irish secretary, Edmund Burke, from the portrait by Sir Joshua Reynolds. Rockingham was First Minister in 1765–6 and in 1782.

31. Augustus Fitzroy, third Duke of Grafton. A descendant of Charles II, he seemed more interested in women and racing than in politics. He became First Lord of the Treasury in 1766.

32. George Grenville, who became the King's First Minister in 1763.

33. The White House at Kew, where the King was treated as being insane in 1788–9. It was largely demolished in 1802, only the mid-eighteenth-century wing surviving.

34. Queen's Lodge, Windsor, in 1783, from an engraving by James Fittler after George Robertson. The King and his family are walking on the South Terrace. In the middle of the picture is Queen's Lodge, built for the King's large family in 1776–8 on the site of Queen Anne's almost entirely demolished house. Behind it is Burford House, which the Queen bought from the Duke of St Albans, Nell Gwynn's grandson.

22

THE MOVE TO WINDSOR

I am a little of an Architect.

During the earlier years of the war in America, the King was still spending most of his time either at Buckingham House or at Kew; but he was already thinking of building another, larger, house in the country to accommodate his ever-growing family. And in helping him to formulate his plans he turned to his favourite architect, William Chambers.

Chambers was born in Stockholm, the son of a rich merchant of Scottish descent whose family firm had helped to supply the armies of King Charles XII. Returning to England for his education, Chambers went back to Sweden at the age of seventeen for service with the Swedish East India Company, in whose employment at Canton he developed that interest in Chinese architecture and gardens which was to influence much of his later work. Deciding against a career as a merchant adventurer, he went to study architecture in Paris, then in Italy, where he met his future rival, the Scottish architect Robert Adam, who rather reluctantly conceded that Chambers drew 'exquisitely' and was 'superior' to himself 'at present'.

All the English who have travelled for these five years imagine him a prodigy for Genius, for Sense & Good Taste [Adam wrote of him], and in great measure [he] deserves their encomium . . . His appearance is gentell & his person good which are most material circumstances. He despises others as much as he admires his own talents . . . It will require very considerable interest to succeed against Chambers who has tolerable Friends and real merit.

These friends had soon included Lord Bute and Augusta, Princess Dowager of Wales, for whose mausoleum Chambers was the only architect asked to submit designs. His appointment as tutor in architecture to Princess Augusta's son George had initiated a friendship which lasted for the whole of the architect's life. Under Chambers's guidance, Prince George had displayed a real talent as well as enthusiasm for architectural design; and at Kew he had been and continued to be surrounded by work in progress and work proposed in a variety of styles. There were Roman ruins and classical temples, Moorish, Turkish and Gothic buildings, a Chinese pavilion, a mosque and an orangery, a chinoiserie fretwork aviary and a pagoda, ten storeys high, with sparkling glazed tiles and bell-carrying golden dragons, built to Chambers's design and completed in less than six months in the winter of 1761–2. The gardens, as the architect Sir John Soane said, had, indeed, like Hadrian's Villa, 'an infinity of buildings peculiarly characteristic of the taste and manners of the different nations'.

In his study of such structures and in the exercises which Chambers set him the Prince had not been a mere copier: his designs certainly displayed the influence of his master at his most unadorned, but they were his own, and those which have survived, such as his plan for a Corinthian temple at Kew, are covered with compass points indicating the great care he took over them. In 1793 a farm worker's cottage designed by the King was built at Windsor; while some of the doorcases at the Queen's House were made to plans prepared by him. 'I am a little of an Architect,' he said himself with more than a hint of pride; and three months after his accession Horace Walpole had been told that building was the new King's 'favourite study'.

The King confessed that the works of Robert Adam and his brothers did not greatly appeal to him. 'I think,' he wrote, 'that the *Old* school (meaning that of Lord Burlingtons period) is not enough attended to, – that the Adams have introduced too much of neatness & prettyness.' He thought, for instance, that Robert Adam's work at Syon House for the Duke of Northumberland had too much gilding. It put him 'in mind of gingerbread'. 'Mere simplicity' would always 'bear the preference'.

Of the works of William Chambers he offered no such criticism; and he saw to it that his favourite architect progressed in his profession as his talents merited.★

In 1761 Chambers was appointed Architect to the Board of Works; in 1769 he became Comptroller of Works in succession to Henry Flitcroft, and in 1782 Surveyor-General and Comptroller of the King's Works. Acknowledged as the leading architect of the day, he was approached by the King whenever a royal residence was to be built or reconstructed, telling him what was required and supervising and approving the designs. When Buckingham House was transformed into the Queen's House, although Robert Adam and Cipriani were asked to supply certain embellishments such as ceilings and chimney pieces, it was Chambers who was the principal architect; and when a conservatory was required at Richmond in 1769 it was Chambers who designed it. It was also Chambers who was approached to design the new Somerset House on the site of the demolished house which had traditionally been the London home of Queen Consorts from the time of James I's Queen, Anne of Denmark.† And it was Chambers who was asked to submit designs when in 1769 the King decided to build a new palace by the river in Richmond Gardens opposite the grounds of Syon House. Work on this palace

---

★ In 1760 Chambers and Giovanni Battista Cipriani were commissioned to design a magnificently ornate Royal State Coach which, with its carving by Joseph Wilton, its gilding and harness, its upholstery and ironmongery, cost £7,587 19s. 9½d. and is now to be seen in the Royal Mews (Coutu, 'William Chambers and Joseph Wilton', 179).

† It had, however, been little used by Queen Consorts since the death of Charles II's Queen, Catherine of Braganza, and was never used by Queen Charlotte, though the place had been settled on her as custom required at the time of her marriage. In 1788, while building was still in progress, the bronze baroque fountain including a statue of George III by John Bacon the Elder was erected in the courtyard. When Queen Charlotte asked Bacon why he had created such a frightful figure, he replied tactfully, 'Art cannot always effect what is ever within reach of Nature, the union of beauty and majesty.' Bacon, the largely self-taught son of a poor clothworker, also made a bust of the King for Christ Church, Oxford. While sitting for it, the King was impressed by the sculptor's applying water from a syringe on to the clay instead of spitting on it as was the common method of artists trained on the Continent. 'Have you ever been out of England?' the King asked him. 'No? I am glad of it – you will be the greater credit for it' (Blackwood, *London's Immortals*, 42).

was fairly well advanced when there were difficulties with the Richmond authorities over a disputed piece of land; and the King called a halt to the construction and turned his attention instead to Windsor, never considering the possibility of either Kensington Palace or Hampton Court, both of which he still associated with the unhappiest days of his childhood. Hampton Court, where he was believed to have been chastised by his grandfather, was in particular anathema to him: when fire broke out there in 1770 he told Lady Hertford he would not have been sorry if the whole place had burned down.

Unfortunately, since his grandfather and George I had both preferred Hampton Court and Kensington Palace to Windsor, most of Windsor Castle had remained neglected since the death of Queen Anne in 1714, and various parts of it were occupied by families with real or pretended claims upon royal favour. The ditch, courtyards and terraces had become playgrounds for local children, while beggars, idle soldiers, sightseers, 'disorderly persons, women in red clogs or pattens' and higglers selling fish and vegetables wandered through the gates into the courts. Some of the buildings were in ruins; and St George's Chapel was 'totally neglected', several of its monuments being cracked and dusty, others tied up with rope.

Instead of instituting immediate repairs and turning out the Castle's unofficial occupants, the King decided in 1776 to build a new house on the site of the one on Castle Hill which Queen Anne had occupied. This house had recently been relinquished by the Lord Steward, Lord Talbot; and, on its becoming vacant, the Queen had 'expressed a strong wish' to have it, 'as Queen Anne lived there' and Windsor was 'just the place for us'. But, since it was considered too small to extend, Chambers was instructed to design a much larger house making what use he could of any features in the original structure. The new building, constructed at an eventual cost of £70,000 was, at the King's instigation, extremely plain, more like a barracks than a country house, although the interior was not so modest: there were a splendid Portland-stone staircase, Portland-stone or marble fireplaces in most of the hundred rooms, and a fine drawing-room with an elaborate allegorical ceiling, designed by Benjamin West and executed by a Dutch artist expert in the application of 'stained marble dust'. Known as Queen's Lodge, it was more often referred to by local people as Upper Lodge, to differentiate it from Lower Lodge, the new name given to the house two hundred yards down the slope which Charles II had given to his mistress Nell Gwynn, and which had formerly been known as Burford House after her son the Earl of Burford, later Duke of St Albans. This house, to the south of Queen's Lodge, was purchased by the Queen from Nell Gwynn's great-grandson, the third Duke of St Albans, for the younger Princesses. The price was £4,000 – a figure which, so the Duke was told, was considered 'far above the Value', but the Queen did 'not chuse to Negociate'.

By the summer of 1778 the King and Queen were able to move into Queen's Lodge and to settle down to that life of quiet regularity which was so much to their taste, the elder sons being found apartments in the Castle, their younger daughters being established with their governesses and ladies in Lower Lodge. The Princesses' lives had long been supervised by Lady Charlotte Finch, known as Lady Cha, the kindly, competent, religious daughter of the first Earl of Pomfret, whose wife's correspondence was published in three volumes after her death. Lady Charlotte, who had been appointed Governess in 1762, was also a gifted woman: Horace Walpole, who had met her in Florence years before, described her as the 'cleverest girl in the world', adding that she spoke 'the purest Tuscan, like any Florentine'. She was well suited to her post in the Royal Household, which she held for thirty years, organizing the girls' lessons in English and French, grammar and spelling, geography and music, needlework, drawing and dancing. She was ably assisted in her duties by another well-liked woman, the Sub-Governess, Martha Caroline Goldsworthy, 'Gooly' to her charges, the sister of Colonel Philip Goldsworthy, the King's Clerk Marshal of the Mews, whose amusingly woeful descriptions of life as one of His Majesty's equerries at Windsor were so much to entertain his fellow members of the Royal Household.

Yet if life at Windsor for the young Princesses was pleasant enough, for the King's and Queen's attendants it was an existence of scarcely supportable boredom. Its tedium weighed with exceptional heaviness upon the Assistant Keeper of the Wardrobe to the Queen, Miss Fanny Burney (daughter of Dr Charles Burney, the music historian), a woman in her mid-thirties whose contemporaries considered it quite extraordinary that she should have been offered, and accepted, this demanding and humdrum post in the Household. At her parents' house, in Leicester Square, Miss Burney met many of the leading musicians, actors, painters and writers of the day – among them Sir Joshua Reynolds, Samuel Johnson, Garrick and Burke – and she had herself written two novels, to the great surprise of her father, who did not even know that she was the author of the more successful of the two, *Evelina*, until six months after it was published. She was a rather nervous young woman, delicate and extremely short-sighted; and the long, introspective entries in the journal she kept at Windsor reveal a good deal more than she can have intended to expose. Her extreme shyness and frequent blushing, her nervous uncertainty and occasional absentmindedness were, for instance, disabilities of which she seems to have been unconsciously proud; and Mrs Schwellenberg, her immediate superior as Keeper of the Wardrobe, may well have been justifiably irritated by what appeared to be wilful efforts to exaggerate them. Certainly Mrs Schwellenberg much resented Miss Burney's having been chosen to occupy a post previously held by Mrs Hagedorn, who, like Mrs Schwellenberg, had accompanied the Queen from Strelitz. Fanny Burney was consequently made to feel that she was invading territory previously regarded as a German province.

The King and Queen, however, were initially well satisfied with their choice. For one thing Miss Burney was a friend of an old lady of whom they were particularly fond, Mrs Delany, who – after the death of the Duchess of Portland, with whom she had lived for much of every year – had been installed as a life tenant in a house near Queen's Lodge which the King had made over to her and fitted up for her, personally supervising the workmen and arranging for the supply 'not only of plate, china, glass and linen, but even of all sorts of stores – wine, sweetmeats, pickles, etc.'. He was there to welcome her when she moved in.

I threw myself at his feet [she told a friend], indeed unable to utter a word; he raised and saluted me, and said he meant not to stay longer than to desire I would *order* everything that could make the house comfortable and agreeable to me and then retired. Truly I found *nothing wanting* . . . [The next day]

Her Majesty came about 2 o'clock. I was lame and, therefore, could not go down, as I ought to have done to the door; but Her Majesty came up stairs . . . She repeated in the strongest terms her wish and the King's, that I should be as easy and happy as *they could possibly make me*; that they waved all ceremony and desired to come to me like *friends*! The Queen also delivered me a paper from the King; it contained the first quarter of £300 per annum which His Majesty allows me.

It was not only because she was Mrs Delany's friend that Miss Burney was welcomed into the Royal Household: her father had been disappointed when he had not been made Master of the Royal Music, so her becoming one of the Queen's attendants was an opportunity of 'benefitting Dr Burney through his daughter'. She was to be given a salary of £200 a year, the services of her own footman and her own maid, and the use of a coach. She was to dine at Mrs Schwellenberg's table.

She had been in two minds as to whether or not to accept the appointment; but, assured that there were 'thousands of candidates of high birth and rank' ready to take it if she did not, and in the belief that by doing so she might be able to help her father, she agreed to enter the Queen's service.

23

AT MRS DELANY'S

*Was there ever such stuff as great part of Shakespeare? Only one must not
say so! But what think you? . . . What – what?*

Before Miss Burney took up her duties, she met the King for the
first time at Mrs Delany's house, where the old lady had already
given her a short lecture on how to talk to the Queen, who frequently
complained that she could not get any conversation and, when she
did, she not only had to 'start the subjects, but, commonly, entirely
to support them', since people could often think of nothing to reply
to her except 'Yes' or 'No'. Miss Burney experienced a similar
difficulty with the King.

She and Mrs Delany's great-niece, Georgiana Port, and some other
visitors were playing a Christmas game in the old lady's drawing-room
one day when a large man in deep mourning with a glittering star
on his chest appeared in the doorway. 'The King! Aunt, the King!'
Georgiana called out nervously, while Miss Burney retreated to the
nearest wall, intending to slip out of the room as soon as she had
sidled near enough to the door. But before she could escape she
heard the King's loud whisper: 'Is that Miss Burney?' Told that it
was, he approached her with 'a countenance of the most perfect
good humour' to ask her a question, to which she replied in an
inaudible voice. He repeated the question; she answered it again,
though whether or not he heard her this time one could not tell,
for he made 'a little civil inclination of his head and went back to
Mrs. Delany'.

Miss Burney was to become well accustomed to the King's unnerv-
ing manner of conducting a conversation, his habit of walking
restlessly about the room to ask a question of one person followed
by a 'What? what? what?' in a tone of voice at once good-natured

and hectoring, then turning away to repeat the answer to someone else.★ She had, indeed, already been warned about his eccentricities on the advice of Dr James Lind, Physician to the Royal Household, who had said to Mrs Delany, 'I hope, Ma'am, you will apprise Miss Burney of the King's quick manner of speaking, for fear it should disconcert her.' Even so, Miss Burney was to be much disconcerted.

After talking 'with the strongest emotion' to Mrs Delany about the recent illness of his dear daughter, the tragically fat Princess Elizabeth, who had undergone blistering and been blooded 'twelve times in a fortnight', the King mentioned, as he often did, that the fault of his own constitution was a tendency to corpulence which he combated with the most vigorous exercise and strictest attention to a simple diet. Mrs Delany was beginning to 'praise his forbearance', when he stopped her. '"No, no!" he cried "'tis no virtue. I only prefer eating plain and little to growing diseased and infirm."'

The King then went up to the table [recorded Miss Burney who, like everyone else in the room, was standing quite still as though frozen in the middle of their Christmas game] and looked at a book of prints . . . He turned over a leaf or two, and then said, 'Pray does Miss Burney draw, too?'

The *too* was pronounced very civilly.

'I believe not, sir,' answered Mrs. Delany; 'at least, she does not tell.'

'Oh!' cried he, laughing, 'that's nothing! she is not apt to tell; she never does tell, you know! – Her father told me that himself. He told me the whole history of her *Evelina*. And I shall never forget his face when he spoke of his feelings at first taking up the book – he looked quite frightened . . .'

Then coming up close to me, the King said,

'But what? – what? – how was it?'

'Sir?' – cried I, not well understanding him.

'How came you – how happened it – what? – what?'

'I – I only wrote, sir, for my own amusement, – only in some odd, idle hours.'

'But your publishing – your printing – how was that?'

'That was only, sir – only because –'

★ As Mrs Delany had already observed when she had encountered him while staying with the Duchess of Portland at Bulstrode, 'the King hardly ever sits' (*Autobiography and Correspondence*, i, 480).

I hesitated most abominably, not knowing how to tell him a long story, and growing terribly confused at these questions . . .

The *What!* was then repeated, with so earnest a look, that, forced to say something, I stammeringly answered –

'I thought – sir – it would look very well in print!'

I do really flatter myself this is the silliest speech I ever made! I am quite provoked with myself for it, but . . . he laughed very heartily himself, – well he might – and walked away to enjoy it, crying out,

'Very fair indeed! that's being very fair and honest!'

Then, returning to me again, he said,

'But your father – how came you not to show him what you wrote?'

'I was too much ashamed of it, sir, seriously.' . . .

'And how did he find it out?'

'I don't know myself, sir. He never would tell me.' . . .

'What entertainment you must have had from hearing people's conjectures, before you were known! Do you remember any of them?'

'Yes, sir, many.'

'And what?'

'I heard that Mr. Baretti laid a wager it was written by a man; for no woman, he said, could have kept her own counsel.'

This diverted him extremely . . . 'But you have not kept your pen unemployed all this time?'

'Indeed I have, sir.'

'But why?'

'I – I believe I have exhausted myself, sir.'

He laughed aloud at this, and went and told it to Mrs. Delany, civilly treating a plain fact as a mere *bon mot*.

Then, turning to me again, he said, more seriously, 'But you have not determined against writing any more?'

'N–o, sir –' . . .

A very civil little bow spoke him pleased with this answer, and he went again to the middle of the room, where he chiefly stood, and, addressing us in general, talked upon the different motives of writing, concluding with,

'I believe there is no constraint to be put upon real genius; nothing but inclination can set it to work. Miss Burney, however, knows best.' And then, hastily returning to me, he cried, 'What? what?'

'No, sir, I – I believe not, certainly,' quoth I, very awkwardly, for I seemed taking a violent compliment only as my due; but I knew not how to put him off as I would another person.

He then made some inquiries concerning the pictures with which the room is hung, and which are all Mrs. Delany's own painting; and a little discourse followed, upon some of the masters whose pictures she has copied. This was all with her; for nobody ever answers him without being immediately addressed by him.

Soon afterwards 'a violent thunder was made at the door'. Miss Burney, who was almost certain that it was the Queen, would, she said, have given anything to escape; but, having been told that 'nobody ever quitted the royal presence, after having been conversed with, till motioned to withdraw', she remained where she was while Georgiana Port, 'according to established etiquette on these occasions', slid her hand behind her back to open the door and crept out backwards into the hall to let Her Majesty in.

On catching sight of her husband, the Queen 'made him a low curtsey and cried, "Oh, your Majesty is here!"' She then hastened to Mrs Delany with both her hands held out, saying, 'My dear Mrs Delany, how are you?'

Instantly after I felt her eye on my face [continued Miss Burney, who knew that etiquette forbade a formal introduction except at a court drawing-room]. I believe, too, that she curtsied to me; but though I saw the bend I was too near-sighted to be sure it was intended for me. I was hardly ever in a situation more embarrassing; I dared not return what I was not certain I had received.

Miss Burney was saved from further embarrassment by the King, who, she fancied, saw her distress and 'most good-humouredly' said something to the Queen which she was too flurried to remember except the words 'I have been telling Miss Burney . . .'

Relieved from so painful a dilemma, Miss Burney dropped a curtsey to the Queen, who made one to her at the same moment and, 'with a very smiling countenance', came up to her as if to talk to her. This, however, she could not do, 'for the King went on talking, eagerly, and very gaily, repeating to her every word I had said during our conversation upon *Evelina*, its publication, &c., &c.'.

When tea was brought in and the Queen went to sit down, the King began all over again on a different tack:

'Are you musical?'

'Not a performer, sir.'

He rushed to the Queen with this intelligence: 'She does not play.'

187

He remained with the Queen a few minutes to tell her some encouraging news he had been given by the doctor about Princess Elizabeth, and then returned to Miss Burney.

'Are you sure you never play? – never touch the keys at all?'

'Never to acknowledge it, sir.'

'Oh! that's it,' he cried, flying to the Queen. 'She does play – but not to acknowledge it.' He went back once more to Miss Burney and began to examine her more closely and with increased eagerness. She, terrified that she might be asked to perform in public, vehemently denied that she had ever done so. Recognizing her distress, he then made a 'complying little bow and said no more about it', continuing, however, to talk about music.

'To me,' he said, 'it appears quite as strange to meet with people who have no ear for music, and cannot distinguish one air from another, as to meet with people who are dumb. Lady Bell Finch once told me that she had heard that there was some difference between a psalm, a minuet and a country dance, but she declared they all sounded alike to her! There are people who have no idea for difference of colour. The Duke of Marlborough cannot actually tell scarlet from green!' And so the King talked on, while in another part of the room the Queen spoke in a low voice.

Soon afterwards Their Majesties departed and, following the common practice, all the people to whom they had spoken saw them to their carriage to 'receive their last gracious nods'.

The King provided another sample of his eccentric discourse in Mrs Delany's drawing-room three days later. He appeared in the evening, unexpected; and at his approach the ladies in the room – in observance of a procedure practised in all houses at Windsor at which he called – started up from their books and needlework and fled to their agreed posts, Georgiana Port to the door, Fanny Burney to the wall opposite the fire. Mrs Delany also stood up, but, because of her age, was always asked to sit down again. Miss Port then backed out of the room, first to fetch candles, then to carry in tea upon a large salver containing, sugar, cream, bread and butter, and cake. She had a napkin over her arm for the King's fingers.

The King talked of a pamphlet by Richard Cumberland about his recently deceased neighbour Lord Sackville, upon which no one else could comment, not having read it. He then alluded to the comtesse de Genlis, author of children's books, who had not long since been in England and whom Miss Burney had met.

'Did she speak English?' the King asked eagerly.

'Yes, sir.'

'And how?'

'Extremely well, sir; with great felicity.'

'Indeed? That always surprises me in a foreigner that has not lived here.'

He then spoke of Voltaire [Fanny Burney recorded], and talked a little of his works, concluding with this strong condemnation of their tendency: –

'I,' cried he, 'think him a monster, I own it fairly.'

Nobody answered. Mrs. Delany did not quite hear him, and I knew too little of his works to have courage to say anything about them.

He next named Rousseau, whom he seemed to think of with more favour, though by no means with approbation. Here, too, I had read too little to talk at all, although His Majesty frequently applied to me . . . He [related various anecdotes] all charging him with savage pride and insolent ingratitude.

Here, however, I ventured to interfere; for, as I knew Rousseau had had a pension from the King, I could not but wish His Majesty should be informed he was grateful to him. And . . . I thought it but common justice to the memory of poor Rousseau to acquaint the King of his personal respect for him.

'Some gratitude, sir,' said I, 'he was not without. When my father was in Paris, which was after Rousseau had been in England, he visited him, in his garret, and the first thing he showed him was your Majesty's portrait over his chimney.'

The King paused a little while upon this; but nothing more was said of Rousseau.

The sermon of the day before was then talked over. Mrs. Delany had not heard it, and the King said it was no great loss.

Some time afterwards, the King said he found by the newspapers that the [comic actress] Mrs. [Kitty] Clive was dead . . .

This led on to . . . Mrs. Siddons [who] took her turn, and with the warmest praise.

'I am an enthusiast for her,' cried the King, 'quite an enthusiast. I think there was never any player in my time so excellent – not Garrick himself; I own it!'

Then, coming close to me, who was silent, he said,

'What? what?' . . . But I still said nothing; I could not concur where I thought so differently, and to enter into an argument was quite impossible; for every little thing I said, the King listened to with an eagerness that made me always ashamed of its insignificancy . . .

From players he went to plays, and complained of the great want of good modern comedies, and of the extreme immorality of most of the old ones.

'And they pretend,' cried he, 'to mend them; but it is not possible. Do you think it is? – what?'

'No, sir, not often, I believe . . .'

Then he specified several; but I had read none of them, and consequently could say nothing about the matter; – till, at last, he came to Shakespeare.

'Was there ever,' cried he, 'such stuff as great part of Shakespeare? Only one must not say so! But what think you? – What? – Is there not sad stuff? What? – what?'

'Yes, indeed, I think so, sir, though mixed with such excellences, that –'

'O!' cried he, laughing good-humouredly, 'I know it is not to be said! but it's true. Only it's Shakespeare, and nobody dare abuse him.'

Then he enumerated many of the characters and parts of plays that he objected to; and when he had run them over, finished with again laughing, and exclaiming,

'But one should be stoned for saying so!'★

★ The King elaborated his views upon Shakespeare in a conversation with Miss Burney's father, who mentioned a German translation of the plays by J. J. Eschenburg. 'The Germans translate Shakespeare,' exclaimed the King, laughing. 'Why, we don't understand him ourselves. How should foreigners?' The Queen remarked that she thought the soliloquies very well rendered by Eschenburg.

'Aye,' said the King, 'that is because, in those serious speeches, there are none of those puns, quibbles and peculiar idioms of Shakespeare and his times for which there are no equivalents in other languages' (d'Arblay, *Memoirs of Dr Burney*, iii, 18–20).

24

THE SQUIRE OF WINDSOR

He had an extraordinary facility for recognizing everybody, young or old.

Disjointed and discursive though it was, the King's talk revealed the breadth of his reading and the wide range of his interests. He was knowledgeable about botany and agriculture as well as architecture, genealogy, astronomy and horology. He made himself conversant with the state of the country's manufacturing industries, which he discussed at Windsor with Josiah Wedgwood, the porcelain manufacturer, who was appointed Potter to the King and who made a celebrated green and gold service for the Queen, the design of which was influenced by the King's taste for simplicity. Wedgwood's partner, Thomas Bentley, was also summoned to Windsor and said after his audience, 'The King is well acquainted with business, and with the characters of the principal manufacturers, merchants and artists and seems to have the success of all our manufacturers much at heart, and to understand the importance of them.'

At the same time the King was devoted to the history and traditions of Eton College, and spoke of the school in an almost proprietary way. 'You Westminsters must now look to yourselves,' he once said to the Earl of Onslow, Outranger of Windsor Forest, who had been at Westminster School in the 1740s, 'or we shall get ahead of you very soon.' During his later years he sometimes imagined he had actually attended the school himself. 'Look, my Lord,' he said to the Duke of Wellington's eldest brother, Lord Wellesley, whose affection for the place was quite as great as his own. 'Look, there is the noble school where we were all educated!'

He went to look round the buildings almost every year, never failing to ask the boys about their most recent flogging, and taking the greatest interest in the appointment of suitable headmasters and provosts: when a successor to the inadequate Dr Sleech had to be found as Provost, he insisted that the new man must be a sound and eminent scholar. 'At Eton,' he said, 'I must not have any but an able man.'

He provided regular entertainments for the Eton boys, such as an automaton dancing on a rope and a 'species of phantasmagoria consisting of dancing figures'; and with equal regularity he attended Montem – the rowdy triennial festival during which the boys exacted gratuities to defray the expenses of the senior scholar at King's College, Cambridge – permitting the boys who had taken part to appear on the East Terrace of the Castle in their fanciful costumes. 'He was hospitable to the boys in his odd way,' in the words of an account of Etonian life. 'On one occasion he sent to invite them in a body to the Terrace and kept them all to supper – "remembering to forget" to extend the invitation to the masters who had accompanied them and who returned home in great dudgeon.' The school's celebrations on 4 June, his birthday, were inaugurated in his lifetime, while the present uniform of Etonians was introduced during the long mourning after his death.

He loved fireworks, military bands and uniforms; and any suggested alteration in the details of a soldier's dress disturbed him just as profoundly as any proposed change in the prescribed customs and particularities of etiquette. When the shape of the hats worn by the Guards at Windsor was changed, he was deeply shocked. 'What!' he protested to the Duke of Richmond, Master-General of the Ordnance. 'What, Richmond! Who ever saw Guards in round caps?' 'Oh yes, Sire,' said the Duke. 'My own hat is round.' 'Aye! And so is my night-cap!'

He spent hours studying military prints until he could recite the details – as he could recite the names of all the ships in his Navy – by heart. He often wore the uniform of the Royal Horse Guards because he liked the colours so much, and he created a special Windsor troop and made himself a captain. Also, borrowing perhaps an idea of Frederick the Great's, he designed a personal uniform, known as the Windsor uniform, the colours of which, 'dark blue and gold turned up with red', were those of a hunting livery which had been designed by his father in 1729. This uniform, which, according to Fanny Burney, was by 1786 worn 'by all men who belong to His Majesty and come into his presence at Windsor', was often worn by the King not only at Windsor but in London also. While notoriously derisive of fashionable attire and often criticized for the 'ill made coats' of his civilian clothes – which often resulted in his not being recognized when walking about in the countryside – he was far from averse to dressing up when occasion demanded, and then his appearance could be, and was described as, 'majestic beyond description', 'quite superb'.

He liked his daughters to dress up too; and when he went hunting with them they all wore 'blue habits faced and turned up with red, white beaver hats and black feathers'. Sometimes he himself, taking 'the most dangerous leaps with the utmost indifference', wore a black jockey's cap, for eighteenth-century rides were often fast and long – eighty miles being a not uncommon distance. They were also, by modern standards, ferociously cruel to the horses. At the end of one ride from Windsor which lasted six hours, the 'stag dropped down dead before the hounds; not twenty of the horses out of 150 were in at the death; several horses died in the field, and tired ones were seen crawling away to every village'. Sometimes the King could be seen hurtling home in a phaeton, driving at a speed that terrified his daughters. Once he was seen being driven back to Windsor in a butcher's cart, 'holding affable conversation with the butcher all the way'.

The King had a passion for pottering about with bits of machinery, and was constantly adding to his collection of scientific instruments, barometers and hygrometers, microscopes and orreries, models of engines, steam pumps and the ingenious devices constructed by his Mathematical Instrument Maker, George Adams.*

---

* In 1766 Adams presented a copy of his *Treatise Describing and Explaining the Construction and Use of New Celestial and Terrestial Globes* to the King, 'who had given him permission to bring the volume out under the royal sanction. His Majesty looked over the dedication and said, "This is not your writing." "No, Sire," replied Adams, "it was composed for me by Dr Johnson." "I thought so," answered the King; "it is excellent – and the better for being void of flattery which I hate."' The pair of eighteen-inch globes illustrated in this book are probably those now in the King

He had long been fascinated by such instruments and had been stimulated in his interest by Lord Bute, who had himself a superb collection of them in cabinets at the fine house built for him by Robert Adam at Luton Hoo in Bedfordshire. Indeed, according to Louis Dutens, Bute's collection could be 'reckoned the most complete of its kind in Europe'.

Encouraged by Bute, the King constantly added to his own collection. 'His Majesty's Collection of philosophical instruments increases daily,' Stephen Demainbray assured Bute in November 1760, 'and, as it is finely chosen, requires one assistant to keep it in Order; would it be advisable, My Lord, to apply . . . to be nominated as Keeper of the same?'

Demainbray's application was not successful on this occasion; but he was later given a more responsible appointment; and in the meantime several other men of science were rewarded by the King, for example James Ferguson, the astronomer, and George Adams's assistant, John Miller, who, having demonstrated to the King that a guinea and a feather would fall at the same rate if there was no air to hinder them, noted His Majesty's sparingness in small matters:

Mr Miller . . . used to tell that he was desired to explain the airpump experiment of the guinea and feather to Geo. III. In performing the experiment the young optician provided the feather, the King supplied the guinea and at the conclusion the King complimented the young man on his skill as an experimenter but frugally returned the guinea to his waistcoat pocket.

The King delighted in showing visitors the mechanism of machines and tools, and could himself use a lathe with skill; he even managed, so it was said, to turn out several respectable buttons. Predictably in a man who so disliked unpunctuality, uncertainty, untidiness and change and who set such store by exactitude and regularity, he was fascinated by timepieces as well as by optical instruments, and spent pleasant hours taking them to pieces and putting them together again,

---

George III Collection at the Science Museum in London. This collection, which is believed to include items inherited from the King's uncle, the Duke of Cumberland, was formerly kept at Kew until most of it was passed to King's College, London, shortly after its foundation in 1828; there it was exhibited in the King George III Museum until 1927, when the bulk of it was handed over to the Science Museum. (Morton and Wess, *Public and Private Science*, 17–37).

making a careful record of how this was done. He was proud to accept a fine and remarkably accurate chronometer from the horologist, a Yorkshire-born carpenter's son, John Harrison, upon whose behalf he managed to extract from a dilatory Board of Longitude the balance of the reward which Harrison had won for making a chronometer which could determine longitude at sea to within a maximum of thirty miles. The King also patronized two of the finest clockmakers of the day, Alexander Cumming of Bond Street and Christopher Pinchbeck, who carried on business at the sign of the Astronomico-Musical Clock in Fleet Street and who constructed a four-sided astronomical clock for which the King assisted Sir William Chambers in designing a case. To both Pinchbeck and Cumming he paid over £1,000 for splendid examples of their work; while to John Arnold, the son of a Bodmin clockmaker and himself an expert horologist, he paid £500 for a curious watch so small it could be set in a ring. He also patronized Thomas Mudge, who made him a watch which automatically adjusted itself to changes in temperature, and Benjamin Vulliamy the Elder, who was responsible for ensuring the accuracy of all the timepieces which were kept ticking away in most of the principal rooms of the royal residences.

It was the King's curiosity about optical instruments which led to his interest in astronomy; and he asked Sir William Chambers to design for him an observatory at Kew to which he became a frequent visitor, showing people round with great enthusiasm, introducing them to his old tutor Stephen Demainbray, who had been appointed Director, and talking knowledgeably about the observatory's telescopes. When the German scientist Georg Christoph Lichtenberg came to England in 1775, the King spent two hours with him in the observatory showing him its instruments. Occasionally he would remain there for most of the night, as he did in 1769 to watch the transit of Venus, having asked Demainbray to provide him with detailed notes on what to expect.*

---

* Having granted £4,000 to the Royal Society to cover the cost of sending observers to the South Seas aboard Captain Cook's *Endeavour* to study the transit of Venus from there in 1769, the King subsequently asked Cook to take a number of animals from his own farms to Polynesia 'with a view of stocking Otaheite and the neighbouring islands with these useful animals' (Hough, *Captain James Cook*, 282). The 1769

The telescopes and reflectors at Kew, however, were poor instruments when compared with those brought by invitation to the Queen's House in the spring and summer of 1782 by William Herschel.

Herschel, who had been born in Hanover five months after the birth of the King in London, had formerly been a musician, an oboist in the band of the Hanoverian Foot Guards. He had come to England in 1757 and, after almost three years struggling to survive by giving music lessons, had eventually been found employment by the Earl of Darlington, who engaged him to train the band of the Durham Militia. Six years later he became organist at the Octagon Chapel in Bath. Yet for all this time he had been studying hard in his spare moments, poring in particular over books on optics and astronomy; and, having bought the tools and patterns of a Quaker optician, he began to make his own instruments, with one of which he observed the Orion nebula and with another discovered the planet Uranus.

The King was intrigued by his history and determined to become his patron. Joseph Banks, the President of the Royal Society, an astronomer as well as a botanist, suggested to the King that Herschel might be placed in charge of the Kew observatory; but this place had already been more or less promised to the present astronomer's son; so, after granting Herschel an audience at the Queen's House in 1782, he gave him a pension of £200 a year. Thereafter he was most generous in his patronage, paying 600 guineas each for four ten-foot telescopes, one of which he presented to the University of Göttingen in Hanover, founded by his grandfather in 1737. The King also contributed a total of £4,000 towards the completion of a huge reflector – which Herschel eventually set up in a field behind his house – giving in addition £200 a year for its upkeep and repair and a pension of £50 for Herschel's sister and assistant, Caroline. 'The King,' Fanny Burney commented, 'has not a happier subject than this man, who owes wholly to His Majesty that he is not wretched.'

---

voyage cost less than the £4,000 the King subscribed to it. The surplus was accordingly spent upon commissioning the bust of His Majesty by Nollekens which now stands in the entrance hall of the Royal Society.

Shortly before the giant instrument was finished the King went to inspect it, taking with him the Archbishop of Canterbury, the amiable John Moore, who was staying at the time at Windsor. 'Come, my Lord,' Miss Herschel heard the King say to the Archbishop as he helped him into the immense tube, 'I will show you the way to heaven.'

The King also took the greatest pleasure at Windsor in going over the three farms of well over a thousand acres in all which he had created in the Great Park and ensuring that they were profitably run. He had a sound knowledge of agriculture and sheep farming and, acting on the advice of Sir Joseph Banks, he imported sheep from Spain and 'played a key role in breeding the ancestors of the Merino sheep of Australia and New Zealand'. He wrote letters under a pseudonym, Ralph Robinson, the name of one of his shepherds, to the *Annals of Agriculture*, edited by the agriculturist Arthur Young, who, greeted with the highly complimentary words 'I consider myself more indebted to you than to any other man in my dominions', was later taken over the farms at Windsor and was much impressed by what he saw:

The King rode with me for two and a half hours, talking farming and reasoning upon points we differed in. Explained his system of crops . . . Recommended me to [write] in short paragraphs, '*as there are many, Mr. Young, who catch the sense of a short paragraph, that lose the meaning of a long one*' . . . His farm is in admirable order, and the crops all clean and fine. He was very desirous that I should see all and ordered [his bailiff] to carry me to two or three other things next morning. I found fault with his hogs; he said I must not find fault with a present to him. The Queen was so kind as to give them from Germany . . . We must not examine them too critically . . . He is the politest of men.

Perfectly at home with Arthur Young, the King was equally at ease with his farm workers, and with poor country people in general. He encouraged their children to play cricket and football and fly kites in the Great Park; and he would stroll into their cottages unannounced and talk to them about simple matters, sometimes alarming them at first by his abrupt manner and the way in which he would stand close to them, peering into their faces, but winning them over in the end by his obvious sincerity and the kindliness of his intent. 'He had an extraordinary facility for recognizing everybody, young or old,' wrote Charles Knight, the Windsor bookseller, who, as a little boy gathering mushrooms in the short grass of the Home Park, often used to bow to the King when he walked quickly by on his way to his dairy at Frogmore. 'He knew something of the character and affairs of most persons who lived under the shadow of the Castle.'

Numerous were the stories of his encounters with them – of, for instance, his coming across a boy in the Great Park. 'Who are you?' he asked him. 'I be pig boy but I don't work. They don't want lads here. All this belongs hereabouts to Georgy.'

'Pray, who is Georgy?'

'He is King and lives at the Castle, but he does no good to me.'

The King immediately saw to it that the boy was given work on one of his farms.

Where had all the other labourers gone? he asked another day of a woman working alone in a field at harvest time. They had all gone to see the King, she said, and added, 'I wouldn't give a pin to see him. Besides the fools will lose a day's work by it, and that is more than I can afford to do. I have five children to work for.' 'Well, then,' said the King, putting some money into her hand, 'you may tell your companions who are gone to see the King, that the King came to see you.'

His own servants became accustomed to being addressed in the same cheerfully familiar or inconsequential way as villagers he met on the road or in the fields. 'Well, boy, what?' he called happily one morning while on his way to make his usual early visit to his stables. 'What do you do? What do they pay you, what?'

Inside the stables another morning he found the grooms arguing so urgently that they did not notice his arrival. 'I don't care what you say, Robert,' one of them said, 'but everyone else agrees, that the man at the Three Tuns makes the best purl in Windsor.'

'Purl? Purl? Purl?' whispered the King in his quick, excited way. 'Purl? What's purl, Robert?'

Robert said it was a tankard of warm beer with a glass of gin in it.

'I dare say a very good drink, grooms,' said the King so loudly that they all turned round and recognized him, 'but, grooms, too strong for the morning. Never drink in the morning, grooms.'

He never expected that they would take his advice, and many years later, arriving at the stables much earlier than usual, he found them deserted except for a small lad who did not know him.

'Boy! Boy!' the King asked. 'Boy! Where are the grooms?'

'I don't know, sir, but they'll soon be back because they expect the King.'

'Aha! Then run, boy, run, and say the King expects them. Run to the Three Tuns, boy. They are sure to be there, boy, for the landlord makes the best purl in Windsor.'

He often went down to the town himself. He liked strolling along the streets, tapping the stones with his long stick, looking in the shop windows, occasionally walking in to give the tradespeople instructions on how to vote in a local election.

He took a real interest in the place and its citizens; and over the years as a private investment he bought seven houses there.* He contributed £1,000 to the paving of the streets of the town; he put up the money for a military hospital; and, when a new organ, a 'magnificent Organ made by Green', was installed at his expense in St George's Chapel, he presented the old instrument to the parish church of St Mary. He gave his support to the reconstruction of the Theatre Royal, which was reopened in 1794 and of which he became patron. He was often to be seen laughing uproariously in the royal box or, to the embarrassment of his wife and daughters, shouting encouragement to the comedians, as he was wont to do to Dickey Suett, the celebrated comic actor, 'the very personification of weak whimsicality', at Drury Lane and the Haymarket. Often also he was to be seen, 'a quiet, good-humoured gentleman in a long blue coat', sitting on a high stool at the counter of Charles Knight's bookshop, looking over the latest publications. One afternoon his eye caught Paine's *Rights of Man*, and he picked it up and began to study it intently. Absorbed, he 'continued reading for half an hour', the

---

* He also owned Gloucester House and four other houses in Weymouth and two small tenements in Pimlico, as well as a public house there (Royal Archives, Privy Purse Accounts, 17105–17290, quoted in Brooke, *King George III*, 212).

bookseller's son remembered, 'and he left the shop without saying anything; but he never afterwards expressed his displeasure'. He might well have felt some displeasure if he had reached the passage in the second volume in which Paine wrote, 'It has cost England almost seventy millions sterling to maintain a family, imported from abroad, of very inferior capacity to thousands in the nation.' In fact, when he returned to the shop later, he was as good-humoured as ever. On another occasion, though, the title of Bishop Watson's *Apology for the Bible* upset him. 'What! What! What! Apologize for the Bible! What! What! What!'

In many respects he was niggardly – the tips he gave to servants frequently amounted to a single penny produced after a long search between the folds of a leather purse – but his heart was moved by poverty and distress and he did his best to help the poor in their adversity. He saw to it that a mill in the Park ground corn at a special rate for the needy; and he would frequently leave money behind him on a chair or table when he left a cottage where the tenants seemed in want of some comfort they could not afford.

In her diaries and letters Fanny Burney described her life at Windsor, which she found as exhausting as it was tedious and which was made all the more so by her not being allowed to wear spectacles, for this would have been a breach of court etiquette. She got up in the morning at six o'clock and waited anxiously for the ringing of the bell which summoned her for the first of her daily attendances upon Her Majesty. Sometimes she was not ready when the bell rang and was seen, half-dressed, racing down the windy corridors of Queen's Lodge to her mistress's apartments. When she arrived there, the Queen's hair had already been dressed by her German wardrobe-woman, who handed Miss Burney the clothes that were to be worn that day. No maidservant was allowed into the room while Her Majesty was there, so Miss Burney had to do all the dressing herself. At this she was evidently not very competent. Indeed, according to Lady Llanover, a relation of Mrs Delany's, she was 'utterly unfit for any place requiring punctuality, neatness and manual dexterity'. It was certainly true that she always found it difficult to tie the bow of the Queen's necklace without getting Her Majesty's hair caught up in the knot; and she was thankful that she did not have the wardrobe-woman's job, for she was sure that she would never remember which piece of clothing to hand over first and, embarrassed as she would undoubtedly be, would 'run a prodigious risk of giving the gown before the hoop, and the fan before the neckerchief'.

By eight o'clock the Queen was dressed and ready to go to prayers with the King and Princesses in St George's Chapel, which had by now been cleaned and restored at a cost of £20,000, the Knights of the Garter, whose place of worship it was, having paid £5,800, the King the rest. After prayers, unless she was asked to look after one of the Queen's dogs, Miss Burney was free to return to her room for breakfast and for the long process of preparing her own clothes for the day. She was then called again to the Queen's apartments to attend her while her coiffure was being arranged by the royal hairdresser, a process which took three hours on Wednesdays and Saturdays, when her hair had to be curled and craped, and two hours on other days. While the hairdresser was at work the Queen read the newspapers, occasionally reciting a paragraph aloud to lessen the boredom of her standing attendants. These were allowed to retreat a few paces during the process of powdering, so as not to spoil their clothes. The deferential Fanny Burney, always far readier to give examples of Her Majesty's 'condescension' and 'consideration' rather than of her selfishness, considered that the grant of this permission was a gesture which one would not have expected from one who 'belonged to the Queen's high station'.

In the afternoon, when her duties in the Queen's apartments were over, Miss Burney returned to her room for dinner, a dispiriting meal served at five o'clock, sometimes eaten alone with the forbidding Mrs Schwellenberg, more often with the attendants of any guests whom the King and Queen might have staying with them, but almost invariably in tedium. After dinner, coffee was served in Mrs Schwellenberg's sitting-room while, in the summer, the Royal Family took their evening stroll up and down the Terrace, the King in his Windsor uniform with the star of the Order of the Garter on his chest and wearing a hat with a gold button and loop, surmounted by a black cockade, which marked him out 'conspicuously from the rest of the company'. As they marched sedately from one end of the

Terrace to the other – the King and Queen arm in arm, their daughters with their governesses and ladies walking two by two, their sons if they happened to be at Windsor at the time also in attendance, two bands playing alternately – the spectators backed away from their path. A police officer was on duty with a little switch to keep 'individuals from pressing too much on the King' when he stopped to talk to anyone. But this was done 'with the greatest urbanity'. Indeed, the presence of the police officer was rarely necessary, though once there was an altercation when a man refused to take his hat off as the King passed by and then flew with flailing fists and kicking feet at the Marquess of Thomond, a Lord of the Bedchamber, who had knocked it off for him; and once there was an unpleasant scene when many persons had to be 'turned off, being in a state of intoxication'.

When the 'Terracing' was over and the King had thanked the bandsmen, as it was his unfailing practice to do, it was time for Miss Burney to go for tea in the dining-room with the equerry on duty and any gentlemen whom the King and Queen might have invited for the evening, as it was 'only a very select few' that could eat with Their Majesties, and those few always ladies, 'no men, of what rank soever, being permitted to sit in the Queen's presence'. An hour later, at about nine o'clock, the equerry led the guests away to the concert room and left Fanny, by now almost stupefied with boredom, with Mrs Schwellenberg for two more long hours during which, nearly every evening, she was obliged to play piquet. At eleven o'clock she had supper and then waited, as after breakfast, for the bell to ring. As soon as she heard it she again hurried along the corridor to the Queen's room, to take Her Majesty's clothes off.

There were few chances to escape from the boredom of her demanding duties, and when she seized a rare opportunity she felt that Mrs Schwellenberg and the Queen were sure to be aware of it and make clear their disapproval. Once James Boswell came to Windsor to stay with the Bishop of Carlisle in the Canons' Lodgings. It was suggested that he might come to see Miss Burney at Queen's Lodge; but, although she 'really wished to see him again', she dared not permit a visit and suggested what might appear to be a chance meeting outside St George's Chapel after evening service.

This proved just as embarrassing. In a loud voice Boswell teased her about her employment, urging her to resign. 'If you do not quit, ma'am, very soon, some violent measures, I assure you, will be taken. We shall address Dr Burney in a body . . . We shall fall upon him all at once . . .' Miss Burney interrupted the flow of his facetious raillery by asking him about Edmund Burke's forthcoming book, *Reflections on the French Revolution*, which Boswell assured her was the best book in the world after his own. He then began to read her one of Dr Johnson's letters. But she was growing increasingly nervous: the King and the Royal Family were approaching them from the Terrace; a crowd was gathering round the railings; and Mrs Schwellenberg was looking out of her window. She made a quick apology and hurried off, immediately to be asked who the unknown and uninvited gentleman was and to be warned that she must never allow such visitors to come beyond the limit of the railings.

It took Miss Burney a long time to grow accustomed to the rigid formality which the King and Queen insisted upon at Windsor. All attendants and even guests were obliged to retire to the nearest wall and stand quite still as soon as any member of the Royal Family appeared in sight. Even among themselves the King and Queen and the Princesses maintained this severe formality. When the King approached one of his daughters' rooms he was preceded by a page who made that 'particular kind of scratch' which had to be used on royal doors instead of knocking. The Princesses were then expected to stand up and to remain silent unless asked a question. Nor were they allowed to leave a room – walking backwards as everyone else did – until they were dismissed with the formal command 'Now I will let you go!' They could sit with permission; but the ladies-in-waiting, whose rules went so far as to forbid them to walk past the open doorway of a room which contained a royal personage, had always to remain on their feet, sometimes for hours on end.

Very rarely was a visiting Minister invited to sit down in the King's presence. After standing for two hours while enduring a painful attack of gout, Pitt was asked by the King if he had suffered any ill effects from having had to stand so long; but the King seems not to have considered the possibility of asking him to sit down. Even in the Park, if visitors happened to come across a member of the Royal Family, they were expected to back away respectfully.

Her Majesty's Reader was obliged to stand up at a lectern while she read to the Queen and the circle of ladies standing around her. As Miss Burney observed, those who formed this circle were expected to maintain a deep and decorous silence:

If you find a cough tickling your throat [she told her sister-in-law in a letter] you must arrest it from making any sound; if you find yourself choking with forbearance, you must choke – but not cough.

In the second place, you must not sneeze. If you have a vehement cold, you must take no notice of it; if your nose-membranes feel a great irritation, you must hold your breath; if a sneeze still insists upon making its way, you must oppose it, by keeping your teeth grinding together; if the violence of the repulse break some blood-vessel, you must break the blood-vessel – but not sneeze.

In the third place, you must not, upon any account, stir either hand or foot. If, by chance, a black pin runs into your head, you must not take it out. If the pain is very great, you must be sure to bear it without wincing; if it brings the tears into your eyes, you must not wipe them off; if they give you a tingling by running down your cheeks, you must look as if nothing was the matter. If the blood should gush from your head by means of the black pin, you must let it gush; if you are uneasy to think of making such a blurred appearance, you must be uneasy, but you must say nothing about it. If, however, the agony is very great, you may, privately, bite the inside of your cheek, or of your lips, for a little relief; taking care, meanwhile, to do it so cautiously as to make no apparent dent outwardly. And, with that precaution, if you even gnaw a piece out, it will not be minded, only be sure either to swallow it, or commit it to a corner of the inside of your mouth till they are gone for you must not spit.

His attendants found the King less demanding than the ladies of the Household found the Queen, even though he evinced little sympathy for them when they were unwell: Fanny Burney recorded how one day he refused to allow that one of his equerries was ill. He had a 'very good colour' and looked strong, so the man *must* be well!

As an example of his consideration in other ways, the story was told that one evening when the fire was getting low he rang for the page-in-waiting and asked him to go for some more coal, as the scuttle was empty. The page considered this task too menial and rang for the footman, an elderly man, to perform it. Immediately and angrily the King picked up the scuttle himself, told the page to show him where the coal was kept, filled the scuttle, went back to the fire, tipped the coal on to it, and, handing the empty scuttle to the page, said, 'Never ask an old man to do what you are so much better able to do yourself.'

The King was also considerate in his care to ensure that all his servants – whose names he knew and to whom he would often speak about their families – received the perquisites to which they were traditionally entitled; and it was for this reason, as well as for economy's sake, that as soon as the last card game was over of an evening the candles were immediately snuffed out, since candles, on which by 1812 the Household was spending £10,000 a year, were, when partly used, the property of the servants. So was all unconsumed food and wine once it had been laid upon a table.

These traditional perquisites compensated the Household servants for their not being allowed to accept the tips (known as vails) from their master's guests which they would have received in other great houses, where, upon the guests' departure, servants were often lined up in rows in the hall to receive gratuities appropriate to their calling and where it was generally understood that failure to be generous in this way might well result in the parsimonious guest being 'a marked man' should he be invited to that house again.

The King's servants had also cause to complain of having to wait, sometimes for long periods, for their modest wages, particularly at times when an exceptionally large proportion of his income was required for the purchase of political support, pensions and annuities, as well as charitable donations. Making up their wages by recognized perquisites and in other ways, however, the royal servants seem not to have been unduly discontented. Certainly the King did his best to make them feel at home. All new servants were likely sooner or later, usually in the first week or so of their employment, to be startled by His Majesty appearing suddenly in front of them to make some cheerfully confusing remark.

The upper servants complained not so much of their salaries as of the almost spartan conditions which the King's austere tastes and habits imposed upon them. One of the equerries, an elderly general, was particularly upset by the King's habit of eating his scanty dinner so quickly that he was ready to go out for a ride or a walk 'ere his equerry-in-waiting, who was always summoned to attend him forthwith, had had time to swallow his soup'. 'Well, thanks to Heaven,' this general exclaimed when disturbed by the summons as he sat down at the equerries' table, 'my waiting will finish tomorrow, and I shall take care to order *two* pounds of rump steaks for my dinner, and to be *two* hours in eating it.'

Another of the equerries, Colonel Goldsworthy, had warned Miss Burney at the outset of her career that she would undoubtedly die of cold. He himself, like every other equerry-in-waiting, had always to be ready to accompany the King whenever he felt like going out for a ride. It was 'the King's delight to mount his horse before the equerry-in-waiting could possibly be aware of it; often in severe or unpleasant weather which rarely deterred him'. Sometimes the King was halfway down Windsor Hill before the equerry had had time 'to pull up his stockings under his boots'.

'Oh, Ma'am, what lives do we lead!' Colonel Goldsworthy – who was, in fact, 'warmly and faithfully attached to the King' – had complained to Miss Burney in his own inimitable 'style of rattle':

It's a wonder to me we outlive the first month [what with] all the labours of the chase, all the riding, the trotting, the galloping, the leaping . . . being wet through over head and soused through under feet, and popped into ditches and jerked over gates . . . Well, it's all honour! That's my only comfort! Well, after all this, fagging away like mad from eight in the morning till five or six in the afternoon, home we come, looking like so many drowned rats, with not a dry thread about us, not a morsel within us – sore to the very bone, and forced to smile all the time! And then after all this what do you think follows? – 'Here, Goldsworthy,' cries His Majesty: so up I comes to him, bowing profoundly, and my hair dripping down to my shoes; 'Goldsworthy,' cries His Majesty. 'Sir,' says I, smiling agreeably, with the rheumatism just creeping all over me! but still, expecting something a little comfortable, I wait patiently to know his gracious pleasure, and then, 'Here, Goldsworthy, I say!' he cries, 'will you have a little barley water?' Barley water in such a plight as that! . . . barley water! I never heard of such a thing in my life! barley water after a whole hard day's hunting!

Fanny Burney was spared the rigours of hunting on a rainy winter's day, but she had to endure the fearful cold of the Windsor corridors. 'Wait till November and December and then you'll get a pretty taste . . . of the joys of this sort of life,' Goldsworthy had told her:

Running along in these cold passages [where] there's wind enough to carry a man of war . . . then bursting into rooms fit to bake you, then back again into all these agreeable puffs . . . and . . . [cold blasts] enough to blow you half a mile off . . . You'll be laid up as sure as fate! you may take my word for that. One thing, however, pray let me caution you about – don't go to early prayers in November; if you do, that will completely kill you!

The Princesses, Goldsworthy had said, got 'regularly knocked up' by the cold of the Chapel, to which the King seemed quite oblivious. 'First the Queen deserts us [then her poor daughters one by one], then all the poor attendants, my poor sister [the Princesses' Sub-Governess] at their head, drop off, one after another, like so many snuffs of candles, till at last, dwindle, dwindle, dwindle – not a soul goes to the Chapel but the King, the parson and myself; and there we three freeze it out together.'

25

'GROSS ABUSES IN THE EXPENDITURE OF PUBLIC MONEY'

Please, your Majesty, that will be setting thy nobles a good example.

On 8 February 1780 the Rev. Christopher Wyvill of Constable Burton Hall, Leyburn, the owner of large estates in that part of Yorkshire, had presented a petition to Parliament on behalf of the Yorkshire Association, of which he was Chairman. Among the petition's demands were a shortening of the duration of Parliaments, an inquiry into 'gross abuses in the expenditure of public money' and an end to 'sinecure places and unmerited pensions'. These demands and their implied criticism of royal finances were neither new nor isolated, and there had already been some success in abolishing various posts in the Royal Household, which at one time in the not far distant past had included not only the Master of the Great Wardrobe, the Master of the Revels and the Master of the Harness but also a Keeper of the Fire Buckets, a Groom of Confectionery and an Embellisher of Letters to the Eastern Princes. In debates in the House of Commons it had been and continued to be alleged by Edmund Burke and others that there was still gross incompetence in the management of public money, that much of this money was used for increasing the power of the Crown, and that, as the Member for Calne, a former Solicitor-General, John Dunning, proposed, 'the influence of the Crown has increased, is increasing and ought to be diminished . . . and it is competent to this House to examine into and correct abuses in the expenditure of the Civil List revenues'.

That there was inefficiency as well as extravagance at Court, and in the payment of pensions and grant of sinecures, could not well be denied.* The dozen Lords of the Bedchamber, whose attendance at Court was required for only one month in the year, all received £1,000 a year. Their assistants, the Grooms of the Bedchamber, also had £1,000 a year; so did the eight members of the Board of Green Cloth, an ancient institution with few remaining duties. The Master of Buckhounds, whose duties were also negligible, had £2,000; so had the Master of Foxhounds and the Master of Staghounds. The King's Librarian, Richard Dalton, whose duties were far more onerous, had £300 a year. Five thousand pounds a year was assigned to the Hanoverian Minister in London, whose salary and those of his staff were met by the King despite his declared lack of his grandfather's interest in the territory which the Minister represented. Salaries were still paid to the holders of obsolete offices; while valuable sinecures were given to men who employed ill-paid clerks to perform such duties as were required of them. Pensions were granted to large numbers of men and women whose past services to the Crown were all but forgotten.

Secret Service money was used for the purpose of providing pensions as well as for bribing foreign politicians and for the employment of such spies as Paul Wentworth, whose reports from Paris the King, who much disliked the whole concept of espionage, 'considered not only quite untrustworthy' but also 'hard labour to wade through'.

Politicians grumbled about both the secrecy of the Secret Service money and its supposedly inordinate cost; but in fact it was scarcely secret – the amounts spent were recorded in the books of the Treasury, and Samuel Johnson's pension was far from being the only

---

* There were estimated to be over a thousand appointees connected with the Royal Household (Porter, *English Society in the Eighteenth Century*, 129). Even so, this was a very small number compared with the 10,000 or so denizens of Versailles in the 1740s, 'an abundance of artists, actors, singers, scientists, huntsman, fencers, mistresses, cooks, courtiers and servants . . . thereby compelling fashionable society to revolve around the inclinations and pursuits of the monarch and enabling him to live free from dependence on his capital city. British court society was quite different. It was on a much smaller scale . . . and because it was situated amidst London's theatres, opera houses, pleasure gardens, clubs and the magnificent town houses of the aristocracy, the court was never the *only* focus for fashionable society' (Colley, *Britons*, 199–200).

one paid from Secret Service money and generally known to be so
– and it was also far from inordinate in cost: about £60,000 a year,
very little more than had been spent in the previous reign.

Indeed, a thorough investigation of royal finances would have
revealed no practices which had not been acceptable in earlier days.
When he came to the throne the King might well have asked for,
and would undoubtedly have been granted, the same Civil List of
£876,000 a year which had been allowed to King George II, who
had far less demanding claims upon his purse than his grandson, a
man with three brothers and two sisters to provide for, as well as
what might well prove to be, and did indeed turn out to be, a
large collection of children. King George III's father, however, had
undertaken not to accept more than £800,000 a year in the event
of his becoming King, and King George himself felt bound by Prince
Frederick's moderation. That was certainly not an extravagant sum,
since the Civil List was intended to meet all the expenses of government with the exception of those of the armed forces. The costs of
the Court and all its denizens had to come out of the Civil List, as
well as the salaries of civil servants, judges, ambassadors and Ministers
of the Crown and also pensions, annuities and occasional payments
to all manner of institutions and individuals, from the Chelsea Waterworks to the Bey of Algiers as an inducement for him not to
countenance piracy off the coasts of North Africa. The Civil List
had also to provide the income, set at £48,000 a year, later raised to
£60,000, for the King's private income, his Privy Purse.

This private income was augmented to a modest extent by revenues
from the King's farms and from the Duchy of Lancaster, a private
property of some 50,000 acres spread all over England which was
mostly acquired in the Middle Ages and yielded about £5,000 a
year. But even with these augmentations the Civil List was never
enough to meet all the demands made upon it; and, with inflation
rising, it became less so as year followed year. By 1769 the debt on
the List had risen to over £500,000, and an approach had to be made
to Parliament to settle it. Nine years later another approach had to
be made to Parliament, and a successful request was made to increase
the annual grant to £900,000.

★

Less widely known than the so-called secrets of the Secret Service were the range and munificence of the King's charity, which, according to Lady Charlotte Finch, was 'prodigious' and which Anthony Highmore, the legal writer and Secretary to the London Lying-in Hospital, described as 'unrivalled'.★ Praised by the philanthropist Sir Thomas Bernard, Treasurer of the Foundling Hospital, as a 'kindly parent' promoting 'the happiness of his subjects' through his benefactions, the King was criticized in the *London Chronicle* for not making it more widely known how much he gave to the poor.

Appearing in the King's accounts were such diverse beneficiaries as the boys at Christ's Hospital, the attendants at the boxes in the London theatres which he patronized, various parish churches whose bells rang on his birthday, the drummers of the regiments of Foot and Horse Guards, the widows and children of former servants, the man who cleaned the locks at Kensington Palace, the servants who brushed and powdered His Majesty's wigs, the Universities of Oxford and Cambridge for the services of preachers, St George's Hospital, the Society for Bettering the Condition and Increasing the Comforts of the Poor, the Royal Jennerian Society, the Hospital for Small Pox Inoculation, the Governors of the Foundling Hospital, King's College in New York, and three daughters of the widowed Lady Molesworth who had survived a fire in their house in Upper Brook Street in which their mother and nine other people perished.

The King concerned himself particularly with the education of the poor, maintaining that 'every poor child' in his dominions 'should be taught to read the Bible'. He invited to Windsor both Mrs Sarah Trimmer, author of *The Oeconomy of Charity*, and Robert Raikes, the promoter of Sunday schools; and he warmly encouraged the work of Joseph Lancaster, who, in order to promote cheap education for the poor, devised the 'Lancastrian' or 'monitorial' system by which older pupils were taught to instruct younger ones. The King promised him financial as well as moral support – an undertaking

---

★ Certainly, as Frank Prochaska has observed, no British monarch since his day has 'given away a greater proportion of his or her private income', a proportion which in today's money would be worth never less than some £850,000 a year and probably more (*Royal Bounty*, 12).

which drew forth a response from the Quaker Lancaster that was said to have caused His Majesty much amusement: 'Please, your Majesty, that will be setting thy nobles a good example.' Also received at Windsor was the prison reformer John Howard, upon whose death the King agreed to head a subscription for a statue of the great philanthropist, the first statue to be erected in St Paul's Cathedral.

While contributing generously to institutions, the King gave even more money away to needy individuals, both poor people whose plight he knew of personally, such as the children of destitute parents whom he had come across starving at Windsor, and those he learned about from others, like the family to whom he sent £200 with the assurance that, if he could but spend all his time in relieving want, he would 'with pleasure live to the age of Methuselah'.

The Queen was equally generous and equally conscientious, going so far as to give up the indulgence of a Sunday hairdresser after reading Hannah More's *Thoughts on the Importance of the Manners of the Great to General Society*. She contributed well over £5,000 a year to charities and poor individuals, to such institutions as the Bible Society, a Sunday school at Windsor founded on the advice of Mrs Trimmer, an establishment for distressed needlewomen at Brentford to which she contributed £25,000 over a period of fifty years, the Magdalen Hospital – a refuge for the 'Reception of Penitent Prostitutes' – and Mrs Wright's school of embroidery in Great Newport Street, where young girls from poor professional families were taught to earn a living from needlework. Often the Queen spent considerably more than she could afford, much to the concern of her advisers, who warned her against 'profuse liberality'. But her appeals to her husband to help her when her accounts were overdrawn in this way were not made in vain.

PART TWO

26

THE GORDON RIOTS

I am persuaded that the King does not know what fear is.

In the summer of the year before the surrender of the British army at Yorktown, the King had been called upon to play his part in the suppression of the most violent riots in London's history. The Wilkes riots in the 1760s had been followed in the late 1770s by riots occasioned by the court martial and acquittal of Admiral Lord Keppel, an outspoken Whig critic of the Government, on charges brought against him by an inferior officer, Vice-Admiral Sir Hugh Palliser, a supporter of the King's unpopular Administration. Hired, so the King believed, by rich young idlers and the kind of aristocratic ruffians known as Mohocks, and encouraged, according to Walpole, by Charles James Fox and his friends Lord Derby and the Duke of Ancaster, mobs broke into Palliser's house in Pall Mall, ransacked and plundered it, attacked the houses also of Lord George Germain and Lord North in Downing Street, and broke down Lord Sandwich's gates at the Admiralty, forcing Sandwich to flee with his mistress, Martha Ray, through the garden to the Horse Guards, where he 'betrayed most manifest panic'.

Men wearing Keppel cockades marched through the streets, demanding the windows of houses be illuminated in celebration of Keppel's acquittal, while so-called Keppel caps were worn by ladies at the theatre. The King had urged Lord North to take care when he went to the House, and offered him his own guard as protection. A few days later, when Keppel was an honoured guest in the City, Fox's windows, together with those of other members of the Opposition, were smashed, 'at the instigation', so Walpole alleged, of the Court.

Both the Keppel and the Wilkes riots were, however, quite mild affrays when compared with the riots which erupted in London in June 1780, ostensibly in protest against the Roman Catholic Relief Act of 1778.

For years Roman Catholics had been subject to restrictions so severe that the laws in which they were contained had been, by tacit agreement, largely ignored; and, as this was so, the repeal of these laws was not contemplated even by the more enlightened Members of a Protestant Parliament, nor was it expected or requested by the Catholics themselves. There was, however, one part of the anti-Catholic law which the Government itself found irksome, and this was a clause in a statute of William III which enforced upon anyone joining the Army the necessity of taking the attestation oath, and thereby swearing that he was a Protestant. There were, of course, Catholics in the Army, but they were enlisted as Protestants and treated as such; and, although when soldiers were badly needed it was customary for certain parts of the attestation oath to be omitted in an attempt to encourage Catholics to enlist, recruiting among Catholics was never very successful.

At the beginning of 1778, when the military operations in America were going badly and it had seemed likely that Spain and France would come into the war on the Americans' side, the Government had decided, with the King's approval, that an attempt must be made to persuade Catholics to join the colours. A profitable area for recruitment was Scotland, where suitable recruits might be found among the poor, hardy men of the Highlands.

A confidential agent was therefore sent to Scotland to inquire of leading Catholics there what hopes there were of men of their faith joining the Army if it were made easier for their consciences to do so, and what favours they would ask in return for their military service. The response to these inquiries was encouraging, so similar approaches were made to leading Catholics in England; and meetings were also arranged with leaders of the Opposition to discover what dissent there was likely to be in Parliament to a Catholic Relief Bill. Reassured that the opposition to it would be negligible and ineffective, since every good Whig could not but agree to uphold the traditional belief of his party in religious toleration, such a Bill was prepared. Accepted as a non-party measure, it passed into law with remarkable rapidity. On 15 May 1778 it was introduced into a poorly attended and not particularly interested House, and little more than a fortnight later it had passed its three readings in both Houses without a division. On 3 June it received the royal assent.

It was neither a generous nor a far-reaching measure. The Catholics were still, in most essential respects, outcasts; and so they were to remain until the Emancipation Act of 1829. It was believed that so limited and conditional a Bill could not possibly cause offence even to those for whom Roman Catholicism was England's most fearsome moral, social and political menace. Yet, as the international situation grew worse, and the most powerful and hated Catholic countries in Europe were once more England's enemies, it became easy again, as it had been in the past, to earn a cheap popularity by speaking out against English papists as untrustworthy representatives of a dangerous international conspiracy and members of a foreign and traitorous religion.

Wild and absurdly improbable stories began to circulate and to be believed. It was said that 20,000 Jesuits were hidden in a network of underground tunnels beneath the Surrey bank of the Thames and were waiting for orders from Rome to blow it up and thus flood London, and that a gang of Benedictine monks in Southwark, disguised as Irish chairmen, had poisoned all the flour in the Borough. For days many of the inhabitants would not touch any bread until it had been tested by a dog. It was even generally supposed, according to Samuel Romilly, at that time a young lawyer in Gray's Inn, that the 'King was a Papist. Some were sure of it; they pretended to know that he heard Mass privately, and that his confessor had the direction of all political concerns.' In a widely distributed print the tonsured King was shown in his private chapel, praying before a crucifix behind which hang portraits of Lord North and Bute. Lying on the floor of the adjoining privy are crumpled Protestant petitions.

Such petitions and pamphlets were issued in their hundreds by various Protestant Associations, spreading fear of 'the progress of that soul-deceiving and all-enslaving superstition, Popery'. The London Protestant Association prepared a petition which contained so many signatures that a strong man could scarcely lift on to his shoulder the enormous roll of parchment on which they were inscribed.

The President of this Association was Lord George Gordon, a younger son of the third Duke of Gordon and Member of Parliament for Ludgershall in Wiltshire, a vain, loquacious, ambitious agitator whose eccentricities verged on madness. For him popery was 'synonymous with arbitrary power', and therefore an enemy to the interests of the people, while the Catholic Relief Act was a most contemptible example of the 'hypocritical, underhand dealings of a despicable' Government which, behind a pretence of generosity and tolerance, was tricking men into fighting a shameful war against the noble American people.

As the son of a duke, he requested an audience of the King in order to express his views; and he presented himself at St James's for this purpose in the last week of January 1780. According to his own account of what took place, the King received him kindly enough – in spite of Lord George's impertinent request that 'some or all of his confidential counsellors', including Lord Bute and the Lord Chief Justice, Lord Mansfield, should be called into the room as witnesses of what passed between them. The express purpose of the interview was to deliver into the King's 'own hand the English appeal against the Popery Bill drawn up by the committee of the Protestant Association', which Lord North had refused to submit himself. Lord George asked if he might report to his committee that His Majesty had received the appeal 'very graciously', and the King 'approved of the expression "very graciously"'.

Horace Walpole's version of the audience was quite different. He had seen a malicious report in the *Morning Post*, an often unreliable newspaper, and his account of the meeting is based upon this. He wrote to the Countess of Upper Ossory, taking pleasure in making the most of a story which put Lord George, of whom he had a very low opinion, in an unfavourable light.

Lord George Gordon, he wrote,

asked an audience, was admitted, and incontinently began reading [a pamphlet], and the King had patience to hear him do so for above an hour, till it was so dark that the lecturer could not see. His Majesty then desired to be excused, and said he would finish the piece himself. 'Well!' said the lunatic apostle, 'But you must give me your honour that you will read it out.' The King promised but was forced to pledge his honour . . . It is to be hoped this man is so mad that it will soon come to perfection unless my plan is adopted of shutting up in Bedlam the few persons in this country that remain in their senses. It would be easier and much cheaper than to confine all the delirious.

The next time Lord George came for an audience the King mentioned this earlier meeting. 'Did you see the account that was given of your last audience in the papers?' he said, again according to Gordon's account. 'It's surprising what things they say! It hurt me exceedingly.' Lord George replied that he had heard of the report but, as he took only the *Public Advertiser*, he had not read it.

At a subsequent audience, on being conducted into the King's room, Lord George's first action was not merely to close the inner door as the lord-in-waiting shut the outer but to lock and bolt it behind him as well. He then advanced towards the King and immediately 'in solemn tones reminded him that the House of Stuart had been banished from the throne for encouraging Popery and arbitrary power; and requested him that he should order his Ministers to support the Protestant Religion', quoting extracts from a pamphlet by John Wesley, who had warned his congregations of the 'chains forging at the anvil of Rome for the rising generation'.

Startled by the direct and unceremonious approach of his long-haired, intense visitor, the King replied evasively that he had 'taken no part with the late Bill. Parliament did it.'

'Please recollect,' Lord George said sternly. 'You *have* taken a part and a very capital part too, by giving your royal assent to it.'

The King made no reply to this, nor to Lord George's subsequent assertion that the 'diabolical purpose' of the Relief Act was 'to arm the Roman Catholics for the American war and not from enlightenment'. But when Lord George went on to complain about the secret, underhand talks which the Government had instigated with the Scottish Catholics, the King denied that he had been 'privy to any secret transactions of that nature'. Then, evidently feeling that the undignified conversation had gone quite far enough, he assured Lord George that he was a Protestant, although in favour of toleration, and, changing the subject, asked after his family in Scotland.

Not to be deflected, Lord George briefly thanked His Majesty for the inquiry and hoped he would excuse him if he returned to the subject in hand: 'Will your Majesty, or will you not, direct your confidential servants to support the Petition?'

'I am in no way pledged in the business.'

'Does that mean you will not speak to Lord North?'

The King declined to answer this last question, and was obliged to bow low several times before Lord George accepted this dismissal and left him in peace. The next time the importunate and disrespectful young man called at St James's he was refused admittance. He returned to the Protestant Association convinced at last that no help could be expected from the 'ill-educated Elector of Hanover'.

On Friday 2 June a crowd estimated as being over 50,000 strong and organized by the London Protestant Association gathered in St George's Fields for a march to Parliament with their petition against the recent Roman Catholic legislation. The demonstration, orderly at first, was soon quite out of hand. Following the burning of Roman Catholic chapels and the destruction of prisons, distilleries were attacked as well as the houses of men who had made themselves unpopular with the mob and whole areas occupied by Irish workmen. At the height of the rioting, Lord George Gordon – concerned that the demonstration which he had planned had been taken over by hundreds of troublemakers, criminals and looters who had adopted his supporters' 'No Popery!' cry – called at the Queen's House to offer his services to the King. Lord Stormont, the Secretary of State, who was there that morning, described how 'a page came and scratched at the door' and said that Lord George Gordon was outside and wished to see the King. Lord Stormont told the page to see that Lord George was shown into a room in the colonnade, and there he joined him. 'What do you want?' Lord Stormont asked.

His answer to me [Stormont reported] was that 'he desired to see the King because he could be of essential or material service or do great service in suppressing the riots'. I went with the message to the King whose answer was 'It is impossible for the King to see Lord George Gordon until he has given sufficient proofs of his allegiance by employing those means which he says he has in his power to quell the disturbances and restore peace to the capital.' To that Lord George Gordon answered that 'if he might presume to reply he would say that his best endeavours would be used'.

The time had long since passed, however, when the rioters were prepared to listen to reason. A firm stand against them was essential, as the King had already written to Lord North on Monday morning:

I think it right to acquaint Lord North that I have taken every step that could occur to me to prevent any tumult tomorrow, and have seen that proper executive orders have been sent to the two Secretaries of State. I trust Parliament will take such measures as the necessities of the time require. This tumult must be got the better of or it will encourage designing men to use it as a precedent for assembling the people on other occasions; if possible, we must get to the bottom of it and examples must be made. If anything occurs to Lord North wherein I can give any farther assistance, I shall be ready to forward it, for my attachment is to the laws and security of my country, and to the protection of the lives and properties of all my subjects.

Having arranged for the Members to get to the House in a more dignified way than had been possible on Friday, the King was annoyed by their apparently forbearing attitude when they had arrived there.

Lord North cannot be much surprised [he wrote that evening] at my not thinking the House of Commons have this day advanced so far in the present business as the exigency of the time requires; the allowing Lord Geo. Gordon, the avowed head of the tumult, to be at large certainly encourages the continuation of it; to which is to be added the great supineness of the civil magistrates; and I fear without more vigour that this will not subside; indeed, unless exemplary punishment is procured, it will remain a lasting disgrace and will be a precedent for future commotions.

There was something at least that the King could do on his own authority without reference to Parliament. From Tuesday onwards there appeared in the press a Royal Proclamation offering a reward of £500 and a 'pardon if necessary' to anyone who would 'discover any other person or persons who, directly or indirectly, were concerned in pulling down . . . the chapel of any Foreign Minister so as that person or persons may be prosecuted for the same'. But by noon on Wednesday not a single informer had come forward to take advantage of this offer, and it was clear that some more drastic measures would have to be adopted. During the morning, threatening messages had been delivered not only at the houses of numerous Catholics who had so far escaped the attention of the mob but also at the houses of almost all the leading members of the Government, warning them of destruction that night.

The Commander-in-Chief, Lord Amherst, was receiving frantic messages every minute; but, with so many regiments in America, he found it impossible to accede to every request for protection; and, even when he was able to send troops to a danger spot, the officers in charge could find on arrival no magistrate prepared to give them any orders. The Commander-in-Chief was naturally enraged by this utter collapse of the civil authority. 'It is the duty of the troops, my Lord,' he explained in an angry letter to Lord Stormont, 'to act only under the authority and by direction of the Civil Magistrate.'

After the troops had marched to the places appointed for them [he went on to complain], several of the magistrates refused to act . . . I leave it to your Lordship to judge in how defenceless and how disgraceful a situation the military are left, and how much such conduct as this tends even to encourage Riots, and how much the public service as well as the troops must suffer by it.

Well aware of the dilemma in which the troops were placed by what he had referred to as the 'great supineness of the civil magistrates', the King was determined to do something to help them. 'There shall be one that I can answer for, that will do his duty,' he told a meeting of the Privy Council on Wednesday, and he threatened to head the Guards himself if the military authorities were not given more extensive powers. Undoubtedly he would have had the courage to do it. 'I am persuaded,' a captain in the Horse Guards whose duties brought him into close touch with the Royal Family told Frederic Reynolds, the schoolboy son of John Wilkes's affluent solicitor, 'that the King does not know what fear is.'

It was generally held at that time that troops had no legal right to open fire on a lawless mob without specific instructions to do so, even after the Riot Act had been read. This belief rested upon the much quoted opinions of Lord Hardwicke, one of the most respected Lord Chancellors of the eighteenth century, and of Lord Raymond, another great and earlier legal authority. Yet this was not, it subsequently transpired, the interpretation put upon the law by the Lord

Chief Justice, Lord Mansfield; and the Archbishop of York, no doubt having discussed the matter with Mansfield, who lived next door to him in Bloomsbury Square, expressed the opinion in a letter to his son that the respect accorded to Lord Hardwicke's opinion was a 'fatal error' – an observation no doubt prompted by the recent horrifying sight of a gang of prisoners who had escaped from Newgate, raging drunk, surging through Bloomsbury Square, shouting their intention of roasting His Grace alive.

'Fatal error' or not, it was undoubtedly the opinion that 'prevailed among the military', and the King insisted upon a new reading of the law at that meeting of the Privy Council which had urgently been convened on Wednesday. The Councillors were mostly in disagreement with the King; only the elderly Lord Bathurst, Lord President of the Council, and one or two others supported him. The Council was about to break up in irritable uncertainty when, very late, Alexander Wedderburn, the Attorney-General, arrived. Immediately the King asked him to give his opinion as to whether officers could use their own discretion in ordering their men to fire upon rioters. Wedderburn said that he thought they could. 'Is that your declaration of the law as Attorney-General?' the King asked him. 'Yes,' replied Wedderburn. 'Then,' said the King, standing up and dismissing the Councillors, 'so let it be done.' A few hours later a Royal Proclamation giving effect to Wedderburn's declaration was issued.

This was not a declaration of martial law in the strictest sense of the term, but it was interpreted as such by the Commander-in-Chief, who issued an order to all officers in London from the Adjutant-General's Office on the morning of 7 June:

In obedience to an order of the King in Council the military to act without waiting for direction from the Civil Magistrates and to use force for dispersing the illegal and tumultuous assemblies of the people.

The civil authorities, however, were not prepared to accept this overruling of their authority; and at a meeting of the Common City Council held in the Chamber of Guildhall a resolution was put 'that this Court doth agree to petition the Honourable the House of Commons against the Act of Parliament lately passed in favour of Roman Catholics'. In spite of the horrors and devastation of the preceding days and nights and the threats of more destruction and murder to come, this resolution was passed unanimously.

Among those who, through either fear or the hope of advantage, had done nothing and intended to do nothing to suppress the riots were the Lord Mayor, a wine merchant and former waiter in a brothel, who excused his refusal to countenance the use of troops by saying he must be cautious what he did lest he bring the mob to his own house, Alderman Frederick Bull, a rich tea merchant, the constables in whose ward wore blue cockades as an emblem of solidarity with the demonstrators, and a marshalman who stood idly by when a mob was setting fire to a Roman Catholic chapel, commenting that he would 'not go to protect any Popish rascals'. There were those among the aldermen, however, who felt compelled to dissociate themselves from their colleagues and to do what they could to suppress the rioting which had already cost so many lives.

One of these who, realizing what further inaction would mean, made up their minds to support the King in his firm stand was Alderman John Wilkes, now the City Chamberlain and a man firmly opposed to religious bigotry. He talked the unwilling Lord Mayor into a promise to call out a *posse comitatus* to quell the rioting; and he himself went back to his ward to form a force which he could put, with himself at its head, under the officer in command of the troops in the City.

There was another night of appalling violence in which many more lives were lost and many other buildings destroyed; but by the morning of Friday 9 June the troops and the militia had quelled the disturbances and, as William Pitt assured his anxious mother, everything seemed likely to subside. And so it did. Encouraged by the display of military power, their fears dispelled by what the *Public Advertiser* termed the 'silence, decency and tranquility of the streets', more and more people came forward with offers to form bands under the leadership of army officers to protect themselves and their neighbours from 'a renewal of the mischiefs so recently experienced from a lawless and licentious Banditti'. An estimated 850 people had lost their lives. Lord George Gordon was arrested and accused of high treason. He was acquitted, but twenty-one ringleaders were found guilty and hanged.

Commenting on the King's firm stand at the Privy Council meeting on Wednesday 7 June, Sir Nathaniel Wraxall wrote, 'Never had any people a greater obligation to the judicious Intrepidity of their Sovereign!'

27

ATTEMPTED MURDER

The poor creature is mad. Do not harm her. She has not hurt me.

The courage which the King had displayed at the time of the Gordon Riots was also evident when attempts were later made on his life. The first of these occurred on 2 August 1786, when he was alighting from his coach at the garden front of St James's Palace to attend a levee. A woman named Margaret Nicholson, a domestic servant, approached him, holding out a sheet of paper which he assumed to be a petition. As he took the paper from her she suddenly produced a knife and with it lunged at his chest. The blade of the knife was weak, however, and the blow clumsy. The King was unharmed, and his linen waistcoat scarcely cut; the woman was seized and roughly handled. 'The poor creature is mad,' the King protested. 'Do not hurt her. She has not hurt me.'

When the woman had been taken away, he walked through the garden into the Palace, giving instructions that no one should tell the Queen what had happened until the levee was over and he had returned to Windsor to show himself to her unharmed.

Upon entering the Queen's dressing-room at Windsor, where she was with their two eldest daughters, he called out, 'Here I am, safe and well!' He then told them what had happened. 'The Queen stood struck and motionless for some time, till the Princesses burst into tears, on which she immediately found relief herself.'

The King himself, however, 'still maintained the most cheerful composure', Fanny Burney recorded, and he insisted upon walking on the Terrace with no other attendant than his single equerry.

The poor Queen went with him pale and silent [Miss Burney continued], – the Princesses followed, scarce yet commanding their tears. In the evening, just as usual, the King had his concert: but it was an evening of grief and horror to his family: nothing was listened to, scarce a word was spoken; the Princesses wept continually; the Queen, still more deeply struck, could only, from time to time, hold out her hand to the King, and say, 'I have you yet!'

The affection for the King felt by all his household has been at once pleasant and affecting to me to observe: there has not been a dry eye in either of the Lodges, on the recital of his danger, and not a face but his own that has not worn marks of care ever since.

A few days later the Royal Family left Windsor for Kew, where the Green was 'quite filled with all the inhabitants of the place – the lame, old, blind, sick, and infants, who all assembled, dressed in their Sunday garb, to line the sides of the roads through which their Majesties passed, attended by the band of musicians, arranged in the front, who began "God save the King!" the moment they came upon the Green, and finished it with loud huzzas . . . The Queen, in speaking of it afterwards, said, "I shall always love little Kew for this!"'

The King was in far greater danger in the autumn of 1795, a year in which he said more than once to Lord Eldon, the Attorney-General, that he thought it 'not improbable that he should be the last King of England'. On 29 October, when driving in the state coach to open Parliament, the King was surrounded by a surly, menacing mob, shouting in that year of want and high prices, 'Peace and Bread! No war! No war! Down with George!' Lord Onslow, a Lord of the Bedchamber, who was among those with the King, recalled:

The multitude of people in the Park was prodigious. A sullen silence prevailed . . . no hats, or at least very few pulled off; little or no huzzaing, and frequently a cry of 'give us bread': 'no war' and once or twice, 'no King', with hissing and groaning . . . Nothing material, however, happened till we got down to the narrowest part of the street called St Margaret's [where] a small ball, either of lead or marble, passed through the window glass on the King's right hand and, perforating it, passed through the coach out of the other door, the glass of which was down. We all instantly exclaimed, 'This is a shot!'

The King showed, and I am persuaded felt no alarm; much less did he fear, to which indeed he is insensible.

'Sit still, my Lord,' he rebuked one of his companions who was fidgetting in alarm. 'We must not betray fear whatever happens.'

In the House of Lords the King 'ascended the stairs, robed, and then, perfectly free from the smallest agitation, read his speech with peculiar correctness, and even less hesitation than usual'. Afterwards, while the King was disrobing, the shot or stone which had passed through his carriage was the 'only topic of conversation, in which the King joined with much less agitation than anyone else; and afterwards, in getting into the coach, the first words he said were, "Well, my Lords, one person is *proposing* this, and another is *supposing* that, forgetting that there is One above us all who *disposes* of everything and on whom alone we depend." '

On the return journey to St James's the crowds surrounding the coach were even greater than before.

It was said that not less than 100,000 people were there [Lord Onslow continued his account], all of the worst and lowest sort . . . and the insulting abuse offered to His Majesty was what I can never think of but with horror . . . They proceeded to throw stones into the coach [breaking all the glass]. Several stones hit the King, which he bore with signal patience, but not without sensible marks of indignation and resentment at the indignities offered to his person and office . . . The King took one of the stones out of the cuff of his coat, where it had lodged, and gave it to me saying, 'I make you a present of this, as a mark of the civilities we have met with on our journey today.'

At a critical moment during this assault on the coach, when the guards surrounding it were in danger of being overwhelmed by the press of the demonstrators, a man sprang forward in front of the coach door, threatening to kill anyone who approached any nearer. The King afterwards made inquiries as to who this gentleman was, and, having been informed that it was a Mr Bedingfield, he instructed one of his Ministers to find the man 'an appointment of some profit'. When he was asked what could be done for him, Bedingfield facetiously replied that the best thing that could be done for him was to make him a Scotchman. So nothing was done until the King, upon inquiring what had become of Mr Bedingfield and being told that no suitable situation was vacant, replied that in that case a situation must be created for him. This was done; and Bedingfield found himself in possession of an office worth £650 a year.

Five years later the King's life was again threatened when, at a review of the 1st Foot Guards in Hyde Park, a bullet struck a clerk in the Navy Office who was standing close to the King. 'When it was proposed to send the Princesses away, he said, "I will not have one of them stir for the world."' That same evening at the packed Theatre Royal, Drury Lane, before a performance of Colley Cibber's comedy *She Would and She Would Not*, a man in the pit fired a pistol at him. 'Do not come forward,' he said turning round to reassure the Queen. 'It's only a squib. We will not stir. We'll stay the entertainment out.' Ignoring the advice of Sheridan, the manager of the theatre, to leave his box in case another shot were to be fired, the King peered calmly round the house through his opera glass.

When he came forward to show the audience he had not been hurt '*les Cris de joie de* God Save the King' filled the air, so the Queen told her brother. The cheering at length gave way to angry demands for the punishment of the would-be assassin, until an actress came on to the stage to announce, 'I have the pleasure to tell you the man is in custody.'

Never shall I forget His Majesty's coolness [wrote Michael Kelly, the Irish actor who was the theatre's musical director and was on stage at the time], – the whole audience was in uproar. The King, on hearing the report of the pistol, retired a pace or two, stopped, and stood firmly for an instant; then came forward to the very front of the box, put his opera-glass to his eye, and looked round the house, without the smallest appearance of alarm or discomposure.

So calm was he, indeed, that he followed his usual practice of having a short doze at the end of the play and before the beginning of the farce that followed it, then listened complacently to the verse which, on the spur of the moment, Sheridan had composed as an addendum to 'God Save the King.'

> From every latent foe,
> From the assassin's blow,
>   God save the King.
> O'er him Thine arm extend,
> For Britain's sake defend
> Our father, prince and friend,
>   God save the King.

Gratified by the thunderous applause that greeted this loyal addition to verses which had become popular at the time of the 1745 Jacobite rebellion as a tribute to his grandfather, the King drove home, where, before going to bed, he said that he had no doubt he would sleep as soundly as usual and expressed the hope that the same could be said for the madman, James Hadfield, a former soldier, who had fired the shot in the theatre. Nor did he lose any sleep over the later discovery of a wild plot to assassinate him formulated by an unbalanced Irish soldier, Colonel Edward Despard, who planned to blow him apart with cannonshot on his way to open Parliament. 'The King's composure on hearing of Despard's horrid designs was remarkable,' commented Lord Malmesbury, 'and evinces a strength of mind, and tranquility of conscience, that prove him to be the best of men.'

28

KING GEORGE VERSUS MR FOX

*It is intolerable that it should be in the power
of one block-head to do so much mischief.*

Few supposed that the Whig Administration which was formed on the resignation of Lord North in March 1782 would last long. Certainly it was not harmonious. At its head was the Marquess of Rockingham as First Lord of the Treasury; and Rockingham's political associate Charles James Fox was Foreign Secretary. Warily suspicious of them both, and having as little as possible to do with either, was the coldly reserved Secretary of State for Home and Colonial Affairs, the Earl of Shelburne, who, much to their annoyance, endeavoured to make himself as agreeable as possible to the King.

The King was thoroughly dissatisfied with all three of them, and with their colleagues, intensely annoyed by their attempts to diminish his influence and limit his rights of patronage. The persistent endeavours of the Paymaster, Edmund Burke – in Fox's later opinion 'a most unmanageable colleague' – to reform the Civil List not only aroused the indignation of the King but were also so hastily and ill considered that, after Burke's resignation, Shelburne was driven to complain about the amount of time he had to spend upon unravelling the problems caused by 'the nonsense' of Burke's Bill. Attempts at parliamentary reform were scarcely less ill-managed; while the conduct of the final stages of the war and the opening gambits of the peace negotiations were overseen by men who were far from agreeing upon the ends to be pursued and who, when in rare agreement upon the means to those ends, almost invariably took what the King considered to be the wrong decision – as, for instance, when, for political reasons, it was decided to recall Admiral Rodney.

'As it is the unanimous recommendation of the Cabinet,' the King wrote on that occasion, 'I shall not object to it; but I hope Lord Keppel [First Lord of the Admiralty] has a proper Admiral in his eye to succeed him.'

It was still the King's opinion that the war could yet be won: France was nearing the end of her financial resources; the Dutch, who had entered the war on France's side, had lost St Eustatius in the Leeward Islands; a British garrison was still holding out in Gibraltar, which had been besieged since 1779; and on 12 April 1782 in the Battle of the Saints, off Dominica, an engagement which ended French threats to British possessions in the West Indies, Admiral Rodney had captured or destroyed seven enemy ships and inflicted 3,000 casualties in a notable victory, the news of which had not reached London at the time of his recall.

While the war dragged on, so did the peace negotiations, which were still in uncertain progress when on 1 July the Marquess of Rockingham died in the influenza epidemic which claimed many other lives in England and on the Continent that year.

Fox pressed for the appointment of the Duke of Portland as Rockingham's successor, knowing that, with the Duke at the Treasury, he himself would be the effective leader of the Government. The King responded to this suggestion by promptly nominating Lord Shelburne as First Lord of the Treasury even though he had never much liked him. Fox, who also much disliked Shelburne, as promptly responded to this appointment by resigning – much to the King's relief, since, as he pointed out to Lord North, the man was aiming at the 'sole direction' of his kingdom. Besides, the contest between the two of them was 'becoming personal'; and Fox himself also saw the contest 'in that point of view'. It was not only a contest of political power: there was deep personal animosity, too.

As obsessive in his dislikes as in his attachments, the King could never bring himself to disregard the fact that Charles James Fox was the son of Henry Fox – the favourite son, whose childhood had been one prolonged indulgence, a child permitted to paddle in an enormous bowl of cream beneath the dining-room table and to urinate on a joint of meat being prepared for that table in the kitchen. The King constantly recalled Henry Fox's unscrupulous jobbery, his bad character, his attempts to have Lady Sarah Lennox installed as a royal mistress, his having secretly married the Duke of Richmond's daughter without her parents' consent. It was with marked reluctance that the King had agreed to Henry Fox being raised to the peerage, as Baron Holland of Foxley, Wiltshire; and he had declined to approve his elevation to the earldom after which he had long hankered and which had been granted to the elder William Pitt. Lord Holland's resentment and dislike was passed on to his son. The King's reciprocal dislike was plain for all to see: at a levee in March 1782 Fox presented to him an address from Westminster. 'The King took it out of Fox's hand without deigning to give him a look even, or a word; he took it as you would take a pocket-handkerchief from your *valet-de-chambre*, without any mark of displeasure or attention, or expression of countenance whatever, and passed it to his Lord-in-waiting.'

Charles James Fox was a hard-drinking gambler who had been known to play hazard at Almack's for more than twenty-four hours at a stretch. In one night he and his brother were said to have lost £32,000 between them. He was consequently almost constantly in debt for almost the whole of his life.

Paunchy, untidy, clumsy, with a swarthy skin and black, shaggy eyebrows, he was a man of extraordinary charm, self-confidence and good temper. His smile was delightful, his intellect extraordinarily acute, his conversation so entrancing and diverting that Georgiana, Duchess of Devonshire, said it was 'like a brilliant player at billiards, the strokes follow one another piff puff'. He may have been selfish and, as George Selwyn said, have had 'no feeling for anyone but himself'; he was undoubtedly slovenly, and seemed to take pride in being so, in appearing in a grubby frock-coat of buff and blue, the colours of Washington's army; his friends pretended not to mind or even not to notice when he hawked and spat on the carpet. But, as Selwyn observed, 'he had no malice or rancour'. His open-hearted good nature was not, however, apparent when talking about the King. Indeed, he and his friends were 'strangely licentious in their conversations about his Majesty' in his lodgings in St James's Street, where, unwashed and unshaven, he received his morning visitors to discuss the topics of the day. He referred to the King as Satan, and spoke openly of his wish that he should die soon. 'It is intolerable,' he once wrote, 'that it should be in the power of one block-head to do so much mischief.'

The King knew only too well how Fox felt about him and how virulently he reviled him; and he disliked him quite as much in return. 'That young man,' he once declared, 'has thoroughly cast off every principle of common honour and honesty.' When the 'odious' and 'contemptible' reprobate had come to kiss hands on his appointment to Rockingham's Cabinet it had been noticed that His Majesty put back his ears like a horse bent on throwing its rider.

Thankful as he was when Fox resigned on Shelburne's appointment as First Lord of the Treasury, the King could not comfort himself with the thought that he would be spared from having to deal with the detested man for long; for Shelburne's Administration appeared so shaky that it was likely to last no longer than Rockingham's, and, if Shelburne were to resign, Fox would then once more be seen as a leading contender for high office. So, indeed, would Lord North; but this was little consolation to the King, since relations between him and North were far from as friendly as they had been in the past. North had not responded as the King would have liked to a request that he should come forward in the Commons to support Shelburne and help to keep the 'constitution from being entirely annihilated which must be the case if Mr Fox and his associates [were] not withstood'. Also, there had been a bitter dispute about payments out of the Secret Service accounts, which North, while never suspected of dishonesty, had kept most carelessly. A large sum had been borrowed in 1780 from Drummond's Bank in North's name, and on the King's authority, and had never been repaid. North, who had failed to notify the King of the amount of money due, proposed that the outstanding debt should be paid out of the Privy Purse. The King, however, insisted that North must himself repay the bank the sum due, which North was unable to do. 'It was not owing to inaccuracy in me,' the King wrote to Henry Drummond, explaining why the money had not been paid before, adding with great injustice, 'but the most bare-faced fraud on the part of Lord North.'

When he wrote this letter, in February 1783, the King was in an aggrieved and bitter mood because Lord North had come to an agreement with Fox to combine their influence in the Commons to push Shelburne out of office and to form a coalition government themselves.

The King's reaction to this coalition was predictable. After Shelburne's expected defeat and resignation, he wrote, 'I am sorry it has been my lot to reign in the most profligate age and when the most unnatural and factious coalition seems to have taken place.' He talked as he had done before and was to do again of abdication and retirement to Hanover, and he went so far as to prepare a speech to be given in the Lords announcing it, as well as a letter setting out the reasons for it to the Prince of Wales.

On reflection, however, he accepted the fact – again as he had done in the past – that his personal feelings must be subjected to the welfare of the country; and accordingly he felt obliged to agree to Fox's return to office in April 1783 as Secretary of State for Foreign Affairs, and to Lord North's appointment as Secretary for Home and Colonial Affairs, with the Duke of Portland as nominal leader of the Administration. He had struggled long to resist Fox's determination that he should have no say in the choice of his Ministers, and he had done his best to persuade other men to form an administration instead; but eventually he had had to submit to Fox's demands and to the establishment of an unnatural coalition which North was soon to regret: it made him, so North told his father, 'perfectly miserable'. Fox also had cause to deplore an alliance that damaged his reputation and gave people reason to believe that the King's distrust of him might be justified.

Fox began his conduct of affairs by writing a conciliatory letter to the King, assuring him that he and the Duke of Portland had nothing so much at heart as to conduct His Majesty's affairs in the manner that would give him the most satisfaction. 'It will be the study of Your Majesty's Ministers,' Fox added, 'to show how truly sensible they are of Your Majesty's goodness.' The King did not answer the letter, preferring to wait to see how Fox would behave in office. All that had occurred in the past weeks had tended to increase his dislike and distrust of the man; and it was all the more galling for the King, and all the more a cause of his intense dislike, that one of Fox's most dissipated intimates and warmest admirers was the Prince of Wales, now approaching his twenty-first birthday and the time when a larger establishment and income would have to be provided for him.

29

THE PROFLIGATE HEIR

The Prince of Wales on the smallest reflection must feel
that I have little reason to approve of any part of his conduct
for the last three years.

Accomplished and attractive, the Prince of Wales was generally agreed to be a handsome young man of taste and discernment and a good deal of vanity. He himself admitted that he was 'rather too familiar to his inferiors . . . too subject to be in a passion . . . rather too fond of wine and women'. To this modest list of weaknesses his father would have added many others, including his thoughtless extravagance, his capricious waywardness, his lack of a strict regard for truth, his neglect of his religious duties, and his fondness for profligate characters of both sexes. For, accomplished as his eldest son was admitted to be, charming as could be his manners and entertaining his conversation, in the eyes of his father the Prince's gifts were not such as to compensate for the many faults to be found in him.

Among the worst of these faults, in the King's opinion, was the Prince's notorious philandering. At the age of sixteen he was supposed to have seduced one of the Queen's maids of honour; he had then fallen in love with one of his sisters' attendants, whom he adored 'beyond the idea of anything that is human'. After this he had a passionate affair with the exhibitionist actress Mary Robinson, for whom £5,000 and annuities for herself and her daughter had to be found when the Prince grew tired of her and she was passed on to Charles James Fox, who later took over another of the Prince's discarded mistresses, Elizabeth Bridget Armistead, a delightful woman of unknown provenance but strong cockney pronunciation. After his affair with Mary Robinson, the Prince became entangled with

Grace Dalrymple Elliott, whose illegitimate daughter may well have been his, then with several other women, nearly all of them older than himself, one of them, with whom he contemplated flying abroad, the wife of a Hanoverian diplomat.

The King heard reports of these sexual escapades and the Prince's extravagance and drunken debauches with increasing concern. He wrote to him to say that he had hoped that the payment of £5,000 on his behalf to rid him of Mrs Robinson might have persuaded him thereafter 'to act in a manner worthy of approbation'; yet whenever he opened a newspaper of a morning it was 'almost certain that some unpleasant mention' of his eldest son and heir would be found in it. 'Draw your own conclusion,' he said, 'whether you must not give me many an uneasy moment. I wish to live with you as a friend, but then by your behaviour you must deserve it. If I did not state these things I should not fulfil my duty either to my God or to my country . . . When you read this carefully over, you will find an affectionate father trying to save his son from perdition.'

The Prince's brother, their father's favourite son, Frederick, Duke of York, who had been sent out to Hanover to improve his German and to complete his military education, urged him to listen to their father's advice and to try to be 'upon as good a footing as possible' with him:

for really it is of so much consequence to yourself that it appears to me quite ridiculous that you do not at least attempt [it] . . . For God's sake do everything that you can to keep well with him, at least upon decent terms; consider he is vexed enough in publick affairs. It is therefore your business not to make that still worse . . . For both your sakes I entreat you to keep as well together as possible. I know you will. Excuse what I write to you because it comes from the heart.

But the Prince of Wales could not bring himself to follow his brother's advice. He continued to miss levees and church services, to drink far too much, to enjoy the company of most unsuitable companions. It was as though their parents' dull domestic way of living, and their constant criticism of his extravagance, incited him to further dissipation and expenditure, just as their father's faithfulness to a physically unappealing wife made it all the harder for the King to bear the Prince's shamefully licentious behaviour with a succession of attractive and amusing women.

The Prince never tired of grumbling about his father's attitude towards him. The King was always so 'excessively cross, ill-tempered and uncommonly grumpy', as well as 'stingy'. The Queen was really quite as bad. She said that she criticized his conduct and accused him 'of various high crimes and misdemeanours' upon her own initiative; but the Prince felt sure, from 'the language she used and the style she spoke in', that the King was behind it all. Indeed, the 'unkind behaviour' of both of them was 'hardly bearable'.

He complained of being kept on 'so tight a rein'; and, to be sure, even after he had been granted his own modest establishment soon after his eighteenth birthday, on 12 August 1780, his father attempted to exercise a strict control over him, still requiring him to live under the same roof as his parents at Buckingham House and in apartments along the east front of Windsor Castle.

As you may be desirous of dining with some of your attendants [the King had written to him in a long letter informing him of the arrangements which had been made for him in 'this middle state between manhood and childhood'], I shall consent when I am in town that you may have a dinner in your apartment on Sundays and Thursdays, but I cannot afford it oftener . . . You may very naturally chuse to go oftener to plays and operas than I may. I shall not object to it when I am in town, provided you give me previous notice that we may not expect you in the evening, but then you must go in your box attended by your regular attendants, as all Princes of Wales have heretofore done. Whenever you are desirous of dancing, on an intimation to the Queen or me, we shall very readily forward it, and shall have no other wish on such occasions but to make the Ball agreeable to you; but I shall not permit the going to balls or assemblies at private houses, which never has been the custom for Princes of Wales. As to masquerades, you already know my disapprobation of them in this country, and I cannot by any means agree to any of my children ever going to them. Of course you will come every Sunday to church and to the Drawing Room at St James's when I appear there, as also at the Thursday Drawing Room. When I ride out of a morning I shall ever expect you to accompany me. On other days I shall not object to your doing it also, provided it is for exercise, not lounging about Hyde Park. Whenever you ride out or go in a carriage, one of your attendants must accompany you . . . Be but open with me and you will ever find me desirous of making you as happy as I can, but I must not forget, nor must you, that in the exalted station you are placed in, every step is of consequence, and that your future character will greatly depend in the world on the propriety of your conduct at the present period . . . I can reason more coolly on paper than in conversation, but should you at any time wish to talk on any subject, you will never find me unwilling to enter into it. Indeed, I wish more and more to have you as a friend and in that light to guide you, rather than with the authority of a parent . . .

The King 'wished to be accommodating' in the matter of the Prince's new residence. There was, unfortunately, no country house available, so the King informed Colonel George Hotham, the Treasurer of the Prince's Household; but such a house was not really necessary, since the apartments at Windsor would 'always be kept ready to receive him'. As for a London house, His Majesty was willing to grant him the use of Carlton House, the house which the Prince's grandmother, the Princess Dowager of Wales, had inhabited on the southern side of Pall Mall, provided he became responsible for 'all repairs, taxes and the keeping of the garden'.

The King's specific proviso about the garden was understandable, for, laid out by William Kent, it was both extensive and beautiful. The house, however, was unremarkable; but the Prince had plans to enlarge it and, with the help of the architect Henry Holland, to make it as grandly imposing as possible. He was now able to afford to do so, since, after lengthy and at times acrimonious discussions, he had been granted a handsome income in anticipation of his twenty-first birthday.

The figure at first suggested by the Cabinet was £100,000 a year. This figure, which would have to come out of the Civil List, horrified the King. It was the sum granted to his grandfather, who had had a wife and nine children to support. The weight of taxes which the people of the country laboured under made it wholly unreasonable. The King wrote to Colonel Hotham to say that he did not think it advisable to apply to Parliament for more than £50,000. This, with the revenues of the Duchy of Cornwall, which amounted to about £12,000 a year, would make the Prince's income about £27,000 more than he himself had received in a similar situation.

The Prince's behaviour, in the King's opinion, did not warrant even this generosity. His womanizing was notorious, but it had proved less difficult to disentangle the Prince from the arms of designing mistresses than to separate him from undesirable male companions such as Anthony St Leger, with whom he had dashed up to Northamptonshire to hunt, absenting himself without permission from one of His Majesty's levees. When the King had insisted upon 'the like not being done again', the Prince had replied that, although his conduct in the world was admittedly 'in great measure different from the limited plan' drawn up for him, he flattered himself that his behaviour, far from deserving censure, 'merited the strictest approbation'. In fact he ignored his father's reprimand and went on behaving as before.

The King's letter to Colonel Hotham ended on a sadly familiar note:

The Prince of Wales on the smallest reflection must feel that I have little reason to approve of any part of his conduct for the last three years; his neglect of every religious duty is notorious; his want of common civility to the Queen and me, not less so; besides his total disobedience of every injunction I had given and which he, in presence of his brother and the gentlemen then about them both, declared himself contented with. I must hope he will now think it behoves him to take up a fresh line of conduct more worthy of his station.

The King wrote also to the First Lord of the Treasury, protesting at the outrageous idea of granting the Prince £100,000 while he remained unmarried. It was 'a shameful squandering of public money, besides an encouragement of extravagance'. It was 'impossible for the King to find words expressive enough' of his 'utter indignation and astonishment'. When the Duke of Portland had come into office His Majesty 'had at least hoped he would have thought himself obliged to have [the King's] interest and that of the public at heart and not have neglected both, to gratify the passions of an ill-advised young man'. Fifty thousand pounds and the revenues of the Duchy of Cornwall were quite sufficient.

As the letters flew backwards and forwards between Downing Street and Windsor in the summer of 1783 and there seemed no hope of a settlement being reached, Fox thought that the dispute would bring down the Government. But at length the King suddenly relented. He sent for the Duke of Portland, regretted that he had gone too far, and broke down in tears, confessing that the 'unfortunate event of the American war' had 'soured and ruined' his temper. Portland called upon Fox, who had written to assure the Prince that he thought himself 'bound by every principle of honour as well of gratitude to take whatever part' His Royal Highness chose to prescribe to him 'in this business'.

Fox went to see the Prince and persuaded him, for the sake of peace within the Royal Family, to accept £50,000 and the Duchy of Cornwall income, provided that he also received from Parliament a capital sum of £60,000, about half of which was to be set aside to settle the Prince's debts.

Thankful that he was thus enabled to get his hands on a decent amount of money at last, the Prince wrote to his father to promise, so far as it lay in his power, not to exceed his income. The King replied that 'not a single word shall be mentioned . . . relative to any past unhappy misunderstandings'.

Yet, if he was prepared to credit his son with the intention of leading a more responsible life, the King was not prepared to overlook Fox's part in the troublesome negotiations. The Secretary for War believed that the Government could never now gain the King's favour. There might be a wary politeness; but there would be 'no peerages, no marks of real support'. As for the King, deeply distressed by the death of his beloved four-year-old son, Prince Octavius, he said that every morning when he woke up he wished that he was eighty, or ninety, or dead.

30

THE DEFEAT OF FOX

We are beat in the House of Lords by such treachery on the part
of the King and such meanness on the part of his friends . . .
as one could not expect either from him or them.

On the opening day of the new session of Parliament in November 1783, Charles James Fox made a speech in the Commons on the treaties recently concluded with France, Spain and the United States – a speech which the *Morning Chronicle* reported as having been 'one of the ablest, and at the same time one of the most fair and honest ever delivered from the mouth of a Minister at the opening of a session of Parliament'.

Among those who listened approvingly to it was the Prince of Wales, exquisitely dressed in black velvet lined with pink satin and embroidered in gold, wearing shoes with pink heels, his abundant fair hair frizzed and curled. But, to the Prince's great disappointment, Fox's days of power were coming to an end. Soon after the opening of the session, he introduced a Bill for reforming the government of India by transferring the political responsibilities of the East India Company to commissioners in London appointed by Parliament.

It was a reform long overdue; and the King, who deplored the vast fortunes made by nabobs, the 'fleecers of the East Indies', warmly approved of its purpose. Yet Fox's opponents had little difficulty in representing it not only as a threat to all charter companies but as a means of obtaining a controlling interest in Indian affairs for the Whig majority in the House of Commons. Fox was alleged to be attempting to make his own fortune as King of Bengal, and in this guise he became a favourite butt of caricaturists. Two caricatures in particular, both by James Sayers, had, as Lord Eldon said, 'a vast effect upon the public mind'. One depicted Fox running off with

India House on his shoulders, transferring patronage and sovereignty from the East India Company and the Crown to himself and his colleagues. The other, *Carlo Khan's Triumphal Entry into Leadenhall Street*, showed him as an immensely fat oriental prince riding through the City on an elephant with the face of Lord North. Edmund Burke, the inspirer of the India Bill, was shown blowing a horn as he led the elephant on its way.

The King, who had come to the view that Fox and his friends were using the Bill to undermine his royal prerogative, did not scruple to make it known that he would not show favour to anyone who supported it. He decided that he could make use of it to rid himself of Fox, and that he had the sanction of the constitution, 'the most perfect of human formations', for doing so. Encouraged in this belief by Lord Thurlow, who had been Lord Chancellor in the previous Administration and was anxious to return to that office, and by Lord Temple, who was to be appointed Home Secretary, the King was also persuaded that he was well within his rights by his reading of the influential *Commentaries on the Laws of England* by the jurist Sir William Blackstone, the last of whose four volumes had been published in 1769.

Before bringing down the Fox–North coalition, however, the King recognized that he must be certain that there was a man he could trust to take its place. There was but one man with the authority and character to do so, the young son of the Earl of Chatham. William Pitt was then only twenty-four years old and had not been elected to Parliament until January 1781. But he had soon established his authority there as a fluent and persuasive speaker, and in July 1782 he had been appointed Chancellor of the Exchequer in Shelburne's Administration. Needing further support, Shelburne had asked him to approach Fox, who had agreed to join the Ministry only if Shelburne resigned as First Lord of the Treasury. Pitt is said to have brought the interview to an abrupt close with the words 'I did not come here to betray Lord Shelburne.' Thereafter Fox and Pitt were political enemies, while the King and Pitt had become potential allies. Pitt's vehement attack on Fox's India Bill and, before that, his remarkable two-and-three-quarter-hour attack on the Fox–North coalition helped to convince the King that he had found a man to lead his Government, even though, as he was later reported to have said, 'Mr Pitt is sometimes in the wrong. Mr Fox often is – but when they both agree they are sure to be so.' So, as soon as Pitt had satisfied himself that he could probably command a majority in the House of Commons, the King authorized Lord Temple, Pitt's cousin, to inform the members of the House of Lords that whoever voted for the India Bill was 'not only not his friend but would be considered by him as an enemy'. And, 'if these words were not strong enough', Temple was told he 'might use whatever words he might deem stronger and more to the purpose'.

Having passed its second reading in the House of Commons by 229 votes to 120, the India Bill had seemed certain to pass into law. It had also passed its first reading in the House of Lords. But the King's intervention was decisive: on its second reading there it was defeated by 75 to 57, the Archbishop of Canterbury, who had been summoned for an audience with the King, and a majority of the bishops all voting against it.

The next day, shortly before midnight, Fox was informed by a special messenger that the King had no further use for his services and would dispense with the formality of receiving back the seals of his office – as he would those of Lord North – since 'audiences on such occasions must be unpleasant'.

The following morning, 19 December 1783, it was announced in the House of Commons to derisive laughter that William Pitt had accepted office as First Lord of the Treasury and Chancellor of the Exchequer. Earl Temple succeeded North as Home Secretary.

Fox put a brave face on his defeat so acutely organized by the King in what His Majesty took to be the best interests of the country. 'We are beat in the House of Lords,' Fox wrote, 'by such treachery on the part of the King and such meanness on the part of his friends . . . as one could not expect either from him or them.' But he expected to be able to destroy the new Cabinet 'almost as soon as it [was] formed'. And certainly Pitt experienced great difficulty in forming it.

Three days after taking up his appointment Lord Temple shocked his colleagues by suddenly resigning. The reason, so it was said, was that he feared that he was going to be impeached for delivering the

King's message to the Lords about voting on the India Bill. Pitt was 'led almost to despair'. As it was, his Cabinet, 'hastily patched together', was 'composed of men wholly inadequate to the work before them'. All its members, apart from himself, were in the Lords, so it would be left to him alone to defend their policies in the Commons.

Fox was sure that 'Master Billy' would not survive; and indeed it seemed for months that he could not possibly do so. Time and again he was defeated; motion after motion called for the resignation of a man who had neither a majority in the House nor its confidence. But with the encouragement and help of the King, who created peerages to oblige him, Pitt clung to office, determined to remain until public opinion was on his side and until his supporters stood a good chance of winning a general election, arguing that, as the right of dismissal did not rest with the Commons, he had a perfectly constitutional right to stay in office even against its wishes.

He had certain advantages which Fox had not: he had access to the King's election fund and organization as well as to the patronage at the King's disposal. Besides, public opinion was, as he had hoped, slowly coming round to his side. He was seen as an honest and conscientious, if unprepossessing, young man of supposedly unexceptionable private life; while the King was known to be a sober, respectable family man, strict in his religious observances, proud of his country; whereas Fox was perceived as a gambler and libertine, a fat, louche opportunist, probably an atheist, and a crony of the Prince of Wales, from whom he had taken at least two discarded mistresses. Pitt had made only one short visit to the Continent (and was never to go there again); Fox had spent many months in Italy and France, and delighted in their literature and art: caricaturists were soon to depict him as relishing the breezes that wafted across the Channel from revolutionary France.

Pitt was encouraged to believe that public opinion was running in his favour when he was widely praised for declining to accept a valuable sinecure, bestowing it instead on Isaac Barré, on condition that Barré gave up an even more valuable pension, thus saving the balance for the nation. Soon afterwards he received great sympathy and his opponents aroused much indignation when, returning from a ceremony in which he had been presented with the freedom of the City, his carriage was stoned and attacked by men wielding bludgeons and sedan-chair poles outside Brooks's Club, the haunt of Fox's Whig friends, obliging Pitt to run for safety up St James's to White's.

The election was held in the spring of 1784. John Wilkes, who now protested that he had 'never been a Wilkesite', was once more returned for Middlesex. Pitt came in for Cambridge, a seat he held for the rest of his life. Fox was narrowly elected for Westminster, following a lengthy scrutiny of the votes during which he was obliged to sit for Kirkwall, a pocket constituency in Scotland. Many of his supporters lost their seats, including men who had never failed to win an election since they had first stood as candidates years before. The tide had turned: the electors, cheered by a healthy expansion of the country's industry and commerce, not least with America, had given a vote of confidence not only in William Pitt but in King George. As the sociable Lord Palmerston, a former Lord of the Treasury, observed, 'an epidemical kind of spirit' had 'gone about the country in favour of the King's prerogative and against the House of Commons'. His Majesty had shown how much he had learned from experience: making full use of the rights which the constitution permitted him to exercise, he had, by skilful management and timing and a sound knowledge of the processes of British government, obtained the services of a First Minister who was – to the nation's general satisfaction – to remain in office for over seventeen years.

31

A SECRET MARRIAGE

No, I will never marry . . . Frederick will marry, and the crown
will descend to his children.

The contentment which the King felt about the election victory of
1784 and his general approval of the conduct in office of Mr Pitt —
with the exception of his First Minister's 'unfortunate' inclination
towards parliamentary reform — were overcast by worry about his
heir. If only, his father admonished him, the Prince of Wales would
spend more time in healthy open-air pursuits instead of living so
debauched a life in London, his character would be less open to
general censure. But, as it was, the King felt obliged to write frequent
letters to his son, 'reprobating in each of them', in the words of Lord
Malmesbury, to whom the Prince showed them, 'his extravagance
and dissipated manner of living. They were void of every expression
of parental kindness or affection.' The Prince himself told the Duke
of York, his brother, that their father was 'so excessively unkind' to
him that there were moments when he felt he could 'hardly ever
put up with it . . . sometimes not speaking to me when he sees me
for three weeks together, and hardly ever at Court, speaking to
people on each side of me and then missing me, and then when he
does honour me with a word, 'tis merely "''tis very hot or very cold"
. . . and then sometimes when I go to his house never taking any
notice of me at all, as if I was not there'. He esteemed his father, he
added; but, although he used him with 'all possible duty, deference,
and respect', he remained unalterably estranged from him. Really,
he concluded on a later occasion, 'he hates me; he always did, from
seven years old . . . He will never be reconciled to me.'

As well as being 'void of every expression of parental kindness or
affection', his father's letters to his son were also void of any suggestion

that the Prince might occupy himself in some capacity that might fit him for his future office. As the Bishop of Llandaff put it to the Duke of Queensberry, 'he was a man occupied in trifles, because he had no opportunity of displaying his talents in the conduct of great concerns'.

So he continued to spend hour upon hour in the company of his cronies, his women, his tailors and his shoemakers, finding the day, as he was said to have bitterly commented on receipt of one of his father's letters, quite long enough for doing nothing. His debts mounted month by month, to such a height, indeed, that in August 1784 he wrote to his father to say that 'the very embarrassed situation of his affairs' made it necessary for him to ask permission to go abroad immediately. The King was appalled by this request. The Prince's whole conduct was 'reprehensible' and had 'grown worse every year, and in a more glaring manner since his removal to Carlton House', upon which well over £1,000 a month had been spent upon furnishings alone since he had taken possession.

Although the Prince had told his father that he 'proposed only painting' the house and 'putting handsome furniture where necessary', in a 'very few weeks this was forgot'.

Large additional buildings erected [the King complained, increasingly indignant and ungrammatical] and, lest these should not waste enough money, the most expensive fêtes given, and at this hour considerable additional [*sic*] are again begun; yet the Prince of Wales chooses to term his difficulties as occasioned by necessary expenses . . . If he has deranged his affairs he ought to take a manly resolution to diminish his expenses and thus establish a sinking fund to clear those debts, which would in some measure palliate with the public for an extravagance which everyone but his flatterers have universally blamed; the Prince of Wales ought to know that every step he takes is of consequence, that if he once loses the good opinion of this nation it is not to be regained.

I have found myself under the disagreeable necessity of showing the Prince of Wales's letter to the Queen, who is as much hurt as me, and coincides in the opinion that if his improper plan [of going abroad] was put into execution his character would be for ever blasted in this country, and also in all Europe. I therefore insist on his giving up a measure that would be a public breach with me.

The Prince replied that he would be 'truly hurt' at a public breach; but, in defiance of his father's strongly worded warning, he repeated his intention of going abroad. It was out of the question for him to make 'sufficient retrenchments' to extricate himself from his difficulties at home. 'It would be merely a drop of water in the sea!'

The King's reply to this was a short, firm injunction to the Prince from 'his father and his Sovereign strictly to charge and command him . . . not to leave the realm without having obtained particular leave'. The King was, however, prepared to see what he could do to help the Prince out of his financial difficulties, and he asked Lord Southampton, as head of His Royal Highness's Household, to ascertain the exact amount of his debts.

The Prince's Treasurer, instructed by Lord Southampton to provide the figure, confessed that he was horrified by the sums he unearthed, even though many items had not been brought to his notice: the 'torrents of expense' had risen to 'an enormous amount', certain debts having gone up 'beyond all kind of calculation whatever'. It would take months to arrive at an accurate estimate of them.

In the meantime, the Prince continued to express to his father his determination to live abroad in order to 'practice a system of economy'. This, however, was not the real reason for his wanting to leave England. He had another, more urgent, secret reason, which he was anxious should not be discovered by his father, who in fact was quite well aware of what it was.*

The Prince was once again in love, and this time more desperately than ever. The object of his passion was Mrs Maria Fitzherbert, a well-to-do widow six years older than himself, who had recently come to live in London after the death of her second husband at Nice. She was not particularly good-looking, but she had a pleasantly rounded figure, a fine bosom, lovely dark brown eyes, and abundant golden hair. Everyone who knew her liked her, though she was 'rather heavy than brilliant in conversation' and had a somewhat quick temper and a certain haughtiness of manner. Soon after seeing

---

* The King was far better informed about matters of this kind than people generally supposed. 'The King talked a great deal about you,' the Duke of Queensberry once told George Selwyn. 'As he knows everything, he is perfectly well acquainted with your passion for Mie Mie [Maria Fagniani, the Marchesa Fagniani's daughter, of whom both Selwyn and Queensberry claimed to be the father and to whom both of them left large sums of money] (Jesse, *George Selwyn*, iv, 86).

her in a box at the opera the Prince was 'really mad for love'. There could, however, be no question of his making her his mistress, for she was devoutly Roman Catholic and irreproachably respectable. Yet, if he could not live with her outside marriage for moral reasons, he could not marry her for legal ones: the Royal Marriages Act stood in the way. The Prince swore that he could not live without her, burst into tears, threatened to kill himself, protested that nothing must stand in their way, neither the Royal Marriages Act nor the Act of Settlement, which provided that anyone who married a Roman Catholic could never become monarch of England. Warned of his excitability and inconstancy, Mrs Fitzherbert, though flattered by his attentions and wild desire for her, was not sure that she wanted to marry him anyway; and in her dilemma she decided to go abroad. On hearing of her intention, the Prince became more frenzied than ever; and in a desperate attempt to stop her he staged an attempt at suicide. Persuaded to go to his bedside, where she found him covered in blood, she weakly assented when he begged her to marry him and declared that, unless she agreed to do so, 'nothing would induce him to live'. Later, regretting the promise that shock had induced her to make to him, she sailed for the Continent.

Prevented by his father from following her, the Prince bombarded her with a series of fiercely passionate, imploring, tearful letters, beginning with one that scrawled its way over eighteen pages and ending with one that stretched to forty-two. After a year, tiring of her exile, Mrs Fitzherbert succumbed to his entreaties. She returned to England, where, ignoring the attempts of Charles James Fox to dissuade him from taking such a 'very desperate step', the Prince found an Anglican parson who conducted a marriage service in Mrs Fitzherbert's drawing-room, having assured Fox that 'there not only is, but never was, any grounds' for reports 'so malevolently circulated' that such a marriage was about to take place – an assurance which misled Fox into declaring in the House of Commons on His Royal Highness's 'direct authority' that there was not the 'smallest degree of foundation' for the 'miserable calumnies' and 'monstrous reports' which had been circulating in society.

Distressed and angered by this declaration, which she could not but feel had been authorized by the Prince with an increased allowance in mind, Mrs Fitzherbert refused to see him for a time; but, encouraged by the sympathy with which she was received and the respect with which she was treated in London society, she soon began to relax in her attitude towards him, while he himself, having once again threatened suicide unless she returned to him, was prepared to make an effort to improve relations with his father now that his financial affairs were being settled at last.

This had not been easy to arrange. When the Prince's Treasurer had finished doing his complicated sums, it appeared that his master's 'load of debts' had risen to the astonishing figure of £269,878 6s. 7¼d. Apprised of this, the King had held it 'impossible to enter on the consideration of any means' to relieve his son until he had received 'a sufficient explanation of his past expenses' and saw 'a prospect of reasonable security against a continuance of his extravagance'. It 'would be necessary to have as clear an explanation as the nature of the thing will admit, of his past expenditure, and above all to ascertain that it will be confined within proper limits in future'.

It had been hinted to the Prince that his father would prove more amenable if the Prince would marry some suitable foreign princess. But, when this matter was mentioned to him, the Prince had burst out vehemently, 'I will never marry. My resolution is taken on that subject. I have settled it with Frederick. No, I will never marry . . . Frederick will marry, and the crown will descend to his children.'

It had also been suggested that the King might prove less intractable if the Prince were to abandon his support of the Whig Opposition. This, however, had been considered equally impossible. He had declared that he would never 'abandon Charles' and his other friends. So the Prince had decided to make a dramatic gesture: he had shut up Carlton House, sold his carriages and his horses, dismissed most of the members of his Household, and gone to live with what for him passed for frugality in Brighton. While there had been many who commended the Prince and sympathized with his decision, the King had felt that he was flaunting his poverty before the world merely to draw attention to his father's meanness.

After Parliament had been induced to come to the Prince's rescue by granting £161,000 towards the settlement of his debts, together with £60,000 towards the completion of Carlton House, and the

King had agreed to contribute another £10,000 a year from the Civil List, which, together with about £13,000 from the Duchy of Lancaster, increased his income to some £73,000 a year, relations between the Prince and his father had begun slowly to improve. The King had read with pleasure and relief such reports as one in the *Morning Post* which informed its readers that the Prince of Wales was gaining 'many hearts by his affability and good humour', that he was 'certainly more sober' and his 'company much better than it used to be'.

The Prince, whose birthday in August 1786 had not been noticed at Court, was once again welcomed at Windsor. Not only did the Queen greet him as affectionately as she had done in the past but the King spoke to him for three hours. His son assured him that he did 'most sincerely mean never to incur any future debts, which must undoubtedly be as disagreeable to the King as painful to himself'. This undertaking was not to be fulfilled, nor was the reconciliation which prompted it to last.

32

THE 'MEDICAL TRIBE'

I am getting into Mr Burke's eloquence, saying too much on little things.

In the summer of 1788 the King suffered from what he called 'a pretty smart bilious attack' which 'forced him to take to his bed, as the only tolerable posture he could find'. Sir George Baker, a learned Old Etonian and authority on lead poisoning, who was nine times elected President of the College of Physicians, and the King's other physicians were all puzzled by his case, giving it as their joint opinion that his bile was not flowing correctly and diagnosing gout. They prescribed various medicines, which the King, having a very low opinion of both his doctors' competence and their prescriptions' efficacy, refused to take. He also declined to follow their advice to give up riding. He did, however, agree to go to Cheltenham for a course of the waters there.

So 'we were all up at five o'clock,' wrote Fanny Burney on 13 July, the day after their departure; 'and the noise and confusion reigning through the house, and resounding all around it, from the quantities of people stirring, boxes nailing, horses neighing, and dogs barking, was tremendous'.

They went by way of Henley-on-Thames, where they had breakfast, and Oxford, where the cavalcade of carriages stopped for 'a sort of half-dinner'. News of his journey had preceded the King, and all along the route crowds of people had gathered to watch him pass.

Every town and village within twenty miles seemed to have been deserted, to supply all the pathways with groups of anxious spectators . . . and all the towns [along the route] were filled with people, as closely fastened one to another as they appear in the pit of the playhouse . . . Their Majesties travelled wholly without guards or state; and [Miss Burney was] convinced, from the time they advanced beyond Oxford, they were taken for their own attendants.

254

Every five miles or so there were bands of the 'most horrid fiddlers, scraping "God save the King" with all their might, out of tune, out of time, and all in the rain'.

Determined to get well as soon as possible, the King rose as early at Cheltenham as he usually did, hurried down to the nearby spa from Bay's Hill Lodge, the modest house, a quarter of a mile from the wells, which had been lent to him and his family by Lord Fauconberg, a Lord of the Bedchamber, who, suffering from 'a violent scorbutic humour in his face', had built the house so as to be near the spa when in need of treatment. At the spa the King drank three large glasses of the unpleasant-tasting, purgative water, went for a brisk walk or a hard ride into the country – he was often in the saddle from eleven o'clock until three – then drank some more water. He found 'a pint and a half the proper quantity to give him two openings'. 'These,' he reported to Sir George Baker, 'only clear him without any sinking; on the contrary he finds himself in better spirits and has never been obliged to take the rhubarb pills.' The Cheltenham waters, he added, gave him an appetite for good mutton. So efficacious did he believe the waters to be, indeed, that he had a well sunk in the grounds of Bay's Hill Lodge to provide him with an alternative supply.

Feeling much improved in health, the King made several excursions into the surrounding countryside: he went to Tewkesbury to look round the Abbey church; he went to Gloucester to see the Cathedral; he visited Croome Court, home of the Earl of Coventry, the interiors of which had been recently designed by Robert Adam, and Hartlebury Castle, episcopal palace of his old friend Richard Hurd, now Bishop of Worcester. He also went to George Selwyn's house, Matson, which had been Charles I's headquarters during the siege of Gloucester in the Civil War.

Yet, while his physical health certainly improved, it was noted that his eccentricities became ever more marked. He bustled about, with the Queen on his arm and his three eldest daughters in train, raising his hat to the passers-by as if to dear old friends and going into houses to talk to their occupants as he was accustomed to doing at Windsor. He took the Queen and the Princesses to the newly built theatre, which was renamed upon their departure the Theatre

Royal, where they saw Mrs Jordan in a play and a farce and as Mistress Ford in *The Merry Wives of Windsor*, and the King displayed all his rumbustious enjoyment of the jokes and sent Colonel Digby backstage with a present for the actress, who was to become the mistress of his third son, William.

During his visit to Worcester he woke up the Dean before dawn for a conducted tour of the Cathedral and, at an equally early hour on another day, he disturbed a maid washing the front door step of his equerries' lodgings, calling out, 'Good day! Good day! Pray show me where the fellows sleep, what? what?' The equerries leaped out of bed; but before they were dressed the King was on his hurried way to the river bank. Coming to the water's edge, he encountered some early risers standing by a bridge.

'This, I suppose,' he said to them, 'is Worcester New Bridge?'

'Yes, please Your Majesty.'

'Then, my boys, let's have a huzza!'

In the Cathedral later on he was seen beating time to Handel's *Messiah* as though conducting an orchestra; and at a reception in the Town Hall the Lord Mayor, notified of His Majesty's sobriety, offered him a jelly before the meal should he not want a glass of wine. 'I do not recollect, Mr Mayor, ever in my life drinking wine before dinner; yet upon this pleasing occasion I will venture.' So he took the wine, offering an apt toast: 'Prosperity to the Corporation and citizens of Worcester!'

When he heard that his son the Duke of York intended to join him in Cheltenham, he ordered the immediate erection of a timber building in the grounds of Bay's Hill Lodge for the accommodation of the Duke's party.

The task had employed twenty or thirty men [Miss Burney recorded], and so laborious, slow, difficult and all but impracticable had it proved that it was barely accomplished before it was wanted. There was no room, however, in the King's actual dwelling, and he could not endure not to accommodate his son immediately next himself. His joy upon his arrival was such joy as I have only seen here when he arrived first from Germany.

After his return to Windsor on 16 August, however, the King's happiness was overcast by a return of stomach pains, which seized him so violently in the middle of the night that he was rendered speechless for several minutes. The attack was attended by other unpleasant symptoms: by agonizing cramp in the legs and a rash on his arms, which he showed to his daughter Princess Elizabeth. She was shocked to discover how very red it looked, 'and in great weals, as if it had been scourged with cords'. Early the next morning his pages were astonished to see the Queen running out of the royal apartments 'in great alarm, in her *shift*, or with very little clothes'. The pages turned away to save her embarrassment, but she ran towards them and told one of them to go immediately to Richmond to fetch the surgeon David Dundas, who, upon his arrival, proved to be quite as puzzled by the King's complaint as were the other medical men in attendance. Sir George Baker expressed the opinion that His Majesty's illness was caused by his having 'walked on the grass several hours; and, without having changed his stockings (which were very wet) went to St James's; and that at night he ate four large pears for supper', having had no dinner. It was generally supposed that the complaint might well be gout, and Lady Harcourt, the Queen's Lady of the Bedchamber, hoped that it would prove to be so, for gout would preclude other diseases and would surely not be fatal unless it flew to the brain.

One morning in October, Baker was summoned to the King's bedside after he had suffered a particularly painful 'spasmodic bilious attack'. The doctor was asked to bring with him 'one of the opium pills in case the pain should not have entirely subsided'. He found his patient 'sitting up in his bed, his body being bent forward'. The King complained of 'very acute pain in his stomach, shooting to the back and sides and making respiration difficult and uneasy'. He had also been 'much tormented in the night by a cramp in the muscles of his legs', and had 'suffered much from the rheumatism which affected all his limbs and made him lame . . . The pain continued all day and did not cease entirely until [strong laxatives having been administered] the bowels had been emptied.' The laudanum he was then given counteracted the purgatives; so these were repeated, which necessitated a second dose of the anodyne. 'Within twenty-four hours,' Lady Harcourt recorded, 'he took three doses of each.'

By the end of this period of twenty-four hours the King was

feverish; his feet were swollen and painful; the whites of his eyes had turned yellow, and his urine brown. Yet, even so, with characteristic conscientiousness, he tried to attend to business by writing a letter to Pitt on official business. But he found he could not concentrate: he made numerous mistakes; he repeated himself; his handwriting grew big and shaky, until he was forced to conclude, 'I am afraid Mr Pitt will perceive I am not quite in a situation to write at present.'

Two days later, on 22 October, his 'agitation and flurry of spirits gave him hardly any rest'. He flew into a rage with Sir George Baker over the medicines he had been given, and harangued him for three hours.

The look of his eyes, the tone of his voice, every gesture and his whole deportment represented a person in a most furious passion of anger [Sir George recorded]. One medicine had been too powerful, another had only teased him without effect. The importation of senna ought to be prohibited, and he would give orders that in future it should never be given to the Royal Family . . . Having no opportunity of speaking to the Queen, I wrote a note to Mr Pitt immediately on my return to town, and informed him that I had just left the King in an agitation of spirits nearly bordering upon delirium.

In spite of his deplorable condition, after spending a quieter night than usual the King insisted on appearing at the levee on 24 October, to demonstrate that there was no cause for alarm, to 'stop further lies and any fall of the Stocks'. His appearance at St James's Palace, however, exacerbated rather than quietened the disturbing rumours that were flying about London. His dress was so disordered that the Lord Chancellor, Lord Thurlow, was obliged to advise him to retire to the Closet to readjust it; his legs were wrapped in flannel; his speech was slurred and hurried; his agitated impatience and muddled thoughts were obvious to all. 'You too, my Lord, forsake me and suppose me ill beyond recovery,' he said angrily, turning on Lord Thurlow. 'But whatever you and Mr Pitt may think and feel, I, that am born a gentleman, shall never lay my head on my last pillow in peace and quiet so long as I remember the loss of the American colonies.'

On his return to Kew, it seemed that he was quite unconscious of the effect his appearance at the levee had had upon those who had seen him there. 'I am certainly stiff and weak,' he said, 'but no wonder. I am certain air and relaxation are the best restoratives.' He hoped to find both these at Windsor, where the Royal Family and Household were due to go next day.

Yet at Windsor, where he returned on 25 October, it was obvious to all that came into contact with him that the King's insistence that he was not seriously ill could not possibly be credited. 'As the coach drew up at the door,' Lady Harcourt reported, 'the King saw his four younger daughters waiting to receive him, and was so overcome that he had a hysteric fit.'

'He assures everybody of his health,' wrote Fanny Burney. He was 'all benevolence and goodness, even to a degree that [made] it touching to hear him speak'. Yet he spoke in 'a manner so uncommon, that a high fever alone could not account for it; a rapidity, a hoarseness of voice, a volubility, an earnestness – a vehemence, rather – it startled me inexpressibly ... The Queen grows more and more uneasy.'

He talked to Miss Burney incessantly about his health. He hardly ever slept, he told her, 'not one minute, all night'. Once, in the Queen's dressing-room, she heard him beg his wife 'at least a hundred times' not to speak to him when he got to bed, 'so that he might fall asleep as he felt great want of that refreshment'.

He need scarcely have made such a request of the Queen, for she could scarcely bring herself to talk to him at all. 'More and more uneasy' on his behalf, she seemed to be quite frightened of him in his present alarming state, and kept out of his way as much as she could. Frequently she burst into tears. 'How nervous I am!' she exclaimed to Miss Burney. 'I'm quite a fool. Don't you think so?'

The King's dependence upon the Queen, however, was evident to all. 'The Queen is my physician,' he announced in a hoarse voice to the former Lady Effingham, now the wife of General Sir George Howard and one of Her Majesty's Ladies of the Bedchamber, 'and no man need have a better. She is my *Friend* and no man *can* have a better.' One day in chapel, so it was reported, he stood up suddenly in the middle of the sermon and, throwing his arms round the Queen and the Princesses, exclaimed raucously, 'You know what it is to be nervous. But, was you ever as bad as this?' Princess Elizabeth answered, 'Yes,' and he fell into silence.

Worried to distraction by his 'great hurry of spirits and incessant loquacity', the Queen sent urgently for Sir George Baker, who, on his arrival at Windsor, found the King attending a concert throughout which, 'not seeming to attend to the music', he talked continually, 'making frequent and sudden transitions from one subject to another . . . He was lame, and complained of rheumatic pain and weakness in the knee, and was continually sitting and rising.' He later told Baker that his vision was impaired by a mist floating before his eyes whenever he tried to read; and he 'likewise mentioned' as a 'cause of great distress that, having in the morning selected a certain prayer, he found himself repeating a prayer he had not proposed to make use of'. He also feared that he was going deaf.

'I feel, sir, I shall not long be able to hear music,' he confided to the conductor at a Handel concert. 'It seems to affect my head, and it is with difficulty that I hear it.'

'My dear Effie,' he said in one of his lucid moments to Lady Howard, 'you see me, all at once, an old man.' He lifted up his walking-stick. 'I can't get on without it, Effie. My strength diminishes daily.'

He had no doubt that he was in danger of losing his reason; and one day when the Queen made some comment about the necessity of bearing up under afflictions, and in believing that God would not impose burdens impossible to bear, he put his arm round her waist and said, 'Then you are prepared for the worst.'

'They would make me believe I have the gout,' he complained, kicking one foot against the other; 'but if it was gout how could I kick the part without any pain?' He knew only too well that he was excessively loquacious, but once he had started talking he found it almost impossible to stop. He told his attendants to keep him quiet by reading aloud to him, but he kept on talking just the same. He also suggested that he should be taken to Stoke Place, General Sir George Howard's house in Buckinghamshire, where, as he said, 'Sir George would give him an account of the campaigns he made in Germany, and that will keep me from talking.'

One day, apparently, he burst into tears on the Duke of York's shoulder and cried out in anguish, 'I wish to God I may die, for I am going to be mad.'

The Prince of Wales and the Duke of York had both been attentive to their father up till now. The Prince, so his father said, had wept to see him so ill when he came to Windsor from Carlton House to visit him; and the Duke, who was at Windsor the next day, assured his brother that the King had spoken of him 'with tears in his eyes and with the greatest affection', saying how happy he had made him by coming to see him.

On 5 November, however, when the Prince returned to Windsor from London, the King was in no mood for such sentiment. He had gone out for a drive in his chaise with the Princess Royal before his son's arrival, stepping in and out of the carriage with such agitation that Miss Burney, who was watching the scene from an upstairs window, said that her fear of 'a great fever hanging over him grew more and more powerful'. When they returned, to Miss Burney's relief the Princess Royal came in 'cheerfully and gave, in German, a history of the airing, and one that seemed comforting'.

Later that day the Prince arrived and, after a conversation with the Queen, they went in to dinner. During the course of the meal, the King became more and more agitated until, the conversation turning ill-advisedly to murder, he suddenly rose from the table and in a delirium of rage seized the Prince by the collar, pulled him out of his chair, and hurled him against the wall. The Queen fell into violent hysterics; the Prince burst into tears, and was prevented from fainting only by his distracted sisters, who rubbed his forehead with Hungary water.

On examining the King after this outburst, Sir George Baker decided he was now 'under an entire alienation of mind and much more agitated than he had ever been. The pulse was very quick', though just how quick he was unable to determine, because the patient was so restless. The next morning the rate was 'at least 120; but after bleeding it fell to 100'. His eyes, the Queen told Lady Harcourt, were like 'black currant jelly, the veins in his face were swelled, the sound of his voice was dreadful. He often spoke till he was exhausted, and, the moment he could recover his breath, began again, while the foam ran out of his mouth.'

It was decided that he should be moved out of the Queen's bedroom into a dressing-room next door, being warned that Her Majesty was ill herself, otherwise he would be sure to refuse to go. As it was, he insisted on getting out of bed in the middle of the night to make sure the Queen was still in the house. For half an hour he stood by her bed, staring down at her, the curtains in one hand, a candle in the other.

He appeared in the room the following night also; but the Queen was not there, having been moved to an apartment further down the corridor. In her place, sitting on chairs and sofas around the walls, were the Prince of Wales and the Duke of York, together with various equerries, physicians, pages and other attendants. The King demanded to know what they were all doing there; and, ignoring the Prince of Wales, he began rambling on about the Duke of York, his dear Frederick, his favourite son, his friend. 'Yes,' he said in a croaking voice, 'Frederick is my friend.' Then, catching sight of him, he cried out in anguish, 'Oh, my boy!'

Under pressure from the others, Sir George Baker made a few hesitant attempts to persuade the King to return to his room; but his nervous shilly-shally so exasperated his patient that he turned upon him in a fury, upbraiding him as 'a mere old woman' for knowing nothing of his complaint. 'I am nervous,' he had insisted earlier, 'I am not ill, but I am nervous. If you would know what is the matter with me, I am nervous.'

Whispering anxiously and gesturing to the pages, the Prince of Wales endeavoured to persuade someone else to lead the King back to his room; but no one dared approach him until Colonel Stephen Digby, the Queen's Vice-Chamberlain, who had some experience of insanity in his own family, took him firmly by the arm and drew him away, saying, 'You must come to bed, sir: it is necessary to your life.'

Thereafter the King's condition grew progressively if erratically worse. On 5 November Sir George Baker reported that his patient was still extremely agitated, sweating profusely and complaining of 'burning'. Occasionally overcome by convulsions of his arms, legs and hands, he became ever more violent and uncontrollable. He talked endlessly, one day rambling on 'for nineteen hours without scarce any intermission', and sometimes talking 'much unlike himself', that was to say 'indecently'. Often he spoke longingly of Lady Pembroke, the second Duke of Marlborough's daughter, who had married the tenth Earl of Pembroke and had adorned the Court of his youth, an attractive, virtuous and stately woman, described by Walpole at the King's coronation as being 'the picture of majestic modesty'.

He suffered from strange delusions, imagining that London was flooded and that he could see Hanover through Herschel's telescope. He gave orders to people who were long since dead or who did not exist; he composed dispatches to foreign courts on fantastic events; he lavished honours on all who approached him 'elevating to the highest dignity ... any occasional attendant'. It was noted with surprise by Sir George Baker that he no longer interrupted his talk with ejaculations of 'What? What?' and 'Hey! Hey!'

Baker, indeed, was quite out of his depth, wholly at a loss to account for his patient's symptoms and close to nervous collapse himself. It was decided that other medical advice would have to be sought from men less apprehensive and less frightened of his patient than he was. This was, indeed, something that Baker, anxious to share his responsibility, had 'often in vain solicited'. But, when other members of what General the Hon. William Harcourt, a Groom of the Bedchamber, called the 'medical tribe' were called in, they proved of little help. First came Dr William Heberden, an old, highly respected and scholarly physician living in retirement in Windsor; then Dr Richard Warren, an urbane Fellow of the College of Physicians with a highly lucrative practice, who was sent by the Prince of Wales. After him came Dr Henry Revell Reynolds, who had resigned as physician to St Thomas's Hospital to devote himself to an exclusive and profitable private practice; then, a fifth doctor, the Old Etonian Sir Lucas Pepys, a future President of the College of Physicians.

The arrival of Dr Warren – who was not only the Prince of Wales's physician but also attended several other members of that fashionable society so frowned upon at Court, including Charles James Fox and the Dukes of Devonshire and Portland – was accepted with obvious distaste by the Queen. Much disliking and distrusting him, she was soon describing him as 'that black spirit', a spy for the Whigs. As for the King, he ordered Warren out of his room, pushed him when he would not go, and, 'pale with anger and foaming with rage', turned his back on him. As though in revenge for the indignity of this treatment, Warren advocated an extremely painful remedy for the King's illness: the blistering of his shaven scalp so as to draw out the poisonous matter from his brain. At the same time his legs were blistered with plasters of cantharides and mustard, to draw the humours in the opposite direction, while leeches were applied to his forehead. He was also given strong purges and emetics, followed by sedatives, while his room was kept so cold, its fire unlit, that no one other than the patient, who was required to remain there, could bear to stay in it for more than half an hour at a time.

The King had his calmer, more lucid days, when he was composed enough to enjoy a hot bath and to be shaved by Mr Papendiek while the Queen anxiously watched the operation out of sight. On such days he spoke of his garrulity with a kind of wry and weary amusement, commenting for instance, 'I am getting into Mr Burke's eloquence, saying too much on little things.' But there was no sign of continued improvement. He suffered from insomnia and from paroxysms that shook his limbs so violently that his pages could control him and 'overpower his turbulence' only by sitting on him.

The behaviour of the pages, some of whom began to treat him with insulting familiarity, exasperated and on occasions enraged him. He gave one a 'smart slap on the face', he pulled another by the hair, and he tried to kick a third. But then he would be overcome by remorse and call for a page he had struck or endeavoured to strike and take him by the hand and 'ask his pardon twenty times'. He was painfully thin, so emaciated indeed that looking-glasses were covered with green cloth or removed altogether lest the sight of his shrunken frame should shock him grievously.

News of the progress of the King's malady was eagerly sought in London by members of the Whig Opposition to Pitt's Administration who hoped that, if he were to be declared incurably insane or were to die, they might be called upon to form a government by the Prince of Wales when he became Regent or King in his father's place. Indeed, newspapers, including the *Morning Post* and *The Times*, printed lists of probable Ministers in the new Administration.

Charles James Fox had gone abroad in the summer with his mistress, Mrs Armistead. They had travelled to Italy, where, Mrs Armistead having sprained her ankle, they had stopped longer than they had intended. Since they saw no newspapers – except upon one occasion when Fox was anxious to learn the results of the races at Newmarket – and since they had left no address, they had as little knowledge of what was going on in England as their friends in England had of them.

In Fox's absence, Richard Brinsley Sheridan, the dramatist and Member of Parliament for Stafford, who had been Secretary to the Treasury in the Duke of Portland's coalition Administration, became the Prince of Wales's confidential adviser and the recipient of a series of letters from the Prince's intimate friend John Willett Payne, a naval officer and Comptroller of the Prince's Household.

Member of Parliament for Huntingdon, Payne was a brave and respected naval officer who was to become a rear-admiral; but his dissipated private life and irregular financial dealings were such that he was blackballed when proposed by the Prince for membership of Brooks's Club. Having been brought to Windsor by the Prince and promised that, were the King to be pronounced incurably insane and a regency established, he would be appointed a Lord of the Admiralty, he gleaned as much information as he could about the King's condition from His Majesty's attendants and sent unreliable and garbled accounts to Sheridan, who showed them to his friends at Brooks's and to Fox's friend the Duchess of Devonshire. On 5 November Payne reported:

I arrived here about three quarters of an hour after Pitt had left . . . Pitt desired the largest delay in the declaration of the present calamity. The Duke of York, who is looking over me, bids me add that His Majesty's situation is every moment becoming worse. His pulse is weaker and weaker; and the doctors say it is impossible he will survive long, if his situation does not take some *extraordinary* change in the next few hours.

The next day, according to Payne, the King was given a dose of James's Powder, a compound of antimony prescribed for the reduction of fever which had been invented by Robert James, a physician who had been at school with Samuel Johnson and who compiled a medical dictionary in three stout volumes and was said to have been drunk every day for twenty years. After taking a strong dose of this powder the King had 'a profuse stool, after which he fell into a profound sleep. He awoke with all the gestures and ravings of the most confirmed maniac, and a new noise in imitation of the howling of a dog.'

Some of the King's doctors agreed that the King was incurably mad. Dr Warren told Pitt that there was 'every reason to believe that the disorder was no other than direct lunacy' and that the King might, indeed, 'never recover'. In Latin, on 12 November he confidentially assured Lady Spencer, the Duchess of Devonshire's mother, that '*Rex noster insanit.*' This was not, however, an opinion shared by all the physicians who had been called in to examine and treat the King. To be sure, on 19 November Sir George Baker told Pitt that the patient was 'in a perfectly maniacal state'; but on the same day Sir Lucas Pepys reassured Miss Burney that there was 'nothing desponding in the case', and that the King would 'certainly recover, though not immediately'. Another doctor who was called in for consultation towards the end of November agreed with Pepys and announced that he was 'favourable as to a possibility, and even a prospect of recovery'. This was Pitt's family physician, Dr Anthony Addington, who, when in practice in Reading, had gained a high reputation for his methods of treating mental breakdowns and had built a house next to his own for the reception of the insane – a species of patient of which, so he maintained, Reading had a larger than average share.

While the doctors disagreed, wrote contradictory reports, and dropped inconsistent hints, newspapers printed stories which added to the confusion. Rumours of the King's imminent death became so rife that the *Morning Chronicle* was induced to print a categoric denial. But the rumours continued to circulate as wildly as ever. Even if the King were not dead already, it was 'a probability amounting almost to certainty', so the Marquess of Buckingham was informed, that His Majesty's insanity was now fixed. In fact, as the Duchess of Devonshire was told, 'nobody [could really] get at the truth'. In the meantime, ridiculous stories spread about the town. A characteristic one, which found its way into print, had it that the King had walked up to an oak tree in Windsor Great Park, took a branch in his hand, shook it, and entered into a conversation in the belief that he was talking to the King of Prussia.★ The Duchess of Devonshire filled her diary with equally more or less spurious stories which were spread about in her circle:

The King shew'd his backside to his attendants saying that he had not the gout. He pull'd off Sir George Baker's wig and made him go upon his knees to look at the stars; he begins by beating the palms of his hands, then crying and then howling; he got naked out of bed but C[olonel]. Digby threaten'd him back.

Since the doctors' confused and confusing daily bulletins were of great political importance, were read by the Royal Family, and would be seen by the King himself if he recovered, they were understandably cautious and equivocal. This naturally added to the public disquiet and to a popular feeling that the King was in the hands of a bunch of designing charlatans. Sir Lucas Pepys actually feared for his life if the King did not recover. He and his colleagues received threatening letters by almost every post; and Sir George Baker's carriage was stopped by a mob who demanded to know what the King's present condition was. On being told it was a bad one, a man cried out to general approval, 'More shame to you!'

For the convenience of the doctors, who had their practices in London to consider, it was decided that the King should be moved from Windsor to Kew, where he might take exercise in the garden

---

★ The King's malady has been diagnosed by the psychiatrists and historians of medicine Drs Ida Macalpine and Richard Hunter as a particularly virulent form of a rare hereditary disorder known as porphyria, endemic in the Stuarts and transmitted to the Hanoverians by the Electress Sophia, granddaughter of James I and mother of George I. Its victims suffer from abdominal pain, discoloured urine, weakness of the limbs, neuritis and mental derangement leading to rambling speech, hallucinations and symptoms of hysteria, paranoia and schizophrenia which a layman might loosely term madness. (Macalpine and Hunter, *George III and the Mad Business*, 172–6). The diagnosis has been questioned (*The Times Literary Supplement* 8, 15, 22, 29 Jan. 1970) by a few historians and various experts in porphyria research, but it has been found convincing by most historians of the period, as, for instance, Ian R. Christie, *History*, xxxi, No. 232, 1986.

'without being overlooked and observed'. Since it was well under-stood that he would resist it, the Cabinet was summoned to the Castle on 27 November by the Prince of Wales to approve the move and to hear what the physicians had to report on the progress of the King's malady. The Cabinet gave their consent to the move, and so did the Queen – though she did so with great reluctance, knowing how strongly the King would oppose it.

The Queen was becoming increasingly distraught and disgusted by her husband's unpredictable behaviour and the rambling, continuous talk degenerating into obscenities. One day, his vision so blurred he could not clearly distinguish her features, he evidently 'almost set her on fire by pushing the candle in her face to see if it was she'. On another occasion he endeavoured to get into her room and, finding the outer door locked, burst into tears. 'Surely,' he said, 'they might have thought one door enough to stop me.' 'We've been married twenty-eight years,' he said to her later, 'and never separated a day until now; and now you abandon me in my misfortunes.'

To her attendants the Queen seemed on occasions to be in danger of suffering a nervous breakdown herself. She was frequently in tears, sometimes to be seen walking up and down her room shaking her head or sitting 'with her hands and arms stretched across a table before her, with her head resting upon them'. Lord Harcourt was told that she 'neither ate nor slept, that she passed a great part of the day in prayer, the rest in weeping and walking backwards and forwards'.

On 30 November, the day of his proposed removal from Windsor, the King refused to move from his bed; and it was decided to persuade him to get up and go to Kew by telling him that the Queen had already gone there. Pitt was called upon to impart this information to him.

She had gone without his leave, the King angrily responded, and she must 'return to supplicate his pardon'. Soon afterwards he consented to follow her, but he would do so only if he could drive in his own carriage, which he knew had gone with the Queen's entourage. He then pulled the bed curtains shut and remained behind them for the rest of the morning, deaf to the pleas of General Harcourt and an equerry, Colonel the Hon. Robert Fulke Greville, who begged him to come out. In the afternoon – having jumped out of bed in an attempt to assault Dr Warren for pressing him to go to Kew without further delay – he was at last persuaded to leave, having been threatened with removal by force, on the understanding that he would be allowed to see the Queen and his daughters as soon as he arrived there.

He dressed in his Windsor uniform, and paused for a moment to talk to the postilions. He then said goodbye to the footmen, porters and other Castle servants who had gathered to watch him depart and were clearly distressed to see him go. He then drove off with three equerries and an escort of cavalry, preceded by Colonel Stephen Digby, who galloped ahead to warn the Queen of His Majesty's approach. By the roadside a crowd of people, hearing rumours of his removal, had gathered to wish him farewell. They 'bowed respectfully and took a melancholy leave'. The King on seeing them 'bowed most kindly' in return and 'putting his hand before his face he said with much feeling, "These good people are too fond of me," and then he added with affecting sensibility, "Why am I taken from the place I like best in the world?"' He seemed quite content during the journey, however, evidently cheered by the prospect of seeing the Queen and the Princesses again.

At Kew, where the Prince of Wales had allocated all the rooms, writing the names of their intended occupants in chalk on the doors, the King stepped down from the carriage, exchanged a few words with the porter, walked through the hall, then made a dash for the room where he had been told he would find the Queen. Finding instead that the door was locked, he lashed out at his pages, pulling one about by the hair and kicking at another. Furious too with Harcourt and Greville for having deceived him, he told them he would wear them out by refusing to go to bed; and to prove he had the strength to resist them he began hopping about his room in a pathetic demonstration of agility.

From now on the King's disorder grew progressively worse. He ate little and 'refused all medicine, throwing what he could away'. At night he was almost unmanageable, and pages had to sit on him while he was tied to his bed. By day he swore, uttering strange indecencies and 'oaths which had never yet been heard from his lips', begging his attendants to put an end to his miserable life. Moods of deep depression alternated with spasms of childish mischievousness in which he would get his pages to wheel him about the room or he would lie on his bed to 'defend himself by gathering up his feet, and then darting them forward with violence against those who pressed against him'. As at Windsor, he was allowed no fire in his uncarpeted downstairs room, though some attempt was made to keep out the draughts by placing sandbags at the bottom of the doors and the floor-length windows. Even so, the house was 'in a state of cold and discomfort past all imagination'.

On 3 December his doctors were examined on oath by the Privy Council in an attempt to ascertain the present 'situation of the King'. They all agreed in confirming that their patient was for the time being incapable of public business and that it was impossible to say how long this state would continue. But whereas Baker, Pepys, Reynolds and Addington all gave it as their distinct opinion that the King would probably recover his wits, Warren was far more hesitant. In a confused, halting manner he answered the questions put to him, using the word 'insane', mentioning an 'unknown distemper', and nervously suggesting that at the moment it was impossible to say whether or not the King would recover.

The Times complained of the 'truly ridiculous' contradictions in the doctors' bulletins; while Colonel Greville was of the opinion that they appeared 'to shrink from responsibility' and had not 'established their authority, though pressed by every attendant to do so'.

Relying on reports reaching her from John Payne and others, the Duchess of Devonshire continued to disseminate more or less unreliable stories about the King's wild behaviour at Kew:

The King is as mad as ever, for he ordered a tie-wig and danced a minuet with Dr. Reynolds . . . The King has taken the Duke of York's regiment from him because he said the Duke of York had taken pokers and tongs from his room . . . [He] engaged a page to pretend sleep . . . and immediately picked his pockets – it is supposed in search of keys . . . [He] tore two of his attendants almost to pieces, and is so ill he is held down by force. The Prince and the Duke came with this account.

There were also malicious stories enough about the behaviour of the Prince of Wales. It was said that he had taken his friend Lord

Lothian into the King's room when it was darkened, so that he could 'hear his ravings at a time when they were at their worst'; and that he had spied on the King through a hole in a screen. Sheridan's sister Betsy said that, as the Prince peered through the hole, his father looked up, saw the eye, and called a page, whereupon the Prince hastily withdrew. 'I have seen my son,' the King said. 'They assured him that he had not. However he persisted, and when he found they still denied it, gave no answer but a most significant glance at the screen.' Thomas Rowlandson, in an exceptionally offensive print entitled *Filial Piety*, depicted the drunken Prince leading two equally drunken companions, Sheridan and another of the Prince's cronies, the dandy the Hon. George Hanger, into the King's bedroom calling out, 'Damme, come along, I'll see if the Old Fellow's [mad] or not.'

In fact at this time the Prince did not behave nearly as badly as his detractors maintained. Certainly he and the Duke of York much offended the Queen, whose passion for precious stones was undiminished, by taking charge of the King's jewels together with his papers and loose money which were scattered about unlocked in various rooms; but these were all handed over to the Lord Chancellor for safe keeping.

Sir Gilbert Elliot, the future first Earl of Minto and Governor-General of India, said that the Prince's general behaviour had been 'exemplary'. Lord Loughborough, a former Attorney-General and now Chief Justice of the Court of Common Pleas, confirmed that it had gained the applause of all men, even of those who were secretly glad that the Prince remained so unpopular; while Edward Gibbon's friend Lord Sheffield, an Irish peer who sat in the House of Commons as Member for Bristol, agreed with them that the Prince's conduct had won him 'great credit'.

As the King's mental state showed no signs of maintained improvement, however, and the prospect of becoming Regent became ever closer and ever more alluring, the Prince could not resist the excitement of political intrigue. He sent an urgent message to Charles James Fox, wherever he might be, pressing him to return from the Continent as soon as possible. Immediately on receipt of this message in Bologna, Fox set out for England, leaving Mrs Armistead at Lyons in order to travel more rapidly himself; and after nine days of rattling along in carriages over bumpy roads at a rate of over a hundred miles a day he arrived home on 24 November, looking quite worn out by the arduous journey.

By then Pitt had recognized that his Government would have to introduce a Bill providing for a regency, and that the Regent would have to be the Prince of Wales. Pitt accepted that this would probably mean the fall of the Government and the installation of the Prince's Whig friends in its place. It was clear to all that the Prince could not disguise the excitement he now felt at the prospect of influence and money; and, eagerly discussing with his friends who was to have what office when the Whigs came to power, he displayed a readiness 'to go to all the lengths to which that party [was] pushing him'. Yet no one knew for sure who was to be given office and who was not. There were suggestions that the Prince would send for both Pitt and Fox and 'endeavour to make his time quiet by employing them jointly'. There were also rumours that Lord Thurlow, the Lord Chancellor, who was not on good terms with Pitt, was ready to desert to the Whigs in order to retain his office. Some believed the Duke of Portland would surely be chosen as First Lord of the Treasury; others began to doubt that the Prince was worthy of being placed in a position to appoint anyone at all. Day after day, night after night, at Carlton House and Brooks's, at Devonshire House and at the Duke of Portland's mansion, Burlington House, the Opposition continued their discussions, their intrigues and their feuds; and then, on 10 December 1788, the question of the Prince's regency was the subject of a heated debate in the House of Commons.

Sheridan and Burke both vehemently defended those doctors who maintained that the King was insane; while Fox, still looking ill and astonishingly thin after his exhausting rush home from Italy, cut across the arguments about the credibility of the respective doctors and roundly declared that the Prince of Wales, as heir to the throne, of full age and capacity, had 'as clear, as express a right to assume the reins of Government and exercise the power of sovereignty' as he would have had if the King had 'under-gone a natural and perfect demise'. This was an extravagant claim, and it was widely believed that Fox had gone too far for the Opposition's good in putting forward so high a Tory doctrine. As Pitt listened to Fox's expression

AFFABILITY.

"Well, Friend, where a'you going, Hay?_ what's your Name, hay?_ where d'ye Live, hay?_ hay?"

35. The King alarming a cottager at Windsor by his persistent questioning and close inspection on one of his walks around his farms. A caricature by Gillray entitled *Affability*.

The Constant Couple

36. 'Farmer George' and his wife as though returning to Windsor from market. A caricature by Gillray, entitled *The Constant Couple*.

37. In his caricature *Carlo Khan's triumphal Entry into Leadenhall Street* (1783) James Sayers portrays Charles James Fox as a turbaned Grand Mogul riding towards the offices of the East India Company on an elephant with the features of Lord North, and preceded by Edmund Burke as herald.

39. Dr Francis Willis, from a pastel by John Russell. This old clergyman, who had shown skill in the treatment of symptoms of madness in his asylum in Lincolnshire, was called in to give advice upon the King's strange malady in December 1788.

40. Dr John Willis, a mezzotint by William Say after Richard Evans. Dr Francis Willis's son, together with Dr John's brother, Dr Robert, and three of their father's keepers, came down from Lincolnshire to help in controlling and treating the King.

38 (*opposite*). James Gillray's 1792 caricature *Anti-Saccharrites, – or – John Bull and his Family leaving off the use of Sugar*. The move to boycott sugar as a protest against the slave trade gives the parsimonious King and Queen an opportunity for petty saving.

41. *Filial Piety*, a 1788 caricature by Thomas Rowlandson showing the Prince of Wales bursting into the King's bedroom with two of his drunken cronies, Colonel the Hon. George Hanger and R. B. Sheridan.

42. Sir William Beechey's *George III at a Review* was painted for the King in 1797–8. The King on his white horse, Adonis, is pointing towards a mock battle in which the 3rd Dragoon Guards and the 10th Light Dragoons are engaged. Behind the King is the Prince of Wales, in the uniform of the Light Dragoons.

43. An engraving by
John Condé of Richard
Cosway's drawing of
Mrs Maria Fitzherbert,
whom the Prince of
Wales secretly and
illegally married on
15 December 1785 in
the drawing-room of
her house.

44. The marriage of the Prince of Wales to Princess Caroline of Brunswick
on 8 April 1795 in the Chapel Royal, St James's, by Henry Singleton.
Behind the bride and the bridegroom are the Archbishop of Canterbury,
and the Bishop of London. On the left under the canopy sits the King.

45. The King's second and favourite son, Frederick, Duke of York, wearing uniform as Colonel, the Coldstream Guards. A miniature on ivory by Richard Cosway.

46. William, Duke of Clarence, later King William IV. A miniature on ivory by Richard Cosway.

47. Edward, later Duke of Kent, the future father of Queen Victoria, in Hanoverian uniform. A miniature on ivory, possibly by Maria Cosway.

48. Augustus, later Duke of Sussex, in Hanoverian uniform. A miniature on ivory, possibly by Anne Mee, a follower of Richard Cosway.

49. The King and Queen with their six daughters followed by a footman carrying parasols. A contemporary painting on glass attributed to William Rought of Oxford.

The BRIDAL-NIGHT

50. *The Bridal-night*, by James Gillray. The Princess Royal was married to the extremely fat Hereditary Prince of Württemberg on 17 May 1797. The Lord Chamberlain, the Marquess of Salisbury, holds open the door. The King, his face obscured by a pillar, and the Queen, in a poke bonnet and covered with the jewels of which she was so fond, lead the procession. The Prince of Wales follows his sister, and behind him are the Dukes of York and Clarence. Pitt, the First Minister, stands in the background with the dowry.

51. P. E. Stroehling's portrait of Princess Augusta, the King's second daughter, who died unmarried in 1840, after having conceived a romantic admiration for one of her father's doctors and then a passion for an Irish general.

52. Princess Elizabeth, painted at Windsor in 1807 by P. E. Stroehling, when she was thirty-seven. In 1818, at the age of forty-eight, she married Friedrich, Hereditary Prince of Hesse-Homburg.

53. Princess Sophia, a portrait of the King's second-youngest daughter by Sir William Beechey. The favourite sister of both the Duke of Clarence and the Duke of Kent, she gave birth to an illegitimate child at Weymouth in 1800.

54. Their Majesties' youngest daughter, Princess Amelia, from a miniature by Andrew Robertson. The death of this beloved child in 1810 was said to have brought on the King's final mental breakdown.

of it, he is said to have smiled, slapped his thigh in triumph, and proclaimed that he would '*un-Whig* the gentleman' for the rest of his life. The Prince certainly had a *claim* to the regency, but hardly an *inherent right*. To assert such a right, Pitt argued, amounted to an unwarranted interference with parliamentary privilege. It was almost treason to the constitution of the country.

Fox's speech was as strongly condemned outside the Commons as in it; but, encouraged by the number of uncommitted Members who were coming over to the Whig side – several of them tempted by the promises or hopes of honours, perquisites and titles – he assured Mrs Armistead that in a fortnight the Prince would be Regent and his friends would come to power, even though he expected yet further 'hard fights' in the Commons.

So, indeed, there were; and at the end of each debate the arguments were continued with comparable fury outside the House. 'The acrimony is beyond anything you can conceive,' Lord Sydney told Lord Cornwallis. 'The ladies are as usual at the head of all animosity and are distinguished by caps, ribands, and other such ensigns of party.' Supporters of the King wore what they called 'constitutional coats'; ladies displayed their approval of the Prince and the Opposition by sporting 'Regency caps' decorated with three feathers and inscribed with his motto, '*Ich Dien*'.

On the day of the final debate the Duchess of Devonshire – whose husband had been invited to accept office when the Prince formed a new government – sat up until four o'clock in the morning, highly agitated and suffering from a terrible headache, to hear the result. At last her brother and the Duke of Bedford came to Devonshire House with the long-awaited news: by a majority of sixty-four the Opposition had been defeated.

Fox and his friends had failed not only on the issue of the Prince's inherent right to the regency but also on the restrictions to be imposed upon his powers if he were to become Regent; and the comfortable majority which Pitt was able to command was greeted with relief by most people in the country at large.

The Prince, who had earlier told the Duchess of Devonshire that he would not agree to a restricted regency, had now to accept that, if he were to be nominated, his authority would be severely limited, even with regard to the disposition of the Royal Household, since the King was to be entrusted to the care of the Queen.

The Prince unavailingly protested against these proposed restrictions. But he had, in the end, to accept the fact that, if he were to be Regent, he would have to be so on Pitt's terms. On 12 February 1789 Pitt's Regency Bill passed the Commons, and the Lords were on the point of passing it also when unexpected news arrived from Kew.

33

THE LINCOLNSHIRE MAD-DOCTOR

I hate all the physicians, but most the Willises.

On 5 December of the year before yet another physician had been called in to give an expert opinion on the King's strange malady. This was Francis Willis, who had been sent to Kew with the recommendation of both Lady Harcourt, who gave him the credit of curing her mother's acute mental disorder, and the Lord Chancellor, several of whose wards in chancery had been entrusted to Willis's care with satisfactory results.

Dr Willis was a clergyman, seventy years old, who had been Vice-Principal of Brasenose College, Oxford. Drawn to the study of medicine, he was said to have first practised as a physician without a licence, but the University had been prevailed upon to grant him the degrees of M B and M D. In 1769 he had been appointed physician to a hospital in Lincoln, which he had attended twice a week, driving over from his house at Branston, ten miles distant. At this hospital he had been so successful in treating a succession of cases of mental derangement that he had opened an asylum at Gretford, near Stamford.

His arrival at Kew was not welcomed by the other doctors, who agreed with Lord Sheffield that Willis was 'not much better than a mountebank' and not far different from some of those 'who were confined in his madhouse in Lincolnshire'. His professional qualifications were suspect, since he was not a member of the Royal College of Physicians; and, although his father and father-in-law were both clergymen, his social rank was also considered to be questionable.

The King did not welcome him any more agreeably than the other doctors did. He contrived to appear calm when Willis was brought into his room and presented to him, assuring him that he had undeniably been ill of late but was now quite well again. When it later transpired that Willis was in holy orders the King was given further grounds for disliking him. 'I am sorry for it,' he said emotionally. 'You have quitted a profession I have always loved, and you have embraced one I most heartily detest.'

'Sir,' Willis is said to have replied, 'Our Saviour Himself went about healing the sick.'

'Yes, yes,' conceded the King crossly, adding a riposte which was to be much quoted thereafter. 'But He had not £700 [a year] for it, hey!'

The King then 'launched out in strong invective' against all physicians, and demanded that Dr Willis should take Dr Warren under his care instead of himself and drive back with him to his Lincolnshire madhouse. It was not long, in fact, before Dr Willis became as violently disliked by the King as ever Warren had been.

With the members of the Royal Household, however, Dr Willis soon became a favourite. Miss Burney described him as 'open, honest, dauntless, light-hearted, innocent, and high-minded', 'not merely unacquainted with Court etiquette, but wholly, and most artlessly, unambitious to form any such acquaintance'; while Hannah More, the philanthropical bluestocking, thought him 'the very image of simplicity, quite a good, plain, old-fashioned country parson'.

Even the members of the Opposition, who referred to him as Dr Duplicate, because he was a parson as well as a doctor, and who soon grew to distrust him because of his declared belief that the King's condition was certainly curable, gave him the credit of treating his madmen in Lincolnshire, as the Duchess of Devonshire put it, 'with kindness, even keeping a pack of hounds and allowing them to hunt and shoot'.

Certainly his patients at Gretford, who paid up to twenty-five guineas a week for their care, were treated far more humanely than they were at most other lunatic asylums in the country. Dressed in a kind of uniform of black coats and breeches and white waistcoats, so as to obliterate outward signs of social distinction, and given numbers and badges, they were employed in various capacities about the house and in the grounds. They all had meals together, and Dr

Willis would encourage them to talk to him and to each other, to engage in rational conversation. Yet, tolerantly as they were treated by Dr Willis and his 'extremely handsome' son John, a qualified physician, a graduate of both Oxford and Edinburgh, who accompanied his father to Kew, the patients were subjected to a strict discipline. When faced with the disorderly, the insubordinate or the violent, old Dr Willis, so the Duchess of Devonshire was told, became 'a fierce-looking man with a commanding eye' and did not hesitate to use force on his charges, constricting them in straitjackets when necessary.

He intended to use such restraint upon the King when he considered it called for, determined to master his unruly will and to force him into submission. He did not hesitate to threaten him with a straitjacket when he was at his most ungovernable, and he frequently ordered the three keepers whom he had brought with him from Lincolnshire to force their patient into it. Whenever the King refused his food, either because he found it difficult to swallow or because he had no appetite, whenever he became too restless to lie quietly down on his bed, whenever the terrible pain from his septic and suppurating blisters was such that he thrashed about and tore off the bandages, whenever he sweated so much that he threw off his bedclothes, the straitjacket was held up before him or he was strapped into it with a band across his chest and his legs tied to a bedpost. No ruler in the world except a British king, he once protested, could be so utterly confined.

He was also confined in a specially made chair – his 'coronation chair' he called it – to ensure his 'compliance with whatever [was] thought proper'. And once, when he was tied in the chair to be given a severe lecture on his improper and repetitive remarks about Lady Pembroke, a handkerchief was stuffed in his mouth to keep him quiet until the reprimand was completed.

When he was allowed to speak, his talk was as rambling as ever. He rattled on about horses and hunting, the English constitution – 'the finest in the world' – Roman Catholics, Edmund Burke, who was 'flowery and dishonest', and Fox, whom he liked least of all the Whigs. 'I always hated an ambitious man,' he said in one of these circuitous soliloquies.

277

I hate a minion, too [he continued] . . . I wish my son were more steady. The people like me, because they are afraid to trust my son. He has behaved like a boy. He has disinherited himself by marriage . . . I prefer horses under 15 hands . . . I love hunting, but I'm afraid of leaping, and even on a road I think of my neck and my family. A king should not ride bold.

The younger Dr Willis – Dr John, as he was known at Kew – kept a diary in which he recorded the King's words and the erratic progress of his complaint. 'Ungovernable through night,' runs one characteristic entry. 'Constrained at 5. Tongue whitish. Pulse 108. Under constraint most of the day. High spirits, jocose and pertinent.'

Fanny Burney also recorded how the patient 'went on now better, now worse, in a most fearful manner', sometimes sweating so profusely that his clothes were drenched, 'very irritable and easily offended', at other times in 'good humour' and 'high spirits', occasionally lying down on his bed and singing, always having to suffer confinement when he was deemed in need of either punishment or coercion, sometimes even asking for the straitjacket to be put on so that he might be forced to lie still and get to sleep. As well as with blistering, he was doctored with a formidable variety of medicines. He was given calomel and camphor, digitalis, quinine and, as an emetic, tartarized antimony, which made him so sick that he knelt on his chair fervently praying that he might either be restored to health or be allowed to die.

One morning Dr John heard him moaning 'in a wild, monotonous, delirious way, "Oh Emily [Princess Amelia], why won't you save your father? I hate all the physicians, but most the Willises . . . Digby, Greville, you are honest fellows, come to relieve me. Take off this cursed waistcoat."'

Colonel Greville noticed that, while he might claim to hate Dr Willis more than the other doctors, the King was certainly more in awe of the old man than he was of his younger colleagues. It was almost as though he had a kind of respect for him. When the King became agitated and argumentative,

Dr Willis remained firm and reproved him in determined language . . . He conducted himself with wonderful management and force. As the King's voice rose, attempting mastery, Willis raised his and its tone was strong and decided. As the King softened his, that of Dr Willis dropped to softening unison . . . The King found stronger powers in Dr Willis, gave way and returned to somewhat of composure.

Greville also noticed that in Dr Willis's presence the King's talk was curbed, that, if he were rambling on while Willis was out of the room, as soon as he returned, the King 'turned more to the subject and talked more cautiously'. 'The King himself manages in some degree his conversation when before him. Dr Willis always interposes and stops him when he is beginning to talk wildly or inconsistently and thus turns his ideas.'

As Dr Willis gained mastery over his patient, he allowed him to do things previously forbidden. He permitted him to shave himself under careful supervision, whereas the other doctors had 'put every-thing out of his way that could do him any mischief'. He was also allowed to cut his nails. His little spaniel, Flora, was returned to him from Windsor. He was allowed to see the Princesses at a window and, when he was calm enough, to have the Queen and Princess Amelia brought into the room.

I led Princess Amelia myself [Dr Willis reported]. His Majesty showed the greatest mark of parental affection I ever saw. The other physicians protested, but I told them I was sent to make use of my own discretion, and they could not think themselves proper judges of it. That or the next evening he had a quarter-hour interview with the Queen . . . Such occurrences can scarce be too frequent, as it comforts the patient to think that he is with his family and that they are affectionate to him.

Dr Thomas Gisborne, another of the physicians in attendance, reported that the 'Scene when the Queen came to the King was very affecting – he kiss'd her hand passionately & said he held then what was dearest to him in the world – the Queen kiss'd his hand, but could not speak. The K. pressed the Ps. Emily in his arms who cried very much & was frightened.'

Lord Ailesbury was told that the King was 'much agitated' after this visit of the Queen and Princess Amelia. He had 'a bad night, and wore the strait-waistcoat from 4 p.m. to 9 a.m.'. But, according to Dr Willis, it was 'the blisters, not seeing the Queen, that gave him a bad night'.

As the days went by the King gradually became less incoherent in his talk. When Lord North, who had gone blind, called to see him, he said quite coherently:

North might have recollected me sooner. However, he, poor fellow, has lost his sight, and I my mind. He meant well to the Americans – just to punish them with a few bloody noses, and then make bows for the future happiness of both countries. But want of principle got into the Army, want of energy and skill in the First Lord of the Admiralty [the Earl of Sandwich], and want of unanimity at home. We lost America. Tell him not to call again.*

On other days he talked rationally about David Garrick and Samuel Johnson among other people and subjects; and, if he did begin to ramble, he 'turned more to the subject . . . and talked more cautiously' when Dr Willis came into the room. He played backgammon and piquet 'tolerably well'; he occasionally picked up a book, even one in Latin; and, when needing new spectacles, he wrote a perfectly accurate order to the optician.

There were lapses from time to time: on Christmas Eve 1788 he believed his pillow was his young son Prince Octavius, who had died in 1783 and who, he said nursing the pillow, 'was to be new born this day'.

Soon after Christmas, Colonel Greville heard the King talking once more about Lady Pembroke and singing a saucy ballad, 'I Made Love to Kate.' A day or two before this he had 'cried very heartily' when told he could not see the Queen; yet, when permission was granted, after kissing her hand and weeping over it, he seems to have told her that he did not like her, that he preferred another, that 'She was mad & had been so these three years, that He would not on any Account admit Her to his Bed till the year 1793 for reasons he then improperly explained', using words 'such as it was improper for her to have heard'. He referred to himself as Ahasuerus, King of Persia, to the Queen as Vashta, whom Ahasuerus put away as being a bad

---

* After his recovery the King spoke far more kindly of Lord North, whose visit, he was to say, did him 'more good than all the physicians had done for him'. 'I love you all,' he declared in 1801 to North's daughter Lady Sheffield, according to Lord Glenbervie, the former Minister's son-in-law. 'I love you all. I had a great kindness for your grandfather and great affection for your father. You are a good race' (Glenbervie, *Diaries*, i, 231, 394).

example to other wives, and to Lady Pembroke as Esther, whom Ahasuerus promoted to her place. The King eventually announced that all marriages would soon be dissolved by Act of Parliament. He took down the *Tribuna of the Uffizi* which had been commissioned by the Queen from Zoffany and was hanging in his room.★ It was reported that he had said that he wondered how she could 'allow that ugly, old Fumbling fellow [Francis Willis] to go to bed with her'.

★ The King had never cared for this picture and 'during this day [22 December 1788] . . . he had it immediately off the Nails on the Floor, before He was perceived to be busy with it. The Picture was directly moved into the Next room' (Millar, *Later Georgian Pictures*, Text, 155; Millar, *Zoffany and his Tribuna*, 1967).

The King and Queen had fallen out with Zoffany over payment for the picture. Mrs Papendiek, a friend of Mrs Zoffany, wrote, 'Mr. Zoffany was to be paid for his journey to Florence and back, and was to be allowed £300 a year while painting the "Tribune" . . . Alas, poor Zoffany! The moment the question of money was raised, all sorts of objections were made to the work; as to the different persons introduced that could not interest the King, and might even be unpleasant to his Majesty to look at; that he had deviated from the order given to him, simply to copy the "Tribune"; that he had painted portraits of the Imperial Family of Vienna, and others, thereby having lengthened his stay, and retarded the business upon which he left England and so forth' (*Court and Private Life*, i, 83–4).

34

DOCTORS' DILEMMA

He talked much of Lady Pembroke as usual – much against the Queen.

On 11 January 1789 a page delivered to the King's apartments 'a fine Bunch of Grapes from the Hothouse . . . He asked who had sent them. He was told the Queen – He asked what Queen, & if it was Queen Esther who had sent them. The Page answered that Her Majesty His Queen had sent them, upon which he order'd Them away . . . [That evening] he talked much of Lady Pembroke as usual – much against the Queen.'

Two days later the King asked that the Queen's dog, Badine, should be brought to him, because it was fond of him and not of her. Indeed, he added, he himself didn't like the Queen either: she had a bad temper, and her children were afraid of her.

When the Queen had left the room after seeing the King on 28 December, she had 'seemed to make an effort to look up, & by her countenance to show that She was not overcome'. In fact, however, she was becoming increasingly exhausted and distraught. She was 'so dreadfully reduced', it was said, 'that her stays would wrap twice over'. She was 'very low and eats nothing'. She was suffering from toothache, as well as from an inflammation of her eyes which obliged her to sit in a darkened room, where she was often found to be in tears.

She was all the more distressed because she had not only her husband's dreadful state of mind to worry her but also the behaviour of her sons. At Windsor the Prince of Wales had assumed full responsibility and, as Miss Burney said, 'nothing was done but by his orders, and he was applied to in every difficulty. The Queen interfered not in anything.'

Irritated by her sullen complaints and grumbles, her morose and sulky moods, the Prince had been provoked to behave towards her in a way that her Keeper of the Robes described as most heartless and high-handed. He gave his orders 'without any consideration or regard for his mother's feelings', she said, knocking his stick on the floor, condemning everything that had been done before he took control, and retiring from the Queen's presence without kissing her hand.

Lord Bulkeley told the Marquess of Buckingham that once the Prince had taken command at Windsor there was 'no command whatsoever'. It had consequently been resolved that the Prince should be given no opportunity of managing the Household at Kew, a duty which had eventually therefore devolved upon the unwilling Queen. It was bad enough, the Queen complained, to live at Kew at all, for it had never been intended to serve as a winter residence, but to be placed in the position of having to give her consent to measures which she knew could only infuriate the King was intolerable. Even more intolerable was the fact that both her two eldest sons accepted the opinion of Dr Warren, who continued to insist that the King was still in 'a decided state of insanity', and dismissed the contradictory reports of Dr Willis as 'mere fabrications' concocted for a 'sinister purpose'.

The official bulletins sent to St James's were undeniably misleading, since the doctors could never agree on how they should be worded and the Queen, insisting on the right to see them before they were dispatched, asked for alterations in them when she thought them insufficiently discreet.

One day, for example, the draft of the bulletin, written by Dr Warren, had said that His Majesty had had a good night and was calm the next morning. Dr Willis had wanted this to read a 'very good night'; Warren, supported by Baker, had objected, but eventually had given way. Then Dr Willis had proposed that the King's condition the next morning should be described as 'as [it] was yesterday', pointing out that the Queen was sure to ask for such an alteration and asking what was the point of sending up something which would 'only be sent down to be altered'. The draft had accordingly been changed, but it had still not satisfied the Queen, who had wanted it to read, 'and in the morning he continues to mend'. Warren had refused to agree to this alteration, insisting upon 'in the morning he is in a comfortable way'. Warren had privately told the Prince of Wales that His Royal Highness would need a glossary to understand the bulletins: 'calm' meant 'not absolutely raving'; 'rather disturbed' could be translated 'in an outrageous frenzy'. The Prince was also told that the Queen had pressed Warren to tell her something that she understood the King had said to him, and that when Warren hesitated to reply she had commented, 'I suppose it was *indecent.*' Lady Charlotte Finch and Lady Harcourt were sent to Dr Warren to make further inquiries, whereupon Warren said the actual expressions were too gross to repeat.

Since the official bulletins were so unreliable, Warren suggested that he and those colleagues of his who shared his view of the King's condition should make independent reports to the Prince of Wales. All the other doctors agreed to this except Willis, who informed Warren that such a procedure would be totally against his normal practice.

Soon after his arrival at Kew, Willis had expressed his conviction that His Majesty's illness could be attributed to worrying business, severe exercise, too great abstemiousness and little rest, perhaps when the mind was 'upon the stretch with very weighty affairs'. Of his being able to treat the King successfully Willis had and continued to have no doubt.

At the beginning of 1789, indeed, Dr Willis went so far as to express the opinion that the King was 'much better'; and he appeared to be even more confident when he and the other physicians were examined by a committee which began its questioning of them on 7 January.

He was asked, 'Can Dr Willis see any signs of approaching conva-lescence?'

'Yes,' he replied. 'A fortnight ago the King would take up books and could not read a line of them: he will now read several pages together and make, in my opinion, very good remarks upon the subject.' (He had, so Colonel Greville said, spent most of one morning recently reading Pope's *Essay on Man* with 'a fair degree of concentration'.) 'I think, in the main,' Willis continued, 'His Majesty does everything in a more rational way than he did, and some things exceeding rational . . . He is still exceedingly irritable, but not so irritable as he was, nor does the irritation continue one tenth so long.'

Sir Lucas Pepys tended to agree with Dr Willis. His Majesty was now 'more easily controlled', Pepys declared, 'and therefore advancing towards recovery'.

'Can Sir Lucas Pepys,' he was asked, 'speak with more certainty than at the last examination when you say His Majesty will recover?'

'Yes, I think I can.'

To the satisfaction of the Opposition, however, Dr Reynolds maintained that, although Dr Willis and his son were admittedly making the King more manageable, they were certainly not curing him; while Dr Warren still insisted that the King displayed no signs of improvement. 'I have heard from some attendants that His Majesty is *not* in a state of amendment,' Warren announced emphatically. 'There is *no* return of reason. Dr Willis has written to the Prince of Wales declaring progress I could not discover.'

'I see no symptoms of convalescence,' Warren reiterated at a subsequent meeting of the committee on 9 January. 'Sleep has produced no amendment: nor has control and coercion.'

The next day, on being questioned again by the members of the committee, Dr Willis stuck firmly to his stated belief that the King was getting better. Indeed, he now displayed not one symptom that could be described as incurable. 'Certainly,' he added, 'I have much more influence and control over His Majesty than the other physicians; and people visiting the King without me tend to irritate him.'

'Has the King ever conversed with you on a subject which he has read? And how long after?'

'Very often, and sometimes several hours later, for His Majesty never forgets what he reads.'

'When did Dr Willis last employ coercion?'

'Coercion has not been used for a week, and in the previous fortnight much less frequently than before.'

The next day, regrettably, coercion had to be used again. The King had had an extremely disturbed night and 'recourse was obliged to be had to the waistcoat'. His Majesty remained turbulent the next day also; and, as the month progressed, it became clear that he was almost as ill as he had ever been and that the doctors were as divided as before as to the method of treating him and even as to the symptoms their patient displayed. 'Pulse 96 I say,' Dr John wrote in his diary. '106 said Dr Warren – more said Sir Lucas Pepys.'

On 12 January Sir George Baker informed the committee that the King had relapsed into a 'state of total alienation'; while Dr Warren replied sharply to the Lord Chancellor, who had asked him whether or not the King would recover, 'I'll be damned if he does, and there you have it in your own words.'

There were thereafter more rational interludes: the King spoke sensibly again of Lord North, with whom he confessed he had once been 'very angry' but for whom he now felt 'only compassion'. He amused himself by drawing, and once showed the results of his efforts to a page. 'Not bad,' he commented ironically, 'for a madman.' Remembering the builders had not been paid for some work they had done at Kew, he asked that their bill should be settled. The account books had been kept from him, so as not to worry him, so, according to Colonel Greville, 'he made a calculation out of his head'.

On another occasion he seemed so calm and collected that the Queen insisted upon accompanying him on a proposed drive through Richmond Park which had earlier been promised him; but when it was decreed that he ought not to go for the drive the King became agitated again, shouted at the Rev. Thomas Willis, Dr John's younger brother, who had recently arrived at Windsor, warning him that he had been born to command, not to be told what to do, and then once more fell into rambling indecencies about Lady Pembroke.

The next day he again started talking about Lady Pembroke, his adored Eliza, his 'Queen of Hearts'. In the evening he was persuaded to play a game of piquet; but this brought on further outbursts about Lady Pembroke. Holding up the King of Hearts, he called out, 'Oh, if the Queen of Hearts would fall to the King.'

There was further trouble on 15 January, when the planned drive to Richmond Park was once more proposed. Colonel Greville warned Dr Willis against the excursion: when the carriage approached Lady Pembroke's house His Majesty would be sure to demand that he call there and would be violent when the visit was forbidden him.

He was violent anyway when the drive was consequently cancelled, and had to be strapped in the straitjacket for an hour or so. That evening he seemed to have forgotten his disappointment and joined the Willises in singing catches. But the next day he was violent again and was once more forcibly restrained, as he was also the following day, when he was not only tied up in his straitjacket but also given an emetic to quieten him. This made him so sick that he prayed to God, as he had done more than once in the past, to restore him to his senses or let him die.

Instead of to Richmond Park, the King, in calmer mood, was escorted on 19 January to Sir William Chambers's pagoda in Kew Gardens. He tried to run off to Richmond Park but was restrained; and he had again to be prevented from running off when he expressed a determination to climb to the top of the pagoda. Thwarted in his endeavour, he threw himself to the ground and refused to get up, and 'so powerful was his resistance that it was three-quarters of an hour before Willis and four assistants could raise him'. He was carried home and strapped in his straitjacket. Three days later he was thus confined yet again.

But, as Dr John noted, these wild and struggling rages were becoming less common. One day he was seen quietly feeding the Queen's dog and tying a blue ribbon round its neck; another day the Queen herself sat with him for an hour and emerged from his room looking so composed it was clear that there had been no weird or embarrassing talk about Eliza. On the eve of the day celebrated as the Queen's birthday he was described as being 'as mild as milk' and 'better than ever before': he read Gray's 'Elegy' and fell asleep peacefully over it. On the day itself he was wild in the morning, hurling a chair at one of the Willises' keepers; but he was quite calm again in the evening, when the Queen and the three eldest Princesses were allowed to sit with him and sing catches. He had been reading *King Lear*, he told them and was thankful that he was 'better off', since he had neither a Regan nor a Goneril but three Cordelias. 'Poor, dear Angel,' the Princess Royal later commented, 'how good of him to say this.'

35

THE KING'S RECOVERY

I'll take your advice, Dr John

On 23 January 1789 the King walked on the terrace in front of the house, beneath the window of the Queen's room. He called up to her to come down and join him. She did so, and they walked up and down together for an hour, as they had done in the past at Windsor. Perhaps the promenading reminded him of Windsor, for he spoke of the Castle often, longing to return. A few days later, as he was walking on the terrace, he caught sight of Colonel Greville and hurried up to him, calling 'Greville! Greville!' He took him by the arm and said urgently, 'You will walk with me, and I shall not part with you again today ... Remember your promise to be my friend. Now, what will you have? Will you have the Treasurership of the Household? No, that was your brother! One of you shall be Treasurer, the other Comptroller. Take your choice of these.'

'The dear King was as usual, well-intentioned and most kind to me,' Greville said, 'but alas he was much hurried, and there was much wildness in his countenance and manner.'

He was rarely to be so described again. When Miss Burney encountered him unexpectedly the following week in the garden she was 'alarmed past all possible expression', at least partly because the Queen had told all her ladies firmly that they must have no contact with him whatsoever. And as he lumbered towards her, calling hoarsely, 'Miss Burney! Miss Burney!', she fled headlong away from him, with the King shouting, 'Stop! Miss Burney! Stop!' and the Willises also calling out to her. When she did stop, she soon found that there was no reason for her terrified alarm.

'Why did you run away?' he asked her.

Shocked at a question impossible to answer, yet a little assured by the mild tone of his voice, I instantly forced myself forward, to meet him [she recorded] ... I looked up, and met all his wonted benignity of countenance, though something of wildness in his eyes. Think, however, of my surprise to feel him put both his hands round my two shoulders and then kiss my cheek! I wonder I did not really sink, so exquisite was my affright when I saw him spread out his arms! Involuntarily, I concluded he was about to crush me: but the Willises ... simply smiled and looked pleased ...

He told her he was 'quite well – as well as he had ever been in his life'; and asked her how she was getting on, telling her not to be put down by the dreaded Mrs Schwellenberg. 'Never mind her,' he said. 'Don't be oppressed. I am your friend. Don't let her cast you down. I know you have a hard time of it. But don't mind her ... I am your friend.'

'Almost thunderstruck with astonishment', Miss Burney merely curtsied by way of reply. 'Stick to your father,' he then said. 'Stick to your own family. Let them be your objects.'

He then repeated all that he had said: 'I will protect you. I promise you that. And therefore depend upon me!'

At this point, the Willises, 'thinking him rather too elevated', came up to suggest that Miss Burney should walk on. But '"No! No!" he cried, a hundred times in a breath; and their good humour prevailed, and they let him again walk on with his new companion.'

He then told her about his pages and how he had grown to dislike them all, particularly Ernst; he spoke also about her 'dear father, and made a thousand inquiries concerning his *History of Music*. This brought him to his favourite theme, Handel.' He told her innumerable anecdotes about him, then 'ran over most of his oratorios, attempting to sing the subjects of several airs and choruses, but so dreadfully hoarse that the sound was terrible'.

Dr Willis, becoming 'alarmed at this exertion, feared he would do himself harm and again proposed a separation. "No! No! No!" he exclaimed, "not yet; I have something I must just mention first."' Willis again gave way.

The good King then greatly affected me [Miss Burney continued]. He began upon my revered, old friend, Mrs Delany [who had died the year before]; and he spoke of her with such warmth – such kindness! 'She was my friend!'

he cried, 'and I loved her as a friend! I have made a memorandum when I lost her – I will show it you.'

He pulled out a pocket-book, and rummaged some time, but to no purpose. The tears stood in his eyes – he wiped them, and Dr Willis again became very anxious. 'Come, sir,' he cried, 'now do you come in and let the lady go on her walk, – come, now you have talked a long while, – so we'll go in, – if Your Majesty pleases.'

As soon as the King had taken leave of her, Miss Burney hurried to the Queen to tell her what had passed between them and of the King's being 'so nearly himself'. The Queen's 'astonishment, and her earnestness to hear every particular, were very great'. Miss Burney told her 'almost all', leaving out, of course, what had been said about Mrs Schwellenberg.

The next day the King's improvement was maintained. He was allowed to shave himself and to receive a visit from the Queen and the Princesses, who all sang catches with him, the King then assailing them with 'Rule, Britannia' rendered with great vigour. When he was told it was time for them to depart, he protested, pleading pathetically, 'I might surely stay a few hours with my family, when I must stay so many with footmen.' But in the end he parted from them 'very quietly'.

In the morning he was still quite calm and reasonable. Dr John, indeed, thought the King was better than he had ever been since he himself had come to Kew. He went to see how his animals were getting along on his farm; he played his flute, enjoyed a game of piquet with the Queen, and sang again in the evening. On 5 February Colonel Greville agreed with Dr John that the King had never been better – an opinion which Dr Warren still refused to share: in his view the patient was 'as deranged as ever'.

By the 6th Dr Warren's was a lonely voice. On that day the King shaved himself again without mishap, removing not only his beard but also the hairs on his head. By now he had reverted to his old habit of punctuating his talk with 'What? What? Hey! Hey!' He spoke animatedly to Stephen Rigaud, his astronomer, at the observatory, delivering a volley of questions and comments in his familiar manner, then hurried off to discuss the Botanic Gardens with Eaton, the head gardener, and his merino sheep with Sir Joseph Banks. He took some books and music out of the library, asked for some pictures to be replaced on the walls of his room, and was permitted the use of a knife and fork, instead of a spoon, at dinner. After dinner he elaborated his plans for an Order of Minerva, an award to be bestowed upon men of letters and learning.

He was perfectly amenable now to his doctors, readily giving way to Dr Willis, who told him he ought not just yet see the Lord Chancellor to find out what had been happening in the political world while he had been ill. 'I will not see him,' he said, 'until you think fit.' He gave the same assurance that he would not yet concern himself with politics to Dr John, whom he had asked whether or not Parliament was sitting. 'I'll take your advice, Dr John,' he said. 'But I adjourned Parliament and if it is now assembled, 'tis totally illegal.' Even Dr Warren was forced to concede that the patient was better when he had been asked to feel his pulse. 'How does it beat?' the King had asked him with a hint of triumph. 'And how many strokes did it beat three days ago? I think there is some amendment is there not?' Dr Warren was forced to agree that there was. Sir George Baker and Sir Lucas Pepys both thought so too. Dr Willis said there was 'a shade' of delirium left; but, as Lady Harcourt said, that 'shade' was no doubt his own natural manner which – being unknown to the Willises and 'different from that of the generality of the world, and very unlike what they may expect from a King' – might perhaps be 'considered by them as some remains of disorder'.

Those who had known the King in the past now considered that he had returned to his usual state. Lord Herbert, who spent some time with him on 10 February, said that if he had not known that the King had been ill he would not even have noticed how thin he was, though his usual weight of over fifteen stone had been reduced to little more than twelve.

As for the King himself, he felt he had no more need for doctors. Upon coming across Eaton, who was preparing a basket of fruit for Dr Willis, he said to him cheerfully and without the least malice, 'Get another basket, Eaton, and pack up the doctor in it and send him off at the same time.' The official bulletins now tended to confirm the King's own confidence in his recovery. On 10 February the bulletin described him as having 'passed the day before in a state of composure'. The next day he was said to be 'better this morning than he was yesterday'; and on the 12th he was 'in a progressive state of amendment'. Two days later Sir George Baker for the first time declared his belief that the King would 'get quite well'; and by 15 February even Dr Warren was sufficiently convinced of this amendment to state that if His Majesty continued through the day in the same state in which he had seen him in the morning 'he might be said to be well'.

On that day – it was a Sunday – the King played piquet with the Queen. Someone suggested to the Rev. Thomas Willis that, if the King had truly recovered and could tell one day from another, he would surely not play cards on a Sunday. 'He knows it's wrong,' Willis answered, 'but he says he thinks it may now be excusable, for he has no other way of entertaining the Queen.' Three days later the King and Queen went for a walk together, and when they returned he led her up to her room with evident affection; and before long, according to Lady Charlotte Finch, he was showing her 'every mark of tenderness'.

The Lord Chancellor expressed the opinion that the intelligence from Kew was so favourable that 'it would be indecent to proceed further with the Regency Bill when it might become wholly unnecessary'.

This was certainly not the view of the Opposition. In a debate on the Bill in the House of Commons on 5 February, Edmund Burke had declared unequivocally that the King was 'insane'. 'His faculties are totally eclipsed,' he said, 'not a partial but an entire eclipse . . . I maintain the utter impossibility of adducing proof whether a person who has been insane is perfectly recovered or not. The whole business is a scheme, under the pretence of pronouncing his Majesty sane, to bring back an insane King.'

Burke continued to propound this view despite the bulletins emanating from Kew which announced His Majesty's steady improvement. On 11 February, in one of his more frantic tirades, he declared:

Do we recollect that the Almighty has hurled [the King] from his throne, and plunged him into a condition that may justly excite the pity of the meanest peasant . . . Ought we to make a mockery of him, put a crown of

thorns upon his head, a reed in his hand, and cry 'Hail! King of the Britons!'
. . . I have visited the dreadful mansions where these unfortunate beings are
confined. Some, *after a supposed recovery*, have committed parricide, butchered
their sons, hanged, shot, drowned, thrown themselves from windows.

To shouts of protest the Irish voice ran on: 'Such is the danger of
an uncertain cure – such is the necessity to see that a sane sovereign
is put in possession of the Government.'

Yet, having been to see the King, the Lord Chancellor was perfectly
satisfied that, while certainly rather nervous, he was quite in command
of his faculties. Accordingly he postponed the third reading of the
Bill until 23 February.

36

PRAYERS AND CELEBRATIONS

The populace huzza'd Mr Pitt, but hooted and hissed Mr Fox.

Charles James Fox, who had been ill and had been advised by his doctor to leave London for Bath, clung to the hope that the regency would still come to pass. He told his friend Richard Fitzpatrick, Member of Parliament for Tavistock, that he rather thought Dr Warren had been frightened into joining the other doctors in giving favourable reports of the King; and he urged him to do his best to crush rumours that these reports had stopped the Prince and himself making plans for the regency. Fitzpatrick must endeavour 'to cure that habitual spirit of despondency and fear that characterizes the Whig party'. He had already drawn up a list of the men whom he expected to form part of the new Administration, placing the Duke of Portland as First Lord of the Treasury and himself as Foreign Minister; and he still professed himself confident that this Administration would very shortly be in office.

The Prince of Wales also was reluctant to abandon this hope, and, accompanied by the Duke of York, he went to Kew to find out whether or not his father was really as convalescent as the medical bulletins maintained. He was assured that His Majesty was well on the way to recovery; but Dr Willis asked him not to go into his room, as 'such a step might be of the utmost mischief to the King'.

The Prince and the Duke made several other visits to Kew and, denied access to the King's room on these occasions also, they asked that the doctors set out in writing their reasons for refusing them a visit which had been granted to the Lord Chancellor. They also wrote a formal letter to their mother, requesting permission to see His Majesty and to express their 'respectful joy' in his presence. He did not want to see them yet, distressed as he was by reports of their dealings with Fox and his friends. 'I propose,' he told the Queen, 'avoiding all discussions that may in their nature agitate me and consequently must for the present decline entering on subjects which are not necessarily before me.'

Towards the end of February 1789, however, he felt well enough to see his two sons; and the Queen wrote to tell them so, warning them to steer clear of contentious political affairs.

When they arrived, on 23 February, they were obviously very nervous; and so was the King, who hesitated at the door of the room in the Queen's apartments where the interview was to take place, 'crying very much'. He controlled himself before entering the room; but at the sight of his sons he burst into tears again and could not at first speak. When he began to talk he spoke of everyday matters, of the games of piquet he had played and the Latin he had read, of horses to the Prince and of his regiment to the Duke. The Queen remained in the room, so Sir Gilbert Elliot heard. She was suffering from severe toothache, and walked 'to and fro with a countenance and manner of great dissatisfaction, and the King every now and then went to her in a submissive and soothing sort of tone, for she [has] acquired the same sort of authority over him that Willis and his men have'.

As soon as her dinner was announced she left the room, taking curt leave of her sons, who were by now quite convinced of their father's recovery. They also had cause to believe that the Queen was not prepared to forgive them for their collusion with the Whigs during the last terrible months, and that she was particularly angry with the Duke of York, because he was the son whom his father loved most of all. They grew ever more exasperated by her petulant ill temper, until she and the Prince had a blazing quarrel in which he accused her of plotting with his enemies to disgrace and destroy him and she, so Elliot said, 'was violent and lost her temper'. The Queen had 'much to answer for', the Prince said. It was neither 'decent nor just' that Ministers were allowed to see the King – Mr Pitt had seen him the day after the unsatisfactory conversation with his two sons on 23 February – while he, his heir, was not permitted to explain his conduct during his father's illness.

When asking her sons to attend a concert to celebrate the King's recovery, she made it clear on the invitation that she was doing so only for propriety's sake: the entertainment was really intended for those who had remained loyal to His Majesty and herself during his illness. It certainly turned out to be a political and embarrassing occasion. The King was perfectly agreeable; but the Queen, more forbidding than ever, remained 'sour and glum' throughout, making it clear to her daughters that they were expected to behave as distantly to their brothers as she herself did.

The King was remarkably attentive and kind to the Princes [Sir Gilbert Elliot reported], the Queen quite the contrary, and it is said appeared dowdy and glum at the King's behaviour to them . . . At the concert the music had most of it some allusion to politics. All this is quite new at Court, and most excessively indecent, as the King is always expected to be of *no party*, and it is unconstitutional . . . that he should even express openly either favour or disfavour on account of any vote in Parliament . . . It is also said that the King showed very marked attention to Lady Pembroke; – that the Queen seemed uneasy, and tried to prevent it as often as she could; but that the Queen being at last engaged with somebody in conversation the King slipped away from her, and got to the other end of the room where Lady Pembroke was, and there was extremely gallant, and that Lady Pembroke seemed distressed and behaved with a becoming and maidenish modesty.

Although the Prince and the Duke did the best they could during the next few weeks to improve relations with their mother, it was made obvious to them that their overtures were unwelcome. When the King suffered a bad fall from his horse, having turned abruptly in his saddle to hear something Colonel Goldsworthy said to him, the Prince complained of being 'kept in perfect ignorance' of the incident; and when the Duke of York, having been publicly insulted by Colonel Charles Lennox, and having returned the insult, was challenged to a duel in which he was nearly killed by a bullet that shot off a curl from his wig, the Queen displayed not the least emotion on being informed of her son's narrow escape, merely remarking that Frederick was more likely to be in the wrong than Lennox, whose mother was one of her ladies.

She insisted on inviting Colonel Lennox to the King's birthday party. The Prince of Wales was also there, and when he caught sight of his fellow guest he took the Princess Royal, his sister, off the ballroom floor. Fox told Mrs Armistead that he thought the Queen's behaviour towards the Duke and the Prince went far beyond that of the 'worst woman we ever read of'.

The public made no secret of where their sympathies lay. When his coach was stopped in a jam of other carriages in a narrow street, 'the mob soon knew the Prince', Sir Gilbert Elliot recorded. 'They called "God save the King!" while the Prince letting down his glasses, joined them in calling very heartily, and hallooed, "Long live the King!" and so forth with the mob.'

The King's health continued to improve. He was still, as a precautionary measure, given doses of tartar emetic concealed in milk or even in bread and butter; and he still occasionally talked longingly of Lady Pembroke, once, in Dr John's hearing, saying to the Queen, 'If I pay respect to you, why need it affect you, my loving another?' He accepted that his head was not yet quite strong enough to talk about politics, and he told Pitt that for the moment he 'must decline entering upon pressure of business'. 'Indeed for the rest of my life,' he added, 'I should expect others to fulfil the duties of their employments, and only keep that superintending eye which can be effected without labour or fatigue.' But he had rational and enjoyable conversations about timepieces with Benjamin Vulliamy the Elder, the clockmaker, about sheep and farming with Sir Joseph Banks, and about his hothouse flowers with Colonel Greville. He spent evenings of quiet domesticity in the Queen's apartments; he read *The Merchant of Venice* to her and their daughters, adopting different tones and accents to suit the various parts; he played the flute; he went for walks around his farmyard and down by the river, where some boatmen called out to him, 'God bless your Majesty! Long life and health to you! We're glad to see you abroad again.' He went to visit his apothecary, who had been injured in a fall, and he said to him, 'You took care of me in my illness, 'tis my turn to nurse you now.' He even went to a lunatic asylum in Richmond and asked questions about the treatment of the inmates and the use of straitjackets. One day he saw the straitjacket which had been used on him hanging on the back of a chair, regarding it with composure and observing to a nervous equerry, who was fearful of the effect the sight might have on him, 'You needn't be afraid to look at it. Perhaps it is the best friend I ever had in my life.' He read the evidence which the physicians had given before the Commons Committee with equal imperturbability.

On 1 March Fanny Burney had the 'great gratification' of seeing him 'for a few moments in the Queen's dressing-room'. He said to her, 'Pray, are you quite well today?'

'I think not quite, sir,' she answered.

'She does not *look* well,' he said to the Queen. 'She looks a little – yellow, I think.'★

'How kind,' Miss Burney commented, 'to think of *anybody* and their looks, at this first moment of reappearance.'

The doctors' bulletins had remained optimistic throughout February. Dr Warren reported that 'His Majesty continues to advance in recovery.' On the 25th both Warren and Dr Reynolds announced that the King was now 'free from complaint'. The following day Sir George Baker and Sir Lucas Pepys concurred that there was 'an entire cessation of His Majesty's illness'. Thereafter no more bulletins were issued; and the First Minister assured his mother that the King was 'perfectly well'. On 3 March the King and Queen shared a bed together for the first time since the onset of his illness.

The Queen gave Fanny Burney a copy of the 'Prayer of Thanksgiving upon the King's Recovery' which was to be distributed to all the churches in the country. 'It kept me in tears all the morning,' Miss Burney wrote in her journal – 'that such a moment should actually arrive! after fears so dreadful, scenes so terrible. The Queen gave me a dozen to distribute among the female servants; but I reserved one of them for dear Mr. Smelt [Leonard Smelt, Sub-Governor to

---

★ The King was much given to making such personal remarks, which he did seemingly quite oblivious of the embarrassment they caused. 'How do you do, Dr Burney,' he greeted Fanny Burney's father one day in 1799, 'Why, you are grown fat! . . . Why, you used to be as thin as Dr Lind!' James Beattie, the Scottish poet and essayist, was also told he had grown fat (Forbes, *Account of the Life and Writings of James Beattie*, iii, 21). And he later told Fanny Burney herself, after she had left the royal service and become the wife of the French soldier General d'Arblay, that she too had become fat. He reckoned her arm had become 'half as big again as heretofore and then he measured it with his spread thumbs and forefingers' (d'Arblay, *Diary and Letters*, v, 87, 440).

the Princesses], who took it from me in speechless extacy – his fine
and feeling eyes swimming in tears of joy.'

Mr Smelt's thankfulness was most widely shared. From Naples,
Sir William Hamilton wrote to his friend Sir Joseph Banks:

What a train of evils and confusion have we escaped by this happy recovery.
The day after Tomorrow there shall be such a sirloin of Beef on my table as
I am sure never appear'd before at Naples. I have invited all the English,
factory and all, to partake of it and they shall drink His Majesty's health in
the best wines I have, which I can assure you are not despicable and are rare
in this country where nobody seems to give themselves any trouble to be
well served.

London displayed a blaze of light from one extremity to the other [Sir
Nathaniel Wraxall recorded]; the illuminations extending, without any meta-
phor, from Hampstead and Highgate to Clapham, and even as far as Tooting;
while the vast distance between Greenwich and Kensington presented the
same dazzling appearance. Even the elements seemed to favour the spectacle:
for the weather, though rather cold, was dry. Nor were the opulent and the
middle orders the only classes who came conspicuously forward on this
occasion. The poorest mechanics contributed their proportion; and instances
were exhibited of cobblers' stalls decorated with one or two farthing candles.
Such was the tribute of popular attachment manifested in March 1789 towards
a sovereign who, only seven years earlier, in March 1782, after losing a vast
empire beyond the Atlantic, seemed to stand on a fearful precipice.

There were balls at the Pantheon and at the Duke of York's. A
fête was held by White's, where Colonel Manners, who had taken
over as equerry on the expiration of Colonel Greville's tour of duty,
sang 'God Save the King' so lustily that he was asked not to be so
loud. 'They pretended I was out of tune,' Manners said. 'But it was
in such a good cause I did not mind.' At other parties, ladies appeared
in gowns of white and gold with purple bandeaux round their heads
with the words 'God Save the King' picked out in diamonds. The
French Ambassador gave a splendid entertainment at his Embassy in
Portland Place; the Spanish Ambassador an even more magnificent
one at Ranelagh.

Houses and public buildings all over London were illuminated,
and emblazoned with crowns, the letters 'G. R.' and the words 'God
Save the King'. Coaches were decorated, and even sedan chairs were

lit up. Shouting their congratulations, people poured through the streets, abusing those 'rats' who had deserted the King – notably the Duke of Queensberry, the Marquess of Lothian and Lord Rawdon – and breaking the windows of houses which were not illuminated. To the surprise of passers-by, candles flickered in the windows even of Brooks's. The house of Samuel Johnson's friend Mrs Thrale blazed with light, and she herself expressed her profound relief that the King had escaped from the clutches of the doctors, some of whom, she feared, were quite capable of putting an end to his 'sacred life' and then saying 'he did it himself'.

Even Sheridan toasted the King's health, to the annoyance of his sister Betsy, who strongly disapproved of the celebrations. 'All for what?' she asked. 'For truth to say I do not think the recovery exists.' Her brother, however – even though he was giving a dinner to celebrate the imminent regency when he was told that the Bill inaugurating it had been withdrawn – drank a bumper to the King's long life and prosperity.

The doctors too rejoiced, for they were most handsomely rewarded, being given £30 for every one of their visits to Windsor and £10 for their calls at Kew. Sir George Baker had £1,380, Dr Willis £1,000 a year for twenty years, and Dr John £500 a year for life. The King told Pitt that these sums seemed 'very large' to him, but, he added, 'I will not enter upon a subject that cannot but give me pain.'

On 23 April 1789, St George's Day, there was a service of thanksgiving in St Paul's Cathedral. Doubts had been expressed as to whether the King was yet well enough to attend such a service. He himself had told Pitt two days before that he still felt 'more strongly the effects of [his] late severe and tedious illness' than he had expected. He suffered, he said, from 'a certain lassitude and want of energy both of mind and body which must require time, relaxation and change of scene to restore'. Yet, when the Archbishop of Canterbury suggested that such a service as was proposed might be too much for him, he said, 'My Lord, I have twice read over the evidence of the physicians on my case, and if I can stand that I can stand anything.' He had taken the Sacrament before reading the reports, so that he might be helped into a frame of mind ready to forgive 'those who might have acted in a manner' he could not approve. There was, indeed, he decided when he had read them, much to forgive: not only the doctors, but some of his Ministers and certain members of his family had also appeared to have been prepared to write him off as a lunatic. At least most of them were now ready to share the people's enthusiastic gratitude for his recovery.

The crowds lining the approaches to St Paul's sang 'God Save the King' with gusto. 'What pleased us most,' the diarist Mary Frampton told her sister, 'was that the populace huzza'd Mr Pitt, but hooted and hissed Mr Fox – at least, the greatest number did so. Mr Fox, in consequence, sat quite back in his coach, not to be seen.' He was, however, recognized as his coach passed through Temple Bar, according to *The Times*, and he 'received an universal hiss which continued with very little intermission until he alighted at St Paul's'.

The Prince of Wales was also driven to St Paul's to the accompaniment of the jeers and catcalls that now almost invariably greeted his coach. Inside the Cathedral he was reported to have further antagonized his critics by entering into a whispered conversation with his brother and uncles in the middle of the service, by munching biscuits during the sermon, and by making some observation to the Duke of York that made his brother laugh so much he had to cover his face with his hands. Nor was the King's behaviour above reproach. Sir Gilbert Elliot, who was in one of the galleries above the choir, said that 'he looked about with his opera glass and spoke to the Queen during the greater part of the service, very much as if he had been at a play'. At one moment he covered his face with his handkerchief; and then wept when a prayer for him was read.

Elliot himself wept when six thousand children from the charity schools in the City 'set up their little voices and sang part of the Hundredth Psalm'. 'This was the case,' he added, 'with many other people. I had not seen the King since his illness and I was much struck with the alteration in him . . . He is quite an object of thinness and appears extremely weak by his manner of walking . . . He was dressed in the Windsor uniform, had on a greatcoat which reached to his ankles and was probably intended to conceal his legs which are extremely thin.'

★

Lord Cornwallis, now Governor-General of India, expressing a widespread sentiment, wrote home to say, 'The King's recovery gave me the most heartfelt contentment. I rejoiced very sincerely on his account, and I cannot wish to see poor old England in the ravenous jaws of the Buff and Blue squad', the party distinguished by the colours of Fox's supporters. Sharing Cornwallis's contentment, Princess Augusta wrote to her brother Prince Augustus in France, 'I'm sure it is quite impossible for anybody to be more adored and respected and esteemed than the King is at this moment. It would do your heart good to be witness of it. Well! Thank God he is so much *loved*.'

Equally thankful, and much cheered by the demonstrations of loyalty to the Crown, the Queen became almost skittish in her relief. She crept up one day behind the Princesses' friend the Hon. Georgina Townshend and tapped her on the bottom. 'I started round and to my astonishment saw the Queen,' Miss Townshend commented. 'She laughed and said, "I believe you never was whipped by a Queen before."' Yet the past dreadful weeks had aged her. When Thomas Lawrence, then at the outset of his distinguished career, asked if he might paint her, she refused him: she was, she said, not yet sufficiently recovered 'from all the trouble she had gone through'. Eventually she was persuaded to change her mind; but she sat to him impatiently, and once the preliminary work was done her place was taken by Mrs Papendiek for the completion of the picture. The portrait when finished revealed a woman of severe expression whose eyes – 'sure index to the human soul', as her biographer Olwen Hedley put it – 'are oppressed and bleak'. The King, complaining that she was depicted without the head-covering which she always wore in the daytime, did not buy the picture, which now hangs in the National Gallery.

The King continued to behave most considerately and fondly towards her. His old friend Lord Ailesbury had recently written of his 'exceedingly affectionate' behaviour and his description of his wife as the person he loved most in the world. He was well aware how deeply distressed she must have been if she had heard all that he had said about Lady Pembroke during his illness. 'He very feelingly said to one of his pages he hoped nobody knew what wrong ideas he had had, and what wrong things he had said respecting her,' Colonel Greville wrote. 'He observed at this time that in his delirium he must have said many very improper things, and that much must have escaped him then which ought not.'

He later thought it as well to write to Lady Pembroke, and she replied with understanding fondness: 'Your Majesty has always acted by me as the kindest brother as well as the most gracious of sovereigns . . . If I might presume to say that I felt like the most affectionate sister towards an indulgent brother it would exactly express my sentiments.'

37

WEYMOUTH *EN FÊTE*

They have dressed out every street with labels of
'God Save the King'.

Passing through Datchet on his way back to Windsor, the King was much gratified to see the inhabitants drop to their knees in welcoming him. At other villages they gathered in the streets to cheer him as he rode by, looking fifteen years younger, according to George Hardinge, the Queen's Solicitor-General, 'and much better in the face, though as red as ever'.

At Windsor the military guard at the Castle were reduced to tears at the joyful sight of his homecoming. Yet, happy as he was himself to be home again, he did not remain at Windsor for long, for it was decided that his convalescence would be accelerated by the beneficial effects of sea air. So in the summer of 1789 it was decided that an attenuated Royal Household should move to Gloucester House, on the seafront at Weymouth, a house which belonged to the Duke of Gloucester, his brother, and which the King eventually bought from him.

Their journey was 'one scene of festivity and rejoicing', as Miss Burney described it, with the cheers of the crowds and the boom of bands along the route ringing in their ears. 'Carriages of all sorts lined the roadside: – chariots, chaises, landaus, carts, waggons, whiskies, gigs, phaetons – mixed and intermixed, filled within and surrounded without by faces all glee and delight.'

They stayed first for a few days at Lyndhurst, in a house belonging to the King but lent to the Duke of Gloucester, a 'straggling, inconvenient, old house,' as Fanny Burney described it, 'but delightfully situated in a village, – looking indeed, at present, like a populous town, from the amazing concourse of people that have crowded into it'.

During the King's dinner, which was in a parlour looking into the garden [Miss Burney continued], he permitted the people to come to the window; and their delight and rapture in seeing their monarch at table, with the evident hungry feeling it occasioned, made a contrast of admiration and deprivation, truly comic. They crowded, however, so excessively, that this can be permitted them no more. They broke down all the paling, and much of the hedges, and some of the windows, and all by eagerness and multitude, for they were perfectly civil and well-behaved.

In the afternoon the royal party came into my parlour; and the moment the people saw the star [of the Order of the Garter on the King's coat], they set up such a shout as made a ring all around the village . . .

[The royal party] all walked out, about and around the village, in the evening, and the delighted mob accompanied them. The moment they stepped out of the house, the people, with one voice, struck up 'God Save the King!' I assure you I cried like a child twenty times in the day, at the honest and rapturous effusions of such artless and disinterested loyalty . . . The King's popularity is greater than ever. Compassion for his late sufferings seems to have endeared him now to all conditions of men. These good villagers continued singing this loyal song during the whole walk, without any intermission, except to shout 'huzza!' at the end of every stanza.

On Sunday they sang 'God Save the King' in the parish church, which Miss Burney thought misplaced but 'its intent was so kind, loyal and affectionate' that she believed there was 'not a dry eye amongst either singers or hearers'.

From Lyndhurst the royal party drove on to Salisbury, where the King's coach passed under a magnificent arch festooned with flowers and the inhabitants welcomed him 'dressed out in white loose frocks, flowers, and ribbons, with sticks or caps emblematically decorated from their several manufactories'. Approaching Blandford, 'At every gentleman's seat which we passed, the owners and their families stood at the gate, and their guests or neighbours were in carriages all round.' At Dorchester the crowds seemed even more dense than they had been elsewhere: windows had been removed from their frames to give a clearer view; and the roofs above them were covered with cheering spectators. After that, 'Girls, with chaplets, beautiful young creatures, strewed the entrance of various villages with flowers.'

'The bay here is most beautiful,' Miss Burney reported to her father on 13 July, having eventually reached Weymouth some days before; 'the sea never rough, generally calm and gentle, and the sands perfectly smooth and pleasant.'*

The town was *en fête*. 'They have dressed out every street with labels of "God Save the King,"' she continued: 'all the shops have it over the doors; all the children wear it in their caps, all the labourers in their hats, and all the sailors in their voices, for they never approach the house without shouting it aloud, nor see the King, or his shadow, without beginning to huzza, and going on to three cheers.'

The bathing machines had 'God Save the King' emblazoned over their windows; and the professional dippers who helped the bathers into the sea wore the motto in bandeaux on their bonnets as well as in large letters round their waists. And, when the King himself appeared at the door of one of the machines and climbed down the steps into the water, a band concealed in a neighbouring machine struck up the National Anthem.

One thing, however, was a little unlucky [Fanny Burney added in her letter to her father]; – when the Mayor and burgesses came with the address, they requested leave to kiss hands; this was graciously accorded; but, the Mayor advancing, in a common way, *to take the Queen's hand*, as he might that of any lady mayoress, Colonel Gwynn, who stood by, whispered, 'You must kneel, sir!' He found, however, that he took no notice of this hint, but kissed the Queen's hand erect. As he passed him, in his way back, the Colonel said, 'You should have knelt, sir!'

'Sir,' answered the poor Mayor, 'I cannot.'

'Everybody does, sir.'

'Sir, – I have a wooden leg!'

Poor man! 'twas such a surprise! and such an excuse as no one could dispute. But the absurdity of the matter followed; – all the rest did the same; taking the same privilege, by the example, without the same or any cause!

The King and Queen, accompanied by their three eldest daughters, spent their days bathing, walking along the Esplanade or on the

* Described as 'but little' in 1733, Weymouth had since been expanding as its reputation as a watering-place grew. By 1801, twelve years after the King's first visit, its fame had been assured and it was as much as half the size of Brighton. Fifty years later, however, it 'had shrunk relatively to one eighth of Brighton's population' (Thompson, ed., *The Cambridge Social History of Britain, 1750–1850* i, 22).

sands, drinking tea in a private apartment off the Assembly Rooms with the doors left open so they could be seen, visiting country houses and nearby ruins, driving about in the Queen's open carriage, and taking trips in the frigate anchored for the purpose in the bay. In the evenings there were card parties and plays, with the King's favourite actress, Mrs Siddons, to see at the theatre; and on 8 September, the anniversary of the wedding of the King and Queen, they gave a ball.

When the holiday was over and the Household returned to Windsor by way of the Marquess of Bath's house, Longleat, ('very grand and fine but not comfortable' in the Queen's opinion) and Lord Ailesbury's Tottenham Court, Savernake Forest ('abominable, built by the late Lrd. Burlington, whose architecture is the very worst one can see'), the Queen told Prince Augustus that his father was 'much better and stronger for the sea bathing'. 'He began his levees yesterday [23 September 1789],' she added, 'and bore it very well, but little fatigued and seemed very cheerful at night, so I have hopes that we shall soon come to go on in our old way.'

38

WAR WITH FRANCE

*Duty, as well as interest, calls on us to join against
that most savage as well as unprincipled nation.*

'How much the greatest event it is that ever happened in the world!'
Charles James Fox had written on hearing of the assault on the
Bastille in Paris in July 1789. 'And how much the best!' Thereafter,
to the King's disgust, Fox warmly advocated the revolutionary cause
and praised the French soldiers for joining their fellow citizens and
taking part against the Crown.

Just over three years later, through the thin patches of a drifting
mist at Valmy, Goethe watched the well-trained Prussian army of
King George III's cousin Frederick William II falter, halt and turn
aside, demoralized before the massed forces of the French Revolution.
'On this day, at this place,' said Goethe, 'a new era opens in the
history of the world.' The next day the French National Convention
declared that the monarchy was abolished; and a few hours afterwards,
on 22 September 1792, there dawned the first day of Year One of
the Republic. Before Year One was out, the head of Louis XVI was
held up to the crowds at the foot of the guillotine. The reaction of
Europe to this fierce provocation was immediate. Within less than
a fortnight France found herself at war not only with Prussia and
Piedmont but also with Spain, Holland, the Austrian Empire and
Britain.

'The Kings in alliance try to intimidate us,' Danton cried defiantly.
'We hurl at their feet the French King's head.'

The British King had no doubt that, in joining the war against
France, his country would be fighting in a just cause for the sake not
only of the monarchy but of the established order in Europe and the
'preservation of society' and of Britain's constitution, which he

devoutly prayed would remain 'unimpaired to the latest posterity'. 'Every tie of religion, morality and society not only authorises but demands' resistance to the French threat, he declared. 'Now is the hour to humble France, for nothing but her being disabled from disturbing other countries . . . will keep her quiet . . . I confess I am of opinion that in the actual state of things [war] seems the most desirable conclusion of the present crisis.' Although his 'natural sentiments' were 'strong for peace', he told Pitt, he was 'decidedly of opinion that duty, as well as interest, calls on us to join against that most savage as well as unprincipled nation.'

For once the Prince of Wales agreed with the King. The outbreak of the French Revolution and the execution of Louis XVI had sent the Prince scurrying from Charles James Fox towards his father, his 'good and gracious father', to whom, so he told his mother, he felt 'a species of sentiment' which 'surpassed all description'. He let it be known that he now supported the King's Ministers and shared the King's views about Edmund Burke's *Reflections on the Revolution in France* – a book which his father, much gratified by Burke's having turned his back on his old friends to support Pitt, considered a 'good book' and one that 'every gentleman ought to read' as an antidote to *The Rights of Man* by that seditious republican Thomas Paine.★

Although he had said that in future his role as monarch would merely be to keep a 'superintending eye' upon the process of government, the King took the same energetic interest in the conduct of the war as he had done during the American conflict, lamenting

---

★ The publication of the two parts of Paine's *Rights of Man* in 1791 and 1792 coincided with an outbreak of exceptionally malicious ridicule of the King and Queen by caricaturists. Gillray's *Taking Physick; – or – The News of Shooting the King of Sweden!* (M. D. George, *Catalogue*, vol. 6 (BM 8080)) is a characteristic example. In this Pitt is seen bursting into the King's privy, brandishing a paper inscribed 'News from Sweden' and announcing 'Another Monarch done over!' The King, seated on the latrine with the Queen at his side and his breeches round his knees, clutches his stomach as he cries out in alarm, 'What! Shot! What! What! What! Shot! Shot! Shot!' 'It has been claimed that the very familiarity of such images, their emphasis on the humdrum ordinariness of palace life, made possible the affectionate identification of the people with the "father of the nation" . . . However, they excited the ire and alarm of the loyalists' (Donald, *The Golden Age of Caricature*, 146).

failures and rejoicing in victories, his joy tempered, however, by the realization of the dreadful loss of life, as it was to be, for example, after Admiral Duncan's victory over the Dutch fleet at Camperdown in October 1797.

The King seemed overpowered with its magnitude [wrote a friend of the Royal Family who was at Windsor when the news of the battle was brought there], and, pacing up and down the long dark room in which he usually sat, appeared occasionally to ejaculate something in a low voice when the Princess Augusta said to him – 'Papa, you are not half happy enough, so many of the Dutch have fallen, and so few of our English!' Repeating her observation, he turned short, as if awakened from a reverie, and said, with a sharpness not usual with him, 'Remember Augusta, there are just as many widows and orphans as if they were all English.'

The King at this time had the health and strength to keep his 'superintending eye' alert. 'He is quite an altered man, and not what you knew him even before his illness,' Lord Auckland had written not long before. He had 'never been better'. 'His manner is gentle, quiet, and, when he is pleased, quite cordial. He speaks even of those who are opposed to his Government with complacency and without either sneer or acrimony; at the same time he is most steadily attached to his Ministers.'

He was never close to Pitt as he had been to North. But they had a perfectly satisfactory working relationship; and whenever difficulties arose they were settled without acrimony. When, for instance, in 1792 Pitt wanted to dismiss the irritable Lord Chancellor, Lord Thurlow, for whom the King had much respect, and threatened to resign if Thurlow did not go, His Majesty decided that Thurlow would have to depart, at the same time doing all he could to make his departure less painful. Similarly, when the name of Pitt's friend Henry Dundas, the Home Secretary, was put forward as a possible candidate for a governorship of the Charterhouse and the King objected – since these enviable governorships were traditionally granted to men of rank, and Dundas, who spoke with 'a broad Scotch accent', came from a line of Scottish lawyers of no remarkable social distinction – Pitt urged him not to upset the King by pressing his claim: he would undoubtedly be given the appointment in the end – as, indeed, he was.

Closely watching Pitt and his other Ministers in their conduct of the war, the King did not hesitate to give them his advice, which was almost always as well considered as his warnings were justified. He strongly advocated, for example, an assault upon France's colonies in the West Indies, and persistently advised the Secretary for War not to 'have too many irons in the fire' nor to 'attempt too many objects at the same time' – advice he had pressed upon the Government in the earlier war. He regularly discussed operations with the Commander-in-Chief, Lord Amherst, and with the Duke of York, who, at his instigation, was appointed to take command of the British contingent dispatched to Flanders to cooperate with the Austrians. The King also continued to take the interest he had always taken in the promotions and pensions of army officers, in the fortunes of the regiments in which they served, and in the process and verdicts of courts martial. When the likelihood of defeating the French seemed remote, he urged his Ministers not to lose heart. 'Unless the French are thoroughly reduced,' he declared, 'no solid peace can be obtained.' Hastily rushing into a precipitate peace would 'for ever close the glory of this country'. Yet, when Pitt's Cabinet concluded that negotiating for a peaceful settlement would have to be initiated – if only because, as Lord Grenville, the Foreign Secretary, put it, the enemy could not be resisted 'without resources of finance' – the King did not stubbornly resist, remarking that, while he deplored the Cabinet's decision, he would accept it 'with sorrow'. Indeed, he was in the habit of giving way without further argument when confronted by a firm Cabinet decision. A case in point was the King's opposition to an attack upon Copenhagen to force the Danes to withdraw from the Armed Neutrality of the North, an alliance – inspired by Bonaparte's admirer the deranged Tsar – between Russia, Sweden, Prussia and Denmark, countries exasperated by British ships stopping and searching their merchant vessels and occasionally seizing cargoes intended for unloading in French ports. The King argued strongly against this proposed attack upon the Danes as 'a very immoral act' which, in addition, would probably induce the Crown Prince of Denmark to become a supporter of the 'Corsican usurper' – as, in the event, it did. The Duke of Portland, the Home Secretary, was sent down to Windsor to explain the Cabinet's policy to the

King, who, without approving of it and making clear his reasons for that disapproval, raised no further objections to it.

As with the war, so with the problem of Ireland, where the Irish Parliament had been granted legislative independence in 1782: the King concerned himself more deeply than he had thought possible at the time of his convalescence. He lamented the encouragement which the French Revolution had given to Irish nationalism, and he dreaded the thought that he might be asked to accede to demands for the emancipation of Roman Catholics. It was not that he was prejudiced against individual Catholics. He was on perfectly friendly terms with many of them – as he had been, for instance, with Edward Weld, Mrs Fitzherbert's first husband, whom he rode over to see when staying at Weymouth, and Lord Petre, who had entertained the King at Thorndon Hall in Essex in 1779; and when Prince Henry Benedict, the Cardinal Duke of York, the pretender to the English throne as King Henry IX, had been rendered penniless by the French occupation of the Papal States, the King responded at once to a plea for help. He sent £500 at once from the Civil List for the Cardinal's immediate necessities, and settled upon him a pension for life of £4,000. The Cardinal was deeply grateful to the man to whom he had always referred as the Elector of Hanover, and he wrote to the former Sir Gilbert Elliot, now Earl of Minto, British Plenipotentiary in Vienna, to express his gratitude for this 'noble and spontaneous generosity'.

Yet, kindly disposed as he was to individual Catholics, and never denying their right to worship as they pleased, the King could never forget that at his coronation he had taken an oath to maintain the rights and privileges of the Anglican Church. He had solemnly undertaken to exclude adherents to the faith of his Roman Catholic predecessor King James II from any position of authority under the Crown; and if he violated that undertaking, he told his family, having read his coronation oath to them, 'I am no longer legal Sovereign of this country, but it falls to the House of Savoy.' There was no power on earth, he insisted, which would absolve him from 'the due observance of every sentence' of the oath which he had made 'to maintain the Protestant reformed religion established by law'. He had discussed the matter with the most learned of lawyers and the most devout of bishops; and the matter was 'beyond the decision of any Cabinet of Ministers'. It was, in fact, the duty of Ministers, as he had once told Lord North, 'as much as possible to prevent any alterations in so essential a part of the Constitution as everything that relates to religion'. There was no more to be said upon the subject. His opinions on it had 'not been formed on the moment' but were such as he had 'imbibed for forty years'.

The great majority of his subjects were of the same opinion. He made clear at a levee on 28 January 1801 that anyone who proposed or voted in favour of emancipation would immediately forfeit his friendship; when Henry Dundas, by now Secretary of State for War, attempted to propose that there was a distinction between the King in his private and in his constitutional capacity, he cut him short sharply: 'None of your Scotch metaphysics!' He would rather beg his bread 'from door to door throughout Europe' than consent to any measure which would be a betrayal of his solemn oath.

His answer to Pitt's request that he might have His Majesty's agreement to his bringing a measure of emancipation before Parliament could not, therefore, be in doubt. Accordingly, on 3 February, Pitt announced his intention of resigning. The King accepted the resignation with some relief, since it was not only the question of Roman Catholic emancipation which had come between them: Pitt had not been very attentive of late. 'Other Business and want of Health,' as Pitt himself confessed, 'had often made him postpone both written and personal communication with the King', while for six weeks at a time he had not attended the levees at St James's as was expected of all Ministers, most particularly the First.

Henry Addington, the amiable, unremarkable Speaker of the House of Commons and son of one of the doctors who had attended the King in his illness, was nominated Pitt's successor after some pressure had been put upon him by the King, whose talent for persuasion, as Lord Glenbervie said, was 'universally known to be very great'. 'My dear Addington,' the King said to him after he had accepted the appointment, profoundly relieved to have found a First Minister who shared his views on Roman Catholic emancipation. 'My dear Addington, you have saved your country.'

The King and Pitt parted quite amicably. The former Minister, who was also kindly disposed to Addington, possessed His Majesty's 'highest esteem and good opinion'. 'You have acted throughout this business like *yourself* and more I cannot say,' the King told him on 11 February, when Pitt put in his first appearance at a levee for several weeks. 'I don't care who hears me . . . I cannot say too much of your conduct.'

Addressing him as 'My Dear Pitt' – a familiar form he had never employed in the past – he assured him that it was 'much to [his] sorrow' that his Minister was now closing his 'Political Career'; and, well aware of how severely Pitt's finances, as well as his health, had suffered during the seventeen years he had been in office, the King offered to pay his debts, assuring him that he hoped that they would always be friends and that Pitt would feel free to come and see him whenever he felt inclined to do so. Indeed, Pitt said, His Majesty behaved with 'unbounded kindness'. The King acted with equal generosity in his dealings with Addington, to whom he offered White Lodge, King George I's former hunting lodge in Richmond Park, with furniture for it and sixty acres of land around it. Addington said that he would be quite content with five acres but would be most pleased to accept the house.*

---

* George Canning, who had been Paymaster General in Pitt's Administration and had a very low opinion of the new First Minister, the Reading doctor's son, referred to White Lodge sardonically as the Villa Medici.

39

RELAPSE AND RECOVERY

I should like to fight Boney single-handed. I'm sure I should.
I should give him a good hiding. I'm sure I should. I'm sure of it.

On 20 February 1801 Lord Eldon, Lord Chancellor in Addington's Administration, was received by the King, whom he found calm and rational throughout the two hours they spent together. Eldon was surprised by this, since three days before Addington had described the King as being worryingly 'heated' and 'hurried' in his manner. He had caught a chill on 13 February, and soon afterwards suffered from painful cramps, constipation, sickness and hoarseness of voice. It was feared that he was to relapse into the illness the return of which he so much dreaded, for these, indeed, had been the early symptoms of the past affliction. He warned the Queen of his apprehension, and told his daughters that they might not be able to see him for a time. A message was sent to the Willises to come to London to attend the King. Dr Francis Willis, now eighty-two years old, had retired; but Dr John obeyed the summons with his brother the Rev. Thomas, who was later followed by another brother, Robert Darling Willis.

'I do feel myself very ill,' the King told Thomas Willis on 21 February, convinced that he was so because of worry about the Roman Catholic question. 'I am much weaker than I was, and I have prayed to God all night that I might die, or that He would spare my reason . . . For God's sake keep me from your father and a regency.' That night he became delirious and, although helped by two other doctors, Gisborne and Reynolds, Willis took over an hour to get his distracted patient into bed.

Two days later he was worse than ever, and in the night he fell into a coma. As in 1788 the Willises expressed their confidence in the King's recovery, but the other doctors expected him to die. On 27 February, however, he showed signs of improvement, and the following day Henry Addington reported to his friend Charles Abbot, at that time Chief Secretary for Ireland:

[The King] slept two and a half hours last night uninterruptedly and his former mode of talking, his 'what, what, what?' returns. He undresses himself in the usual way, and eats as usual. They now give him bark [quinine] and port wine. Mr Pitt thinks it unnecessary to deliberate on modes of Regency ... The Willises think the King may recover very speedily indeed.

This prognosis proved too sanguine. Soon afterwards his pulse rose to a furious rate, and on 2 March the Prince of Wales and the Queen were both called to his bedside. All manner of remedies were employed: hot vinegar was applied to his feet, and blisters to his head; he was given musk as well as quinine, and tartar emetics; and, as a cure for his insomnia, at Addington's suggestion, a pillow of warm hops was placed under his restless head. Having slept for several hours, he awoke feeling rather better, but for days thereafter he was nervous and irritable, found difficulty in swallowing, and convulsively clenched his teeth, while 'his state of nerves seemed to compel him to roll up his handkerchiefs'. He found it difficult to concentrate his mind, and his failure to do so often reduced him to tears. However, by 5 March he was sitting up in bed and eating his meals unaided. The next day he was allowed to see the Queen, and the day after that the Duke of York, whom he questioned about public affairs. When the Duke hesitated to trouble his father's mind with such matters, he said, 'Frederick, you are more nervous than I am. I really feel quite well and know full well how ill I have been.'

He was gratified to learn how many people had been to the Queen's House to learn about his condition and to wish him well, among them several members of the Opposition who had behaved so callously in 1788. But when he learned that Pitt had called he told Thomas Willis 'to tell him I am quite well – quite recovered from my illness; but what has he not to answer for, who is the cause of my being ill at all?' When told what the King had said, Pitt hastily replied to the effect that he would 'not bring forward the Catholic question' in future, whether in or out of office, and that he would try to defer it should it be 'agitated' by others. This message was immediately passed on to the King, who, so Willis reported, 'exclaimed, "Now my mind will be at ease."'

The King's convalescence was a long one. He slept badly; he looked tired and shrunken, older than his sixty-two years; his eyes, growing dim, appeared more prominent than ever in that strained face. Three months after the onset of his illness, Lord Glenbervie, the joint Paymaster General, described him as being emaciated, 'with the clothes hanging upon him'. He insisted upon reading the Cabinet minutes and signing papers; but this tired him and made him grumpy and, on occasions, 'extremely nervous, low spirited . . . and unequal to business'.

Pressed by Ministers to do so, the Willises endeavoured to prepare him satisfactorily for appearances at St James's Palace, placing more blisters on his legs and administering emetics to combat his excitable moods, so that he would not appear too flustered and garrulous. He was, however, not presentable enough to attend the first of these proposed appearances, on 26 March at the Queen's drawing-room, where the Princesses were seen to be in tears and the Queen, so Lady Malmesbury said, 'looked like death'.

Deeply resenting the painful and exhausting treatment to which they subjected him, the King grew increasingly angry with the doctors – particularly with Dr John Willis, who lectured him on his conduct and told him that his abuse of those who had brought him out of a 'very dangerous and severe fever' was a 'proof of the remnant of his disorder'.

The King responded by ordering the Willises out of his house and driving off to the White House at Kew. The Willises were, however, not prepared to let him escape so easily from their care. With the approval of the Queen and the Cabinet, they proposed to detain him by force. Entering the King's room with their men, they told him bluntly of their intention. Thomas Willis described the scene:

On the King getting sight of me he seemed surprised and would have hastily passed and escaped out of the room but I prevented him . . . I spoke to him at once of his situation and the necessity there was that he should be immediately under control again. His Majesty sat down, turning very pale . . . and exclaimed, 'Sir, I will never forgive you whilst I live.'

For a month thereafter he was kept confined in the White House, denied access to the Queen and his daughters at the Dutch House, his daily routine and behaviour carefully monitored by the Willises. In fact this supervision was quite unnecessary. He wrote sensible letters, conducted rational conversations, played chess and cards, and signed documents until, in the middle of May, he announced to the Lord Chancellor, who had come to see him, that, unless he was allowed 'to go over to the house where the Queen and his family were, no earthly consideration should induce him to sign his name to any paper or to do one act of government whatever'.

Forced by this threat of a royal strike, the Willises gave way; and the King was permitted to visit the Queen and their daughters. His recovery thereafter was spasmodic. By 21 May he appeared to be much better. Indeed, Sir William Grant went so far as to describe him as looking 'extremely well, stout and upright' at a Privy Council meeting on that day. He 'spoke to all his Council individually, going round as at a levee . . . and joked as usual with the Ministers'. Four days later, however, Thomas Willis reported to the Lord Chancellor:

He had but three hours' sleep in the night, which upon the whole was passed in restlessness, in getting out of bed, opening the shutters, praying at times violently, and in making such remarks as betray a consciousness in him of his own situation, but which are evidently made for the purpose of concealing it from the Queen. He frequently called out – 'I am now perfectly well, and my Queen, my Queen has saved me.' Whilst I state these particulars to your Lordship, I must beg to remind you how much afraid the Queen is lest she should be committed to him; for the King has sworn he will never forgive her if she relates anything that passes in the night.

The King woke on most mornings feeling tired and, most unusually for him, was reluctant to get out of bed. Believing that his lassitude was the consequence of his not taking enough exercise, he went out hunting for hours on end and returned more tired than ever, talking little in the evening and going to sleep in his chair.

I have nothing to say that is in truth very favourable [Thomas Willis reported to the Lord Chancellor on 16 June]. His Majesty rode out this morning at ten o'clock and did not return till four. He paid a visit in the course of the day to Mr Dundas [at Wimbledon]. His attendants thought him much hurried, and so think his pages. He has a great thirst upon him, and his family are in great fear . . . His body, mind, and tongue are all upon the stretch every minute; and the manner in which he is now expending money in various ways, which is so unlike him when well, all evince that he is not so right as he should be.

Towards the end of the month, however, he appeared to be so much improved that it was decided that he should complete his convalescence at Weymouth with the Queen, the Princesses and Prince Adolphus, then aged twenty-seven. On their way, the King called on his friend George Rose, Member of Parliament for Lymington, at Cuffnells near Lyndhurst, a house which Rose had bought some years before and for which Sir John Soane had recently provided a new south front. Rose and the King rode together into Lymington, where they were caught in a heavy shower; but, although His Majesty's clothes were soaked,

no entreaties could prevail with him to put on a great coat [Rose told Lord Eldon] and he was wet through before he reached the Town Hall where he remained about three quarters of an hour, speaking to the Mayor and several gentlemen. He then went to Sir Harry Neale's [Admiral Sir Harry Neale at Walhampton] and dined without changing his clothes; then rode back here, and was again wet . . . There is no describing the uneasiness I felt at his Majesty keeping on his wet clothes because I recollect Mr Pitt telling me that his first illness in 1788 was supposed to be brought on by the same thing; but there was no possible means of preventing it.

The King's obstinacy in such matters was the despair of his doctors. As Thomas Willis had recently written, 'His Majesty still talks much of his prudence, but shows none.' He was still, Willis added, 'not quite as right as he should be'.

The King recognized this himself. 'I cannot boast of the same strength and spirits I enjoyed before,' he told his old friend Dr Hurd, the Bishop of Worcester. However, he assured him, his health was 'daily improving' and he hoped that, with quiet and the sea-bathing at Weymouth, he would soon be quite well again.

From Weymouth he wrote on the same optimistic note to both Lord Eldon and Henry Addington. He was now sleeping perfectly, he assured them; he had given up taking medicines and was quite well, provided he did not allow himself to become hurried and troubled. Lord Auckland, who saw him at this time, confirmed that he had become 'much more composed'. 'He might at times appear to those who have always seen him in high spirits to be rather low,' Auckland added. 'But . . . he is always ready to enter into conversation when it is going on, though he does not always start it'.

When autumn came he was judged to be greatly improved, having at last been persuaded to admit that it was possible to take too much exercise. In the first week of October, Lord Chichester declared that he had never seen him 'in better health and spirits'; and by November he seemed to be quite well again, although, as he confessed to Dr Hurd, he still tired easily and had to be 'very careful, and to avoid everything, of fatigue, either of mind or body'. 'But I feel I am gradually gaining ground,' he went on. 'The next week will be rather harassing as I must open the Session of Parliament . . . but I shall return every day to Kew that I may be more quiet.'

'He appeared rather more of an old man,' wrote Lord Malmesbury, who went to see him at this time. 'He stooped rather more, and was apparently less firm on his legs, but he did not look thinner, nor were there any marks of sickness or decline in his countenance or manner.'

The King spent much time this year in studying, with characteristic attention to every detail, plans for a house at Richmond, a Gothic castle with turrets and crenellations, tall keeps and towers, and a large courtyard surrounded by a high curtain wall. It was designed by James Wyatt, who had succeeded Sir William Chambers as Surveyor-General and Comptroller of the King's Works; and, from what they heard of it, architectural critics, like the public at large, did not think much of either the design or the site. 'The foundation,' wrote Sir Nathaniel Wraxall, comparing the building to the Bastille, 'is in a bog close to the Thames and the principal object within its view is the dirty town of Brentford.'

'I am building at Richmond,' the King told the Princess Royal:

It advances but slowly partly owing to a certain want of diligence in Wyatt and partly to the present want of workmen . . . I never thought I should have adopted Gothic instead of Grecian architecture, but the bad taste of the last forty years has so entirely corrupted the professors of the latter I have taken to the former from thinking Wyatt perfect in that style, of which my house will I trust be a good example.

It never proved to be any kind of example, good or bad. The building was never finished, and the incomplete structure, by then an intriguing folly, was demolished on the orders of King George IV in the late 1820s.

During the early course of its slow construction the King continued to improve in health; he remained well throughout 1802, and in the summer of 1803 he was said to be perfectly fit again.

War with France broke out again that year; and Bonaparte, seizing Hanover, made plans for the invasion of England, while the English took energetic measures to resist it: by the end of the year nearly 400,000 men had been enlisted in Volunteer and Yeomanry corps, and coastal defences including Martello towers – 'capital things' in the King's opinion – were hastily built along the south-eastern coasts of the country. The King himself responded to the threat with energy, almost, it might be said, with enthusiasm. 'I should like to fight Boney single-handed,' he told a German officer at Weymouth. 'I'm sure I should. I should give him a good hiding. I'm sure I should. I'm sure of it.'

Should the invasion take place, he said, he intended to put himself 'at the head of his troops' and 'other armed subjects' to repel the enemy's forces. He would move to Chelmsford if the landing took place in Essex, to Dartford if the French came ashore in Kent, and there he would stand 'to repel the usurper's forces'.

Should the enemy approach too near to Windsor [he wrote to Dr Hurd], 'I shall think it right the Queen and my daughters should cross the Severn, and shall send them to your Episcopal Palace at Worcester. By this hint I do not in the least mean they shall be any inconvenience to you, and shall send a proper servant and furniture for their accommodation. Should such an event arise, I certainly would rather that what I value most in life should remain during the conflict in your diocese and under your roof, than in any other place in the island.

40

A DISASTROUS MARRIAGE

The vilest wretch this world ever was cursed with . . .

The Prince of Wales's visits to his parents were far from common events. Hopes that the relationship between him and his father would be improved after the outbreak of the French Revolution and the war with France had not been realized. Thereafter, on his rare appearances at Windsor in the 1790s he had been in the habit of dining at the White Hart, spending the night at his apartments in the Castle and returning to Carlton House without troubling to call on either of his parents.

By then described in *The Times* as a hard-drinking, swearing, whoring man, 'who at all times would prefer a girl and a bottle, to politics and a sermon', whose 'only states of happiness' were 'gluttony, drunkenness and gambling', he seemed more and more inclined to live down to his reputation. Gillray's most frequently reproduced caricature, *A Voluptuary under the Horrors of Digestion*, which shows him, grossly fat, picking his teeth with a fork, slumped in a chair surrounded by evidence of his debauchery, and hints of venereal disease, had been issued in July 1792. A few weeks later, following other caricatures of the King and Queen contrasting the Prince's extravagance with the supposed parsimony of Their Majesties, whose court dinners had long since been abolished, came Gillray's *Temperance Enjoying a Frugal Meal*, which depicts them sitting at a table eating a meal of boiled eggs and salad in a comfortless room in which there is no fire in the grate, the King's chair is covered with a dust sheet, and there is even a protective bag on the handle of the bell-pull. The King has tucked the corner of the table cloth into his collar to protect his coat and patched breeches. Lying on a padlocked chest is a book entitled *Dr Cheyne on the Benefits of a Spare Diet*.

In a caricature, *Anti-Saccharrites – or – John Bull and his Family leaving off the Use of Sugar*, published a few months earlier, Gillray had portrayed the King and Queen seated around a frugal tea-table with their daughters, who are looking either surprised or disconsolate. The King declares the sugarless tea to be 'delicious! delicious!' The Queen, addressing the Princesses through the gaps in her ill-shaped teeth, says, 'O my dear creatures, do but taste it! You can't think how nice it is without sugar: – and then, consider how much work you'll save the poor Blackeemoors by leaving off the use of it! – and above all, remember how much expense it will save your poor Papa!'

The deriding of the King's parsimony was also carried on by John Wolcot, a former parson turned physician, who wrote under the name of Peter Pindar and ridiculed the King and Queen with comic zest in verses which his victim was said to have found as amusing as the rest of the nation. Certainly, towards the end of his life, Wolcot confessed that 'the King had been a good subject to him, and he a bad one to the King'.

A characteristic sally by Peter Pindar lampooned the King's alleged meanness to the German soprano Gertrud Elisabeth Mara, who was asked to sing at Court while she was living in London between 1784 and 1802.

> To Windsor oft, and eke to Kew,
> The r–y–l mandate Mara drew.
> No cheering drop the dame was asked to sip –
> No bread was offer'd to her quivering lip:
> Though faint, she was not suffer'd to sit down –
> Such was the *goodness* – grandeur of the crown.
> Now tell me, will it ever be believ'd,
> How much for song and chaise-hire she receiv'd?
> How much pray, think ye? Fifty guineas. 'No.'
> Most surely forty. 'No, no.' Thirty. 'Poh!
> Pray, guess in reason, come again!' –
> Alas! you jeer us! – twenty at the least;
> No man could ever be so great a beast
> As not to give her twenty for her pain –
> 'To keep you, then, no longer in suspense,
> For Mara's chaise-hire and unrivall'd note,
> Out of their *wonderful* benevolence,
> Their bounteous Majesties gave – not a groat.'

As though drawn together by being, in their different ways, the butt of satirists, the King and the Prince had both made an effort to overcome their differences in the summer of 1790. On 10 August the Prince had written to the Duke of York from Brighton, asking him to find out from the King whether or not the Prince's birthday was to be celebrated that year, since the '*only reason*' for his not having paid his respects the previous year was his not having received 'the smallest intimation on that head'. The King had signified that he was ready to receive the Prince once more.

The Prince had again been at Windsor for the King's birthday the following 4 June, and, according to the *St James's Chronicle*, he had never made a more splendid appearance. That year the Queen had written in good time to assure him that she and his father 'certainly' expected him at Windsor in order to keep his own birthday on 12 August, 'which', she had added, 'none will do with greater pleasure than, my dearest son, than [*sic*] your very affectionate mother and sincere friend'. The assurances of affection and sincere friendship were to some extent formalistic, but at least the breach between mother and son which had threatened to become permanent eighteen months before had now become bridgeable.

Certainly the ball at Windsor on 12 August 1791 was a distinct success. The following day even *The Times* had praised the charming manners of the Prince, once more reconciled with his parents.

The reconciliation, like previous rapprochements, had not lasted long. When his thirty-first birthday approached, the Prince was in camp with the 10th Light Dragoons near Brighton. The King had reluctantly given way to his son's repeated requests to be allowed to take a more active part 'in the military line' by appointing him Colonel Commandant of this regiment, in which the King took so personal an interest that he later invited William Beechey to paint a portrait of himself reviewing it. On the Queen's authority, but without the King's knowledge, according to a story preserved in the Beechey family, Beechey included in the picture a prominent portrait of the Prince of Wales brandishing a sabre. The King was so angry when he saw what had been done, so the Beecheys' legend has it, that he ordered the canvas to be burned or thrown out of the window. Fortunately, the order was not carried out; and some time later, father and son being on rather better terms, the picture was hung at the Royal Academy. Nevertheless, when the King had a copy made to present to Henry Addington, he gave instructions that the figure of the Prince should be left out.

The Prince's delight in being given his colonelcy had been expressed in letters to his parents which he himself conceded were written in that effusive 'tone of insanity' which so often characterizes them. He was beside himself with joy and gratitude; his father had given him not only life but 'the greatest of all blessings . . . the enjoyment of life'. Were he not at that moment unwell, he would come to his 'good and gracious father' to throw himself at his feet.

Unfortunately he had been given command of the 10th Light Dragoons on the understanding that he must not expect further promotion, nor serve abroad against the French, as he had expressed a wish to do. Nor yet was he to be permitted to leave camp to come to Windsor for the usual birthday celebrations in 1793: it would be 'against all military rules' for him to do so. Denied his birthday party at Windsor, the Prince did not intend to remain in camp for long, despite the comforts afforded by his most elaborate tent; and within a month he was back living amid the grander pleasures of Carlton House, though more concerned than ever that unless there were soon to be a dramatic improvement in the state of his finances those pleasures could not much longer be enjoyed.

The amount of his debts had risen once more to unconscionable heights; and, having borrowed money from anyone who would lend it to him and despairing of getting any more either from Parliament or from the King, he had decided he would have to marry. In August 1794 he went to Weymouth to tell his father so; 'very abruptly' he informed him that he had severed all connection with Mrs Fitzherbert and that he was ready to enter 'a more creditable line of life'.

The bride chosen, without the least enthusiasm on his part, was his cousin Princess Caroline, daughter of the Duke of Brunswick and of the King's sister Augusta. No one considered it an ideal choice, except perhaps the Prince's new mistress, Lady Jersey, who, being unable to marry him herself, had no objection to his marrying a woman of supposedly 'indelicate manners, indifferent character, and not very inviting appearance, in the hope that disgust for the wife would secure constancy to the mistress'.

Certainly Princess Caroline was well calculated to disgust the Prince, who seemed almost to have accepted her, hastily and petulantly, as a protest against having to choose any wife at all. She was rumoured to be dirty and extremely indiscreet, and was undeniably no beauty. Lord Holland said that any young English traveller who had been through Germany on the Grand Tour could, if asked, have told the Prince that the character of his intended bride was considered to be 'excessively loose', even in that country where 'they were not very nice about female delicacy'.

The Queen strongly disapproved of the match. 'Her opinions she would not give,' the Prince of Wales was told by Prince Ernest, who was then on a brief visit to England from the Continent. 'God knows what is the matter with her, but she is sullen. I sounded her tonight about you, but no reply soever was made.' She did, however, confide the reasons for her disapproval in a letter to her brother:

They say that her passions are so strong that [her father] himself said that she was not to be allowed even to go from one room to another without her Governess, and that when she dances, this lady is obliged to follow her for the whole of the dance to prevent her making an exhibition of herself by indecent conversations . . . All her amusements have been forbidden her because of her indecent conduct . . . There, dear brother, is a woman I do not recommend at all . . . The fact is that the King is completely ignorant of everything concerning [the Duke of Brunswick's] family, and that it would be unseemly to speak to him against his niece.

Indeed, the King, when told of his son's choice, was quite happy to accept it. Dismissing all previous prejudice against marriages between first cousins, and evidently ignoring reports that two of her brothers were mad and that their own mother thought that their sister was not much saner herself, he expressed himself much satisfied that his niece had been selected. 'Undoubtedly she is the person who naturally must be more agreeable to me,' he wrote to Pitt when informed of the proposed match. 'Provided his plan was to lead a life that would make him appear respectable, and consequently render the Princess happy . . . I expressed my approbation of the idea.' However, he thought it as well to write to his sister, her mother, to say that he hoped that his niece would not prove to be too vivacious when she arrived in England, that she would be prepared to lead a life both 'sedentary and retired'.

The tactful, wily Lord Malmesbury, who had been sent out to Brunswick to bring the Princess to England, was convinced that she was not in the least suited to such a life. She was undeniably well meaning and well disposed, he noted in his diary, she had great good humour and much good nature, but she had 'no judgement'. She was 'caught by the first impression, led by the first impulse . . . fond of gossiping . . . loving to talk, and prone to confide and make missish friendships which lasted twenty-four hours . . . In short, the Princess in the hands of a steady and sensible man would probably turn out well, but where it is likely she will find faults perfectly analogous to her own, she will fail.'

When Malmesbury returned to England with the Princess and made his report to the King, His Majesty's only question was, 'Is she good-humoured?' to which Malmesbury could honestly give a favourable reply; but when the King commented, 'I am glad of it,' and then fell into silence, it was clear to him that His Majesty had already heard from the Queen what their son thought of the person of his bride.

The Prince had, in fact, made no attempt to hide his initial distaste. Having embraced her 'gracefully enough', he immediately turned round, withdrew to a corner of the room, and asked for a glass of brandy. 'My God!' the Princess exclaimed to Malmesbury in French, since English did not yet come naturally to her, 'Does the Prince always act like this? I think he's very fat and he's nothing like as handsome as his portrait.' That evening at dinner her behaviour was as distressingly embarrassing as Lord Malmesbury had ever known it. It was 'rattling, affecting raillery and wit, and throwing out coarse vulgar hints about Lady [Jersey] who was present'. The Princess later excused herself on the grounds that it was the sight of the Prince with Lady Jersey, who had been appointed one of her Ladies of the Bedchamber, that made her behave like this. Listening to her vulgar, impetuous, defensive chatter while Lady Jersey remained loftily silent, the Prince, Malmesbury noticed, was disgusted. Nor were his mother or sisters in the least welcoming. The Queen was cold, the Princesses wary; only the King was prepared to welcome the gauche and lonely young woman. He, indeed, greeted his niece affectionately, with 'tears of joy . . . as if she had been born and bred his favourite child'.

The wedding took place in the Chapel Royal at St James's Palace on the evening of 8 April 1795. The King had refused permission for Prince Ernest, Prince Adolphus and their cousin Prince William, Duke of Gloucester, to come home from the Continent to attend the wedding, as 'the Army was the only place where an officer ought to be, particularly when he commanded a regiment'. But he approved 'greatly of [the] choice' of the Princess's pretty attendants.

He did not approve, however, of the behaviour of the Prince, who appeared to be extremely nervous and agitated and, in the words of the first Viscount Melbourne, who was in waiting, was obviously 'quite drunk'. At one point he stood up suddenly in the middle of a prayer, and the Archbishop of Canterbury paused for a moment until the King stepped forward and whispered something in his son's ear. Then, as he reached that point in the service when he had to ask the question whether or not there was any impediment to lawful matrimony,

the Archbishop laid down the book, and looked earnestly at the King, as well as at the bridegroom, giving unequivocal proof of his apprehension that some previous marriage had taken place . . . Not content with this tacit allusion, the Archbishop twice repeated the passage in which the Prince engages to live from that time in nuptial felicity with his consort . . . The Prince was much affected, and shed tears.

After the ceremony the King and Queen held a drawing-room in the Queen's apartments, where the Prince appeared still rather drunk, looking 'like death and full of confusion', while the bride appeared in the 'highest spirits', smiling and nodding to everyone. Lady Maria Stuart commented, 'What an odd wedding!'

Four days after the wedding the bride seemed quite as cheerful as ever as she walked up and down the Terrace at Windsor on the arm of her father-in-law, who, since the bridegroom sulkily declined to be present, escorted her with evident 'delight' and 'entire gratifica-tion'. The King was even more gratified when, nine months later, almost to the day, he received a letter from the Prince to say that the Princess had borne him a granddaughter, Princess Charlotte. He replied to say that he was 'highly pleased' and that he had 'always wished' that the first child should be a girl. 'You are both young,' he added, 'and I trust will have many children and this newcomer will equally call for the protection of its parents and consequently be a bond of additional union.' 'He talks of nothing but his grand-child,' his daughter Princess Elizabeth said, 'drank her health at dinner and went into the Equerries' room and made them drink it in a bumper.'

The mother was not so content. The 'lively spirits' she had brought over with her from Germany were all gone, and she was now 'a most unhappy woman'. 'I don't know how I shall be able to bear the loneliness,' she wrote to a friend in Germany, 'the Queen ["Old Snuffy" and "de old Begum" as she also called her] seldom visits me and my sisters-in-law show me the same sympathy . . . The Countess [of Jersey] is still here. I hate her and I know she feels the same towards me. My husband is wholly given up to her, so you can easily imagine the rest.'

Only the King was kind to her; but he declined to contemplate the formal separation for which both husband and wife ardently wished within a few months of their marriage. 'You seem to look on your disunion with the Princess as merely of a private nature,' the King wrote to his son, 'and totally put out of sight that as Heir Apparent of the Crown your marriage is a public act, wherein the Kingdom is concerned, that therefore a separation cannot be brought forward by a mere interference of relations.' The public would have to be informed of the whole business, and the public were 'certainly not prejudiced' in the Prince's favour. Parliament would also have to be informed as a matter of course, and Parliament would think itself obliged to secure out of his income the jointure settled on the Princess in case of her husband's death. The King was 'certainly by no means inclined to think the Princess [had] been happy in the choice of conduct' she had adopted; but, if the Prince had 'attempted to guide her, she might have avoided those errors that her uncommon want of experience and perhaps some defects of temper' had given rise to. 'I once more call on you,' the King concluded, 'to have the command of yourself that shall, by keeping up appearances, by degrees render your home more respectable and at the same time less unpleasant . . . In a contrary line of conduct nothing but evils appear.'

Tormented by the enthusiastic support which the public accorded to her out of dislike for her husband and his 'most disgraceful connexions', the Prince's hatred of his wife grew more virulent than ever. And it was all made much worse for him by the attitude of most of his family, who, unnerved by the public reaction, seemed to think he ought to make some sort of attempt at reconciliation with the Princess.

The Prince begged the Queen, who disliked Princess Caroline intensely, to make his father realize what a dangerous woman his wife was – 'the vilest wretch this world ever was cursed with'. In letters scarcely less than hysterical, he pleaded with his 'dearest, dearest, dearest mother' to persuade the King 'to take a firm line' in defence of his son, otherwise 'the fiend' would prove the ruin of the whole family. He had a right to ask this, since, so he now absurdly claimed to believe, it was only his 'unalterable devotion' to his father which had induced him to marry the woman in the first place.

The King must be resolute and firm [he wrote] or everything is at an end . . . I know you will fight for me to the last, and I will for you, and by you till the last drop of my blood, but if ever you flinch, which I am convinced is impossible, I shall then despair . . . God bless you ever dearest mother. I am so overpowered with unhappiness that I feel quite light headed. I know not where to turn to a friend now but to you . . . I wrote at considerable length to the King yesterday to tell him that nothing but his resolution and support can bring *us all* through at this moment . . . *If I* fall, *all* must fall also . . . Nothing can equal what I go through nor can anything paint it strong enough for your imagination . . . By the by I see by Ernest's letter that the Princess has been at the Queen's House. For God's sake let me know everything that has past, tell me nothing, or conceal nothing from me. I suppose she has made the best of her own story and told her lies as usual . . . The thought makes me quite frantic.

He grew even more frantic when he learned that, on the occasion of Fox's re-election for Westminster on 13 June 1796, the Princess had not only held up their baby at the window in response to shouts from Fox's supporters but had 'actually afterwards drove in her carriage through the mob, to pay her devoirs to Mr Fox . . . and to get herself applauded'. Surely the King must now see the Princess 'in her true colours, how false, how mischievous, how treacherous' she was, how much she was made the tool 'of the worst parties at this moment, the democratick'.

THE ANGRY FATHER

*I shall be most happy if I find you seriously turn your thoughts
to your future situation.*

The King certainly did not agree that his niece deserved the abuse
which the Prince of Wales heaped upon her. He believed that, if
she received proper guidance, all might yet turn out well, that the
Princess was quite right to insist that, so long as 'Lady Jerser' – as
she occasionally spelled the name in her badly constructed letters –
held the place she occupied in her Household, there could be no
peace between herself and her husband. It was eventually conceded
that the troublesome Lady Jersey should give up her place, on the
understanding that the Princess was willing, in the Queen's words,
to have a 'complete reconciliation' with her husband and refrain
from all reproaches.

Yet, far from breaking with Lady Jersey as the King had hoped
he would, and as Princess Elizabeth begged him to do 'for the sake
of the country and the whole Royal Family', the Prince saw even
more of her than before, while his wife continued to show as little
restraint as ever when talking about her husband. Indeed, she went
on behaving in a way that well justified her own father's warning
that she must be watched very strictly, otherwise she would 'certainly
emancipate too much'. When he heard rumours that George Canning, Member of Parliament for Newtown and one of Pitt's most
promising supporters, had become her lover the Prince declared that
rather than take the detested woman back as his wife, or even sit at
the same table with her, he would prefer to see toads and vipers
crawling over his food. It was unendurable to him that his father
and the public generally saw her as a wronged wife while he was
condemned as a selfish philanderer. Even his brothers, while offering

him sympathy in private, did not hesitate, in conversation with others, to apportion the blame for his predicament. 'My brother has behaved very foolishly,' Prince William observed to a lady at a ball in Richmond. 'To be sure he has married a very foolish, disagreeable person, but he should not have treated her as he has done, but have made the best of a bad bargain, as my father has done. He married a disagreeable woman but has not behaved ill to her.'

Aware in a general way of the Princess's indiscretions, the King agreed to support his son in his endeavours to ensure that she did not receive or entertain persons of whom her husband did not approve. The Princess declared that she would refuse to obey this rule unless told to do so directly by the King. The Prince appealed to his father, who wrote to his daughter-in-law confirming that it was his opinion, too, that she should 'not receive any society but such as the Prince approved of'.

The Princess then marched off to her husband's apartments at Carlton House, where, addressing him in French, she said that in two and a half years of marriage she had been treated neither as his wife nor as the mother of his child, nor as the Princess of Wales; and she gave him notice 'here and now' that she had nothing more to say to him and no longer regarded herself as subject to his orders.

In reporting this declaration to his father, the Prince added that he thought it 'highly unnecessary to offer at this moment to his Majesty one single comment on this most extraordinary conduct on the part of the Princess'. And, in a subsequent letter, he said that, though it was now obvious that she intended to move out of Carlton House and live in a separate establishment, he did not intend to raise any objection to this intention.

The King, however, objected to this proposal: the Princess might take a small house outside London, but she must certainly not altogether quit her apartments in Carlton House. There must be no kind of formal separation, as this would, as the Lord Chancellor, Lord Loughborough, confirmed, be 'incompatible with the religion, laws, and government' of the kingdom. The Prince was already so unpopular in the country that any step which might increase that unpopularity could not be undertaken without danger to 'the publick safety'; it was therefore of the 'utmost moment' to preserve 'even the outward appearance of cohabitation'. The King wrote to his son to say that he entirely concurred with the Lord Chancellor's view.

By now, though, it was difficult to believe that the Prince could possibly be more disliked than he already was. So strongly did feelings run against him, indeed, that the King, who was believed not to protect his daughter-in-law in the way that he should, had already been contaminated by his son's unpopularity. On his way to the House of Lords in October 1795 the state coach had been stoned by a mob, additionally aggrieved by the rising price of bread, and shouts of 'Down with George!' had filled the air.

The Prince hoped that he might become better liked and more respected if he were to be given some military command other than that of the 10th Light Dragoons. He had been bitterly disappointed not to be given the command of the Royal Horse Guards on the death of Field Marshal Conway in July 1795. He had begged his 'dearest Mama', his 'ever dearest and best beloved' mother, to intercede for him. It had long been his wish to have it. Besides, it was '3000 pretty little shiners every year, which as times go now are no small consideration'. 'I thought,' he added, 'it would be more delicate not to put myself too forward, & if it does come, that it should appear to arise from the King's own idea, than from any solicitation on my part.' The King, however, had other ideas: when he heard the news of Conway's death he 'put down his tea, went into the next room, returned with a letter in his hand, ordered a servant to be sent to the Duke of York & said "After 30 years promise I have given the vacant Guards to the Duke of Richmond."'

Bitterly disappointed, the Prince persisted in his request for some other responsible military command. Were the country to be invaded, he might be employed, he wrote, in a 'real and important trust', professing that, since there were so many alternative heirs to the throne, his own life was of 'little political importance'. But the King refused to reconsider a decision he had already made. 'My younger sons,' he repeated in a letter to the Prince, 'can have no other situation in the State . . . but what arise from the military lines they have been placed in. You are born to a more difficult one, and one which I shall be most happy if I find you seriously turn your thoughts to; the happiness of millions depends on it as well as your own.'

In 1797 the Prince renewed his request; but his father remained as unresponsive as the King's grandfather had been when he himself had made a similar request. His Majesty had, he said, given his son command of a cavalry regiment because the Prince had quite rightly pressed him to place him in a situation in which he could 'manifest his zeal in defence of his country . . . That command . . . should the enemy succeed in their intentions of invading this island, will enable you, at the head of that brave Corps, to show the valour which has ever been a striking feature in the character of the House of Brunswick.' But there could be no question of 'the Prince of Wales being considered as a military man'.

The Prince, having had his suggestion that he be appointed Lord Lieutenant in Ireland peremptorily dismissed by both the King and the Cabinet, refused to be satisfied with such an answer. In 1801, in the following year and again in 1803 he renewed his request, repeating his arguments in ever more impassioned terms, pleading that he might be allowed to 'come forward in a moment of unexampled difficulty and danger', begging to be allowed 'to share in the glory of victory' when he had 'everything to lose by defeat'.

The King, unresponsive as ever, desired that 'no further mention should be made to him on this subject'. Undeterred by the repetition of this familiar rebuke, the Prince turned for help to his brother the Duke of York, by now Commander-in-Chief, complaining of the 'degrading mockery' of being told that the only way he could display his zeal was at the head of his regiment. As he had remarked to the Duke of Devonshire, he fully recognized he was not capable of commanding an army, but he could collect 'the best generals around him and they might in fact command and direct him'. But the Duke of York declined to interfere. 'Surely,' he replied to his brother's request, 'you must be satisfied that your not being advanced in military rank proceeds entirely from his Majesty's sentiments respecting the high rank you hold in the State, and not from any impression unfavourable to you.'

42

A DREADED INTERVIEW

See what he has done, he has published my *letters.*

In resentful desperation, the Prince decided that the whole of his correspondence with the King on the subject should be published. He was strongly advised by all his more responsible friends to do no such thing; but, ignoring their advice, he allowed the letters to be printed on 7 December 1803 in the *Morning Chronicle*, the *Morning Herald* and the *Sun*. *The Times* was also offered the material, but declined to use it, because of the 'delicacy of the subject'.

The Prince protested that he had had 'nothing to do with the business'; but few believed him. 'See what he has done,' the King was heard repeatedly lamenting in a hoarse and hurried voice, 'he has published *my* letters.' For weeks, during which father and son did not meet and the Prince was ostentatiously absent from his parents' levees and drawing-rooms, the King referred to him as 'the publisher of *my* letters'.

After the publication of his correspondence with his father, the Prince still hankered after active employment in the Army; and, in order to placate him, Lord Moira, Master General of the Ordnance, proposed that he should be given command of a specified military district for which he would be directly responsible to the Commander-in-Chief. In the event of a French landing he would surrender command of the district and report to the King's headquarters, where he would assume the nominal responsibilities of a second-in-command. Nothing, however, came of this strange plan, which would certainly not have recommended itself to the King; and thereafter the Prince resignedly abandoned all ideas of 'any military rank or command whatever'. The disappointment still rankled, though, while the King's increasingly cordial attentions to Princess Caroline – who had rented the Old Rectory, Charlton, near Blackheath, and had been granted by His Majesty the profitable rangership of Greenwich Park – angered the Prince beyond measure and made him reluctant to consider the reconciliation with his father which was being urged upon him on all sides, most strongly by his family.

'The Queen and all my sisters *without exception*,' the Duke of Kent wrote to him, 'Adolphus to a *certainty*, and Ernest, *at least to all appearances hitherto*, are full of nothing but the urgency of bringing you together *without* delay.'

The Prince gave way; and on 4 July 1804 he wrote to the Queen to say that he heartily lamented not having paid his duty to the King of late and had long grieved that 'misrepresentations' had estranged His Majesty's mind from him.

Doubting the sincerity of this submission, and protesting that no good would come of an interview, the King was as reluctant to see the Prince as the Prince was to see him; and it was with great difficulty that His Majesty's Ministers and, most persuasively, Lord Eldon, the Lord Chancellor, eventually prevailed upon him to agree to it. Even then the Prince made various stipulations about the meeting, including its venue and its witnesses, which, he insisted, must include the Queen and all his sisters and 'at least, the Duke of Cambridge'. 'I will not see him at Windsor for there he will stay,' the King insisted for his part. 'I will see him at Kew for there he must go about his business when it's over. I know him . . . Yes, yes, I'll see him, and I'll be very civil to him; but I'll never forgive his publishing my letters, and I'll never correspond with him.'

His Majesty is willing to receive the Prince of Wales on Wednesday at Kew [the King wrote in a coldly formal letter to the Lord Chancellor], provided no explanation or excuses are attempted to be made by the Prince of Wales, but that it is merely to be a visit of civility; as any retrospect could but oblige the King to utter truths which, instead of healing, must widen the present breach. His Majesty will have the Queen, Princesses, and at least one of his sons, the Duke of Cambridge, present on the occasion. The Lord Chancellor is to fix on twelve o'clock for the hour of the Prince of Wales's coming to Kew.

337

As the day for the interview approached the Prince became more and more apprehensive, since he was warned that his father's manner was likely to be alarming.

43

'AN ASTONISHING CHANGE FOR THE WORSE'

In his family and usual society his manners and conversation were far from steady.

At the beginning of that year, 1804, the King had suffered a relapse serious enough for the Willises to be summoned once more. He had displayed the by now familiar symptoms of a cold, slight gout, weakness in the legs, and agitation of mind. Since the Queen and the Princesses were nervous of accompanying him in this condition, and the doctors in attendance made the excuse that they did not like being watched by people at the windows in Grosvenor Place, Lord Eldon offered to take the King for a walk round the garden of the Queen's House. When the King was asked if he would care for Lord Eldon's company, he eagerly accepted it, so Eldon said, crying excitedly, 'With all my heart!' and calling for his hat and cane.

We walked two or three times round Buckingham House Gardens [Eldon wrote]. There was at first a momentary hurry and incoherence in His Majesty's talk, but this did not endure two minutes. During the rest of the walk there was not the slightest aberration . . . [But] when we returned into the house, His Majesty, laying down his hat and cane, placed his head upon my shoulder and burst into tears.

Thereafter he grew progressively worse. Lord Malmesbury, who saw him at an assembly at the Queen's House, said that he was 'too lame to walk without a cane' and his manner was 'so unusual and incoherent that [he] could not help remarking on it to Lord Pelham'. On 14 February his fever was 'very high', and that night he talked for five hours without pause. By the 17th, according to Charles Abbot, Speaker of the House of Commons, his disorder had taken the 'decided character of a complete mental derangement'. The Cabinet consequently decided that the dispatch of the Willises to the Queen's House could no longer be delayed.

When the brothers arrived, however, they were forbidden to see the patient. It was explained to them that a solemn promise had been given to His Majesty that, in the event of his being afflicted again, every means would be used 'to prevent anyone of the Willis family from being placed about him'. Both Sir Francis Milman and Dr William Heberden the Younger supported the Dukes of Kent and Cumberland in their contention that forcing the Willises upon the King would result in an even greater 'irritation of his mind'.

And another evil of the greatest magnitude would in all probability ensue [the Duke of Kent warned Addington] – no less a one than that of his Majesty taking up a rooted prejudice against the Queen, for that no argument however strong, no proof however direct, would be sufficient, after his recovery, to persuade him that her Majesty had not been privy to the doctors Willis being placed about his person.

So Addington sent instead for Dr Samuel Foart Simmons, physician to St Luke's Hospital for Lunaticks and an acknowledged authority on mental diseases, who promptly made use of a straitjacket. This constraint imposed on the King by 'that horrible' Dr Simmons was not necessary for long. By 26 February, Addington felt able to announce in the House that His Majesty was quite restored to health and perfectly capable of taking up his duties again. This, indeed, the King demonstrated a few weeks later by calmly accepting the resignation of Addington – whose Administration had been a weak and undistinguished one – and recalling Pitt to office in May 1804.

The King was sorry to part with Addington, whom he liked and respected, though he had to admit that he was not really 'equal to the government of the country'.★ But, when Pitt went to the Queen's

★ The King's affection for Addington was warmly reciprocated. 'The arcane mysteries of a crown blended with the bluff good nature of a worthy *père de famille* were even more irresistible to [Addington] than to the rest of George III's faithful subjects,' Addington's biographer has written. 'Himself credulous, warm-hearted and inclined to servility, he never for an instant questioned the authenticity of the public image' (Ziegler, *Addington*, 242–3). The King offered to create Addington an earl. This offer was declined. Addington did, however, accept the King's suggestion that he

House for an audience to discuss the formation of his Cabinet, the King was perfectly agreeable. When Pitt observed how much better His Majesty appeared to be than after his illness in 1801, the year in which Pitt had resigned as First Minister, the King replied that this was not to be wondered at, since at that time he had been parting with an old friend, and now he was about to regain one.★

The King was not, however, as well and stable as this exchange, his friendly manner and his firm control of the situation suggested. Two days after it, following another audience, Pitt commented on His Majesty's 'hurry of spirits' and 'excessive love of talking'.

His manners and conversation were far from steady [Lord Malmesbury confirmed]. He dismissed and turned away, and made capricious changes everywhere, from the Lord Chamberlain to the grooms and footmen. He turned away the Queen's favourite coachman, made footmen grooms and vice versa and what was still worse, because more notorious, had removed lords of the bedchamber without a shadow of reason. This all afflicted the Royal Family beyond measure. The Queen was ill and *cross*; the Princesses low, depressed and quite sinking under it.

A few days after this was written, on 17 May, the Duke of Kent reported to the Prince of Wales that their father's 'hurry' when with his family 'and [his being] consequently either wholly or nearly without control' continued 'much the same', and 'a variety of shades, some of these highly unpleasant', manifested themselves. The 'great coolness' of the King towards their mother, the Duke added, was 'predominant'. Colonel John McMahon, the Prince of Wales's fac-totum, told the Prince that his father was, indeed, reported to be

---

should remain at White Lodge, as well as the gift of a copy of His Majesty's portrait by Sir William Beechey as a token of the King's esteem for his 'truly beloved friend' (Pellew, *Life of Henry Addington*, ii, 288).
★ 'This courteous and astute rejoinder – assuming at the start that Pitt would be coming in – set the tone for the long talk that followed, in which the recent invalid appears to have displayed a striking example of his kingcraft,' John Ehrman has commented. 'It was small wonder that on emerging Pitt told Eldon that the monarch had never so baffled him in any conversation that he had had with him in his life.' Where suggestions as to the choice of Ministers were made which did not please him, he digressed 'a good deal', returning 'exactly at the parts from which he went off' (Ehrman, *The Younger Pitt: The Consuming Struggle*, 657).

'quite outrageous' with the Queen, to whom he now manifested the 'greatest aversion'.

Lord Grenville learned more from the Marquess of Buckingham about the 'highly unpleasant shades' to which the Duke of Kent had referred. When the King went for his daily drive, Buckingham said, one of his sons now always accompanied him, the Queen and Princesses following in another carriage, *having found it impossible to control the King to any propriety of conduct in their own coach*.

All manner of rumours and 'proofs of the King's madness' spread abroad: 'in ecstasies at seeing her', he had locked himself in a room with Sally, a housemaid at Cumberland Lodge in the Great Park; he had threatened to take a mistress, since the Queen would not pleasure him any more – failing Lady Pembroke, he would have either the Duchess of Rutland or Lady Georgiana Buckley; he had made improper advances to ladies in public at Weymouth; in the stables at Windsor his behaviour had been 'indecent and obscene'.

No one knew how many of these stories to believe; but what could not be doubted was that throughout the year the King was prone to abrupt bouts of irritation and impatience, to occasional disabilities, sudden fevers and pains and inexplicable swellings, and to strange and uncharacteristic conduct. One day in September, according to Prince William, he would have ridden his horse into a church had not an equerry prevented him.

A few weeks later, while staying with George Rose at Cuffnells, he rode down to Southampton accompanied by the Princesses. Cantering down a hill, Princess Amelia's horse fell and 'threw her Royal Highness [then aged twenty-one] flat on her face. She rose without any appearance of being at all hurt, but evidently a good deal shaken . . . and not desirous of getting on horseback again.' The King insisted that either she must do so or return in a carriage to Cuffnells to be bled. Obediently she remounted and rode on to Southampton, where Rose made some suggestion about her return to Cuffnells which was 'certainly not well received' by her father, who sharply told him that he could not bear the thought that any of his children lacked courage. Rose bravely replied that precautions to prevent ill effects after an accident had happened could scarcely be described as a lack of courage. 'Perhaps it may be so,' the King answered crossly. 'But I thank God there is but one of my children that wants courage – and I will not name HIM, *because he is to succeed me.*'

The heir to whom the King referred was growing increasingly anxious about his long-delayed interview with the King. The Duke of Kent warned him that there was 'an astonishing change for the worse, as [the King's] manner was so much more hurried, his conversation so infinitely more light and silly, his temper so much more irritable, besides a strong indication of fever on his cheek, a return of that dreadful saliva, of the strong bilious eye, and of numberless symptoms that manifested themselves last February and were the forerunners of the serious attack'.

From others, the Prince heard that the King was 'so violent with his family that they all dread him beyond description'. An encounter with Sir William Beechey was characteristic of the King's unpredictable behaviour at this time. The King accused Beechey of not understanding colouring, and consequently no more work from his hand was required. There was then some misunderstanding about work already ordered; and the King suddenly burst out in a passion of fury, 'West is an American, & Copley is an American, & You are an Englishman, and were you all at the Devil I should not care.' Beechey was so upset by this terrifying outburst that he fled to the apartment of a maid of honour, where he fainted on a sofa.

The more the Prince heard of such behaviour, the less inclined he became to attend at Kew for the interview; and he wrote to Lord Eldon to say that the information he had received led him to suppose that his proposed visit would merely 'irritate' the King's mind. Unwilling to submit such an excuse to His Majesty, Eldon suggested that the Prince should write to his father merely pleading illness.

When the King was handed the letter he saw from the cover that it came from Carlton House, and it was some time before he opened it, 'evidently seeking to command himself'. When he had read it, he announced, 'The Prince is ill.' He then remarked that he supposed the illness had been brought about by apprehension, adding that the interview would now have to be postponed until he got back from a planned visit to Weymouth.

At Weymouth he was as energetic as ever. Although he did not arrive until five o'clock in the morning, he was seen walking on the Esplanade as usual soon after seven. After breakfast he mounted his horse and rode off to inspect some of the four thousand troops stationed in the area for his protection should there be an invasion. In the afternoon he reviewed the King's German Legion, the Somersetshire Militia and the Weymouth Volunteers. In the course of the following days he was seen chatting to the sailors serving on the frigates and smaller vessels riding in the bay, and talking animatedly to farmers, naval officers and, in their own language, to men of the German regiments; he attended a fête and a ball organized by Princess Elizabeth; he gave a party on board one of the yachts in honour of his eldest daughter's birthday; he paid visits to Milton Abbey and to Lord Rivers at Rushmore Lodge, before going on to stay at Cuffnells with George Rose.

On occasions, however, his behaviour was very strange, not to say alarmingly odd. During performances at the theatre he spoke loudly and inconsequentially before going to sleep, and once vigorously applauded some slighting reference to Members of Parliament. On his yacht he voiced his prejudices in the presence of the crew, condemning all reforms and attacking Roman Catholics. He added Lady Yarmouth, the former Maria Fagniani, to the list of his proposed mistresses; he made indecent suggestions 'with peculiar emphasis and strength of voice' to one of the Queen's most respectable ladies; and one day in the fish market while buying six mullets he talked so incoherently to the fishwives that 'they scarcely believed they had their own senses'. Sir Francis Milman, who was in attendance at Weymouth, warned the Queen that he 'apprehended an immediate apoplexy'.

On his return to London the King looked extremely ill and worn. He had developed a kind of stumbling walk and, increasingly short-sighted, he peered into the faces of people he was talking to, his protuberant eyes unnervingly close to theirs. When Lord Eldon came to see him at the Queen's House the King opened a drawer to take out a watch and chain which he had worn for twenty years and asked Eldon to 'wear them for his sake'. Eldon thought it as well to refuse the offer, whereupon the King burst into tears.

When the nervous Prince of Wales arrived, five minutes early, for the dreaded interview, on 12 November 1804, the King acknowledged his arrival in a gruff, unwelcoming manner, treating him 'much as he would a foreign minister'. 'You have come, have you?' he said. He spoke a little about the weather and much about scandal, dwelling particularly upon Sarah Siddons's reported elopement with Thomas Lawrence, 'running wildly from topic to topic, though not absolutely incoherent'.

Although the Queen welcomed her son with a show of affection, and the Princesses all kissed him as fondly as ever, Princess Amelia in tears of joy at seeing her brother again, the weekend at Windsor was not a success. The King seemed much better than he had been at Weymouth; but the Prince was 'evidently much out of spirits and in ill-humour – hardly spoke a word to anybody and looked very ill'. William Fremantle, the politician, who was then at Windsor, thought it 'quite impossible' that the reconciliation could last, certainly so long as the King continued to make his regular and lengthy visits to his daughter-in-law, Princess Caroline, at Blackheath.

Pitt was now responsible for the care of the King, since the Queen and most of her children had signed a declaration to the effect that the Cabinet, not the Royal Family, must make all necessary decisions about His Majesty's treatment in future. Pitt accordingly approved of the doctors' decision that, while the King was obviously much better than he had been, he should for 'a short time longer [submit himself] to proper management'. It was accepted that, while he was 'generally recovered', it was prudent that he should be spared 'all unnecessary exertion of mind'; that he must 'strictly and uniformly exert himself to correct those ideas which occasionally show themselves in less guarded moments'; and that he must also 'avoid as much as possible any hurry or excess of fatigue'.

The King himself was only too anxious to cooperate. He had come to believe that his mental disturbance had been brought upon him by worry and concern about public affairs, just as the terrible anxiety about being called upon to break his coronation oath and consent to the emancipation of Roman Catholics had been responsible, so he thought, for his relapse in 1801. Those around him were inclined to believe this, too, and consequently were desperately concerned to ensure that nothing should be allowed to agitate his mind again, that unpleasant matters likely to disturb him should be kept from him, and that, as Pitt had assured him, the Roman Catholic question would not be brought up again during his reign.

He was constantly, nervously watched for indications of an agitated mind. It was noticed that when he had appeared at the Queen's birthday drawing-room, leaning on a crutch, she 'never left her eyes off the King during the whole time the party lasted'.

Anxiety had exhausted her. She was thinner than ever, and increasingly given to bouts of sulkiness and ill temper. She had been much relieved to have been able to make the Cabinet responsible for the King's treatment when he was ill; but it was she who still had to put up with his alarming behaviour in her bedroom. She became more and more nervous in his presence, and, well aware of this, he himself became increasingly hurt and upset by her apprehension and more irritated by her than he had ever been. The way to make him well, Dr Heberden told Lord Camden, was for his wife to treat him as though he *were* well, but this she could not bring herself to do.

Aware that the Queen had great faith in the Willises, with whom, indeed, she was in clandestine correspondence, the King constantly insisted to her that he had no need of their attentions, that he was perfectly in control of himself. And, in conversation with his Ministers, he contrived to make it appear that this was in fact the case. Yet, as Mrs Harcourt said, 'in his family and usual society his manners and conversation were far from steady', and the Queen was consequently persuaded that the strict treatment which the Willises had advocated was a painful necessity.

As the months went by, the Queen found it more and more difficult to contain her irritation, anxiety and distaste. In the summer of 1804 Lord Glenbervie said that her temper had become 'intolerable', that her daughters were 'rendered quite miserable by it', and that, as he was told by a lady at Court, she was now showing 'great peevishness and tartness of behaviour to the King', whom she now 'never saw but in company', and then, when he spoke to her, she sometimes did not answer him.

Later that year it was observed that, while never mentioning her with disrespect, the King showed clearly that he was, in Lord Auckland's phrase, 'dissatisfied with her' and much annoyed that in his recurring differences with the Prince of Wales she now took her son's side, not his. The Duke of Kent, the Prince's brother, remarked upon their father's 'great coolness' towards their mother. When they returned from Weymouth that autumn the King kept to his own apartments, while she contrived to ensure not only that he did not sleep with her but also that she was never left alone with him even in the daytime, requiring at least one of her daughters to be in the room whenever he was present. At the Queen's House she locked the door of her boudoir against him.

To people outside the family, however, he still seemed both well in health and cheerful in spirit, despite his failing sight. He had a cataract on the left eye, while the right, 'though not so bad', was 'bad enough'. In the summer of 1805 he had to give up a proposed tour through various counties in England because his eyes, to which leeches had been applied, were so inflamed that he had been obliged to ask others to write letters for him.

Soon it became impossible for him to distinguish the features of people on the other side of the room, and difficult for him to read even with the help of the powerful spectacles he wore for playing commerce. Before long he could not read letters at all, and for dealing with all his correspondence he had to rely on Lieutenant-Colonel Herbert Taylor, who, formerly Private Secretary and Aide-de-Camp to the Duke of York, became the King's Private Secretary in June 1805. 'The patience, resignation and unutterable good humour with which he submits to so great a calamity daily increase,' Taylor wrote the following year. 'It is impossible to be with our good King without finding every hour fresh cause to love and admire him.' 'The King,' confirmed Lord Hawkesbury on 5 July, 'has borne this *last calamity*. . . with all the fortitude and resignation which belongs to his character; and his spirits are cheerful.'

Lord Henley, the former Envoy Extraordinary to Vienna, gave a similar report:

Our good King continues, mind and body, the sight excepted, better than I have seen him for years ... This morning I met him in the park at ten o'clock and rode with him until a quarter past one. He was cheerful, and we had more than one of his hearty laughs which I have not heard for some time. He talked to me, indeed, in an affecting manner of his situation, saying that he had tried this morning, but in vain, to read the docket of one of his dispatches, but is convinced that he perceived an amendment, and that even with the left eye he can perceive the light. Lady Henley says that he presented the muffins to the ladies last night in his old jocose and good-humoured manner.

By now the Royal Family had moved from Queen's Lodge at Windsor into the Castle itself, which was made habitable for them by James Wyatt. With the encouragement of the King, Wyatt replaced the windows of the apartments that Hugh May had designed for Charles I with well-made Gothic ones, a transformation prompting His Majesty to remark to Benjamin West that 'he should have thought it impossible thirty years ago that he should ever encourage Gothic architecture'.

The move was much lamented by the Queen, who had to exchange what she described as 'a very comfortable habitation' for an apartment in the tower at the south-east corner of the Upper Ward, the 'Coldest House, Rooms and Passages that ever existed'. So cold, indeed, was it sometimes that the Queen and her daughters had to huddle together in their fur-trimmed coats, so Her Majesty said, 'to prevent our being frozen'. The move was also much regretted by the King's servants, who had to attend upon their master in his bachelor rooms in the sunless north front of the Castle in which there were no carpets on the floors since carpets, His Majesty insisted, harboured dust.

Disliked though it was, the move was celebrated with uncommon festivities: a concert of music by Handel was given at Frogmore, the Queen's country house in the grounds of Windsor Park, and a 'Splendid Ball' was held in the Castle, where the Queen appeared looking 'Most Magnificent, in a Gold Stuff with Broad Loops of Diamonds'. The Princesses, in 'Silver Tissues', were also as regal as 'Jewels, Gold and Silver could make them'.

Soon afterwards, on St George's Day 1805, there was 'A Most Splendid Procession' of the Knights of the Garter to St George's

Chapel in a day's ceremonial which, costing an estimated £50,000 and witnessed by the numerous foreign ambassadors and Ministers who had been invited to Windsor for the occasion, was intended as a riposte to the Corsican upstart who had assumed the title of Emperor the year before.

The Prince of Wales was present and all the King's other sons, every one of them a duke now and all Knights of the Garter. Accompanied by the other Knights, they paraded up the new, wide Grand Staircase, designed by James Wyatt, which led from the vault beneath the Queen's Guard Chamber to the state apartments. The dinner, which began at six o'clock, was even more splendid than that held in the Castle to celebrate the King's recovery in 1789. The Prince of Wales and his brothers sat at the Sovereign's table, on which were thousands of pounds of gold plate and 'a variety of splendid ornaments . . . composed wholly of silver'. It was noticed that the Prince of Wales 'did not exchange one word with the King during the whole of the banquet. As soon as the Prince was seated he asked for a tumbler of claret. It was brought but [it was whispered to him] that it was a part of the ceremony that no one should drink till the herald had proclaimed the first toast. He therefore declined the tempting cup, much as he appeared to need it.'

After the Knights' banquet, eighteen tables were laid out in the Castle yard with provisions and hogsheads of ale. Police officers from Bow Street had been brought to Windsor to keep the crowds in order; but when the gates were opened the scene of confusion which ensued exceeded 'all description. Everyone being more anxious to plunder than to eat, they carried off that which came soonest to hand.'

The King, watching the tumult from one of the windows of the Queen's apartments, was seen to be extremely agitated. For him it had been a long and anxious day. He had, as was his usual practice, been to the kitchens that morning to supervise the spicing and roasting of a baron of beef, weighing over 160 pounds; and he had seemed as flustered then as he had afterwards appeared to be in St George's Hall, where, 'unusually red and anxious', he appeared in an old-fashioned periwig of astonishing size. It was, said a spectator of the scene, 'an enormous, well-powdered flowing wig, such as we may see in some old pictures as worn by the Lord Chancellors and Judges of those days. The ends of the wig flowed down his shoulders, and nearly covered his chest.'

44

PRINCESS CHARLOTTE AND
HER MOTHER

*When he said he was alone and had come [to Kew]
merely to see the Princess of Wales and Princess Charlotte
I was quite stupefied.*

The Princess of Wales, so she claimed to a Lady of the Bedchamber, Lady Glenbervie, found the King's visits a severe trial. 'She says,' Lady Glenbervie told her husband, 'the freedoms he took with her were of the grossest nature, that those visits always put her in terror, that she could not refuse to see her uncle, her father-in-law and King, alone in her room, without declaring that he was still mad, while the Ministers . . . wished it to be understood that he was in his senses.' Lord Glenbervie was told by the Princess – never a very reliable witness – that the King's 'discourse and actions' while he was not yet fully recovered from his illness, 'could not be repeated'.

He insisted on seeing her alone [Glenbervie continued] and ordered the Duke of Cumberland [who had followed him from the Queen's House] to remain in another room. I wonder her Royal Highness had a scruple on this occasion about telling me all. She had told Lady Glenbervie, on a former occasion, that on one of these visits, being alone with her in the room, he threw her down on one of the sofas and would certainly have ravished her, if, happening to be without a back, she had not contrived to get over it on the other side.

The King told the Princess that, on an occasion when the Queen was lying in, the late Lady Harcourt had humbly offered to supply her Majesty's place till her recovery.

Despite his alleged behaviour, when she heard that the King was coming to see her a few days after his interview with her husband the Princess wrote a characteristically ill-composed letter of welcome:

351

I am this moment Honor'd with your Majesty gracious intention of coming to Black-Heath; and beg leave to express how much I feel myself gratified of the very distinguish'd, and condsending mark of your Majesty favour and goodness towards me and my dear Daughter. my future Conduct will I trust proof to your Majesty, my gratitude and sincere devotion with which sentiments of Dutyful Respects, Veneration and truly attachment, I have the Honor to remain my whole like Sir your Majesty most humble and obedient Servant Niece and Subject Caroline

For the King, his visits to Montague House in Greenwich to which the Princess of Wales had moved from the Old Rectory at Charlton, were particularly pleasurable when he found his little granddaughter there on a visit to her mother. Princess Charlotte was now eight years old, a bright and appealing little girl with blue eyes, blonde hair and a skin badly pitted by smallpox. 'Very lively, intelligent and pleasant . . . amazingly, clever and engaging,' was the opinion of the Earl of Minto, who wished that his own girls were 'so accomplished'. She was 'quite an angel', confirmed Princess Amelia, who never enjoyed 'anything so much' as the little girl's summer visits to Weymouth, where she was taken down to the beach to bathe every day, rode about in her carriage, and collected shells on the sands at Portland. Admittedly she was something of a 'pepper-pot', excitable and temperamental, given to sudden tantrums and a pronounced stammering when thwarted or exhilarated; but it was hoped that she would grow out of these, provided she was kept as much as possible from the *'continual bad examples'* provided at Blackheath. Her father, whose talent for mimicry she had inherited, confessed that he 'doted upon her' and gave constant warnings about the dangers of exposing the child to evil influences 'from a certain quarter'. In London she was provided with her own extensive Household, presided over by a governess in the reliable person of the Countess of Elgin, at Warwick House, a gloomy mansion in a cul-de-sac near Carlton House from which she made periodic visits to Windsor as well as to Blackheath.

The King was entranced by her.* He declared there 'never was so perfect a little creature'. He talked of her endlessly and, so Princess

---

* She was at this time his only legitimate grandchild, though at the time of her death in childbirth in 1817 he was believed to have had fifty-six illegitimate grandchildren.

Elizabeth told the child's father, whenever the King saw her he was in 'extacys of joy'. On one visit she 'delighted the King with singing Hearts of Oak, as also with her reluctance' to leave the Castle. She pleaded often, 'Me go again to Grandpapa', who had delighted her by the present of a 'very large Rocking Horse'.

Not only would the King have liked to see more of her, he expressed the opinion that her mother ought to see more of her, too; and, now that she had reached an age when new arrangements would have to be made for her future education, he proposed that her visits to her mother should be more frequent. He also suggested that she should live at Windsor and be brought up under his eye and protection. The Prince agreed to this, making the significant proviso that the child should be placed under his father's 'sole and exclusive care'. So the King drew up a detailed plan for Princess Charlotte's future education, providing for a governess, a sub-governess and an assistant sub-governess, for tutors in writing, history and geography, in 'belles lettres and French', music and dancing, for a clergyman to teach Latin as well as divinity and to conduct daily prayers, and for a bishop to superintend them all.

The King had no intention, however, of excluding the mother from these arrangements. On 18 August 1804 he had written to her from the Queen's House, telling her that he could not bring himself to set out for Weymouth without first seeing her and his 'ever dear granddaughter'. Would they both, therefore, come over to Kew the following Monday? 'I trust,' he added, 'I shall communicate that to you that may render your situation much more happy than you have as yet been in this country, but not more so than your exemplary conduct deserves. Believe me ever with the greatest affection . . .'

'This moment I have received your Majesty most gracious letter,' the Princess immediately and excitedly replied, with even less regard than usual for the rules of her adopted language, 'which the contents mak's me so happy that I am afraid it will be impossible for me to express my sentiments of gratitude upon paper . . .'

Lady Elgin presented herself and her charge at Kew before the Princess of Wales's arrival and, in view of all she had heard of the King's strange behaviour of late, she was horrified to find the King quite alone. 'He was waiting to receive Princess Charlotte and took us into the dining-room,' she reported. 'Yet when he said he was alone and had come [to Kew] merely to see the Princess of Wales and Princess Charlotte I was quite stupefied. He then added he was to take Princess Charlotte to himself as the Prince wished it, but he could say nothing yet. His Majesty was going on when the Princess of Wales came.'

Immediately the King took his daughter-in-law and his 'little darling' into an inner apartment, from which the child soon emerged, carrying the King's private key to the garden gate, saying that he wanted her and her Governess to go for a walk while her mother and grandfather had a talk. When Princess Charlotte and Lady Elgin returned, all four of them had dinner together, the King eating his pudding and dumplings with a good appetite, but 'overexerting' himself.

The Prince of Wales was appalled to discover what his father had done, threatening to withhold his consent to the arrangements which had provisionally been made for his daughter's future education; and it was only after lengthy negotiations, conducted through the Lord Chancellor, that he agreed to Princess Charlotte living at Windsor from June to January. For the rest of the year she was to remain at Warwick House with a new Household, including a coachman, a postilion, a porter, a page, an errand-boy, a gardener, three footmen, six maids and an educational staff superintended by John Fisher, Bishop of Exeter, a firm but patient man whose chief concern was 'to train the Princess in the self-command naturally foreign to her'. The Princess of Wales was to be allowed to see her daughter from time to time, but only as a visitor.

The limitations placed upon the Princess of Wales's access to her daughter came as no surprise to those who had heard stories of her recklessly indiscreet behaviour at Montague House, where she was said to indulge in conversations which degenerated into 'low nonsense and sometimes gross ribaldry'. She sat on the floor and talked scandal to her ladies, went for picnics at which she ate raw onions and drank large quantities of ale (pronounced 'oil'), and flirted with any presentable man who came to the house, some of whom were entertained behind locked doors. She was rumoured to have had affairs with both Rear Admiral Sir Sidney Smith and Captain Thomas Manby of the Royal Navy, as well as George Canning, the Duke of Cumberland, William Scott and Sir Thomas Lawrence, and to have suggested to Lady Douglas, a neighbour in Blackheath, that she should go over to her house to attend her *accouchement*, taking a bottle of port and a tambourine with her to keep up the expectant mother's spirits. She went so far as to hint that one of the several children whom she adopted was her own child. 'I have a bedfellow whenever I like,' she was reported to have said. 'Nothing is more wholesome.' In the autumn of 1801 and again in 1802 there had been reports that she was pregnant. She herself was supposed to have said that, 'if the worst came to the worst and she were discovered, she would give the Prince of Wales the credit for she had slept two nights in the year she was pregnant at Carlton House'. There were those, like William Lamb and Bishop Hurd, who thought she was more or less insane, or if not actually mad 'a very worthless woman', as Lord Holland said. Lady Hester Stanhope described her as a 'downright whore', Lady Bessborough thought her levity 'inconceivable', while Mary Berry wrote of her, 'Such an exhibition! . . . Such an overdressed, bare-bosomed, painted-eye-browed figure one never saw.'

It was suggested to her husband that her conduct must be the subject of an official investigation. The Prince hoped that this could be avoided if possible; but the First Minister told him, 'I do not know, Sir, what your Royal Highness must do; but I do know what *I* must do. I must lay the whole business, Sir, before His Majesty without delay.' Lord Thurlow, the former Lord Chancellor, agreed with him. 'Sir,' Thurlow said, 'if you were a common man, she might sleep with the Devil; I should say, let her alone and hold your tongue. But the Prince of Wales has no right to risk his daughter's crown. The accusation must be examined into.'

The King, with evident regret, agreed to be 'entirely guided by his Ministers'. A Commission of Inquiry was consequently appointed in the summer of 1806 to consider the Princess of Wales's case.

Having listened to a great amount of conflicting evidence – having heard one witness, a maidservant, declare that she had never noticed any difference in the Princess's shape during the relevant months, another depose that she had in fact been very large, and a footman quoted as having expressed the opinion that the Princess was 'very fond of fucking' – the Commissioners announced their 'perfect conviction' that there was 'no foundation for declaring that the child now with the Princess [was] the child of her Royal Highness or that she had been delivered of any child in the year 1802'.

Having read the Commissioners' report, the Prince discussed it with Lord Thurlow, who persuaded him that they had shown 'too great a lenity to the Princess'. In Thurlow's opinion there might not have been 'quite sufficient' evidence to 'commence an action for High Treason, still, from the circumstances of imprudence, amounting nearly to positive proof, they ought to follow it up by a recommendation to the King (which he ought instantly to sanction) of bringing in an Act of Parliament to dissolve the marriage'.

Yet there was in fact no positive proof of adultery; and the King accepted there was not. He had to concede, however, that his daughter-in-law had undoubtedly been guilty of much 'levity and profligacy'; and he wrote to her to say that there had appeared 'circumstances of conduct' which he could not overlook. The Cabinet's draft had suggested that he viewed these circumstances with 'severe disapprobation'; but he softened this to 'serious concern'. However, she was told that she could no longer be received as an intimate of the family, 'and no nearer intercourse [could be] admitted in future than outward marks of civility'.

If it had been a matter of 'one attachment and even a child', he would have been prepared to have her behaviour hushed up, he told Lord Grenville, but in view of all the evidence which had been presented 'she was not worth the screening'. She had not only been shown to be morally unstable but also a 'female politician', interfering in matters that did not concern her, and this in the King's eyes was quite as bad.

So, well aware that the investigation might be reopened, the Princess was left with what she called the sword of Diogenes still hanging over her head, while the King declined to have any further discussions with her about the education of Princess Charlotte; and when, thereafter, he went to Greenwich he did so to see not the Princess but her mother, his sister, the Dowager Duchess of Brunswick, who had sought a haven in England after her husband had been mortally wounded at the Battle of Auerstädt and Brunswick had been incorporated by Napoleon into the Kingdom of Westphalia. Her brother had sent a ship to bring her back to England from Brunswick; he had arranged for pensions to be paid to her and to all her three sons; and he had found a house for her at Blackheath.

Her gratitude and affection knew no bounds, she said: her 'dearest brother' was 'a father to all'. She died at the age of seventy-six, six years after her arrival in England.

45

THE ROYAL DUKES

Fatherly admonitions at our time of life
are very unpleasant and of no use.

Disappointed as the King was in his heir, he was almost equally distressed on occasions by the behaviour of the Prince of Wales's younger brothers, always excepting his 'valuable' second son, his 'dearest' son, Prince Frederick, Duke of York, who had been gazetted a colonel in the Army at the age of seventeen and the next year sent to Hanover for a rigorous course of training, from which he had returned in 1787 to the great delight of his father. Indeed, the King, so Fanny Burney said, was 'in one transport of delight' at seeing him again. 'So delighted he looked,' she said – 'so proud of his son – so benevolently pleased that everyone should witness his satisfaction' as he paraded his son on the Terrace at Windsor. Leonard Smelt went so far as to say that the King's pleasure was not mere pleasure, 'it was *ecstacy*'.

The Duke had been promoted major-general before he was twenty; and he was not yet thirty when placed in command of the army dispatched to Flanders to cooperate with the Austrian army against the French republicans. The appointment had soon been shown to be most ill-advised: the Duke, while brave and conscientious, had displayed no talent as a field commander, while his dissipations in the mess were none too extravagantly exaggerated by James Gillray, who, in one of his caricatures, depicted him sitting at the head of his table on a drum, a full glass in his hand, while a fat Flemish woman sits on his knee playing with his sword. His foot rests on a tattered British flag, beside which is scattered a pile of muskets.

Although he returned home almost in disgrace, he had been promoted field marshal at the insistence of his indulgent father, who had with great reluctance accepted the Cabinet's advice that he should be recalled.

Overlooking his son's extravagance, his gambling, his notorious womanizing and the enormous expense of his racing stables, in 1793 the King had gone so far as to suggest to Henry Dundas that the Government should feel in duty bound to help him settle the Duke's debts because of the 'very creditable part' he had played when in command in the Low Countries. The Duke's behaviour during the Regency Crisis was soon forgotten. In 1798 he had been appointed Commander-in-Chief; and in that appointment he fulfilled his father's hopes of him by displaying a real talent for administration and a genuine concern for the reform of the Army. As though in recognition of his success as Commander-in-Chief, his father went out of his way to help him when in 1808 the Duke was again troubled by some 'very urgent and extraordinary demands' for the settlement of new debts.

The following year it came to light that the Duke's witty, flamboyant and wildly prodigal former mistress, Mrs Mary Anne Clarke, had been accepting money from officers who trusted her to use her influence with the Duke to get them promotion or employment. The King did not doubt for one moment his son's 'perfect integrity and his conscientious attention to his public duty'; yet charges were brought against the Duke in the House of Commons, where Mrs Clarke captivated Members by her poise and cheerful impudence. When one Member – alluding to her reputation and the Duke's recent abandonment of her for another woman – asked, 'Pray, Madam, under whose protection are you now?' instead of 'condescending to answer the offensive question directly, she calmly and gracefully addressed herself to the Chairman: "At present, Sir," she said, "I believe I am under yours."'

To the profound relief of his father, who had been in 'great agony of mind' over the Prince of Wales's reluctance to make it clear that he supported his brother, the Duke was acquitted of corruption by a majority of eighty-two. It was the widely shared private opinion of Lord Wellington, however, that the Duke had 'manifested so much weakness and had led such a life' that there were grounds for doubting that he was 'a proper person to be trusted with the execution of the duties of a responsible office'. The King, continuing to insist on his son's great worth and probity – and, so Sir William Fremantle heard, 'indignant at his Ministers for [allowing the inquiry] to come forward at all' – acceded to demands for his resignation with marked disinclination, choosing the dour old General Sir David Dundas to succeed him, knowing that, because of his friendship with the Duke, as well as his age, Dundas would be quite prepared to hand the post back to him as soon as the scandal subsided. The King warmly welcomed his son's reappointment to the office two years later. In 1791 he had also approved his marriage to Princess Frederica, eldest daughter of Frederick William II of Prussia, the first acknowledged marriage in the immediate Royal Family since that of the King himself. She was very small, dumpy and rather plain, with bad teeth, 'a little animated woman, talks immensely and laughs still more . . . She disfigures herself by distorting her mouth and blinking her eyes.' But, in Lord Malmesbury's words, she was 'lively, sensible' and, unlike her future sister-in-law, the Princess of Wales, 'very tractable'.

The King took far less satisfaction in his younger sons than he did in his beloved Duke of York. Prince William had been sent to sea at the age of thirteen, his father having written to Rear Admiral Samuel Hood to say that 'the young midshipman will be at the dockyard between one and two on Monday [14 June 1779]. I desire he may be received without the smallest marks of parade. I trust the Admiral will order him immediately on board . . . The young man goes as a sailor, and as such, I add again, no marks of distinction are to be shown unto him; they would destroy the whole plan.'

To the boy himself the King had given instructions not only to study with diligence the profession of a naval officer but also to continue, under the guidance of his tutor, Dr John James Majendie, his academic schooling, to taste the beauties of Latin and 'read it with ease', to speak French and German, to study history, and above all to remember his religious duties and not to neglect 'the habitual reading of the Holy Scriptures'. He must always behave like the son of a king and not as other boys might. 'It must never be out of your thoughts,' his father had told him, 'that more obedience is necessary from you to your superiors in the Navy, more politeness to your equals, and more good nature to your inferiors, than from those who have not been told that these are essential for a gentleman.'

Prince William was not a boy likely to profit from such injunctions. He was good-natured in a rough kind of way, but truculent, boorish and obstinate, sometimes a bully and often a buffoon, much given to swearing and to practical jokes. But it had to be conceded that, for all his faults, he was not an incompetent seaman, though scarcely deserving the high praise which, in reports to his father, his seniors thought it as well to bestow upon him. Captain Horatio Nelson, a man with a high opinion verging upon reverence for royalty, encountered him on the North American station and reported him as potentially 'an ornament to our Service . . . superior to near two thirds of the List'. Yet Nelson grew to know him as a martinet with a firm belief in the efficacy of the lash and an insatiable appetite for coarse and scatological jokes as well as for making long, boring and often quite irrelevant speeches at every opportunity. Nelson also knew that the Prince was a notorious womanizer, picking up girls in every port, frequenting brothels, contracting venereal disease, making reckless proposals of marriage to the most unsuitable women. One of these was the daughter of the Spanish admiral commanding in Cuba; and it was evidently 'a question whether his Royal Highness would have seen England again, had it not been for Captain Nelson, who plainly saw the danger that impended over his royal friend and urged his immediate departure', much to the gratitude of the King, who, warmly approving of the young Captain's friendship with his wayward son, invited him to Windsor after greeting him at a levee at St James's Palace.

The reports about Prince William from his tutor, who wrote of his 'unconquerable aversion' to Latin, were not as encouraging as those from his naval superiors had been; and upon his return home the King was obliged to agree with the Duke of York that Prince William was 'excessively rough and rude', while the Queen reprimanded her son for 'disliking everything which had been thought of as necessary towards [his] improvement'.

He certainly disliked being sent to Hanover for lessons in French and German and in the hope that a supervised sojourn there would do more for his manners and bearing than life in a rough and rowdy midshipmen's mess had done. His letters home to his brothers were full of complaint: Oh! how he wished he was returned to England,

and the 'pretty girls of Westminster'. His circumstances were 'very narrow'. How did his father expect him to live on £3,000 a year?

He had returned to England in the summer of 1785, and soon afterwards had gone back to sea as lieutenant of the *Hebe*, becoming captain of the frigate *Pegasus* in April the following year. He was not much liked, it being said of him that 'no officer could serve under the Prince but that sooner or later he must be broke'. Nor, if his letters home were a true reflection of his mood, was he contented with his lot. He continued to grumble about the inadequacy of his allowance and of his father's attitude towards him. What could be the use of 'our worthy friend our near relation keeping us so close?' he asked the Prince of Wales. 'Does he imagine he will make his sons his friends by this mode of conduct? If he does he is sadly mistaken. He certainly wishes us all well and thinks he is doing his best. I am convinced he loves me by his way of receiving me last. I cannot but regard him, and would do anything to please him, but it is so difficult to satisfy.' 'My Christmas box or New Year's gift,' he wrote in 1787, 'will be a family lecture for immorality, vice, dissipation and expense.' A few weeks later he understood that 'the old boy' was 'exceedingly out of humour', and he was 'in hourly expectation of a thunderstorm from that quarter'. Nor was he left long without receipt of a letter castigating him for doing what he knew would displease his father 'and then thinking to get off like a child' by saying he would not do so again. 'It is by proper conduct,' his father advised him, 'that my opinion of you is to be regained. You have in Frederick an excellent example; follow it.'

'Fatherly admonitions at our time of life [he was twenty-two] are very unpleasant and of no use,' Prince William told his brother. 'It is a pity he should expend his breath or his time in such fruitless labour.' Nor did Prince William think that motherly admonitions were any more pleasant or useful. 'I yesterday morning received a set-down from two persons that were concerned in begetting me,' he once wrote to the Prince of Wales. 'The female was more severe than the male. I do not mention names,' he added with heavy humour, 'for fear the letter should be opened.'

Twice he came home and twice he was promptly sent back to sea again, on the second occasion having failed in his reckless attempt to obtain his father's permission to marry the daughter of a Plymouth merchant.

After the Prince, by then reluctantly created Duke of Clarence and promoted rear admiral, had stepped ashore as an active sea officer for the last time, in 1790, he settled down as Ranger of Bushey Park, a profitable office bestowed upon him by his father – after the death of Lord North's widow – as a means of helping him to settle his debts. At Bushey he lived with the actress Dora Jordan, a beautiful, good-natured and generous Irish woman, who, three years younger than himself, already had four illegitimate children by two previous lovers. The Duke's enforced retirement from active service in the Navy was rendered less unpalatable by the prospect of a life of pleasant domesticity with this attractive and understanding woman, by the appearance of a succession of little FitzClarences, ten in number, five sons and five daughters, and by Mrs Jordan's ability still to command large sums for her theatrical performances.

The King, who for years ignored his son's liaison with Mrs Jordan, turned a deaf ear to the Duke's repeated requests to serve at sea against the French, just as he rejected the appeals of the Prince of Wales to lead a force to fight them on land; but he could not affect ignorance of the Duke's inexplicably immense continuing debts, nor could he pretend to be unaware of his son's exasperatingly ill-considered interventions in debates in the House of Lords, his attacks on Pitt, his clumsy defence of the slave trade and denigration of Wilberforce and other 'hypocritical' abolitionists – which earned him the freedom of Liverpool – and, in the presence of his two adulterous elder brothers, his pious castigation – although known as the 'fornicator-in-chief' – of adulterers in general, those 'insidious and designing villains who would ever be held in disgrace by an enlightened and civilised Society'.

The King's next son, Prince Edward, was also entangled with a woman and was also in debt. After completing his education in Germany, he had been gazetted brevet colonel at the age of eighteen in May 1786; and, having overspent his allowance in Hanover, he had been sent in disgrace by his father to Geneva with a severe military tutor, Colonel Baron von Wangenheim. He had hated

Geneva, the 'dullest and most insufferable' of all the 'villainous dull' places he had ever seen. He had been kept there, 'buried alive', month after miserable month, 'without a single line from the King and only one from the Queen'. He had repeatedly asked to be sent home and for enough money to settle his debts. The King, who considered the young man the least worthy of all his sons, did not answer his letters. So Prince Edward gave Wangenheim the slip and, to the King's fury, returned home without permission, having fathered a daughter whose existence was notified to the world by the *General Evening Post*.

He was summoned to an interview which lasted a bare five minutes, then packed off to Gibraltar, which he disliked even more than Geneva and where, in what he described as 'a cruel state of banishment', he carried out his duties as commanding officer of the Royal Fusiliers with as pertinacious an insistence on the rigidities of discipline and etiquette as his brother William had shown in the Navy. The Governor of Gibraltar felt constrained to report not only upon his 'unbounded ideas of [his] independence' but also upon his 'wild propensity to expense': inordinate amounts of money had been lavished on redecorating his apartments, the recruitment of a private orchestra and the purchase of four new carriages for the reception of a mistress whom a friend had been sent to procure for him in France or Switzerland.

This mistress, Thérèse-Bernardine Mongenêt, known as Mlle Saint-Laurent, was a good choice – pretty, good-natured and sensible; but her well-publicized arrival in Gibraltar frustrated the hope which her lover had entertained of being allowed to return to England. The King still declined to answer his letters; and, far from allowing him to go home, sent him to Quebec, 'the most gloomy spot on the face of the earth', where his parents still continued to ignore his existence. Eventually in January 1794, through the influence of his brother the Prince of Wales, who sympathized with his plight while not much liking him as a person, he was promoted major-general and placed on the staff of the Commander-in-Chief in the West Indies. Here he pleased his father at last by taking an active part in the reduction of Martinique and St Lucia, for which he was mentioned in dispatches. He also received the thanks of Parliament, which in 1799 granted him an annual income of £12,000 a year on his becoming Duke of Kent.

Having returned to Canada from the West Indies, he was invalided home to England, where his father received him with more cordiality than he had expected in view of the fact that he had brought home with him Mlle, or as he now referred to her Mme de, Saint-Laurent, with whom he 'went everywhere in a public manner', much to the annoyance of his brother the Commander-in-Chief, who told him that this might be acceptable behaviour abroad but could not be done by an officer in his position at home.

The Duke of Kent did not, however, remain at home for long. In 1802, to general astonishment, he was appointed Governor of Gibraltar, where, it was hoped, his known reverence for military discipline would help to restore order to a lax and unruly garrison.

The unnecessarily and provocatively severe manner in which the Duke attempted to carry out his instructions led to a mutiny, after which he was recalled in disgrace for a stormy interview with the Duke of York, who denied him a formal investigation of his conduct, which was condemned from 'first to last as marked by cruelty and oppression'. Both brothers lost their tempers; and, to the King's evident grief, Kent called York a rascal to his face in public.

Thereafter the Duke of Kent played little part in either military or State affairs, though exasperating his father from time to time not only by his financial incompetence, which, having embroiled him with moneylenders, eventually obliged him to assign most of his property to his creditors and retire to Brussels, but also by his support of causes, such as Roman Catholic emancipation, known to be opposed by his father.

The King was no less exasperated by the Duke's younger brother, Prince Ernest. Handsome, tall, aggressively self-confident, Prince Ernest had been sent at the age of fifteen to the University of Göttingen, where military subjects formed a major part of the curriculum; and he was still abroad, training with the Hanoverian Army, in 1792, disgruntled by his father's determination to keep him and his brothers out of England and far away as long as possible from the baleful influences of Carlton House.

Mortified also by his having to serve with a heavy cavalry regiment in which most of the other officers were blackguards, he longed to return home. 'No man ever desired more to return to his family, to his country than I do,' he wrote to the Prince of Wales from Hanover in 1792. He had been kept abroad for almost six years now, and had 'not seen a single one out of England except Frederick . . . I should even be pleased if my father would permit my coming over to you if I even was only to stay there but a short time. Nothing can equal the pleasure I should have of seeing you all again; that we all should be again together there I do not believe will ever happen again.'

Certainly it was not to happen yet. The following year, 1793, Prince Ernest was serving at the front with the 9th Hanoverian Hussars; and in 1794 his renewed request that he might be allowed to come over to England on a fortnight's leave to see his family after an absence of eight years was again refused by his father. A few months later, however, he was at last given permission to return, after severe wounds had almost cost him the use of an arm and did eventually cost him the use of his left eye, imposing upon his features a menacingly saturnine cast. His father, deeply gratified by this son's display of bravery, granted his request for an increase in his allowance, a favour which Prince Ernest acknowledged in a characteristically self-congratulatory letter: 'Sir, if your Majesty will only have the goodness and enquire of all those who know me, they will tell you that I am a man who can never go round about to do or get anything.' His way was to go 'straight forward'.

Pleased as he was to have gained his father's favour, however, his short stay in England was not a happy one. Anxious to keep him away from Carlton House, the King insisted upon his accompanying his parents and sisters to Weymouth, where he was bored to death with the 'humdrum' existence there, complaining that nothing was so 'terrible as a family party'. His father, to whom he referred with heavy humour in letters to the Prince of Wales as 'the honoured author of our days', was in good spirits, as he usually was at Weymouth, but their mother was as gloomy and sullen as could be.

Before he was fully restored to health Prince Ernest was back on the Continent once more, proving himself as talkative, opinionated and brave as ever, and bitterly resentful of his father's order that, when the Army went into winter quarters, he must stay with his regiment rather than go on leave to Hanover. The order was couched in a kind enough way; but he would, he said, 'rather be damned than remain as I am now'.

He was still on the Continent when in December 1795 he wrote to complain to the Prince of Wales about his seemingly endless exile: 'It is hard to have lost the use of an eye in doing my duty and exposing myself for my country, and not to have got an answer from His Majesty, though I have wrote four times for leave to return to my country . . . Now I am determined, if I do not get an answer . . . to return without leave, for I have already sacrificed enough.'

The next month the King relented at last and gave permission for Prince Ernest's return home. By then a confirmed reactionary of the most vehement kind, the Prince became increasingly embittered and increasingly strange. Granted a most generous allowance of £18,000 a year by Parliament, he had also received some highly lucrative military appointments in England; but his hopes of a command abroad were thwarted, and his criticisms of those whom he believed to be in the way of his ambitions grew ever more outspoken and vituperative. The Prince of Wales was sympathetic, but as for the Duke of York, who declined to appoint him to the command of a corps, 'By God . . . How different can *brothers* be?' Spurned by the Duke, he wrote twice to their father requesting promotion to the rank of lieutenant-general in the British Army. Neither letter was answered. He threatened to enlist as a volunteer in the Yeomanry. The letter to the King in which this proposal was contained was not answered either. At length, having declared that honour would not permit him to remain in the Hanoverian service under General von Wallmoden, an illegitimate son of George II, he did accept the rank of lieutenant-general in Wallmoden's army; and in 1799, having been created Duke of Cumberland at last, he achieved his ambition of being promoted lieutenant-general in the British Army.

Cumberland was an intelligent man with a cruel, sardonic humour, 'very sarcastick, very comical though very impudent', in the words of the Prince of Wales, whose feelings for him alternated between the deepest distrust and dislike and the closest intimacy. The Duke of Clarence observed that if anyone had a corn he was sure to tread on it. To another of his brothers, the Duke of Kent, Cumberland was 'alias the *Black* Sheep'.

So long as he remained in England he was immediately and inevitably suspected of involvement whenever there were rumours of quarrels in the Royal Family or of scandal or crime in high places. Not only was he said to have been one of the Princess of Wales's many lovers, when his sister Princess Sophia gave birth to a child at Weymouth in August 1800 he was even said to have seduced her; and when his Corsican valet, Sellis, was found dead in bed with his throat cut in the early morning of 31 May 1810 it was promptly spread abroad that the Duke – who was supposed either to have been caught in bed with Sellis's wife or to have been blackmailed after having made homosexual advances to the husband – had murdered him. In fact, as the jury at the inquest decided, Sellis, whose wife said 'he frequently complained of a giddiness in the head', had attacked the Duke with a sabre, had fled when his master's other servants appeared on the scene, and had cut his own throat as guards had appeared in the corridor outside his room. It was the opinion of Colonel Henry Norton Willis, the well-informed Comptroller of Princess Charlotte's Household, that Sellis, his mind deranged by illness, had been goaded into fury by the Duke, who, 'in his violent, coarse manner', had taunted him for being a Roman Catholic.

Like the Duke of Cumberland, his younger brother Prince Adolphus was sent to Göttingen University. Also like Cumberland, he was commissioned in the Hanoverian Army and stationed in the Low Countries under the command of the Duke of York, serving with his regiment, as the King required, rather than at headquarters. Again like Cumberland he was wounded; and he was not allowed home for an even longer period than his brother, being on the Continent uninterruptedly for no fewer than fifteen years. He was a kind, good-hearted man, a capable soldier, prudent in both financial and social affairs, as unlike his brother Ernest in character as it was possible to be, respectable and obedient. He was saddened and puzzled rather than disgruntled when his mother behaved so coldly towards him when she was worried about her eldest son becoming engaged to marry into the family of the Duchess of Brunswick, whom she had never liked; and he had asked in puzzlement, 'What can possess her to be so odd? And why make her life so wretched when she could have it just the reverse?'

55. Joseph Nollekens's bust of the King, which the Queen considered the best likeness of all.

56. *A View of the Wilderness, with the Alhambra, the Pagoda and the Mosque in Kew Gardens, c.* 1763–5 by William Marlow. William Chambers was appointed Architect to Augusta, Princess of Wales, in 1757 and continued designing buildings for the gardens of Kew for several years.

57. *George III and his Family at the Spa Well, Cheltenham.* Having suffered a succession of abdominal spasms in the summer of 1788, His Majesty was advised to take a course of the waters at Cheltenham.

58. *The Republican Attack*, a caricature of 1795 showing the King's coach being attacked as he was being driven to open Parliament at the end of October.

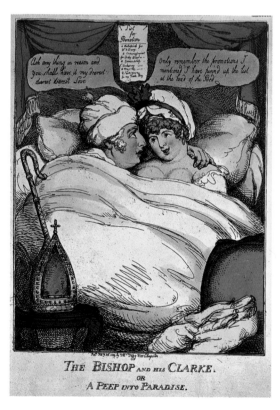

59. *The Bishop and his Clarke – or – a Peep into Paradise.* The Duke of York is shown in bed with his mistress, Mary Anne Clarke, who was accused of making money out of her intimacy with him by promising promotion to officers who paid her for her recommendations.

60. William Pitt the Younger, from the portrait by John Hoppner. Pitt became the King's First Minister in 1783 and remained in office for seventeen years until succeeded by Henry Addington.

62 (*opposite*). *John Bull Humbugg'd, alias Both Ear'd*, a 1794 caricature by Isaac Cruikshank. Pitt and Fox are represented using the horns used by newsboys to cry their wares, Pitt trumpeting the 'Great News' as presented by the government paper, the *True Briton*, Fox giving contrary reports of 'Horrid, Bloody News' from the Whig Opposition's *Morning Chronicle*. In the middle is John Bull, represented by the King, muddled and dismayed.

61. The House of Commons in 1793, from the painting by K. A. Hickel. Henry Addington is in the Speaker's chair; Pitt is making a speech. Charles James Fox is in the front row of the Opposition bench, wearing a hat.

63. The King relished hunting. This etching after Robert Pollard shows him returning from a hunt, with Windsor Castle in the background, St George's Chapel to the left.

TEMPERANCE enjoying a Frugal Meal.

64. James Gillray's *Temperance Enjoying a Frugal Meal*, 28 July 1792. The King and Queen dine most modestly on boiled eggs, sauerkraut, salad and water. They are surrounded by evidence of their parsimony.

65. The Prince of Wales by William Beechey, who presented the picture to the Royal Academy as his Diploma work in 1798. The Prince is portrayed in the uniform of the Tenth, the Prince of Wales's Light Dragoons.

66. Queen Charlotte by William Beechey. The Queen, aged fifty-two, is shown in the grounds of Frogmore House, which can be seen in the distance.

67 (*below*). The King portrayed towards the end of his life in an engraving by Charles Turner after Joseph Lee; blind and deaf, he is living in a strange world of his own imagining.

Prince Adolphus himself, the Duke of Cambridge from 1801, wished to marry his cousin Frederica of Mecklenburg-Strelitz, his mother's niece, the young widow of Prince Frederick of Prussia. The King granted his permission, but suggested that the wedding should be delayed until after the war. Prince Adolphus dutifully agreed; but in the meantime Princess Frederica fell in love with the Prince of Solms-Braunfels, whom she married shortly before giving birth to their child. After her second husband's death, Princess Frederica was in 1815 married for a third time, to Prince Adolphus's brother the Duke of Cumberland. Prince Adolphus remained a bachelor until 1818, when he married, most conventionally, Princess Augusta of Hesse-Cassel, the future grandmother of Princess May of Teck, consort of King George V.

Prince Augustus was also sent to Göttingen University, where, like all his brothers except Adolphus, he was soon in debt; but he earnestly apologized for it with such contrition that his father replied with unexpected leniency: 'You seem so sensible to the impropriety of such a conduct that it is not necessary for me to enlarge upon it.' The King was also understanding when he was advised that Prince Augustus's health would not permit his following his brothers into the Hanoverian service, for which he was in any case temperamentally ill-suited. Because of his weak chest it was considered necessary for him to live in Switzerland and Italy, where he was pitifully homesick. While still abroad, in 1792 he wrote to the Prince of Wales of his longing to return home 'after an absence of so many years'. 'I have frequently wrote to His Majesty on this subject,' he said; 'the Physicians have also informed the King it would be highly advantageous to my health – not a line on the subject nor even a hint.' He had not, he said, heard from his father for almost three years, though he wrote to him once a fortnight, sending him interesting accounts of his travels and displaying an intelligent appreciation of art and architecture. After three years wandering on the Continent with a travelling tutor he decided he would like to marry and be ordained; but his father, while no doubt pleased by the thought of his having a son in the Church, replied that he ought to stay abroad for the sake of his health for the time being.

But the Prince longed to go home and, as his brother Ernest had done, sought the Prince of Wales's help in persuading his father to agree to it:

Perhaps a word thrown in by you on a favourable occasion might have the desired effect – the more so as he knows my wish is not to remain near the Metropolis, from which both physical and political reasons drive me . . . Happy in being a quiet spectator of the prosperity of my country I should be glad with some quiet corner of it where I might give myself up to the recovery of my health and the forming of my mind.

The King did not trust the habits of Prince Augustus's mind, which were often as confused as the high-flown phraseology of his letters. At the age of six he had already displayed political views quite at variance with his father's, and had had the impertinence to wear the election colours of the perversely Whiggish Admiral Keppel, a precocious declaration of political independence which had been punished by his being locked up in his nursery.

Nor was it only his suspect political views to which the King had cause to object. In 1793, when he was twenty, Prince Augustus, without reference to his father, had the temerity to marry in Rome a woman some ten years older than himself, Lady Augusta Murray, the plain and rather bossy daughter of the fourth Earl of Dunmore, who could trace his descent from Henry VII of England, Charles VII of France and James II of Scotland. Having been warned of the possibility of this marriage by a courtier whose son happened to be in Rome, the King ordered Prince Augustus's immediate return to England. Taking the pregnant Lady Augusta with him, he obeyed his father's summons; but fearing lest objection might be raised to the previous ceremony of their marriage on the grounds that, although it had been performed by an Anglican clergyman, it had taken place in Roman jurisdiction, he married Lady Augusta a second time on 5 December 1793 at St George's, Hanover Square, appearing in the register as Mr Augustus Frederick. Soon after his second marriage, Lady Augusta – 'Goosy' as her husband called her – had a son who was to take the name of d'Este, that of Italian ancestors, rulers in the Middle Ages, common to both parents. This birth was followed in 1801 by that of a daughter.

The King would have been prepared to tolerate if not openly to acknowledge Lady Augusta as a mistress. After all, his other sons had

had mistresses enough between them and, when not pretending to be unaware of their existence, he had tolerated them, eventually acknowledging, for instance, Mrs Jordan as the Duke of Clarence's, taking notice of her children and accepting them as FitzClarences. But Mrs Jordan made no claim to be the Duchess of Clarence. It was Lady Augusta's pretensions in breach of the Royal Marriages Act of 1772 which the King found unforgivable.

He declared the marriage – the 'shew or effigy' of a marriage – null and void, and forbade the Prince, who had returned to Italy soon after Christmas, to see Lady Augusta, who was required to stay in England. The King thereafter more or less ignored his son's existence – as from time to time he had chosen to ignore the existence of others of his disobedient children – and when he did take notice of him he pronounced himself bitterly disappointed in his sixth son. By the end of October 1794 Prince Augustus was miserably asking the Prince of Wales to 'cast one moment of compassion on an unhappy being . . . wandering among the ruins of Ancient Rome'.

A few years later, in defiance of the King's arbitrary order, Lady Augusta joined Prince Augustus on the Continent; and in 1800 he returned to England, where his father, angry with the young man for 'coming over without permission', declined to see him until he had abandoned his 'absurd ideas' of being married legally. If he would give up all thoughts of presenting Lady Augusta to the world as his lawful wife, his father would look after both her and her offspring financially. He was prepared to give her the same sort of help as he had promised to Mrs Fitzherbert should the Prince of Wales die before her. But Prince Augustus refused to consider such an arrangement. 'Whoever thinks I will give up the partner of my misfortunes insults my feelings,' he declared indignantly.

The following year, however, he had made up his mind to swallow the insult: he agreed to separate from Lady Augusta; and the King, in return, consented to his being raised to the peerage as Baron Arklow, Earl of Inverness and Duke of Sussex. But thereafter he was a constant annoyance to the King by his support of all manner of progressive causes, while Lady Augusta was as tiresome an annoyance to both of them, insisting that the Duke proclaim their marriage in the face of all opposition, badgering the King, demanding money and a peerage in her own right, threatening to publish all the letters and documents she possessed unless justice were done, insisting on being known as Princess Augusta and returning, unopened, letters addressed to her as Lady Augusta Murray.

On his eventual return to England from the Continent, the Duke of Sussex applied to be appointed to some important military or civil appointment, preferably at the Cape or in the West Indies, where the climate would suit him. But the King supported the Government in its reluctance to place so sickly and inexperienced a man in a position of responsibility; and their persistent refusal of his request, combined with his creditors' 'threats of an execution upon all the little property' that he possessed, dismayed Sussex to such an extent that the Duke of Kent feared it might actually 'derange his intellect' – not that there was all that much intellect to derange, so Thomas Creevey said: 'There is a *nothingness* in him that is to the last degree fatiguing.'★

★ The Duke of York died at the Duke of Rutland's house in Arlington Street in January 1827. He was succeeded as Commander-in-Chief by the Duke of Wellington. His next brother, the Duke of Clarence, after a prolonged search for a suitable bride, married Princess Adelaide, the Duke of Saxe-Coburg-Meiningen's eldest daughter, whom Charles Greville described as 'frightful', 'very ugly with a horrid complexion'. He succeeded his eldest brother, King George IV, as King William IV in 1830. The fourth of King George III's sons, the Duke of Kent, married the widow of the Prince of Leiningen-Dachsburg-Hardenburg in 1818. Their child, the future Queen Victoria, was born at Kensington Palace the following year. The Duke died at Sidmouth in 1820. Having made a nuisance of himself in England, the Duke of Cumberland, under the regulations of the Salic law prohibiting female inheritance, succeeded to the German possessions of his family as King Ernest I of Hanover on the accession of his niece Victoria to the throne of England in 1837. He died at his palace of Herrenhausen at the age of eighty in 1851. Augustus, Duke of Sussex, having contracted a second marriage with the ninth daughter of the Earl of Arran and widow of Sir George Buggin, died of erysipelas in 1843. Wayward to the end, he directed in his will that he should be buried in the public cemetery at Kensal Green rather than at St George's, Windsor. The youngest surviving brother, the Duke of Cambridge, was promoted field marshal in 1813, but when it was suggested that he should be appointed Commander-in-Chief the proposal was dismissed out of hand by the Duke of Wellington on the grounds that the man was 'as mad as Bedlam'. However, he took an active part in public life, and was described in the *United Service Gazette* in 1850 as 'emphatically the connecting link between the throne and the people'. He died at Cambridge House, Piccadilly, in 1850. His widow outlived him for almost forty years.

46

THE CONSERVATIVE GENTLEMAN

I owne I rather encline too much to John Bull.

While his younger sons, willingly or unwillingly, spent years abroad, their father never evinced a desire to travel as his granddaughter Queen Victoria was to do. He had no taste, he once said, for the 'fine wild beauties of nature'; he did not like 'mountains and other romantic scenes, of which he sometimes heard much'. He saw little even of England, content to spend his holidays at Weymouth, to take the waters at Cheltenham when in need of a cure, and to drive not too far from these places to visit country houses in the neighbourhood or to go to see a nearby town. When he did make such an excursion he behaved with notable generosity: on a visit to Salisbury, for example, he contributed £1,000 to the Cathedral funds and £200 for the discharge of debtors. Debtors were also discharged at his expense at Gloucester and Dorchester; at Worcester he gave £550 to the city's poor; and at Plymouth he contributed £1,950 to the workers in the docks.

His travels in England were largely limited to the West Country. He never went to Wales or Ireland, and probably not to Scotland, though he may have been as far north as that during a tour incognito when he was Prince of Wales. He never went to the Continent either, much disliking the idea of France, and distrusting the Prussia of Frederick the Great; and, while often speaking of doing so, he never visited his territories in Hanover, although he was proud enough of his German descent, once being heard to declare as he 'laid his hand upon his breast with fine, manly frankness', 'Oh! my heart will never forget that it pulses with German blood.' To the end of his life he and the Queen spoke German when they were alone together; and all his sons, apart from the Prince of Wales, received part of their education in Hanover.

Yet, proud as he professed to be of his German blood, his sympathies and prejudices remained essentially those of the English landed aristocracy and of ordinary conventional English citizens. He was well aware of this himself. 'I owne I rather encline too much to John Bull,' he had once observed to Lord Bute, 'and am apt to despise what I am not accustom'd to.' He believed that the old ways were the best ways, that an honest Englishman should love his country and his family, always speak the truth and lead a life of orthodox morality. He had no doubt not only that the English constitution — the 'most beautiful combination that ever was framed' – was incapable of improvement but also that society and social rank in England were ordered as they should be ordered, and that such people as moneylenders, City financiers and arrivistes generally should not sit in the House of Commons, the members of which should be 'gentlemen of landed property'. As for the House of Lords, so Sir Nathaniel Wraxall said, 'throughout his whole reign, George the Third adopted as a fixed principle that no individual engaged in trade, however ample might be his nominal fortune, should be created a British peer. Nor do I believe that in the course of fifty years he infringed or violated this rule except in the single instance' of Robert Smith, the banker, a friend and supporter of Pitt, who, 'after a long resistance on the part of the King', was created Baron Carrington of Upton in the English peerage in 1797.

When it was proposed that a certain commoner should be appointed to an office instead of a member of the aristocracy, the King expostulated in a letter to Lord North that surely he 'could not seriously think that a private gentleman like Mr. Penton' should stand in the way of an eldest son of an earl. Undoubtedly if that idea held good it was 'diametrically opposed' to what he had believed all his life. Similarly he believed, as the Duke of Wellington was to believe, that officers in the armed services should be gentlemen, and essentially capable gentlemen. He also took the view that persons appointed to positions in the Royal Household should be of suitable social rank. When the Prince of Wales suggested that the respectable daughter of a merchant – whose husband had recently committed suicide when unable to settle debts incurred at the card table – might be found an appointment in his mother's Household, the Queen replied,

'The King from the beginning of my coming to England having desired me to keep every place in my Family as near to the rank in which I found it, must of course preclude the person in question.'

Yet the King was by no means as hidebound as many others who held such views. While an eldest son of an earl might well be considered worthier of a certain office than a private gentleman like Mr Penton, the King insisted that merit must come before birth and influence in the filling of posts of high responsibility. He made it clear, for instance, that bishops must be men of exemplary character and that social connections and family influence should play no part in their selection. He once told Lord North that the qualities to be sought in choosing clergymen for bishoprics were good private character, orthodoxy and learning.

Of the bishops appointed to dioceses in the 1770s, a majority came from quite humble backgrounds. Robert Lowth, Bishop of London, was the grandson of an apothecary; both Thomas Thurlow, Bishop of Lincoln, and John Thomas, Bishop of Rochester, were the sons of undistinguished country parsons; the Bishop of Exeter's father was a Herefordshire attorney, the Bishop of Ely's a King's Lynn merchant; Richard Hurd, Bishop of Lichfield and Coventry, then of Worcester, was the son of a farmer; William Markham, Bishop of Chester and later Archbishop of York, the son of a man who kept a small school in Nottinghamshire. The father of John Moore, Archbishop of Canterbury from 1783 to 1805, was said to have been a butcher.

Determined as he was to have men of unblemished private lives, learning and orthodoxy as bishops in a highly respected Established Church, the King was equally insistent that bishops should not be 'politicians', as he put it. When Pitt wanted to advance his former tutor and unpaid secretary George Pretyman Tomline, Bishop of Lincoln, to the archbishopric of Canterbury, the King strongly objected, pressing the claims of Charles Manners-Sutton, Bishop of Norwich and Dean of Windsor, although Tomline was senior to Manners-Sutton on the Bishops' Bench and had the largest diocese in the country. The dispute became acrimonious: heated arguments ensued; Lady Charlotte Finch heard angry voices raised; and Pitt went so far as to threaten to resign. The King ensured that Pitt was forestalled by going to the Deanery at Windsor, calling out Manners-Sutton from a dinner party, shaking him by the hand, and saying to him, 'My Lord Archbishop of Canterbury, I wish you joy. Not a word. Go back to your guests.'

As with the Church, so with the Army: officers chosen for high command must, the King insisted, be worthy of it and not be distinguished merely by rank, although it could not be denied, as Mrs Arbuthnot, the well-informed wife of Charles Arbuthnot, a former ambassador in Constantinople, said, that His Majesty 'always stood up for old Generals & disliked aspiring young ones'. The Government and the Commander-in-Chief, upon whose recommendations the King had largely to rely, did not, however, always choose well, often preferring a general of respectable seniority and upper-class birth to a younger, more talented officer: Sir Hew Dalrymple, great-grandson of the Viscount Stair, for example, rather than Sir John Moore, son of a Glasgow doctor and grandson of a Presbyterian minister, or Sir Harry Burrard, Member of Parliament for Lymington, as his uncle and grandfather had been before him, rather than the much younger and less well connected Sir Arthur Wellesley, the future Duke of Wellington.*

---

* Having been induced to add his signature to the highly unsatisfactory Convention of Cintra, by which the French were permitted to withdraw from Portugal in British ships, taking their stores with them, after their defeat at Vimeiro in 1808, Sir Arthur Wellesley was called to account – with Generals Dalrymple and Burrard – before a Board of General Officers. Severely criticized in the press, and as virulently lampooned by caricaturists as these two much older and more senior generals, who had been appointed to supersede him, Wellesley was advised by Lord Castlereagh, the Secretary for War, not to put in an appearance at the next levee at St James's. But Wellesley was determined to go. He had intended to do so as 'a matter of respect and duty to the King', and he was not the kind of man to shrink from showing his face on account of 'ill-humour in the public mind'. He now looked upon his attendance as a 'matter of self respect and duty' to his own character. 'I therefore insist on knowing whether this advice proceeds in any degree from His Majesty,' he replied to Castlereagh's letter, 'and I wish you distinctly to understand that I will go to the Levee tomorrow, or I will never go to [another] Levee in my life.' He did go, and the King was 'most gracious' (Arbuthnot, *Journal*, 234; Croker, *The Croker Papers*, i, 344; Stanhope, *Notes of Conversations with the Duke of Wellington*, 243).

47

THE NUNNERY

Poor old wretches *as we are* . . .

While most of the King's sons contrived to lead lives which appalled their father's strong sense of decorum, his daughters had very few such opportunities. Virtually every hour of their day was planned; permission had to be obtained for the pursuit of any activity other than those usually prescribed and permitted. A governess or lady of the Household had to be in the room whenever a man, even a tutor, was present. No work of fiction could be read unless approved by their mother,★ no excursion permitted unless closely chaperoned. Sometimes an actor or actress was summoned to recite or read to them. This was not always a welcome diversion, however: once David Garrick came to give a dramatic reading of the mythological burlesque *Lethe*, which, according to Walpole, 'went off perfectly ill with no exclamations of applause'.

Yet they did not lead such a cloistered existence as these rules might suggest. They enjoyed an occasional ball, a visit to the theatre to see some approved or specially censored play, a birthday party (when they had new clothes). There were summer holidays at Weymouth, and occasional short visits to friends of their parents, such as the Harcourts at Nuneham Courtenay, who evidently found the Royal Family rather tiring guests, as was evidenced when they accompanied them on a visit to Blenheim Palace.

They stayed here from eleven to six [the Duchess of Marlborough told the Archbishop of Canterbury]. We had breakfast for them in the library, and,

★ An exception was made in the case of Fanny Burney's third novel, *Camilla*. 'I've got leave!' Princess Elizabeth told the author in great excitement, 'and Mamma says she won't wait to read it first!' (d'Arblay, *Diary and Letters* ii, 72).

after they returned from seeing the park, some cold meats and fruit . . . Poor Lord Harcourt seemed quite happy to be able to rest himself, and the Duke of Marlborough found him sitting down behind every door where he could be concealed from royal eyes. We were just an hour going over the principal floor as they stopped and examined *everything in every room*; and we never sat down during that hour, or, indeed, very little but while we were in the carriages, which fatigued me more than anything else. Lord Harcourt told the Duke that he had been full dressed in a bag and sword every morning since Saturday.

The Princesses were taken to the races at Ascot and sometimes at Egham, though the Queen did not approve of this, considering racing 'a vulgar business'. And the King himself agreed with her so far as Newmarket was concerned. He never took his daughters there, disapproving of the high stakes ventured and the raffish atmosphere. Nor did he ever consider setting up a racing stables as the Princesses' two eldest brothers did, at enormous expense to them both.

The King once took three of his daughters on a formal visit to Oxford; and once they were taken round Whitbread's brewery. Most of the time, however, they remained at home, at the Queen's House, at Kew or at Windsor, where they could be seen going for drives in the surrounding countryside or for walks accompanied by governesses or ladies, or, on summer evenings on the Terrace while the band played appropriate tunes, promenading in crocodile fashion, two by two with their parents, stopping when the King caught sight of a familiar face or turned aside to talk to someone in the watching crowd. Their behaviour on these occasions did not always win the approval of the spectators, one of whom, the American John Aspinwall, Franklin D. Roosevelt's great-grandfather, described them as being 'not at all handsome and all very impolite as they were continually laughing at all they met'.★

Except at a distance, the Princesses rarely saw a man other than their father and his pages, equerries and attendants; and even these

---

★ Aspinwall had come to Windsor in 1795 from Kew, where he thought 'the pallace very mean. The most remarkable thing was the modesty of the Keeper for when we came away, *he refus'd* a half-Crown we offered him. This is the first time I ever saw an englishman in the lower Stations refuse money . . . The woman that shew'd us the Castle at Windsor *did not refuse money*' (*Travels in Britain*, 94).

they did not see at mealtimes, etiquette still forbidding any man to sit down in the Queen's presence.

In the evenings after dinner they listened to the music of one or other of their parents' bands, or took up their knitting needles or drawing-boards, or turned over the pages of a volume of prints while their mother listened to one of her ladies reading from some improving book, her eyes cast down upon her needlework or upon the spinning-wheel which she had been taught to use by Mrs Delany. When it was time for bed they approached their mother, one by one, to kiss her hand, curtsied to her ladies, and, accompanied by a female attendant, left the room.

When they were young they seemed to be quite contented with their lot. They loved their father and, indeed, undoubtedly continued to love him throughout their lives. To Princess Charlotte, the Princess Royal, he was 'the best of Kings and of fathers'; she described him in 1791 coming home from hunting 'the least fatigued of the party, and always so good-humoured and cheerful'. Princess Elizabeth thought him 'the finest, purest and most perfect of all characters. He was a man after God's own heart.'

The girls were often to be seen laughing in their younger years. They struck those who encountered them as being at once lively, well mannered and good-looking. Gainsborough, who was commissioned to paint them, declared that he went 'all but raving mad with ecstacy in beholding such a constellation of youthful beauty'.

But, as they grew older, rather more thickset and less even-tempered, they were year by year more frustrated by the enclosed life – the 'perpetual tiresome and confined life' as the oldest of the sisters, Princess Charlotte, called it – which they were required to lead in what they called 'the Nunnery'. For years they could see no prospect of escape from this 'nunnery' into matrimony, their father being unwilling to have any of the others married before the Princess Royal was settled, reluctant to approve of a match with any member of a family in their own country, and, as the Duke of Gloucester put it, 'not looking for Continental alliances from a notion [that his daughters] would be unwilling to leave England'.

Holidays at Weymouth eventually became an ordeal rather than a pleasure, 'a *perfect stand*-still of *everything* and everybody', complained

Princess Mary, who found their time there 'more *dull* and stupid' than she could find words to express. 'Mama, I feel, is beginning to feel unwell as she always does whenever she is at Weymouth,' she told her 'dearest dear' brother, the Prince of Wales, in the summer of 1794. 'One thing makes her very happy which is its being *determined* that the *sea* parties are not to take place . . . Whenever the weather will permit we are to row, but *entre nous* mama is so much afraid of *any motion* that I do not think papa will get her to go at all.'

Life at Weymouth became an unchanging round of more or less tedious activities for the Princesses, beginning at six or even five o'clock in the morning, when they got up so as to be ready to go out when their father did. They marched down to the bathing-machines through streets which made Princess Elizabeth wish she had lost 'the sense of smelling'; they were helped by dippers into the sea; they walked on the sands; they rode round the grounds of Gloucester House in a donkey-chaise; occasionally they attended a public breakfast given by some local dignitary, or were taken to watch a military review; regularly they went to the theatre, where they had to endure the same piece performed by '*a very bad sort of actors*' because the King enjoyed it and they had, as Princess Mary, thoroughly disgruntled, complained bitterly to the Prince of Wales, 'nothing to do but submit and admire his being so easily pleased'.

Princess Charlotte was quite as bored by these performances as Mary. She was a rather clumsy girl, not as good-looking as her sisters, ill-dressed, shy and lacking in confidence, though inclined to be managing by nature. She felt sure, with some justification, that her mother did not love her as she should and kept her subdued in the background as though she were still a little girl, 'just like an infant'. She suffered miserably, she once complained, from 'the violence and caprice of her mother's temper'. She told the Prince of Wales, to whom she was as devoted as was Mary, that her parents obviously loved her other sisters more than herself, that they constantly restrained her and made no attempt to find her a husband abroad or give her an establishment of her own at home. She begged him to see what he could do to find her a husband, and mentioned as a possibility Fox's friend the Duke of Bedford.

Knowing that their father would never consent to such a match,

the Prince wrote to the Duke of York to ask his advice about the
possibility of a marriage with someone of whom their father might
approve in Germany. The Duke replied that the Prince of Prussia
was hoping to marry one of their sisters; but, since Charlotte was
nearly five years older than he was, he was not likely to be interested in
her. Prince Peter Friedrich Ludwig of Oldenburg was then suggested,
but, although Princess Charlotte would have welcomed him and
blushed whenever his name was mentioned or her sisters teased her
about him, calling her 'the Dutchess of Oldenburgh', nothing came
of this proposal either; and it was not until she was thirty-one that
she found a husband at last in the extremely plain Hereditary Prince
of Württemberg, a man so fat that Bonaparte said that God had
created him merely to see how far the human skin could be stretched
without bursting.

The immensity of the girth of 'the great bellygerent' was satirized
by Gillray in one of his most celebrated caricatures, *The Bridal Night*,
in which the Prince is shown escorting his wife to bed on the evening
of 17 May 1797, the Prince of Wales – almost as stout as the
bridegroom – walking behind the bride, who demurely attempts to
conceal her features behind a fan. Pitt, beneath a picture of Cupid
on the back of an immensely obese elephant, holds a large sack
containing the dowry of £80,000; the Queen, in a poke-bonnet,
bears a bowl of posset; the King leads the way with a candle in each
hand.

Concerned by reports that his eldest daughter had 'fallen into a
kind of quiet, desperate state, without hope, and open to every fear',
the King had agreed not to oppose any reasonable match. But he
had initially refused to consider the Hereditary Prince as a suitable
husband, since the man was said to have ill-treated his late wife, a
daughter of the King's sister Augusta, Duchess of Brunswick, and
even to have connived at her murder. 'I have sent abroad for
information [as to] whether my opinion on the Prince is well
founded,' the King explained, 'which, if it is, no power on earth can
get me to admit of his marrying a daughter of mine.' Reassured, he
had given way and approved a treaty which stipulated that the
children of the marriage were to be brought up in Württemberg but
might not marry without the consent of the King of England or his

successors, and that the whole of the dowry of £80,000 was to be invested in England and the income from it paid to the Princess half-yearly. She was to be free to attend divine service according to the rites of the English Church, and she was to take with her to Württemberg three English servants as well as a German footman.

The marriage proved to be a reasonably contented one, as she indicated in the letters she wrote regularly from Germany both to the Prince of Wales, to whom she remained 'ever most sincerely attached', and to her father, who had been in tears when she returned from the chapel after her wedding and whom she was never to see again.*

Her next sister, Princess Augusta, was not so fortunate in her search for a husband. The King had been unwilling to consider a marriage for her so long as the Princess Royal remained unattached, and had found fault with all the suitors who had been proposed. Augusta was less self-conscious than Charlotte, lively, even boisterous, affectionate, cheerful and amusing. She had been a tomboy as a young girl, playing cricket and even football with her brothers; but she was studious, too, as Fanny Burney testified. She had conceived a sentimental passion for her father's courtly doctor, Henry Halford, and had then fallen in love with one of the equerries, the Irish soldier Major-General Sir Brent Spencer, a brave officer who was to be appointed second-in-command of the army in the Peninsula, much to the annoyance of Lord Wellington, who had no high opinion of his worth. The King was fond of Spencer; but there could be no question of his giving his approval to Augusta's marriage to him. She was to die unmarried at the age of seventy-one.

It seemed likely that her younger sister Elizabeth would also die a spinster. Still as fat as a young woman as she had been as a girl, she was often ill. Artistic, emotional, bossy and outspoken, she once deeply shocked Lady Sheffield, Lord North's daughter, by asking her whether she really believed some lady of their acquaintance was a virgin. 'Most certainly, Madam,' Lady Sheffield replied. Whereupon

---

* She did, however, return to England as the childless Queen Dowager of Württemberg in 1827, to consult Sir Astley Cooper and other physicians about her abnormal obesity. They were unable to help her, and she died at Ludwigsburg the next year (*Annual Register*, 1828).

Princess Elizabeth turned to her sister Sophia and remarked, 'You know, Sophy, I always say I do not believe there is [such] a thing as a woman being a virgin, unless she stuff herself with lead.' When Lady Sheffield told a lady at Court that she 'never in her life heard from any woman such gross, strange language as she had lately heard used' by Princess Elizabeth, this lady replied, 'I am sure it can have been nothing to the style of her elder sister.'

There had been rumours in the past of a secret affair conducted by Princess Elizabeth with one of her father's pages and even, less believably, of more than one pregnancy. She longed for a husband and children, and beseeched the Prince of Wales, on whom she 'doated', to help her. The name of Louis Philippe, duc d'Orléans, was suggested but was rejected immediately by the Queen, who, strongly opposed to the match herself, declined even to mention it to the King, knowing what would be his reaction to his daughter's marriage to a penniless French Roman Catholic.

Princess Elizabeth resigned herself to the continuance of what she sardonically described as her '*lively, cheerfull and gay life*', while sublimating her longing for babies of her own by looking after other people's and in charitable works for orphans. She also saw to it that she had little unoccupied time to dwell peevishly upon her plight. She wrote verse; she designed a Gothic ruin, a temple and a hermitage at Frogmore; she kept Chinese pigs in a nearby field; she organized *fêtes champêtres* for family birthdays; she produced numerous creditable watercolours, mezzotints and engravings and produced the illustrations for a book entitled *The Birth and Triumph of Cupid*. She became a connoisseur of porcelain; she was an expert japanner; she formed a fine library, which was to fetch good prices at Sotheby's; she wrote letters for her mother; she did what she could to help her father; and, determined not to become undesirable when a suitable husband presented himself, she attempted to keep her weight down by taking long walks in the early morning. She also drank sugar melted in water at night, in the belief that it would keep her temper sweet. At last, shortly before her thirty-eighth birthday, she found a husband in Friederich Joseph Louis, the Hereditary Prince of Hesse-Homburg, who succeeded as Landgrave on his father's death. She died at Frankfurt am Main in 1840.

383

Princess Elizabeth's next sister, Mary, was an affectionate young woman, 'all good humour and pleasantness', in Lord Malmesbury's words, and 'very pretty, full of sense and sweetness', in Lord Glenbervie's. More self-contained than her sisters, she was discreet in her behaviour, though outspoken in her remarks. It was understood that she would one day, marry her cousin, the boring, dense, though conceited Prince William, Duke of Gloucester, of whom she seemed unaccountably fond. Eventually, at the age of forty, she did marry him, and was perfectly content. After her husband's death she lived in seclusion, devoting herself to various charitable enterprises. Outliving all her brothers and sisters, she died at Gloucester House, Park Lane, at the age of eighty-one in 1857.

Neither of the younger sisters was ever to find a husband, though both had affairs with gentlemen about the Court much older than themselves. Princess Sophia was generally considered a delightful though moody girl, pretty, delicate and passionate, as devoted as her sisters to her father, exasperating as she found him at times. 'The dear King is all kindness to me,' she once wrote, 'and I cannot say how grateful I feel for it.'

She seems to have given birth to a child in secret at Weymouth when she was twenty-two. It was whispered that her dreadful brother the Duke of Cumberland, whose watchful affection for her was certainly felt to be unnatural, was the baby's father. But the child was far more probably fathered by one of the King's equerries, General Thomas Garth, uncle of Frances Garth, Princess Charlotte's former Sub-Governess. Thirty-three years older than Sophia, he was a man who might almost have been selected by the King for service at Court, since, of stunted growth and with a face badly disfigured by a purple birthmark, he was surely not likely to appeal to any of His Majesty's daughters, however frustrated and impressionable they might be. The diarist Charles Greville described him as a 'hideous old devil'. But then, Greville added, 'women fall in love with anything – and opportunity and the accidents of the passions are of more importance than any positive merits of mind or body . . . Secluded from the world, mixing with few people – their passions boiling over [the Princesses] were ready to fall into the hands of the first man whom circumstances enabled to get at them.' Evidently not considering the possibility that her father chose to pretend to believe an absurd story, Greville wrote that, when she was pregnant, the King was told that Princess Sophia was dropsical, then that she had suddenly recovered and had been 'cured by *roast beef,* and this he swallowed, and used to tell it to people, all of whom knew the truth, as "a very extraordinary thing"'.

The baby, so Lord Glenbervie said, was christened Thomas and left at the house of the King's Private Secretary, Colonel Herbert Taylor, in Weymouth; while the supposed father, General Garth, remained in favour at Court, being appointed to a responsible position in the Household of the King's granddaughter, Princess Charlotte. Princess Sophia remained under her father's roof. Although in indifferent health, she was to survive all her sisters except Princess Mary, living on well into the reign of her niece Victoria, and, until her mother's death, as oppressed by her restricted life as she had ever been. '*Poor old wretches* as we are,' she wrote to the Prince of Wales in her cramped hand, lamenting the lot of her unmarried sisters and herself and thanking him for his unfailing kindness to the 'old cats' at Windsor. They were not only '*a dead weight*' upon their dear brother, but '*old lumber* to the *country*', like '*old clothes*'. She wondered that he did not vote for putting them all in a sack and drowning them in the Thames. 'Two of us would be fine food for *the fishes,*' she ended her letter. 'All here goes on the same – quiet days do us no good – it only shews the mind more completely gone. God bless you, my dearest G. P. – Ever Your unalterably attached Sophy.'

48

APOTHEOSIS

In solemn prayer and thanksgiving for . . .
the Father of the People . . .

The King continued to follow the course of the war with the greatest interest, rejoicing as the whole country did at the defeat of the Franco-Spanish fleet at Trafalgar on 21 October 1805, but grieving less than most at the death of the victorious Admiral whose private life he so deplored. On receiving the news of Nelson's earlier victory in Aboukir Bay while on holiday at Weymouth, he had read the Admiral's dispatch 'aloud four times to different noblemen and gentlemen on the esplanade'. But he had since then made his disapproval of the man so clear that, on his way to his great victory at Trafalgar, Nelson had been much relieved when his flagship had not been blown into Weymouth by adverse winds as he had feared it might be, since Weymouth, where the King had been on holiday, was, as he told Lady Hamilton, 'the place of all others' he 'should wish to avoid'.

On learning of Nelson's death, the King briefly expressed his regret in a letter dictated to Colonel Taylor, then went on to bestow the most fulsome praise upon Lord Collingwood, Nelson's second-in-command. When the Admiral's tiresome brother, who had been created Earl Nelson, went to restore the great hero's insignia of the Order of the Bath to His Majesty, the King looked at it, fumbled with it a little, and was walking away without a word when Earl Nelson expressed his gratitude for the honours bestowed upon him and his family. Not content with this, the Earl, who had been a pretentious clergyman, proceeded to speak of his brother's religion – 'the true religion that teaches us to sacrifice one's life for one's King and Country' – to which homily the King curtly replied, 'He died the death he wished.'

To Charles James Fox, of whom he had also so strongly disapproved and whom he had never liked, the King could bring himself to behave more charitably after Fox had married his agreeable and much loved mistress Mrs Armistead. To be sure he had refused to consider Fox as a Minister in Pitt's Government in 1804, wishing it to be known that, while he was persuaded to accept other Ministers for whom he did not much care, Fox was 'excluded by his express command'. But then, on 23 January 1806, Pitt died, much to the King's distress; and 'not till after two days had elapsed could he either bear to speak of the event or admit his Ministers to his presence'. Lord Henley 'greatly feared' that the death and the consequent embarrassments into which it plunged him would have a disastrous effect on the King's mind. It was immediately clear that his existing Ministers were unwilling to carry on together;* and the King, for want of a more congenial choice, felt obliged to send for Lord Grenville, who requested that Fox should join the Administration. The King felt constrained to agree to this and to the formation of what became known as the 'Ministry of All the Talents', although it was largely composed of Foxites and there were no Pittites in it. For some days, according to Princess Augusta, the King 'showed considerable uneasiness of mind' on admitting to office a man whom he had earlier said he would exclude 'even at the hazard of a civil war'. 'A cloud seemed to overhang his spirits.' But on his return from London one day it was evident that the cloud had been removed: 'His Majesty, on entering the room where the Queen and Princess Augusta were, said he had news to tell them. "I have taken Mr Fox for my Minister, and on the whole am satisfied with the arrangement."'

Certainly Fox was immediately put at his ease when going to St James's for his first audience as Foreign Secretary. 'Mr Fox,' the King said to him, 'I little thought you and I should ever meet again

---

* When Lord Eldon, Lord Chancellor in Pitt's Administration, came to the Queen's House to deliver up the Great Seal, 'the King,' he said, 'appeared for a few minutes to occupy himself with other things. Looking up suddenly, he exclaimed, "Lay them down on the sofa, for I *cannot* and I *will not* take them from you." "Yet," he added, "I admit you can't stay when all the rest have run away."' (Twiss, *Life of Lord Eldon*, i, 512)

in this place. But I have no desire to look back on old grievances, and you may rest assured I shall never remind you of them.'

'My deeds and not my words,' Fox replied, 'shall commend me to Your Majesty.'

Thereafter the King had no cause to complain of Fox's conduct of foreign affairs, nor of his general demeanour, which was in pleasing contrast to that of another of his Whig Ministers, who, 'when he came into office, walked up to him in a way which he should have expected from Buonaparte after the battle of Austerlitz'. Nor had the King any reason to fear that Fox would agitate his mind by bringing forward once more the dreaded matter of Roman Catholic emancipation, as he had once declared it was his wish to do. When questioned on this point by the Austrian Ambassador, Fox replied that he now had no intention of introducing so controversial a measure. 'I am determined,' he said, 'not to annoy my Sovereign by bringing it forward.'

But less than a year after he had taken office Fox lay dying in the Duke of Devonshire's house at Chiswick. 'No believer in religion', he consented to have prayers said only to satisfy his wife, paying little attention to the ceremony, 'remaining quiescent merely', not liking, as Lord Holland said, 'to refuse any wish of hers, nor to pretend any sentiments he did not entertain'. His last words, on 13 September 1806, were, 'It don't signify, my dearest, dearest Liz.' He died 'without a groan and with a serene and placid countenance'.

'Little did I think,' the King sadly commented to Henry Addington, now Lord Sidmouth,★ when next he saw him after Fox's death, 'little did I think that I should ever live to regret Mr Fox's death.'

★ Henry Addington had been created Viscount Sidmouth in January 1805. On offering him an earldom the year before, the King had written, 'The King's friendship for Mr Addington is too deeply graven on his heart to be in the least diminished by any change of situation. His Majesty will order the Warrant to be prepared for creating Mr Addington Earl of Banbury, Viscount Wallingford and Baron Reading; and will [give orders] for the usual annuity, having most honourably and ably filled the station of Speaker of the House of Commons. The King will settle such a pension on Mrs Addington, whose virtue and modesty he admires, as Mr Addington may choose to propose.' Addington had then declined the pension as well as the earldom (Pellew, *Life of Henry Addington*, ii, 288).

Grenville's Ministry did not long survive it. The King had accepted its anti-slavery legislation; but when it came to a proposal to open all ranks in the Army to Roman Catholics he put his foot down. He had agreed with misgivings to ranks up to colonel in the Army and captain in the Navy being open to Catholics, but the extension to all ranks was too much for him to contemplate, much to the gratification of the signatories of addresses supporting his stand which poured into London and Windsor from all over the country. The Government was forced to capitulate and, when the King asked for a written undertaking that Ministers would never bring up the question of Roman Catholics again, Grenville resigned. The King parted from him and from Grenville's colleagues in perfect amity, assuring them that they had given him satisfaction on all matters other than this one, to which his religious scruples would not allow him to consent.

He got on just as well with the Duke of Portland, who succeeded Grenville at the age of sixty-nine in 1807, and with Portland's colleagues, in particular with the Lord Chancellor, his old friend Lord Eldon. Handing back the Great Seal to Eldon, he said, 'I wish and hope you may keep it till I die.' He was, Eldon wrote the next day, 'remarkably well, firm as a lion, placid and quiet beyond example in any moment of his life. I am happy to add that on this occasion his son, the Prince of Wales, has appeared to behave very dutifully to him.'

Portland and his Cabinet – which included Spencer Perceval as Chancellor of the Exchequer, George Canning as Foreign Secretary and Viscount Castlereagh as Secretary for War – evinced no desire for unwelcome reforms, nor for Roman Catholic emancipation; and they continued the fight against the 'Corsican usurper' with the required determination.

Yet the news that reached England from the Continent about the Corsican's progress was not reassuring. A month after Fox's death Napoleon defeated the Prussians at Jena; on 27 October he occupied Berlin, and on 15 December he entered Warsaw. The next year France defeated a combined Russian and Prussian force at Friedland; in 1808 a French army invaded Spain and occupied Madrid; and in January 1809 Sir John Moore, having been forced to retreat to Corunna, was mortally wounded there.

In the summer of 1809, however, came better news: at the end of July, Sir Arthur Wellesley defeated the French at Talavera; and as the war progressed, in triumph and defeat, the popularity of the King, as a stolid, reliable, honest, dependable monarch as well as a national symbol, increased month by month. One night at Covent Garden the American visitor John Aspinwall found

The house was so full I could get no seat but *peep'd* at their Majesties thro the crowd in the doors of the Boxes – the King, Queen, and five princesses with their Boxes cram'd full of *Maids of honor, lords in waiting, ladies of the bed chamber, and such like.*

I was surprised to see *his Majesty* pleas'd with the flattery so grossly offered, as the whole gang of Actors & Actresses *several* times came out and roard out God Save the King & Rule Brittannia and then the choruses was so charmingly echo'd from the Boxes, Pit and Gallery. A Stranger would have thot the audience a french Army pointing their Guns at the *Royal* Guests – every person having an opera (alias a Spying) Glass leveled at them. All that I could hear was hurra, bravo, encore.

'His popularity is very great,' wrote Lord Berkeley in October 1809, 'for the mass of the people look up to his good moral character, and to his age [seventy-one], and to a comparison with his sons.' The next year his popularity was described as being 'as great as it can possibly be'. At Windsor, respectful crowds were touched to see him walking unsteadily on the Terrace in his blue coat and white breeches, his hat shaped so as to protect his eyes, a daughter on each arm to guide their dimly sighted father towards those who wished to talk to him and to wish him well. When he went down to Weymouth, the people lined the route to cheer him on his way. On 25 October 1810, while Lord Wellington, as Sir Arthur Wellesley had by then become, was holding the French army at bay in the Peninsula in his defensive lines at Torres Vedras, London celebrated the fiftieth anniversary of the King's accession.

The number of people in the street . . . was immense [said George Rose], and the illuminations remarkably beautiful . . . The carriage could only move at a foot's pace through the people; but all most perfectly quiet and civil; not an offensive word or insulting gesture – not even a squib or a cracker thrown by a boy which might frighten the horses. I can truly say I never saw before such a collection of people to give an idea from sight of the population of the metropolis; nor ever witnessed such perfect order and decorum in any great assemblage of the middling and lower order of the inhabitants of it.

The whole country joined in these Jubilee celebrations. Theatre audiences in every county encored 'God Save the King', which was by now becoming known as the National Anthem; bands marched through the streets; balls and receptions were held in assembly rooms; crowds gathered in squares and fields to watch firework displays and illuminations. 'Indeed, the Jubilee of 25 October 1810,' as Professor Linda Colley has written, 'the first royal event of this kind ever held, was celebrated in outposts of the Empire, throughout Scotland and Wales and in well over 650 different locations in England.'

The Jubilee marked the apotheosis of King George III. Writing that year, the law reformer Sir Samuel Romilly commented upon the transformation of the King from 'one of the most unpopular princes that ever sat upon the throne . . . to one of the most popular', dating the beginning of this gradual transformation from 'the coalition between Lord North and Mr Fox'. 'Then followed an attempt upon his life by a maniac,' Romilly continued; 'then the irregularities and dissipation of the Prince destined to be his successor; next his own unfortunate derangement of mind . . . and last of all, but which added tenfold strength to every motive of endearment to the King, the horrors of the French Revolution.'

Yet the new national perception of the King was due not only to these events but also to the determination of the King himself to be, in Linda Colley's words, 'a different kind of monarch than his predecessors' and to the decision, made by him and his Ministers and advisers, to emulate the fêtes and festivals which had become so powerful as national propaganda in revolutionary France and which in Britain were focused upon the monarchy.

For weeks before the day of the Jubilee – which was also fortuitously the anniversary of the Battle of Agincourt – preparations had been afoot in town and country not only to celebrate it with processions, reviews, dinners and galas but also to mark it with some new and permanent monuments or civic amenities. Newspaper columns were filled with details of what was to be done and with readers' suggestions of what should be done. Towns vied with each other in providing their inhabitants both with a day to remember and with permanent facilities to commemorate that day in the future. The celebrations – attended by thousands of people who trusted the Volunteer and Militia regiments to prevent the disorders which had marred earlier occasions of this kind – were judged to be an unqualified success. 'The whole nation', one newspaper reported, was 'like one great family . . . in solemn prayer and thanksgiving for . . . the Father of the People'.

Thereafter it was, indeed, as the Father of his People that the King was perceived by the great majority of his subjects. No longer did satirists and caricaturists portray him as the buffoon, the skinflint or the tyrant of earlier years; and if he was still teased by them on occasion it was done with affection rather than rancour, and often the element of caricature in prints was slight, perhaps unintentional, as in the one entitled *Jubilee* published by I. G. Parry that October. Growing old now, and less involved in public affairs, the King was no longer the unpleasantly caricatured figure of earlier years: he had become the genial-looking gentleman holding a huge extinguisher over the head of a furious, diminutive Bonaparte. He was England's John Bull, even her patron saint, St George.

In these years the King seemed quite content, despite his increasing infirmities: his eyes were now so weak he could not see to write official letters – even the clumsily formed letters of the recent past – and he was obliged to dictate his correspondence to an amanuensis or to ask Taylor to answer letters for him. He had contrived to deliver the Speech from the Throne in 1804, and, in Lord Colchester's opinion, he 'read it well, with great animation but accidentally turned over two leaves together and so omitted one fourth of it. It happened, however, that the transition was not incoherent' and several members of the Cabinet did not realize it had been made. He managed also to deliver the Speech in 1805, reading from a script printed with huge letters; but this was the last time he was able to do so.

Suffering from acute rheumatism, he was persuaded to abandon his early-morning swim in the sea at Weymouth and to take warm sea-water baths instead. Yet in 1808, and again in 1809, Charles

Arbuthnot remarked upon his 'cheerfulness'. He spoke of his sons, even of the Prince of Wales, with affection now; while his daughters were dutiful and loving. The Queen remained remote and grumpy, but he treated her with continued respect; and when she fell into debt he immediately, as in the past, made arrangements with Spencer Perceval – who in 1809 had succeeded the Duke of Portland as First Lord of the Treasury – to have the debts settled.

His daily life at Windsor was perfectly tranquil. He got up rather later than usual, at half past seven; attended an hour-long service in the Chapel, repeating the alternate verses of the Psalms after the clergyman almost as perfectly as if he had been able to read them in the prayer book; went for a ride with the equerries and two or three of his daughters or, if it was too wet to ride, and so long as his eyes allowed him to do so, played chess with an equerry; dined at two o'clock; and at five visited the Queen and their daughters, who had had dinner separately at four. 'After this period public business is transacted by the King in his own study, wherein he is attended by his private secretary, Colonel Taylor,' according to a contemporary newspaper report. 'The evening is passed in the Queen's drawing-room . . . When the Castle clock strikes ten visitors retire. Supper is set out but that is merely a matter of form, and of which none of the family partake. These illustrious personages retire at eleven. The journal of one day is the history of a whole year.'

In 1810 the King's 'cheerfulness' was abruptly dispelled when he learned that his beloved daughter Princess Amelia was fatally ill with pulmonary tuberculosis and in intermittent agony from the devices which the doctors employed to drain her swollen lungs. Having scarcely recovered from the shock of the murder of the Duke of Cumberland's valet, the King became progressively more distracted and unbalanced, talking so loudly while out riding a horse led by a groom that his voice could be heard a long way off, and then relapsing into paroxysms of weeping at thoughts of losing his 'little darling', his youngest child, who in happier times, in celebration of her birthday, had been allowed to march proudly along the Terrace at Windsor in front of the rest of the Family 'in a robe coat covered with fine muslin, white gloves and a fan', turning from side to side to watch the spectators retreat before her. She had long been his dearest child, the recipient of loving letters.

My dearest Amelia [he had written to her three days before her fifth birthday].

As I shall not see you on the dear 7th of this Month I have sent to Gooly a writing-box and a wooden shoe which is a nutmeg grater, as signs of my not having forgot you. Were I to express all the wishes I make for your prosperity in this world and Eternal Happiness in the next in a letter Vollumes would not contain them. I shall on Sunday the 17th be at Kew before you are out of your bed, to bring you to Windsor and to see your two sisters. – Believe me, ever, my dearest Amelia, Your most affectionate father,

GEORGE R.

As often as he could in her last illness, the King would go to Princess Amelia's room and 'hold her hand and bend over her to scan the face in which he was too blind to discern the onset of death'. Her former wet-nurse, who was helping to look after the Princess, said that 'the scenes of distress and crying every day during the hour the King used to be with his daughter were melancholy beyond description'.

He asked Sir Henry Halford to send him bulletins about the Princess's condition three times a day; and when she was taken to Weymouth in her sister Mary's care, in the hope that the sea air would do her good, he dictated letter after letter to her, struggling to express the love he felt for her, and once endeavouring to write in his own hand a letter which was impossible to read. She replied with deep affection and in gratitude to her 'dear papa' for his 'never ceasing but increasing kindness' to her.

When the time came for her return from Weymouth she expressed a wish to go to Kew instead of to Windsor; but the Queen, from whom she did not expect 'much feeling or pity', objected. So, by now suffering from erysipelas as well as tuberculosis, she was installed instead in Augusta Lodge, Windsor, with Princess Mary to look after her there. The Queen raised objections to this, too: it was 'selfish of Amelia to demand so much attention' from her sister. Their mother's behaviour, her 'ill and cross looks', Amelia said, were 'the strongest contrast to the dear King possible'. But she was 'much too used to it to feel hurt by it'. Mary appealed to their father. It would 'half kill' Amelia, she said, if her mother's words were repeated to her. The

King replied that he had taken care to have it understood that the two Princesses were not to be separated.

Your conduct through life [he wrote to Mary] has amply proved how much my satisfaction and comfort have been your object, and every act of yours has tended yet more to endear you to me, none more than the tender love and attention which you have bestowed on a beloved suffering sister, and the cheerfulness with which you have devoted yourself to her service.

REGENCY

I fear we can never make them a real comfort *to each other.*

When she knew she was going to die, Princess Amelia gave instructions to Rundell and Bridges, jewellers to the Royal Family, to put a valuable stone she possessed into a ring for her father to wear in remembrance of her. As well as the jewel, there was a lock of her own hair under a little crystal window, and an inscription cut into the gold: 'Remember me.' The King broke down in tears at the sight of it. Afterwards he tried to write her a letter, but the handwriting was atrocious and only a word here and there is decipherable. He accepted the news of her death, at the age of twenty-seven on 2 November 1810, with a mumble of incoherent talk. At length, in the words of Sir Henry Halford, who had been asked to take the sad news to him, 'he became more composed and mentioned her again, saying, "Poor girl."' She was buried on the evening of 13 November in the new royal vault in St George's Chapel, the work on which was not yet complete. The King was asleep. He did not hear the mournful knell of the death-bell tolling in the Curfew Tower.

The day before Princess Amelia's death the Lord Chancellor had been to see the King, but so irrational was the King's discourse that upon leaving his room Eldon had thrown up his arms in a gesture of despair. Later that day the King was heard murmuring to himself about the causes of his previous attacks of mental disturbance. 'This one,' he said, 'is occasioned by poor Amelia.'

One evening a few days before Princess Amelia died, the King shocked Miss Cornelia Knight, the precise, humourless, literary companion of the Queen, by a 'dreadful excitement in his countenance' when he came into the drawing-room.

As he could not distinguish persons [Miss Knight wrote in her memoirs], it was the custom to speak to him as he approached, that he might recognise by the voice whom he was about to address. I forget what it was I said to him but shall ever remember what he said to me: 'You are not uneasy, I am sure about Amelia. You are not to be deceived, but you know that she is in no danger.' At the same time he squeezed my hand with such force that I could scarcely help crying out. The Queen, however, dragged him away. When tea was served I perceived how much alarmed I had been, for my hand shook so that I could hardly take the cup.

The King then called his sons over to him one by one and 'said things to them equally sublime and instructive, but very unlike what he would have said before so many people' had he been in a more composed state of mind.

A day or so later the King became so difficult to control that Dr Samuel Simmons, the mad-doctor, was summoned to Windsor. He went away again when he was given to understand that he was not to be given sole charge of the case; and thereafter the patient was left in the care of a whole succession of doctors who were already at Windsor or soon to go there – Sir Henry Halford, Matthew Baillie, Henry Reynolds, David Dundas, Robert Battiscombe, William Heberden, and Robert and John Willis. Also in attendance from time to time were John Meadows, a former surgeon-apothecary at St Luke's Hospital, and a Mr Briand, keeper of a madhouse at Kensington, who arrived with two formidable assistants.

The patient's condition improved slightly at the beginning of December 1810, but by Christmas he was believed to be close to death. In the New Year he rallied; he saw Perceval and asked him sensible questions about the progress of the war, though he could not concentrate on the answers; and he seemed to take comfort in playing the harpsichord. The doctors were as baffled by his case as ever they had been in the past, Robert Willis maintaining that the illness had 'never borne the characteristics of insanity'; and Dr Reynolds testifying that, while the King spoke like a man talking in his sleep, his memory was 'entire' and his 'acuteness considerable'.

Certainly he accepted the need for a regency quite calmly when Spencer Perceval explained the provisions of a proposed Bill to him. He was ready to sign or do anything that Perceval should recommend, he said; and when the First Minister warned him that his physicians 'did not think him sufficiently recovered to be troubled with public business' he complaisantly replied that he should conform to their advice. 'He then dwelt upon his own advanced age of seventy-two, that it was time for him to think of retirement. That he must still, however, be "King"; he could not part with that name . . . He should always be ready to come forward if he was wanted.'

So the Prince of Wales was sworn in as Regent on 6 February 1811; and, though it had long been expected that he would dismiss the present Administration and call his friends to office, he kept Perceval's Cabinet in power, explaining that he did so because he was, after all, only acting for his father for the time being.

He pleased his father in other ways too: the doctors had dreaded the King's discovering that, in her will, Princess Amelia had – with a few exceptions, including 'something belonging' to her to 'the dear King' – left all her possessions to Major-General the Hon Charles Fitzroy, a son of the first Lord Southampton and a descendant of one of the illegitimate sons of Charles II. He was one of the King's equerries, and a man with whom she had been passionately in love. He was better-looking than Princess Sophia's lover, General Garth; but, whereas Garth had some charm and wit, Fitzroy was generally reckoned to be a dull, sedate, reserved soldier, interested in little apart from his profession, and not likely to be attractive to women, particularly to those, like Amelia, who were over twenty years younger than himself.

The Queen, who had learned of her daughter's passion for the equerry as early as 1803, kept it a secret from the King, who was devoted to Fitzroy – so much so, indeed, that he was referred to at Court as Prince Charles. But she repeatedly remonstrated with her daughter about 'this unpleasant business', 'this unfortunate indulgence'. To refer to the love of her life in these dismissive terms was, for Amelia, unforgivable; and her mother, whose 'ill and cross looks' were explained by her daughter's distressing passion, never was forgiven. The Princess had become ever more determined to marry her 'blessed and beloved angel', her 'precious darling', as soon as she could. 'O, Good God, why not be together?' she had asked him imploringly. 'I pine after my dear Charles more and more every instant . . . I really must marry you, though inwardly united, and in reality that is much more than the ceremony, yet that ceremony would be a protection.'

She had liked to suppose that Fitzroy was in fact her husband already, and she had assured the Duke of York that she 'considered herself married'. When out riding she had dropped behind the others so as to be near her 'own dear Angel'; she had asked him to sit where she could see him in St George's Chapel; she had begged him to give her a 'kind look or a word' and a lock of his 'dear hair'. She had signed herself dear Charles's 'affectionate and devoted wife and darling'; and, torn between love of her father and her longing to marry Fitzroy officially – which she thought she would be able to do when her brother became King George IV – she drafted letters to be sent to the Privy Council in which she referred to 'the late King'. Shortly before she died she had begged Sir Henry Halford to help her marry Fitzroy before it was too late. Halford had urged her not to consider a step which would entail 'great wretchedness' upon herself and 'misery upon all the Royal Family for years to come', besides delivering a blow to the King's peace of mind that would endanger the loss 'not only of his happiness but also of his health'.

When the King was informed by Halford of the contents of Princess Amelia's will, he appeared, against all expectations, unperturbed, expressing himself gratified that the Prince of Wales had carried out his duties as executor so tactfully. In fact the Princess had little to leave but jewellery and debts. She had been an extravagant young woman, and had borrowed money from both Mary and Sophia, and from her eldest brother, who had once lent her £4,000. The Prince had the jewels valued and presented them to his sisters, mostly to Princess Mary, giving their purchase price to the fund for the settlement of the debts. The unfortunate General Fitzroy, cajoled by the Prince into renouncing his claim, was obliged to content himself with a monetary compensation and a few boxes of worthless effects. Lord Holland thought that, in the circumstances, the Prince could not very well have dealt with the problem of Amelia's will in any other way; throughout the business he had behaved 'with great delicacy and good nature'.

'Thank God,' the King said, 'for so fine a trait. The Prince of Wales has a heart. I always knew he had. I will never call him anything but George in the future . . . How thankful I ought to be to Providence for giving me such a son in the hour of my trial . . . This is so like the Prince of Wales. This is so like my dear son.' When the Prince reappointed the Duke of York Commander-in-Chief, in succession to Sir David Dundas, the King was further gratified by his behaviour; and he asked the Queen to write to the Prince to tell him that he 'never could forget his conduct on this occasion'.

The Queen, into whose care and that of a committee of advisers her husband had now been committed, went to see the King on 8 February 1811, the first time she had done so for several weeks. She found him looking much better than she had expected, and not so much 'fallen away' as in his earlier illnesses. He received her 'very kindly', she wrote, 'and talked much of his family with great affection'. Towards the end of the month he was, in fact, so much better than the Prince Regent, who was 'extremely ill', in an 'agony of pain all over him', that some wag suggested that the King should be appointed Vice-Regent to the Regent.

Yet he was given to worrying delusions. He sometimes seemed to believe that Princess Amelia was still alive, happily married and living in Hanover, where she would 'never grow older and always be well'; and he tried to comfort one of his doctors whose wife had died by assuring him that she was perfectly all right and had gone to stay with Amelia in Germany. From time to time he expressed the belief that he himself was married to Lady Pembroke, 'Queen Esther', whose continued absence from Windsor grieved him deeply. 'Is it not a strange thing, Adolphus,' he said one day to his youngest son, 'that they still refuse to let me go to Lady Pembroke, although everyone knows I am married to her?' And, what was worse, 'that infamous scoundrel, Dr Halford, was at the wedding and now had the effrontery to deny it to his face'.

It was not only in these deluded states that the Queen found her husband increasingly exasperating. She was, indeed, so unsympathetic in her impatience that Princess Elizabeth felt compelled to approach Sir Henry Halford and ask him to beseech her mother to be 'more gracious and soothing to the King when he is reasonable'. 'I think my mother much altered,' she said to the Dowager Lady Pembroke, 'at times very low, & often complaints in her Bowels which worry her.' Having grown so fat in 1807 that an observer who saw her walking on the Terrace that year said that she looked as if she were pregnant 'with all the Princes and Princesses at once', she had now become thin again and was much troubled by headaches.

For most of the time the King was calm and rational, though much given to drawing up plans for the wholesale reconstruction of the royal residences. The doctors thought that he would recover within the year. He played the harpsichord; he went to the Queen's apartments to listen to music; he paid attention when books were read to him, and asked for excerpts from Boswell's *Life of Johnson*; he walked on the Terrace with his sons and other companions; he was taken for rides in the Park; he expressed the hope that he would soon be freed from the attention of the doctors, and was saddened but by no means violent when told that he would have to wait a little while longer yet.

The Archbishop of Canterbury suggested that he might be allowed to attend services in St George's Chapel; but Princess Elizabeth and Halford agreed that he was not really up to this yet. It was 'the *last* place he ought to go'; and he thought so too himself; he told Dr Battiscombe that 'not till he was well should he take the Sacrament or go to church'.

Towards the end of May 1811 'rumours went forth that the King was better', wrote Charles Knight.

On Sunday night, the 20th of May, [Windsor] was in a fever of excitement at the authorized report that the next day the physicians would allow his Majesty to appear in public. On that Monday morning it was said that his saddle-horse was to be got ready. This truly was no wild rumour. We crowded to the Park and the Castle Yard. The favourite horse was there. The venerable man, blind but steady, was soon in the saddle, as I had often seen him – a hobby-groom at his side with a leading-rein. He rode through the Little Park to the Great Park. The bells rang. The troops fired a *feu de joie*. The King returned to the Castle within an hour. He was never again seen without those walls.

In the middle of July he became violent again, and recourse was had once more to the straitjacket. By October he was often uncontrollable; and on the 20th Princess Elizabeth reported 'a great deal of violent action in stamping with his feet on the floor'. By now he was rambling on quite as inconsequentially as he had ever done in the past; he refused to eat. The Queen's Council advised Her Majesty to recall the Willises, who had been allowed to depart; but she was reluctant to do so, since, as she said, if the King recovered she would 'forfeit his good opinion'. She was, however, induced to give way, so Robert Willis returned. The Council asked him if he thought it a good idea to throw buckets of water on the King's head; Willis confessed he 'shuddered' at the idea. Instead his patient was kept in seclusion with his keepers, and the old methods of restraint were used.

Slowly the King became more docile and retreated into a fantasy world in which the past was largely forgotten, the dead were alive, and the alive were dead. On occasions when the Queen went to see him, always accompanied now by a doctor or one or other of her children, he rarely gave any indication that he knew who she was. One day in July 1812 she found him 'very quiet & in appearance thoughtfull, but except asking for His Shoes no other words passed his Lips'. When he was pathetically docile like this her pity for him returned with something of her former affection. The sad plight of her '*Cher Objet*', she told her brother, was the cause of '*Chagrins continuelle*'. 'I went down with the Queen,' wrote Princess Mary after one of these distressing visits, 'and it was shocking to hear the poor, dear King run on so, and her unfortunate manner makes things worse.' Princess Mary thought that this 'unfortunate manner' of their mother's was attributable partly to 'extream timidity', and partly to a deficiency in 'warmth, tenderness, affec.'. Deeply unhappy and, as the months passed, finding her husband more and more distasteful as well as frightening, the Queen made others unhappy too.

Princess Mary proposed to the Prince Regent that it might be suggested to the Council that, when the King was in one of his calmer moods, two of the Princesses might go down to see him together, to spare the Queen this duty and to 'enable us', as she put it, 'to speak kindly of her to the K. and agreeably so of the K. to the Q., repeating all that could do good and give comfort to both'.

'I fear we can never make them a *real comfort* to each other,' she added, 'as all confidence has long gone, but . . . I am clear it is in the power of their daughters, if they are allowed to act, to keep them tolerably together.'

The Council agreed that the daughters might go down to see the King in pairs, provided the doctors gave permission for them to do so; and it seems that, after a brief visit to his apartments in June 1812, the Queen never saw him again.

She quarrelled with the Princess Royal, who decided that she was a 'silly woman'. She quarrelled with the Princess of Wales over the upbringing of Princess Charlotte. She behaved badly to her attendants. She became increasingly ill-tempered, withdrawn and aloof. One day in 1812 she received four letters of protest from her daughters – one each from Elizabeth, Mary and Sophia, the fourth signed by them all. She replied that she would see none of them that day. If she could bring herself to do so, she would appear the following day at breakfast. She had never felt 'so shattered' in her life.

Six months later two of the Princesses went with their niece, Princess Charlotte, to the opening of Parliament, although the Queen had told them that going to 'public amusements', except where duty called, would be 'the highest mark of indecency possible' at this time. Consequently there was 'a dreadful scene', which ended in the Queen accusing Princess Elizabeth of not caring for the King's feelings and in Elizabeth collapsing in hysterics.

The Queen spent much of her time at Frogmore, her small estate in the Park, where, in her 'little paradise', she retreated from the formal and distressing life of the Castle and found pleasure in creating the lovely gardens which still exist. She had long since given up holding fêtes there, and now went only for peace, in order to escape from the miseries of the Castle. Sometimes her daughters went with her, but whenever they could they excused themselves and stayed behind at the Castle, occasionally spending their afternoons in a hexagonal cave in the slopes beneath the North Terrace. This cave, made less gloomy by walls of looking-glass and ventilated by a chimney which opened on to the turf above their heads, was their favourite hiding-place from a difficult mother, who died in 1818, a sad, unloved old woman, after a long and painful illness.★

★ The Queen left all her private property to her daughters. There would have been considerably more to leave had not the medical expenses incurred in the King's last. lingering illness been so heavy. Repeatedly Colonel Taylor, who was appointed the Queen's Secretary after having been the King's, asked the Council to reduce these expenses, since there was no hope of His Majesty's recovery. It was quite unnecessary, Taylor said, for the physicians to call at the Castle so frequently at up to thirty guineas plus travelling expenses a visit. But he pleaded in vain. When the King died the total sum spent since 5 January 1812 came to £271,691 18s. (Royal Archives 50449–50452, quoted in Brooke, *King George III*, 385).

50

LAST DAYS AT WINDSOR

*His people have clung to his memory, with a sort
of superstitious reverence.*

The King was unaware of the Queen's death. He was deaf now as
well as blind, so he did not hear the death-bell nor the sound of the
funeral carriages as they crunched over the straw which had been
laid in the inner court, taking her body for burial in St George's
Chapel, where his own was to lie beside it.

Month after month he lingered on, a pathetic ghost-like figure to
the outside world: in the Whig circles of Thomas Creevey and
Michael Angelo Taylor the 'gentleman at the end of the Mall', as he
had been known in the days before the establishment of the Regency,
was now 'Old Nobbs'. On occasions, on his better days, his attendants
took him for a walk on the Terrace.

I once saw George III walking with his favourite son, the Duke of York,
with whom he talked incessantly, repeating his, 'Yes, yes, yes, Frederick' in
his usual loud voice [Captain R. H. Gronow recorded in his memoirs]. His
beard was of unusual length, and he stooped very much. He wore the
Windsor uniform with a large cocked hat, something like that in which
Frederick the Great is usually represented. The doctors walked behind the
King, which seemed greatly to annoy him, and he was constantly looking
round.

He was still subject to strange delusions – fearing, for instance,
that God had punished the world by decreeing another flood. He
was often in tears, and sometimes gripped by wild and what Princess
Augusta described as 'unpleasant' laughing. There were occasions,
however, when his mind was tolerably, momentarily clear. One day
for instance, so Charles Greville was informed, Sir Henry Halford
called to see the King in order to 'acquaint him with the great events

which had taken place in Europe', although the King had 'always avoided talking of publick affairs, nor [had] the Physicians ever informed him' of them.

Upon the doctor's entering the room, the King immediately asked him, 'What news is there, Sir Henry?'

'Very great news, sir.'

'Indeed!'

Anxious as he might have been to hear this news, the King first asked after Lord Westmorland, the Lord Privy Seal, who had formerly been Master of the Horse and as Lord Lieutenant of Ireland in the early 1790s had been strongly opposed to Roman Catholic emancipation.

'He is very well, sir, and constantly asks after Your Majesty with the greatest affection.'

'Indeed, after me still?' And with these words the King leaned back and 'cried like a child; then said "He is a rough man [Canning called him '*le sot privé*'] but has an excellent heart at bottom . . . But come, what is the news?"'

'Sir, the Emperors of Austria and Russia are at the head of their armies in the heart of France.'

'Indeed,' said the King with great emotion.

'Yes, sir; and Your Majesty's army is in France also.'

At this intelligence the King appeared greatly agitated, and eagerly asked, 'Who commands?'

'The Duke of Wellington, sir.'

'That's a damned lie! He was shot two years ago.'

The King then 'began to talk incoherently'.

There were days when he believed that he himself was dead. The thought did not seem to distress him; often, indeed, he seemed strangely happy. He walked about his rooms in his purple flannel dressing-gown and ermine nightcap, holding conversations with Ministers long since dead, talking to angels, 'relating pleasant things', reviewing imaginary troops, planning musical concerts. He still liked to play his flute and his harpsichords, of which there was one in each of his rooms, and when he had given an uncertain rendering of one of his favourite tunes he would say that he had been very fond of that particular tune when he was in the world. He spent hours tying and untying his handkerchief, buttoning and unbuttoning his waistcoat. He remembered to say his prayers on going to bed at night and on rising in the morning; and, for fear that he might inadvertently say something immoral, blasphemous or unbecoming in the night, he stuffed a handkerchief in his mouth before going to sleep. It was bitten through and through before morning.

His meals often appeared before he was expecting them, and he would say, 'Can it be so late? How time flies!' He now had a good appetite, particularly for mutton, which he usually ate standing up; and Miss Lucy Kennedy, an old lady who had lived in the Castle for over thirty years in the previous century and still heard all the news of it at her house in the town, recorded in her diary with evident pleasure that one 'Tuesday he eat 3 jellys'. His one complaint was that he was not given cherry tart often enough.

He did not lose his appetite and, until the last few weeks of his life, he never lost the pleasure of dressing up, although by then he could no longer walk and had to be carried from room to room in a chair. Every afternoon he changed for dinner, wearing his Orders, up to the date of his death. Occasionally he decided to wear mourning 'in memory of George III, for he was a good man'. He found comfort in praying to God, and on at least one occasion, apparently, he administered Holy Communion to himself. He liked to believe that he possessed supernatural powers, and he would sometimes stamp his foot when one of the doctors annoyed him and say that he would send him down to hell.

But he was rarely upset now. It irritated him when he was denied his favourite meal or when it was proposed to shave his beard. If they insisted on shaving him, he warned them once with magnificent authority, he would have the battleaxes called in. It was a rare outburst, though. Most of his days were passed quietly and without complaint in the dark room overlooking the Terrace, where he refused now to go because he could no longer see the countryside beyond it, which he loved.

Towards the end of 1819 the Duke of York, who had taken over responsibility for the care of the King on his mother's death, reported to the Regent that, 'without any apparent illness', their father, by now aged eighty-one was 'declining fast'. He rarely got out of bed now, and swallowed only liquid food. In December he once talked for fifty-eight hours with scarcely a moment's intermission. On 20 January 1820 the Duke again wrote to the Regent to say that he was 'never more shocked than in perceiving the melancholy alteration' which had taken place in their father's condition during the ten days since he had last seen him. 'The degree of weakness and languor in his looks and the emaciation of his face' struck him more than he could describe. Nine days later, on 29 January, it was his 'melancholy duty' to inform his 'dearest brother that it had pleased Providence to take to himself' their 'beloved King and Father'.★

The Duke was with him when his father died.

A few minutes before he extended his Arms, and bade his Attendants raise him up [so Lady Jerningham was informed]. The doctors signified to his attendants not to do so, in the Supposition that the Effort would extinguish life but upon

---

★ The King left his private property to the Queen under the terms of a will drawn up in 1770. The Duke of York spoke about this will to Charles Greville while they were driving to shoot at Oatlands together on 8 January 1823. By it, so the Duke said, the King left 'all he had to the Queen for her life, Buckingham House [since Queen Charlotte's death known as the King's House, Pimlico] to the Duke of Clarence, some property to the Duke of Kent, and to the Duke of York his second best George [a jewel forming part of the insignia of the Order of the Garter]. He considered the Duke of York provided for by the Bishopric of Osnaburgh [Osnabrück, worth about £20,000 a year] . . . He afterwards resolved to cancel this will and . . . in 1810 made another will but for various reasons he always put off signing it . . . And before the signature was affixed he was taken ill, and consequently the will was never signed . . . Now arose a difficulty − whether the property of the late King demised to [King George IV] or to the Crown. The King [George IV] conceived that the whole of the late King's property devolves upon him personally, and not upon the Crown, and he has consequently appropriated to himself the whole of the money and jewels. The money did not amount to more than £120,000 . . . The consequence is that he has spent the money and has taken to himself the jewels as his own private property . . . He has also appropriated [Queen Charlotte's] jewels to himself, and conceives that they are his undoubted private property . . . She possessed a great quantity' (*The Greville Memoirs*, i, 140−41).

A clause in the 1770 will, a copy of which is in the Royal Archives, stipulated that, if the Prince of Wales wished to buy Buckingham House from the Duke of Clarence, the Duke should agree to sell it for £36,000. There is no record of such a sale taking place; but certainly the Prince treated this house as his own on his mother's death and considered moving into it when he was Regent (Royal Archives; *History of the King's Works*, vi, 263).

his repeating the request, they obeyed and he thanked them. His Lips were parched and Occasionally wetted with a Sponge. He, with perfect presence of mind, said: – 'Do not wet my Lips but when I open My Mouth.' And when done he added, 'I thank you, it does me good.' This was told by the Duke of York, who was present, to the Dutchess of Clarence. She said that it gave her pleasure to see how much he was affected in speaking of his Father.

When the King's death was announced, shops closed their doors all over the country, and the whole nation, so it was said, went into mourning, even the poor of London wearing some token of their sympathy. Over 30,000 people came down to Windsor for the funeral, which took place in St George's Chapel on the night of 16 February. The procession of black-clothed mourners, accompanied by heralds in their brightly coloured tabards, walked by torchlight from the Castle to the Chapel along a specially constructed platform draped in black cloth and lined with soldiers. To the sound of muffled drums, trumpets, minute-guns and the tolling of the death-bell, the mourners passed through the south door of the Chapel as the choir sang the anthem 'I Know that my Redeemer Liveth.'

'The chanting, & indeed the whole service, was most impressive and affecting,' wrote the Duke of Wellington's friend Mrs Arbuthnot, who was there with her husband, '& when the coffin was lowered into the vault Ld. Winchilsea broke his staff of office & threw it in & the Garter King at Arms attempted to proclaim the style; but the poor old man, who is 92, was so much affected that his voice was quite inaudible.' And, as his feeble body tottered on his feet, it seemed to John Wilson Croker that it was as though this frail old man with his 'death-like appearance' was going to his own grave.

And thus has sunk into an honoured grave the best man and the best King that ever adorned humanity [Mrs Arbuthnot wrote] and it is consoling . . . that *such* a sovereign was followed to his last home by countless thousands of affectionate subjects drawn to the spot . . . to pay a last tribute of respect to him . . . who, for sixty long years, had been a father to his people.

This 'affectionate respect' in which the King was held was emphasized in his memoirs by Sir Nathaniel Wraxall:

Never, I believe, did any prince – not even Elizabeth – leave behind him a memory more cherished by his subjects! Confined as he was to his apartments at Windsor, unseen except by his medical attendants . . . deprived of sight, as well as of intellect; and oppressed under the weight of old age; yet his people have clung to his memory with a sort of superstitious reverence; as if, while he still continued an inhabitant of the earth, his existence suspended or averted national calamities.

NOTES ON SOURCES

Full bibliographical details are given on pages 426–443.

Two excellent biographies of George III were published in 1972, John Brooke's *King George III* and Stanley Ayling's *George the Third*, both of which deal more thoroughly with the politics of the King's reign than I have attempted here. The same may be said of W. R. Fryer's 'King George III: His Political Character and Conduct' (1962). Of previous biographies, the best is J. H. Jesse's *Memoirs of the Life and Reign of King George the Third*, which appeared in three volumes in 1867 and was soundly based on what materials were available at that time. More recent biographies are B. Wilson, *George III as Man, Monarch and Statesman* (1907), Lewis Melville, *Farmer George* (2 vols., 1907), J. D. G. Davies, *George III* (1936) and C. E. Vulliamy, *Royal George* (1937), none of which adds very much to Jesse's work.

The chapter on George III in J. H. Plumb's *The First Four Georges* (1956) is a first-class summary, so are Plumb's 'New Light on the Tyrant George III' in his *The American Experience* (1989) and the relevant chapter in *The Oxford Illustrated History of the English Monarchy* (ed. John Cannon and Ralph Griffiths (1988). *Queen Charlotte* (1975) by Olwen Hedley, an assistant in the Royal Library for several years, is a skilful product of a long acquaintance with the Royal Archives.

Of contemporary or near-contemporary accounts the most interesting are John Adolphus, *The History of England from the Accession to the Decease of George III* (1840); John Aikin, *Annals of the Reign of George III* (2 vols., 1816); W. Belsham, *Memories of the Reign of George III* (3 vols., 1802); R. Bisset, *History of the Reign of George III* (1803); J. Galt, *George III: His Court and Family* (2 vols., 1824); Edward Holt, *The Public and Domestic Life of George III* (2 vols., 1820); Robert Huish, *The Public and Private Life of George III* (1821). The various editions of Horace Walpole's memoirs, journals and letters contain much information and gossip. Most useful are his *Memoirs of the Reign of George III* (ed. G. F. R. Barker, 4 vols., 1894).

The political background has been examined in detail in Sir Lewis Namier's *The Structure of Politics at the Accession of George III* (rev. edn, 1957), in his *England in the Age of the American Revolution* (2nd edn, 1963) and in John Brewer's *Party Ideology and Popular Politics at the Accession of George III*

(1976). The validity of the Namierite approach was questioned by Sir Herbert Butterfield in *George III and the Historians* (1957). See also Ian R. Christie's '*George III and the Historians* – Thirty Years On' in *History* (1986) and his 'Was there a "New Toryism" in the Earlier Part of George III's Reign' in *Journal of British Studies* (1965–6).

Most of the material relating to the King in the Royal Archives has been published. Sir John Fortescue, for over twenty years Librarian at Windsor, edited *The Correspondence of King George III from 1760 to 1783* in six volumes (new edn, 1973). The many inaccuracies in vol. 1 of this edition were listed in L. B. Namier's *Additions and Corrections to Sir John Fortescue's Edition of the Correspondence of George III* (1937). The King's correspondence from 1783 was scrupulously edited by Arthur Aspinall in *The Later Correspondence of George III* (5 vols., 1962–70). Professor Aspinall also edited *The Letters of George IV* (3 vols., 1938) and *The Correspondence of George, Prince of Wales* (8 vols., 1963–71), both of which contain references to George III and letters to and from him. Bonamy Dobrée's *The Letters of King George III* (London, 1935) is a useful collection.

CHAPTER 1 Much of the material in this chapter comes from Romney Sedgwick's edition of the memoirs of Lord Hervey, John Brooke's edition of Horace Walpole's *Memoirs of King George II* and George Bubb Dodington's journal. The most recent biography of Prince Frederick is Michael De-la-Noy's; earlier studies are by Averyl Edwards and George Young. The most interesting biographies of George II are by Charles Chenevix Trench and John Van der Kiste's *King George II and Queen Caroline*. J. B. Owen's 'George II Reconsidered' appeared in *Statesmen, Scholars and Merchants*, ed. Anne Whiteman et al. Lord Hervey's life has been written by Robert Halsband. All Lord Waldegrave's observations quoted in this and the next chapter come from *The Memoirs and Speeches of James, 2nd Earl Waldegrave*, ed. J. C. D. Clark.

CHAPTER 2 I have taken material about Francis Ayscough and George Lewis Scott from John Nichols's *Literary Anecdotes of the Eighteenth Century*, about George Lyttelton from Sir Robert Phillimore's *Memoirs and Correspondence of George, Lord Lyttelton* and from Lord Brougham, George Rose and Mme d'Arblay, and about Lord Bolingbroke from H. T. Dickinson's biography and W. S. Sichel's *Bolingbroke and His Times*. The plan for the Princes' education was printed in the *Gentleman's Magazine*, January 1749.

CHAPTER 3 The letter, written in French, which the Princess of Wales wrote to the King on her husband's death (Royal Archives 54237) is quoted in Brooke's *King George III*. There is much about Lord Harcourt in Walpole's *Memoirs of King George II*, about Thomas Hayter in Nichols's

Literary Anecdotes, and about Andrew Stone in Walpole's, Hervey's and Waldegrave's *Memoirs*. The charges against Stone and Scott by Harcourt and Hayter are explained in Chapter 5 of Langford's *A Polite and Commercial People*. Waldegrave's report on his method of instruction of the Prince of Wales and his comments on the Prince's character are quoted in his *Memoirs*. The Duke of Gloucester's comment on the Prince's upbringing comes from Hannah More's letters, Lady Louisa Stuart's on the Prince of Wales as a young man from 'Notes by Lady Louisa Stuart' in *George Selwyn and his Contemporaries* by J. H. Jesse.

CHAPTER 4   For Bute I have relied upon Lovat Fraser's biography, Romney Sedgwick's edition of *Letters from George III to Lord Bute*, Namier's *England in the Age of the American Revolution*, K. R. Schweizer, ed., *Lord Bute: Essays in Re-interpretation* and Sedgwick's account of Bute's correspondence with Pitt in Richard Pares and A. J. P. Taylor, eds., *Essays Presented to Sir Lewis Namier*. Horace Walpole's estimate of him comes from *Walpoliana*, William Warburton's from William Seward's *Anecdotes of Some Distinguished Persons*, Waldegrave's from his *Memoirs*, Lord Shelburne's is quoted in Brooke's *King George III*. The Prince of Wales's expression of pleasure at Bute's appointment as Groom of the Stole is also from Waldegrave's *Memoirs*.
    For the Duke of Newcastle my authorities have been R. A. Kelch and Reed Browning; for William Pitt, Earl of Chatham, Stanley Ayling's biography and O. A. Sherrard's *Life of Lord Chatham*.

CHAPTER 5   The account of the King's relationship with Lady Sarah Lennox given in this and the previous chapter is based on her *Life and Letters*, E. R. Curtis's biography and Stella Tillyard's *Aristocrats*.

CHAPTER 6   The arrangements for the King's marriage to Princess Charlotte and her arrival in England are covered in detail in Olwen Hedley's biography, and in Doran, vol. 1. Colonel Graeme's reports are in the Bute MSS quoted by Hedley. The description of the Princess by the daughter of her page is from Mrs Papendiek's *Court and Private Life*. The Princess's behaviour during her journey is described in the *Annual Register*. The Duke of York's words of encouragement to the Princess on their way to the Great Drawing-Room are quoted in Queen Victoria's journal in the Royal Archives. Colonel Disbrowe's remark about the Queen's ugliness is contained in a letter from Walpole to General Conway. Prince William's observation about his brother wanting his bride to be 'wholly devoted to him alone' is recorded in 'Mrs Harcourt's Diary of the Court of King George III'; the King's warning her of the dangers of 'medling in politics' and the Queen's abhorrence of such meddling as being 'equal to sin' are both in the Harcourt MSS, quoted by Hedley.

CHAPTER 7 The description of the King by Lady Susan O'Brien (the former Lady Susan Fox-Strangways) comes from Lady Sarah Lennox's *Life and Letters*, William Hickey's account of the coronation from Alfred Spencer's edition of the *Memoirs*, vol. 1, Thomas Gray's comment on Their Majesties' appetites at the banquet from his letter to the Rev. James Brown in vol. 2 of his *Correspondence*. The account of the visit paid by the King and Queen to David Barclay was printed in the *Gentleman's Magazine*, 1808. Additional information about this visit is in Mrs Papendiek's *Court and Private Life*. For the Queen's passion for snuff, see the Bute MSS Cardiff, quoted by Hedley, and the Duchess of Northumberland's *Diaries*. The equerry's complaint about his hurried meals comes from Sir Nathaniel Wraxall's *Posthumous Memoirs*, vol. 2. John Wesley's praise for the King is in his journal entry for 25 October 1760.

CHAPTER 8 The Queen's House is well described in Edna Healey's *The Queen's House*, John Harris's 'From Buckingham House to Palace' and his *Buckingham Palace*, written in conjunction with Geoffrey de Bellaigue and Oliver Millar; also in H. Clifford Smith's *Buckingham Palace* and *The History of the King's Works*, vol. 5, ed. Howard Colvin et al. The Duke of Buckingham and Normanby's description of it is from Weinreb and Hibbert, *The London Encyclopaedia*. *The Dictionary of National Biography* has entries on George Thomason by R. E. Graves, on Consul Smith by S. W. Moon and on Stephen Demainbray by William Duna Macray. John Adams's complimentary reference to the King's library is in *The Works of John Quincy Adams*. Samuel Johnson's visit to the library is recounted in Boswell's *Life of Johnson* under the date February 1767. The King's comment about Sydney Smith is quoted in Alan Bell's *Sydney Smith*. For the King's art collection and commissions I have relied upon Oliver Millar's *The Later Georgian Pictures in the Collection of Her Majesty the Queen*, Richard Wendorff's *Sir Joshua Reynolds*, William T. Whitley's *Thomas Gainsborough*, W. B. Boulton's *Thomas Gainsborough*, H. E. Jackson's *Life of Benjamin West*, Von Erffa and Staley's *The Paintings of Benjamin West* and F. Russell's 'King George III's Pictures Hang at Buckingham House'. The Queen's Gallery catalogue *Canaletto: Paintings and Drawings* provides a good account of the King's purchase of Consul Smith's collection. For the King's interest in Hogarth, see Jenny Uglow's *Hogarth*. The background to the formation of the Royal Academy is well described in Jane Roberts's 'Sir William Chambers and George III' and Nicholas Savage's 'The "Viceroy" of the Academy'; the history of the Royal Academy has been written by S. C. Hutchison. The principal source for the birth and early days of Prince George is the Northumberland *Diaries*.

CHAPTER 9 Lord Brougham's observations on the King's conscientiousness are taken from his *Historical Sketches*, vol. 1. The letters concerning the plight of the sailor James Richardson are in the Egerton MSS, quoted in Jesse, *Memoirs*, vol. 1. The quotations from Sarah Siddons are from Roger Manvell's biography of the actress. The King's relations with Charles Burney are discussed in Percy A. Scholes, *The Great Dr Burney*.

CHAPTER 10 The King's interest in Omai, the South Sea islander, and Omai's greeting are recorded in J. C. Beaglehole's *The Life of Captain James Cook*. His Majesty's tactless remark to Sir William Hamilton is quoted in Brian Fothergill's biography of Hamilton. Nelson's various receptions by the King are recorded in Tom Pocock's biography of the Admiral (1987), in E. H. Moorhouse, *Nelson in England* and in Nelson's *Dispatches and Letters*, vol. 4. The journal of the Persian ambassador Mirza Abul Hassan Khan was translated and edited by Margaret Morris Cloake as *A Persian at the Court of King George*. Newcastle's complaint of being treated like a cipher is quoted in P. C. Yorke, *Life and Correspondence of Philip Yorke, Earl of Hardwicke*, vol. 3. Bute's self-congratulatory letter taking credit for the King's education comes from Namier, *England in the Age of the American Revolution*. Pitt's words and behaviour on surrendering his seals of office were reported in the *Annual Register* for 1761. The description of Pitt's reception on his way to the Guildhall is from Mrs Papendiek's *Court and Private Life*.

CHAPTER 11 The most scurrilous of the prints satirizing Bute, Princess Augusta and the King are listed in the British Museum catalogue as BM 3845, 3846, 3851, 3880, 3897, 3911, 3912, 4021, 4329, 4049, 4078 and 4329. Chapter 3, 'Pitt, Bute and George', of M. Dorothy George's *English Political Caricature to 1792* provides details of these as do the relevant volumes of her BM catalogue. The King's attitude to Henry Fox is described in Lord Ilchester's *Henry Fox, first Lord Holland*. His remark about being unable to forgive is quoted in the second volume of George Rose's *Diaries and Correspondence*, his expression of hope that the appointment of Fox would be a temporary expedient is from the first volume of *The Grenville Papers*, ed. W. J. Smith, the description of the mob's assault on Lord Bute from the third volume of the Duke of Bedford's *Correspondence*, ed. Lord John Russell.

CHAPTER 12 Queen Charlotte's philanthropy is discussed in the first chapter of Frank Prochaska's *Royal Bounty* and in the eighth of Olwen Hedley's biography. For the King's comments on the birth of Princess Augusta, see the second volume of Lady Mary Coke's *Letters and Journals*. Mrs Scott's comments on the King's playing with his children come from James Renat Scott's *Memorials of the Family of Scott*. The comment on Dr

Markham is Jeremy Bentham's; that on Dr Hurd, Francis Kilvert's. Prince Frederick's complaint about Cyril Jackson's teaching methods comes from Samuel Rogers's *Table Talk*, the Princess's description of her brother's flogging from the Hon. Amelia Murray's *Recollections*.

CHAPTER 13 Lord Egremont's comment on his appetite is contained in a letter from Horace Walpole to Sir Horace Mann, 1 September 1763, Grenville's accounts of his audiences in *The Grenville Papers*, vol. 1, the King's observations on Grenville in Walpole's *Memoirs of the Reign of George III* and the Duke of Albemarle's *Memoirs of the Marquis of Rockingham*. For Cumberland, see the biographies by A. N. Campbell Maclachlan and Sir Evan Edward Charteris. Lord Chesterfield's comments on the King's relationship with his Ministers is from the fourth volume of his *Letters*. The account of the Duke of Bedford's harangue is based on the King's version in the first volume of Fortescue's edition of his letters. For the Marquess of Rockingham, see the Duke of Albemarle's *Memoirs*, for the Duke of Grafton Sir William Anson's edition of the Duke's *Autobiography*, and for General Conway his friend Walpole's *Letters* (ed. Toynbee) and the Duke of Buckingham and Chandos's *Memoirs*, vol. 2.

CHAPTER 14 The latest biography of Wilkes is by Peter D. G. Thomas. Earlier biographies are by Horace Bleackley, Raymond Postgate and Charles Chenevix Trench. See also G. F. E. Rudé's *Wilkes and Liberty* and Part 3 of Ian Gilmour's *Riot, Risings and Revolution*, in which there is also an account of the Spitalfields weavers' riots. The Earl of Sandwich's biography has been written by N. A. M. Rodger in *The Insatiable Earl*, and his *Private Papers* were edited in four volumes by G. R. Barnes and J. H. Owen.

CHAPTER 15 The King's response to the American challenge was examined in Frank Arthur Mumby, ed., *George III and the American Revolution*. Among the more recent books about the quarrel and war with America are the works listed in the Bibliography by J. R. Alden, Max Beloff, Jeremy Black, Ian R. Christie, Don Cook, Bernard Donoughue, Theodore Draper, Jack P. Greene, B. Knollenberg, Piers Mackesy, J. C. Miller, S. E. Morison, J. R. Pole, C. R. Ritcheson, Peter D. G. Thomas and G. O. Trevelyan. For Grenville there are P. Lawson, *Lord Grenville*, John L. Bullion's *A Great and Necessary Measure* and *The Grenville Papers* (ed. W. J. Smith); for the Earl of Sandwich, N. A. M. Rodger's *The Insatiable Earl* and the Earl's *Private Papers* (ed. G. R. Barnes and J. H. Owen); for Cornwallis, his *Correspondence* (ed. Charles Ross) and Franklin and Mary Wickwire's biography; for Lord George Germain, the biographies by A. C. Valentine and Gerald Saxon Brown; and for Charles Townshend, Percy Fitzgerald's biography and Sir Lewis Namier and John Brooke, *Charles Townshend*.

CHAPTER 16 Boswell's encounters with Wilkes's supporters are recounted in *James Boswell: The Earlier Years* by Frederick A. Pottle. The Wilkes riots are well described in Ian Gilmour *Riot, Risings and Revolution*. The correspondence between the King and Lord Barrington is printed in *The Barrington Papers*, in Shute Barrington's *The Political Life of Viscount Barrington* and in *An Eighteenth-Century Secretary at War: The Papers of William, Viscount Barrington* (ed. Tony Hayter, 1988). The letters of 'Junius' have been edited by C. W. Everett and by John Cannon.

CHAPTER 17 The most recent biography of Lord North is Peter Whiteley's. Previous biographies include those by Reginald Lucas, W. Baring Pemberton, Peter D. G. Thomas and Alan Valentine. See also Roger North's *The Lives of the Norths* and C. D. Smith's *The Early Career of Lord North the Prime Minister*. Thomas Paine's attitude to America is discussed in the biographies by Robin McKown and A. J. Ayer, and Edmund Burke's in studies by Stanley Ayling, Philip Magnus, Nicholas K. Robinson and T. W. Copeland. General Gage's warnings are quoted in John R. Alden, *General Gage in America*, Thomas Hutchinson's advice to the Government in his *Diary and Letters*, vol. 2. Lives of General Burgoyne have been written by George Wrottesley, James Lunt and Gerald Howson. Information imparted about the Howes comes from *The Command of the Howe Brothers during the American Revolution* by Troyer S. Anderson and Ira D. Gruber's *The Howe Brothers and the American Revolution*, and about General Clinton from William B. Willcox, *Portrait of a General: Sir Henry Clinton in the War of Independence*.

CHAPTER 18 Reactions to the American Revolution in England are discussed in J. E. Bradley, *Popular Politics and the American Revolution in England*, John Derry, *English Politics and the American Revolution*, C. R. Ritcheson, *British Politics and the American Revolution*, Paul H. Smith, *English Defenders of American Freedom, 1774–78* and Sir George O. Trevelyan, *The American Revolution*. For Lord George Germain, see the biographies by Alan Valentine and Gerald Saxon Brown.

CHAPTER 19 The resignation of Lord North is covered in detail in Ian R. Christie's *The End of Lord North's Ministry, 1780–82*. The rise of Pitt is described in *The Younger Pitt: The Years of Acclaim* by John Ehrman, whose two later volumes, *The Younger Pitt: The Reluctant Transition* and *The Younger Pitt: The Consuming Struggle*, cover in great detail his subsequent career. John Adams's description of his reception by the King is contained in the eighth volume of C. F. Adams's edition of *The Works of John Quincy Adams*.

CHAPTER 20 Lady Louisa Stuart's comments on the King's brothers come from Lady Mary Coke's *Letters and Journals* and Lady Sarah Lennox's *Life and Letters*. The Duke of Gloucester's and the Duke of Cumberland's entries in the *Dictionary of National Biography* are by W. A. J. Archbold and J. M. Rigg. There is a good deal about both Dukes in Walpole's *Memoirs* and *Letters* and in Wraxall's and Jesse's *Memoirs*.

CHAPTER 21 Princess Augusta's letters in the Royal Archives are quoted by John Brooke in *King George III*. Princess Caroline's biography has been written by Hester W. Chapman, *Caroline Matilda, Queen of Denmark*, and by C. F. L. Wraxall, *Life and Times of Caroline Matilda*.

CHAPTER 22 As well as John Harris's biography of Sir William Chambers, there are several useful essays on Chambers in *Sir William Chambers, Architect to George III*, ed. John Harris and Michael Snodin, including Jane Roberts's 'Sir William Chambers and George III'. The standard work on Windsor Castle is the two-volume history by St John Hope. Sir Owen Morshead's *Windsor Castle* is the best short book; Robert Tighe's and James Davis's *Annals of Windsor* provides many details. The description of the abandoned Castle is from Charles Knight's *A Volume of Varieties*. The Princesses' lives at Windsor are described by Dorothy Margaret Stuart in *The Daughters of George III*. Fanny Burney's account of life in the Royal Household comes from *Diary and Letters of Madame d'Arblay*. Mrs Delany's of the King's and Queen's visits to her house from her *Autobiography and Correspondence*.

CHAPTER 23 The descriptions of the King's talk and manner are all taken from Mme d'Arblay's *Diary and Letters*.

CHAPTER 24 There is much about the King's life at Windsor in the books listed in the bibliography by J. H. Jesse, R. R. Tighe and J. E. Davis, Robert Huish, Charles Knight, Joseph Pote, Hector Bolitho, Lewis Melville, Joseph Taylor and Edward Holt. The Windsor uniform is the subject of an article by Sacha Llewellyn. For the collection of the King's scientific instruments, see Alan Q. Morton and Jane Wess, *Public and Private Science: The King George III Collection*. His intercession on behalf of John Harrison is described in *Longitude* by Dava Sobel, his association with William Herschel in J. B. Sidgwick's *William Herschel* and Constance A. Lubbock's *The Herschel Chronicle*, and that with Sir Joseph Banks in the biographies of Banks by J. H. Maiden and E. Smith. Arthur Young's account of his visit to the King's farms at Windsor is quoted in Averyl Edwards's *Fanny Burney* and in Stanley Ayling's *George the Third*. The complaint of the old equerry about the haste with which he was expected to eat his meals was made to J. W. Croker.

CHAPTER 25 This chapter is largely based upon Ian R. Christie's *Wilkes, Wyvill and Reform*, the biographies of Burke by Philip Magnus, T. W. Copeland and Stanley Ayling and Burke's *Correspondence*, J. E. D. Binney's *British Public Finance and Administration* and E. A. Reitan's 'The Civil List in Eighteenth-Century Politics'. The King's charities are the subject of the first chapter of Frank Prochaska's *Royal Bounty*. The King's support of Joseph Lancaster is discussed in William Corston's *Life of Joseph Lancaster* and the Queen's of Sarah Trimmer in the latter's *Some Account of the Life and Writings of Mrs Trimmer*.

CHAPTER 26 There are accounts of the King's conduct during the Gordon Riots in J. Paul de Castro's *The Gordon Riots*, Ian Gilmour's *Riot, Risings and Revolution* and my own *King Mob*, which also contains the report on Lord George's audiences of the King.

CHAPTER 27 The description of the distress of the Queen and Princesses after Margaret Nicholson's assault on the King comes from the second volume of Mme d'Arblay's *Diary and Letters*, Lord Onslow's of the attack upon him in 1795 from the first volume of Lewis Melville's biography, the King's refusal to send his daughters away when a bullet was fired during the review in Hyde Park from William Marsden's *Brief Memoir* and Michael Kelly's description of the King's coolness after James Hadfield's attempted assassination from his *Reminiscences*.

CHAPTER 28 The correspondence of Charles James Fox was edited by Lord John Russell. The biographies of Fox I have consulted are those by J. W. Derry, Christopher Hobhouse, L. G. Mitchell, Edward Lascelles and Loren Reid. I have also used Sir George Otto Trevelyan's *George III and Charles Fox*. The Earl of Shelburne's biography was written by Lord Edmond Fitzmaurice. The King's treatment of Fox at a levee in March 1782 is taken from the second volume of J. H. Jesse's *George Selwyn and his Contemporaries*.

CHAPTER 29 Biographies of the Prince of Wales, the later George IV, have been written by Robert Huish, H. E. Lloyd, George Croly, Roger Fulford, Joanna Richardson, Shane Leslie and myself. The Prince of Wales's assessment of his own character comes from the fifth volume of Aspinall's *Later Correspondence of George III*, the Duke of York's admonition to his brother and all subsequent letters to and from the Prince from Aspinall's *Correspondence of George, Prince of Wales*. Carlton House is described in Dorothy Stroud's *Henry Holland* and in vol. 20 of the *Survey of London*.

CHAPTER 30 *Carlo Khan's Triumphal Entry into Leadenhall Street* (BM 6273) is described in M. D. George's *Catalogue of Personal and Political Satires*, vol. 5. The King's comment on Pitt and Fox comes from Glenbervie's *Diaries*, vol. 2. The fall of the Administration in December 1783 is covered in John Cannon's *The Fox—North Coalition*, the formation of Pitt's first Administration in the first volume of Ehrman's biography.

CHAPTER 31 Malmesbury's comment on the King's letters to the Prince of Wales are in the second volume of his *Diaries*, the Bishop of Llandaff's to the Duke of Queensberry in vol. 1 of Wraxall's *Posthumous Memoirs*. The Prince's relationship with Mrs Fitzherbert is described in W. H. Wilkins's *Mrs Fitzherbert and George IV*, Shane Leslie's *The Life and Letters of Mrs Fitzherbert*, and Anita Leslie's *Mrs Fitzherbert*; that of the Prince with Fox in vol. 2 of Lord Holland's *Memoirs of the Whig Party*. The Prince's debts are discussed in the fourth chapter of my *George IV: Prince of Wales*.

CHAPTERS 32 AND 33 Charles Chenevix Trench's *The Royal Malady* is based to a large extent upon the unpublished diaries of Sir George Baker and Dr John Willis.

The diary of Colonel Robert Fulke Greville has been edited by F. McK. Bladon. Ida Macalpine and Richard Hunter's authoritative *George III and the Mad Business* has been the basis for all subsequent accounts of the King's illness, including this one. The King's visits to Cheltenham and Worcester were described in Mme d'Arblay's *Diary and and Letters*. Lady Harcourt's reports come from *Harcourt Papers*, vol. 4. The reaction to the prospect of a regency is the subject of J. W. Derry's *The Regency Crisis and the Whigs*. Sheridan's biography has been written by Raymond C. Rhodes, at greater length by Walter S. Sichel, and most recently by Linda Kelly. Sheridan's letters have been edited in three volumes by Cecil Price, and Betsy Sheridan's journal has been edited by W. Le Fanu. Payne's reports are in Thomas Moore's *Memoirs of the Life of the Rt Hon. R. B. Sheridan*. The King's riposte about Our Saviour not being paid for healing the sick is quoted in the fourth volume of the Malmesbury *Diaries and Correspondence*.

CHAPTER 34 The Prince of Wales's disregard of his mother's feelings is recorded in the fourth volume of Mme d'Arblay's *Diary and Letters* and in the second volume of Mrs Papendiek's *Court and Private Life*. Lord Bulkeley's remark about the Prince's incompetent management is quoted in vol. 2 of the Duke of Buckingham and Chandos's *Memoirs*. The extracts from the evidence given by the physicians are taken from *Report from the Committee Appointed to Examine the Physicians*.

CHAPTER 35 As for Chapters 32–4, the principal sources are Macalpine and Hunter, Mme d'Arblay, Colonel Greville and *Report from the Committee Appointed to Examine the Physicians.* The parliamentary debates and Edmund Burke's speeches are fully reported in John W. Derry's *The Regency Crisis and the Whigs.*

CHAPTER 36 The visits of the Prince of Wales and the Duke of York to Kew are described in Robert Fulke Greville's *Diaries,* Minto's *Life and Letters,* vol. 1, and the Buckingham and Chandos *Memoirs,* vol. 2. The Queen's attitude is explained in Olwen Hedley, John W. Derry and in vol. 1 of Auckland; and the King's recovery and the attendant celebrations are described in Charles Chenevix Trench's *The Royal Malady,* Minto's *Life and Letters,* vol. 2, *The Times* of 24 April 1789, Macalpine and Hunter, and Mary Frampton's *Journal.* Sir William Hamilton's letter to Sir Joseph Banks is quoted in Brian Fothergill's biography of Hamilton, the anecdote about Colonel Manners in Chapter 7 of Trench, and Mrs Thrale's remarks in Chapter 5. Betsy Sheridan's comments come from her *Journal.* Fox's reception at St Paul's is described in Mary Frampton's *Journal,* and the Prince's behaviour in the Cathedral in *The Times* (quoted in Hibbert, *George IV: Prince of Wales*), and the Hutton Bland-Burges Papers (quoted in Ehrman's *The Younger Pitt: The Years of Acclaim*). The King's demeanour was observed by Sir Gilbert Elliot (Minto, *Life and Letters,* vol. 1). Lord Cornwallis's letter is quoted in vol. 2 of Aspinall's edition of the Prince's correspondence. The Queen's skittish behaviour is recounted by the Hon. Georgina Townshend in a letter to Lord Combermere's aunt, Mrs Stapleton, in *Memoirs and Correspondence of Field Marshal Viscount Combermere,* quoted by Hedley. Lady Pembroke's letter to the King is quoted by John Brooke in Chapter 8 of his *King George III.*

CHAPTER 37 The King's journey to Lyndhurst and his convalescence at Weymouth are described in Mme d'Arblay's *Diary and Letters.* The Queen's opinions of Longleat and Tottenham Court are quoted in Stanley Ayling's biography of the King, as is her expressed hope that they would now go on in 'the old way'.

CHAPTER 38 The letter describing the King's reaction to the news of the victory at Camperdown is from the Stuart MSS, quoted in the third volume of J. H. Jesse's *Memoirs*; his behaviour towards Thurlow and Dundas is covered in Chapter 22 of Stanley Ayling's biography of the King, and his dealings with the First Minister in Ehrman's *The Younger Pitt: The Consuming Struggle.* His generosity to the Cardinal Duke of York is described in James Lees-Milne's *The Last Stuarts,* his opposition to the attack upon

Copenhagen in Rory Muir's *Britain and the Defeat of Napoleon*, and his reception of Addington in Pellew's and Philip Ziegler's biographies.

CHAPTER 39 Comments by Lord Eldon are taken from Horace Twiss's biography, those by Charles Abbot from *The Diary and Correspondence of Charles Abbot, Lord Colchester*. The King's relapse in 1801 is the subject of Chapter 6 of Macalpine and Hunter; his differences with Pitt over the Roman Catholic question are discussed in the third volume of Stanhope's biography. Thomas Willis's reports are quoted in Twiss, as are George Rose's letters to Lord Eldon. The King's letters to Richard Hurd are in the third volume of Jesse's *Memoirs*.

CHAPTER 40 Gillray's *Voluptuary under the Horrors of Digestion* is BM 8112 in vol. 6 of M. Dorothy George's *Catalogue*; *Temperance Enjoying a Frugal Meal* is BM 8117, and *Anti-Saccharites* BM 8074. Pindar's lampoon of the King's alleged parsimony is entitled 'Ode upon Ode or a Peep at St James's'. The Beechey family story about the artist's painting of the King reviewing the 10th Light Dragoons comes from Oliver Millar's *Later Georgian Pictures*. Princess Caroline's biography has been written by Flora Fraser in *The Unruly Queen*. Queen Charlotte's letter to her brother about the Princess is in the State Archives at Göttingen and, translated by T. S. Blakeney, is printed in vol. 3 of Aspinall's edition of the Prince's correspondence. The reports about Princess Caroline from Germany are printed in vol. 2 of the Malmesbury *Diaries and Correspondence*. The account of the King's cool reception of her is in Royal Archives George IV Box 8 (quoted in my *George IV: Prince of Wales*), that of the Prince's behaviour at the wedding from Wraxall's *Posthumous Memoirs*, vol. 3. The Princess's complaints about Lady Jersey are quoted in Greenwood's *Lives of the Hanoverian Queens*, vol. 2.

CHAPTER 41 Prince William's observation about the Princess of Wales and his mother comes from the first volume of Glenbervie's *Diaries*. The account of the King's decision to give the command of the Royal Horse Guards to the Duke of Richmond is in a letter from the Queen to her son in vol. 3 of Aspinall's edition of the Prince's *Correspondence*.

CHAPTERS 42 AND 43 The King's letter to Lord Eldon agreeing to the interview with the Prince of Wales, Eldon's description of his walk with the King in the gardens of the Queen's House and his refusal of the King's gift are all from vol. 1 of Horace Twiss's biography of Eldon. Lord Malmesbury's reports on the King's unusual manner are quoted in vol. 4 of his *Diaries and Correspondence*; the King's remark to Pitt about his regaining a friend comes from vol. 2 of Rose's *Diaries and Correspondence*, as does his reference to the Prince's lack of courage. The recurrence of the illness which the King suffered in 1804 is the subject of Chapter 4 of Macalpine and Hunter. The Duke of Kent's warning to Addington about the Willises being summoned again is in vol. 1 of Aspinall's *Correspondence of George, Prince of Wales*. Sir William Beechey's discomfiture is from Oliver Millar's *Later Georgian Pictures*. Fremantle's opinion that the reconciliation could not last is in the Fremantle MSS (Aylesbury), quoted in my *George IV: Prince of Wales*.

CHAPTER 44 Lord Glenbervie's accounts of the King's visits to Princess Caroline come from vol. 2 of his *Diaries*; Princess Caroline's letter to the King accepting his offer to visit her at Blackheath is in the Royal Archives (RA 42397) and is quoted in my *George IV: Prince of Wales*. The King's delight in his granddaughter is expressed in various letters in vol. 3 of Aspinall's *Correspondence of George, Prince of Wales*; Thurlow's opinion of the Commissioners' report is quoted in vol. 5. Princess Caroline's behaviour at Greenwich is described in Flora Fraser's biography, in vol. 1 of Lady Charlotte Bury's *Diary* and in *Extracts of the Journals and Correspondence of Miss Berry*. The Princess Charlotte's childhood is described in Dormer Creston's *The Regent and His Daughter*. Evidence presented during the Delicate Investigation is contained in *The Book . . . Proceedings and Correspondence*. The King's comment on the Princess's 'levity and profligacy' comes from vol. 2 of the Granville Leveson-Gower *Private Correspondence*, and his description of her as a 'female politician' from vol. 2 of *The Croker Papers*.

CHAPTER 45 Roger Fulford's *The Royal Dukes* deals succinctly with the King's brothers. There are good biographies of the Duke of Clarence (William IV) by Philip Ziegler and by Tom Pocock. The Duke's liaison with Mrs Jordan is the subject of Claire Tomalin's *Mrs Jordan's Profession*. The Duke of Cumberland's life has been written by G. M. Willis, the Duke of Kent's by David Duff; the Duke of Kent's relationship with Mme de Saint-Laurent is the subject of Mollie Gillen's *The Prince and his Lady*. The Duke of York's career is well outlined in the *Annual Register* for 1827. There is a full column of references to him in the *Memoirs* of Charles Greville, his racing manager. The description of the Duchess of York is from Baron Stockmar's *Memoirs*.

CHAPTER 46 The King's generosity on his travels in England is described by Frank Prochaska. The King's remarks about 'individuals engaged in trade' are quoted in vol. 1 of Wraxall's *Posthumous Memoirs*. Mrs Arbuthnot's remark about the King's preference for old generals rather than aspiring young ones is taken from vol. 1 of her *Journal*, the Duke of Wellington's determination to go to the levee at St James's from vol. 1 of *The Croker Papers*.

CHAPTER 47 Books about the King's daughters have been written by Dorothy M. Stuart and by Morris Marples. The Duchess of Marlborough's account of the King and Queen's visit to Blenheim is taken from vol. 1 of Lord Auckland's *Journal and Correspondence*. The King's views on racing are quoted in vol. 2 of Glenbervie's *Diaries*; the story of Lady Sheffield's shocked reaction to Princess Elizabeth's views on virginity is recounted in vol. 1. John Aspinwall's comments on the sisters' 'terracing' are from his *Travels in Britain*. Gillray's *The Bridal Night* is listed as BM 9014 in vol. 7 of M. D. George's *Catalogue*.

CHAPTER 48 The King's reading the Aboukir dispatch at Weymouth is quoted in Tom Pocock's *Nelson*. Nelson's remark about wishing to avoid Weymouth is contained in a letter to Lady Hamilton in the Llangattock Papers (quoted in my *Nelson*). The account of the King's interview with Earl Nelson is from Dorothy Stuart's *Life and Times of Lady Elizabeth Foster*. Princess Augusta's account of the King's reaction to the appointment of Fox to the Cabinet appeared in the *Quarterly Review* and is quoted in Jesse's *Memoirs*, vol. 3. The comparison of Fox's behaviour with that of another, unnamed, Minister comes from vol. 1 of Twiss's biography of Eldon, Fox's stated intention not to bring forward the Roman Catholic question from vol. 2 of Pellew's life of Addington, John Aspinwall's description of the King's reception at the theatre from his *Travels in Britain*, George Rose's of the celebrations on 25 October 1810 from vol. 2 of his *Diaries and Correspondence*. Linda Colley's observations on the King as Father of the People are taken from Chapter 5 of her book *Britons* and from her 'The Apotheosis of George III'. Lord Colchester's description of the King's Speech comes from the first volume of his *Diary and Correspondence*, the account of the King's day from a contemporary report quoted in vol. 3 of Jesse's *Memoirs*, the letter from her father to Princess Amelia from the Taylor MSS (quoted by Stuart in *The Daughters of George III*), the wet-nurse's report of the King's distress from vol. 2 of Glenbervie's *Diaries*. Princess Amelia's last days are described by W. S. Childe-Pemberton, D. M. Stuart and Morris Marples, and in Aspinall's *Correspondence of George, Prince of Wales*, vols. 6 and 7.

CHAPTER 49 The King's assurance that Princess Amelia was in no danger is taken from Barbara Luttrell's biography of Cornelia Knight. Lord Holland's comments on the Prince's management of the Princess's will is from Holland's *Memoirs of the Whig Party*, Charles Knight's description of the King's last appearance in Windsor comes from his *Passages of a Working*

Life. Chapters 8 and 9 of Macalpine and Hunter deal with the King's last illness.

CHAPTER 50 The King's conversation with Sir Henry Halford about the war is recorded in the first volume of Charles Greville's *Memoirs*. Accounts of the King's last days are to be found in Joseph Taylor, Ingram Cobbin, A. Hayward Wynn, Robert Huish, Lord Carlisle's *Reminiscences* (quoted in vol. 2 of Melville's *Farmer George*) and the *Jerningham Letters*.

BIBLIOGRAPHY

Adair, John, *The Royal Palaces of Britain* (London, 1981)

Adams, John Quincy, *The Works of John Quincy Adams*, ed. C. F. Adams (6 vols., New York, 1850–56)

Adolphus, John, *The History of England from the Accession to the Decease of George III* (London, 1840)

Aikin, John, *Annals of the Reign of George III* (2 vols., London, 1816)

Albemarle, George Thomas Keppel, Earl of, *Memoirs of the Marquis of Rockingham and his Contemporaries* (2 vols., London, 1852)

Alden, John Richard, *General Gage in America: His Role in the American Revolution* (Baton Rouge, 1948)

——*A History of the American Revolution* (London, 1969)

Anderson, Troyer S., *The Command of the Howe Brothers during the American Revolution* (London, 1936)

Angelo, Henry, *Reminiscences* (2 vols., London, 1828–30)

Arbuthnot, Harriet, *The Journal of Mrs Arbuthnot, 1820–1832*, ed. Francis Bamford (2 vols., London, 1950)

Aspinall, A., *Politics and the Press, c. 1780–1850* (London, 1949)

——ed., *The Correspondence of George, Prince of Wales, 1770–1812* (8 vols., London, 1963–71)

——ed., *The Later Correspondence of George III, 1783–1810* (5 vols., Cambridge, 1962–70)

——ed., *The Letters of King George IV, 1812–30* (3 vols., Cambridge, 1938)

Aspinall, A., and Smith, E. A., *English Historical Documents, 1783–1832* (London, 1959)

Aspinwall, John, *Travels in Britain 1794–95: The Diary of John Aspinwall*, ed. Aileen Sutherland Collins (Virginia Beach, 1994)

Atherton, Herbert M., *Political Prints in the Age of Hogarth* (Oxford, 1974)

Auckland, William Eden, Baron, *Journal and Correspondence of William Lord Auckland*, ed. and intro. Bishop of Bath and Wells [Robert, second Lord Auckland] (4 vols., London, 1861–2)

Ayer, A. J., *Thomas Paine* (London, 1988)

Ayling, Stanley, *Edmund Burke: His Life and Opinions* (London, 1988)

——*George the Third* (London, 1972)

——*The Elder Pitt, Earl of Chatham* (London, 1976)

Bailyn, Bernard, *The Ideological Origins of the American Revolution* (Cambridge, Mass., 1967)

Baines, E., *The History of the Reign of George III* (Leeds, 1820)

Bargar, D. B., *Lord Dartmouth and the American Revolution* (Columbia, 1965)

Barnes, D. G., *George III and William Pitt, 1783–1806* (London, 1939)

Barrington, Samuel, *The Barrington Papers, Selected from the Letters and Papers of Admiral the Hon. S. Barrington*, ed. D. Bonner-Smith (2 vols., London, 1937–41)

Barrington, Shute, *The Political Life of Viscount Barrington* (London, 1814)

Barrington, William, Viscount, *see* Hayter

Beaglehole, J. C., *The Life of Captain James Cook* (London, 1974)

Bedford, John Russell, fourth Duke of, *Correspondence of John, fourth Duke of Bedford*, ed. Lord John Russell (3 vols., London, 1842–6)

Bell, Alan, *Sydney Smith: A Biography* (Oxford, 1980)

Beloff, Max, ed., *The Debate on the American Revolution, 1761–83* (London, 1949)

Belsham, W., *Memories of the Reign of George the Third* (3 vols., Dublin, 1802)

Berry, Mary, *Extracts of the Journals and Correspondence of Miss Berry from the Year 1783 to 1852*, ed. Lady Theresa Lewis (3 vols., London, 1865)

Binney, J. E. D., *British Public Finance and Administration, 1774–1792* (Oxford, 1959)

Bisset, R., *History of the Reign of George III* (London, 1803)

Black, Jeremy, *War for America* (Stroud, 1991)

Blackwood, John, *London's Immortals: The Complete Outdoor Commemorative Statues* (London, 1989)

Bleackley, Horace, *Life of John Wilkes* (London, 1917)

Bolitho, Hector, *The Romance of Windsor Castle* (London, 1947)

The Book, or the Proceedings and Correspondence upon the Subject of the Inquiry into the Conduct of the Princess of Wales (London, 1813)

Boswell, James, *Boswell's London Journal, 1762–1763*, ed. Frederick A. Pottle (London, 1950)

—— *Life of Johnson*, ed. R. W. Chapman (Oxford, new edn, 1976.)

Boulton, W. B., *Thomas Gainsborough: His Life, Works, Friends and Sitters* (London, 1905)

Bradley, J. E., *Popular Politics and the American Revolution in England* (Macon, 1986)

Brady, Frank, *James Boswell: The Later Years, 1769–1795* (London, 1984)

Brewer, John, *Party Ideology and Popular Politics at the Accession of George III* (Cambridge, 1976)

—— *The Pleasures of the Imagination: English Culture in the Eighteenth Century* (London, 1997)

Brooke, John, *King George III* (London, 1972)

—— *The Chatham Administration of 1766–68* (London, 1956)

——see also Namier and Walpole

Brougham, Henry Peter, Baron Brougham and Vaux, *Historical Sketches of the Statesmen who Flourished in the Reign of George III* (3 vols., London, 1845)

Brown, Gerald Saxon, *The American Secretary: The Colonial Policy of Lord George Germain* (Ann Arbor, 1963)

Browning, J. D., ed., *Education in the Eighteenth Century* (New York, 1979)

Browning, Reed, *The Duke of Newcastle* (New Haven, 1975)

Buckingham and Chandos, Richard Plantagenet Temple Nugent Brydges Chandos Grenville, Duke of, *Memoirs of the Courts and Cabinets of George III* (2 vols., London, 1853–5)

Bullion, John L., *A Great and Necessary Measure: George Grenville and the Genesis of the Stamp Act* (Columbia, 1983)

Burges, Sir J. Bland, *Letters and Correspondence*, ed. J. Hutton (London, 1885)

Burgoyne, *see* Wrottesley

Burke, Edmund, *The Correspondence of Edmund Burke*, ed. W. T. Copeland et al. (9 vols., Cambridge, 1958–70)

——*The Writings and Speeches of Edmund Burke*, ed. Paul Langford et al. (9 vols., Oxford, 1981–91)

Burney, Charles, *General History of Music* (London, new edn, 1959)

Burney, Fanny, *see* d'Arblay

Bury, Lady Charlotte, *The Diary of a Lady in Waiting by Lady Charlotte Bury*, ed. A. Francis Steuart (2 vols., London, 1908)

Butterfield, Herbert, *George III and the Historians* (London, 1957)

——*George III, Lord North and the People* (London, 1949)

Calder-Marshall, Arthur, *The Two Duchesses* (London, 1978)

Cameron, H. C., *Sir Joseph Banks* (London, 1952)

Campbell, J. C., *Lives of the Lord Chancellors*, vol. 5 (London 1846)

Canaletto: Paintings and Drawings, exhibition catalogue. The Queen's Gallery, Buckingham Palace, 1980

Cannon, John, *The Fox–North Coalition: Crisis of the Constitution, 1782–4* (Cambridge, 1969)

——*Lord North: The Noble Lord in the Blue Ribbon* (London, 1970)

——ed., *The Whig Ascendancy: Colloquies on Hanoverian England* (London, 1981)

——*see also* 'Junius'

Cannon, John, and Griffiths, Ralph, eds., *The Oxford Illustrated History of the English Monarchy* (Oxford, 1988)

Carretta, Vincent, *George III and the Satirists from Hogarth to Byron* (Georgia, 1990)

Cavendish, Sir Henry, *Debates in the House of Commons, 1768–71*, ed. J. Wright (2 vols., London, 1841)

Chapman, Hester W., *Caroline Matilda: Queen of Denmark* (London, 1971)

Charteris, Sir Evan Edward, *William Augustus, Duke of Cumberland: His Early Life and Times, 1721–1748* (London, 1913)

Chatham, William Pitt, Earl of, *Correspondence of William Pitt, Earl of Chatham*, ed. W. S. Taylor and J. H. Pringle (4 vols., London, 1838–40)

Chester, Sir Norman, *The English Administrative System, 1780–1870* (Oxford, 1981)

Chesterfield, Philip Dormer Stanhope, fourth Earl of, *Letters of Philip Dormer Stanhope, fourth Earl of Chesterfield*, ed. Bonamy Dobrée (6 vols., London, 1932)

Childe-Pemberton, William S., *The Romance of Princess Amelia* (London, 1910)

Christie, Ian R., *Crisis of Empire: Great Britain and the American Colonies, 1754–1783* (London, 1958)

—— *The End of Lord North's Ministry, 1780–82* (London, 1958)

—— 'The Family Origins of George Rex of Knysna', *Notes and Queries*, New Series, vol. 22, no. 1 (Jan. 1975), 18–23

—— '*George III and the Historians* – Thirty Years On', *History*, no. 71 (June 1986), 205–21

—— *Myth and Reality in Late Eighteenth-Century British Politics* (London, 1970)

—— *Wars and Revolutions: Britain 1760–1815* (London, 1982)

—— 'Was there a "New Toryism" in the Earlier Part of George III's Reign', *Journal of British Studies*, vol. 5 (1965–6), 60–76

—— *Wilkes, Wyvill and Reform* (London, 1962)

Cloake, Margaret Morris, trans. and ed., *A Persian at the Court of King George 1809–10: The Journal of Mirza Abul Hassan Khan* (London, 1988)

Cobbin, Ingram, *Georgiana* (London, 1820)

Coke, Lady Mary, *Letters and Journals of Lady Mary Coke*, ed. J. A. Home (4 vols., Edinburgh, 1889–96)

Colchester, Charles Abbot, first Baron, *The Diary and Correspondence of Charles Abbot, Lord Colchester*, ed. Charles, Lord Colchester (3 vols., London, 1861)

Colley, Linda, 'The Apotheosis of George III: Loyalty, Royalty and the British Nation, 1760–1820', *Past and Present*, no. 102 (1984), 94–129

—— *Britons: Forging the Nation, 1707–1837* (New Haven and London, 1992)

Colvin, Howard, *A Biographical Dictionary of British Architects 1600–1840* (London, 1978)

—— et al., eds., *The History of the King's Works*, vols. 5 and 6 (London, 1973–6)

Connell, Brian, *Portrait of a Whig Peer* (London, 1957)

Cook, Don, *The Long Fuse: How England Lost the American Colonies* (New York, 1996)

Copeland, T. W., *Edmund Burke* (London, 1950)

Cornwallis, Charles, first Marquess, *The Correspondence of Charles, first Marquess Cornwallis*, ed. Charles Ross (3 vols., London, 1859)

Corston, William, *Life of Joseph Lancaster* (London, 1840)

Court Historian: The Newsletter of the Society for Court Studies (1996–)

Coutu, Joan, 'William Chambers and Joseph Wilton', in Harris and Snodin, eds., *Sir William Chambers* (q.v.)

Creevey, Thomas, *The Creevey Papers: A Selection from the Correspondence and Diaries of the Late Thomas Creevey MP*, ed. Sir Herbert Maxwell (London, 3rd edn, 1905)

Creston, Dormer, *The Regent and his Daughter* (London, 1952)

Croker, John Wilson, *The Croker Papers: The Correspondence and Diaries of John Wilson Croker, Secretary to the Admiralty, 1809 to 1830*, ed. Louis Jennings (3 vols., London, 1885)

Croly, George, *The Personal History of His Late Majesty George the Fourth* (2 vols., London, 1841)

Crowe, Ian, ed., *Edmund Burke: His Life and Legacy* (London, 1997)

Cumberland, Richard, *Memoirs of Richard Cumberland Written by Himself* (2 vols., London, 1807)

Cumberland, Richard Dennison, *The Cumberland Letters: Being the Correspondence of Richd Dennison Cumberland and George Cumberland between the Years 1771 and 1784*, ed. Clementine Black (London, 1912)

Curtis, E. R., *Lady Sarah Lennox* (London, 1932)

Dale, Anthony, *James Wyatt, Architect* (London, 1936)

d'Arblay, Madame, [Fanny Burney], *Diary and Letters of Madame d'Arblay (1778–1840)*, ed. Charlotte Barrett (6 vols., London, 1905)

——*Memoirs of Dr Burney* (3 vols., London, 1832)

Davies, J. D. G., *George the Third* (London, 1936)

de Bellaigue, Geoffrey, *see* Harris, John

de Castro, J. Paul, *The Gordon Riots* (London, 1926)

De-la-Noy, Michael, *The King who Never Was: The Story of Frederick, Prince of Wales* (London, 1996)

Delany, Mary, *The Autobiography and Correspondence of Mary Granville, Mrs Delany, with Interesting Reminiscences of King George the Third and Queen Charlotte*, ed. Lady Llanover (3 vols., London, 1862)

Derry, John W., *Charles, Earl Grey* (London, 1992)

——*Charles James Fox* (London, 1972)

——*English Politics and the American Revolution* (New York, 1976)

——*The Regency Crisis and the Whigs, 1788–9* (Cambridge, 1963)

——*William Pitt* (London, 1962)

Devonshire, Georgiana Cavendish, Duchess of, *Georgiana: Extracts from the*

Correspondence of the Duchess of Devonshire, ed. the Earl of Bessborough (London, 1955)

Dickinson, H. T., *Bolingbroke* (London, 1970)

Dobrée, Bonamy, ed., *The Letters of King George III* (London, 1935)

Dodington, George Bubb, *The Diary of the late George Bubb Dodington*, ed. Henry Penruddocke Wyndham (Salisbury, 1784)

—— *The Political Journal of George Bubb Dodington*, ed. John Carswell and Lewis Arnold Dralle (Oxford, 1965)

Donald, Diana, *The Golden Age of Caricature: Satirical Prints in the Age of George III* (New Haven, 1996)

Donne, W. B., ed., *Correspondence of George III with Lord North, 1768–83* (London, 1867)

Donoughue, Bernard, *British Politics and the American Revolution: The Path to War, 1773–75* (London, 1964)

Doran, John, *The Lives of the Queens of England of the House of Hanover* (2 vols., London, 1855)

Draper, Theodore, *A Struggle for Power: The American Revolution* (London, 1996)

Duff, David, *Edward of Kent* (London, 1938)

Dutens, Louis, *Memoirs of a Traveller, now in Retirement* (4 vols., London, 1805)

Edwards, Averyl, *Fanny Burney* (London, 1948)

—— *Frederick Louis, Prince of Wales* (London, 1947)

Egmont, John Perceval, first Earl of, *Diary of Viscount Perceval, afterwards first Earl of Egmont*, ed. R. A. Robert (3 vols., London, 1920–23)

Ehrman, John, *The Younger Pitt: The Consuming Struggle* (London, 1996)

—— *The Younger Pitt: The Reluctant Transition* (London, 1983)

—— *The Younger Pitt: The Years of Acclaim* (London, 1969)

Farington, Joseph, *The Farington Diary*, ed. J. Greig (8 vols., London, 1922–8)

Fitzgerald, Percy, *Charles Townshend: Wit and Statesman* (London, 1866)

Fitzmaurice, Edmond George Petty, Baron, *Life of William, Earl of Shelburne* (3 vols., London, 1875–6)

Foord, A. S., *His Majesty's Opposition, 1714–1830* (London, 1964)

Forbes, Sir W., *Account of the Life and Writings of James Beattie* (3 vols., London, 1806)

Foreman, Amanda, *Georgiana, Duchess of Devonshire* (London, 1998)

Fortescue, Sir John, ed., *The Correspondence of King George III from 1760 to 1782* (6 vols., London, 1927–8; new edn, London, 1973)

Fothergill, Brian, *Mrs Jordan* (London, 1965)

—— *Sir William Hamilton, Envoy Extraordinary* (London, 1969)

Fox, Charles James, *Memorials and Correspondence of Charles James Fox*, ed. Lord John Russell (2 vols., London, 1853)

Frampton, Mary, *The Journal of Mary Frampton*, ed. Harriot Georgiana Mundy (London, 1885)

Fraser, Flora, *The Unruly Queen: The Life of Queen Caroline* (London, 1996)

Fraser, Lovat, *Lord Bute* (London, 1912)

Fryer, W. R., 'King George III: His Political Character and Conduct, 1760–1784', in *Renaissance and Modern Studies* (Nottingham, 1962)

Fulford, Roger, *George the Fourth* (London, 1935)

—— *The Royal Dukes* (London, 1933)

—— *see also* Knight, Ellis Cornelia, and Greville, Charles

Furber, H., *Henry Dundas, first Viscount Melville* (London, 1931)

Gage, Thomas, *The Correspondence of General Thomas Gage, 1763–1775*, ed. C. E. Carter (2 vols., New Haven, 1931–3)

Galt, J., *George III, his Court and Family* (2 vols., London, 1824)

Gay, John, *The Letters of John Gay*, ed. C. F. Burgess (Oxford, 1966)

George III, *for correspondence, see* Aspinall, Dobrée, Donne, Fortescue *and* Sedgwick

George III, Collector and Patron, exhibition catalogue, The Queen's Gallery, Buckingham Palace, 1974

George, M. D., *Catalogue of Personal and Political Satires . . . in the British Museum*, vols. 5 to 10 (London, 1938–52)

—— *English Political Caricature to 1792* (Oxford, 1959)

—— *English Political Caricature 1793–1832* (Oxford, 1959)

Gibbon, Edward, *The Autobiography of Edward Gibbon*, ed. Lord Sheffield (London, new edn, 1978)

—— *Gibbon's Journals*, ed. D. M. Low (London, 1929)

—— *The Letters of Edward Gibbon*, ed. J. E. Norton (3 vols., London, 1956)

Gillen, Mollie, *The Prince and his Lady* (London, 1970)

Gilmour, Ian, *Riot, Risings and Revolution: Governance and Violence in Eighteenth-Century England* (London, 1992)

Glenbervie, Sylvester Douglas, Baron, *Diaries of Sylvester Douglas, Lord Glenbervie*, ed. Francis Bickley (2 vols., London, 1928)

Gore-Browne, R., *Chancellor Thurlow* (London, 1953)

Grafton, Augustus Henry Fitzroy, Duke of, *Autobiography and Political Correspondence of Augustus Henry Fitzroy, third Duke of Grafton*, ed. Sir William Anson (London, 1898)

Granville, Granville Leveson-Gower, first Earl, *Private Correspondence 1781–1821*, ed. Castalia, Countess Granville (2 vols., London, 1916)

Gray, D., *Spencer Perceval* (London, 1953)

Gray, Thomas, *The Correspondence of Thomas Gray*, ed. Paget Toynbee and Leonard Whibley (3 vols., London, 1935)

Greene, Jack P., *The Reinterpretation of the American Revolution, 1763–1789* (New York, 1968)

—— *Understanding the American Revolution: Issues and Actors* (New York, 1995)

——ed., *The American Revolution: Its Characters and Limits* (New York, 1987)

Greenwood, Alice Dayton, *Lives of the Hanoverian Queens of England* (2 vols., London, 1911)

Grenville, Richard Temple, Earl Temple, *Additional Grenville Papers, 1763–1765*, ed. John R. G. Tomlinson (Manchester, 1962)

——*The Grenville Papers: Being the Correspondence of Richard Grenville, Earl Temple, and the Right Hon. George Temple, their Friends and Contemporaries*, ed. W. J. Smith (4 vols., London, 1852–3)

Greville, Charles, *The Greville Memoirs, 1814–1860*, ed. Lytton Strachey and Roger Fulford (8 vols., London, 1935)

Greville, Robert Fulke, *The Diaries of Colonel the Hon Robert Fulke Greville*, ed. F. McK. Bladon (London, 1930)

Gronow, Rees Howell, *The Reminiscences and Recollections of Captain Gronow* (2 vols., London, 1889)

Gruber, Ira D., *The Howe Brothers and the American Revolution* (Chapel Hill, 1974)

Guttmacher, M. S., *America's Last King. An Interpretation of the Madness of King George III* (New York, 1941)

Guttridge, G. H., *English Whiggism and the American Revolution* (Berkeley, 1942)

Halsband, Robert, *Lord Hervey: Eighteenth-Century Courtier* (Oxford, 1973)

Harcourt, Elizabeth, Countess of, 'Memoirs of the Years 1788–9. By Elizabeth, Countess of Harcourt', in *Harcourt Papers* (*v.i.*), vol. 4

Harcourt, E. W., ed., *Harcourt Papers* (14 vols., privately printed, Oxford, 1885–1905)

'Mrs Harcourt's Diary of the Court of King George III', in *Miscellanies of the Philobiblon Society*, vol. 13 (London, 1871–2)

Harris, George, *The Life of Lord Chancellor Hardwicke* (3 vols., London, 1847)

Harris, John, 'From Buckingham House to Palace: The Box within the Box within the Box', in *Buckingham Palace: A Complete Guide*, Apollo Magazine, 1993

——*Sir William Chambers: Knight of the Polar Star* (London, 1970)

Harris, John, de Bellaigue, Geoffrey, and Millar, Oliver, *Buckingham Palace* (London, 1968)

Harris, John, and Snodin, Michael, eds., *Sir William Chambers: Architect to George III* (New Haven, 1997)

Harvey, A. D., *Sex in Georgian England* (London, 1996)

Harwood, T. E., *Windsor Old and New* (London, 1929)

Hayter, Tony, ed., *An Eighteenth-Century Secretary-at-War: The Papers of William Viscount Barrington* (London, 1988)

433

Healey, Edna, *The Queen's House: A Social History of Buckingham Palace* (London, 1997)

Hedley, Olwen, *Queen Charlotte* (London, 1975)

Herbert, Sidney Charles, Baron, ed., *The Pembroke Papers, 1780–94* (London, 1950)

Herschel, Mrs John, *Memoir and Correspondence of Caroline Herschel, 1750–1848*, (London, 1876)

Hervey, John Hervey, Baron, *Some Materials towards Memoirs of the Reign of King George II by John, Lord Hervey*, ed. Romney Sedgwick (3 vols., London, 1931)

——*Memoirs of William Hickey*, ed. Peter Quennell (London, 1960)

Hibbert, Christopher, *The Court at Windsor: A Domestic History* (London, 1964)

——*George IV: Prince of Wales, 1762–1811* (London, 1972)

——*George IV: Regent and King, 1811–1830* (London, 1973)

——*King Mob: Lord George Gordon and the Riots of 1780* (London, 1958)

——*Nelson: A Personal History* (London, 1994)

——*Redcoats and Rebels: The War for America, 1770–1781* (London, 1990)

——*see also* Weinreb

Hickey, William, *Memoirs of William Hickey*, ed. Alfred Spencer (4 vols., London, 1925)

Hobhouse, Christopher, *Fox* (London, 1934)

Hoffman, Ross J. S., *The Marquis: A Study of Lord Rockingham 1780–1782* (New York, 1973)

Holland, Henry Richard Fox, Baron, *Memoirs of the Whig Party during My Time by Henry Richard, Lord Holland*, ed. Henry Edward, Lord Holland (2 vols., London, 1852–4)

Holt, Edward, *The Public and Domestic Life of George III* (2 vols., London, 1820)

Hope, W. H. St John, *Windsor Castle* (London, 1913)

Horn, D. B., and Ransome, M., eds., *English Historical Documents, 1714–1783* (London, 1957)

Hough, Richard, *Captain James Cook: A Biography* (London, 1994)

Howard, Philip, *The Royal Palaces* (London, 1970)

Howson, Gerald, *Burgoyne of Saratoga* (New York, 1979)

Huish, Robert, *Memoirs of George IV* (2 vols., London, 1831)

——*The Public and Private Life of George III* (London, 1821)

Hutchinson, Thomas, *The Diary and Letters of His Excellency Thomas Hutchinson, Esq.*, ed. P. O. Hutchinson (2 vols., London, 1883–6)

Hutchison, S. C., *The History of the Royal Academy* (London, 1968)

Ilchester, Lord, *Henry Fox, first Lord Holland* (2 vols., London, 1820)

Jackson, H. E., *Life of Benjamin West* (Philadelphia, 1900)

Jarrett, Derek, *England in the Age of Hogarth* (London, 1974)

Jenkinson, Charles, Earl of Liverpool, *The Jenkinson Papers 1760–1766*, ed. N. S. Jucker (London, 1949)

Jerningham, Charlotte Georgiana, Lady, *The Jerningham Letters (1780–1843): Being Excerpts from the Correspondence and Diaries of the Honourable Lady Jerningham*, ed. Egerton Castle (2 vols., London, 1896)

Jesse, J. Heneage, *George Selwyn and his Contemporaries* (4 vols., London, 1883–4)

——*Memoirs of the Life and Reign of King George the Third* (3 vols., London, 1867)

'Junius', *The Letters of Junius*, ed. John Cannon (Oxford, 1978)

——*Letters of Junius*, ed. and intro. C. W. Everett (London, 1927)

Jupp, Peter, *Lord Grenville, 1759–1834* (Oxford, 1985)

Kelch, Ray A., *Newcastle, A Duke without Money: Thomas Pelham Holles, 1693–1768* (London, 1974)

Kelly, Linda, *Richard Brinsley Sheridan: A Life* (London, 1997)

Kelly, Michael, *Reminiscences*, ed. Roger Fiske (Oxford, 1975)

A King's Purchase: King George III and the Collection of Consul Smith, exhibition catalogue, The Queen's Gallery, Buckingham Palace, 1993

Knight, Charles, *Passages of a Working Life* (London, 1864)

——*A Volume of Varieties* (London, 1844)

Knight, Ellis Cornelia, *The Autobiography of Miss Knight, Lady Companion to Princess Charlotte*, ed. Roger Fulford (London, 1960)

Knollenberg, B., *The Origin of the American Revolution* (New York, 1960)

Langford, Paul, *The First Rockingham Administration, 1765–6* (Oxford, 1973)

——*A Polite and Commercial People: England 1727–1783* (Oxford, 1989)

Lascelles, Edward C. P., *The Life of Charles James Fox* (Oxford, 1936)

Lawson, P., *George Grenville: A Political Life* (Oxford, 1984)

Lecky, W. E. H., *The History of England in the Eighteenth Century*, vols. 3–8 (London, 1879–90)

Leeds, Francis Godolphin Osborne, fifth Duke of, *The Political Memoranda of Francis, fifth Duke of Leeds*, ed. Oscar Browning (London, 1884)

Lees-Milne, James, *The Last Stuarts* (London, 1983)

Lennox, Lady Sarah, *The Life and Letters of Lady Sarah Lennox, 1745–1826*, ed. the Countess of Ilchester and Lord Stavordale (2 vols., London 1901)

Leslie, Anita, *Mrs Fitzherbert* (New York, 1960)

Leslie, Shane, *George the Fourth* (London, 1936)

——*The Life and Letters of Mrs Fitzherbert* (2 vols., London, 1939–40)

Lindsay, John, *The Lovely Quaker* (London, 1939)

Liverpool, *see* Jenkinson

Llewellyn, Sacha, 'George III and the Windsor Uniform', in *The Court Historian: Newsletter of the Society for Court Studies*, no. 2 (n.d.)

Lloyd, H. E., *George IV: Memoirs of his Life and Reign* (London, 1830)

Lubbock, Constance A., *The Herschel Chronicle: The Life-Story of William Herschel and his Sister Caroline Herschel* (London, 1933)

Lucas, Reginald, *Lord North* (2 vols., London, 1913)

Lunt, James, *John Burgoyne of Saratoga* (London, 1976)

Luttrell, Barbara, *The Prim Romantic: A Biography of Ellis Cornelia Knight, 1758–1837* (London, 1965)

Lyte, Sir H. C. Maxwell, *A History of Eton College, 1440–1875* (London, 1875)

Lyttelton, *see* Phillimore

Macalpine, Ida, and Hunter, Richard, *George III and the Mad Business* (London, 1969)

McKelvey, J. L., *George III and Lord Bute: The Leicester House Years* (Durham, N. C., 1973)

Mackesy, Piers, *The War for America, 1775–1783* (London, 1964)

McKown, Robin, *Thomas Paine* (London, 1962)

Mackworth-Young, Sir Robin, 'The Royal Archives, Windsor Castle', *Archives*, vol. 13, no. 59 (spring 1978)

Maclachlan, A. N. Campbell, *William Augustus, Duke of Cumberland* (London, 1876)

Magnus, Sir Philip, *Edmund Burke* (London, 1939)

Maiden, J. H., *Sir Joseph Banks: The 'Father of Australia'* (London and Sydney, 1909)

Malmesbury, James Harris, first Earl of, *Diaries and Correspondence of James Harris, first Earl of Malmesbury*, ed. the third Earl of Malmesbury (4 vols., London, 1844)

——*A Series of Letters of the first Earl of Malmesbury, his Family and Friends from 1745 to 1820*, ed. the third Earl of Malmesbury (2 vols., London, 1870)

Manvell, Roger, *Sarah Siddons: Portrait of an Actress* (London, 1970)

Marples, Morris, *The Royal Sisters* (London, 1969)

Marsden, William, *A Brief Memoir of the Life and Writings of William Marsden*, ed. Mrs E. W. Marsden (privately printed, London, 1838)

Marshall, Dorothy, *Eighteenth-Century England* (London, 1962)

Melville, Lewis, *Farmer George* (2 vols., London, 1907)

Millar, Oliver, *The Later Georgian Pictures in the Collection of Her Majesty the Queen* (2 vols., London, 1969)

——*Zoffany and his Tribuna* (London, 1967)

——*see also* Harris, John

Miller, J. C., *Origins of the American Revolution* (New York, 1949)

——*The Triumph of Freedom, 1775–83* (Boston, Mass., 1948)

Minto, Sir Gilbert Elliot, first Earl of, *Life and Letters of Sir Gilbert Elliot, first Earl of Minto from 1701 to 1806*, ed. the Countess of Minto (3 vols., London, 1874)

Mitchell, L. G., *Charles James Fox* (London, 1997)

——*Charles James Fox* and the Disintegration of the Whig Party (Oxford, 1970)

Moore, Thomas, ed., *Memoirs of the Life of the Right Hon. R. B. Sheridan* (London, 1825)

Moorhouse, E. Hallam, *Nelson in England* (London, 1913)

More, Hannah, *Letters of R. B. Johnson* (London, 1925)

Morgan, Edmund S., ed., *The American Revolution: Two Centuries of Interpretation* (Englewood Cliffs, 1965)

Morison, S. E., ed., *Sources and Documents Illustrating the American Revolution* (London, 1929)

Morris, Marilyn, *The British Monarchy and the French Revolution* (New Haven and London, 1998)

Morshead, Sir Owen, *Windsor Castle* (London, 1957)

Morton, Alan Q., *Science in the Eighteenth Century: The King George III Collection* (London, 1996)

Morton, Alan Q., and Wess, Jane, *Public and Private Science: The King George III Collection* (Oxford, 1993)

Mowl, Timothy, *Horace Walpole: The Great Outsider* (London, 1996)

Muir, Rory, *Britain and the Defeat of Napoleon* (New Haven, 1996)

Mumby, F. A., ed., *George III and the American Revolution* (London, 1924)

Murray, Lady Amelia, *Recollections of the Early Years of the Present Century* (London, 1868)

Namier, L. B., *Additions and Corrections to Sir John Fortescue's Edition of the Correspondence of George III* (London, 1937)

——*England in the Age of the American Revolution* (London, 2nd edn, 1963)

——*Personalities and Politics* (London, 1955)

——*The Structure of Politics at the Accession of George III* (London, rev. edn, 1957)

Namier, L. B., and Brooke, John, *Charles Townshend* (London, 1964)

——*The History of Parliament: House of Commons, 1754–1790* (3 vols., London, 1964)

Nelson, Horatio, Viscount, *Dispatches and Letters of Vice-Admiral Lord Viscount Nelson*, ed. Sir Harris Nicolas (London, 7 vols., 1844–6)

Nichols, John, *Literary Anecdotes of the Eighteenth Century* (9 vols., London, 1812–15)

——*Recollections and Reflections, Personal and Political, as connected with Public Affairs, during the Reign of George III* (London, 1820)

Norris, J., *Shelburne and Reform* (London, 1963)

North, Roger, *The Lives of the Norths*, ed. Augustus Jessop (3 vols., London, 1890)

Northumberland, Elizabeth Percy, Duchess of, *Diaries of a Duchess: Extracts from the Diaries of the first Duchess of Northumberland, 1716–1776*, ed. James Greig (London, 1926)

Owen, J. B., *The Eighteenth Century, 1714–1815* (London, 1974)

—— 'George II Reconsidered', in *Statesmen, Scholars and Merchants: Essays in Eighteenth-Century History presented to Dame Lucy Sutherland*, ed. Anne Whiteman, J. S. Bromley and P. G. M. Dickson (Oxford, 1973)

—— *The Rise of the Pelhams* (London, 1957)

Papendiek, Charlotte Louisa Henrietta, *Court and Private Life in the Time of Queen Charlotte: Being the Journals of Mrs Papendiek, Assistant-Keeper of the Wardrobe and Reader to Her Majesty*, ed. Mrs Vernon Delves Broughton (2 vols., London, 1887)

Pares, Richard, *George III and the Politicians* (Oxford, 1953)

Pares, Richard, and Taylor, A. J. P., eds., *Essays Presented to Sir Lewis Namier* (London, 1956)

Patten, Robert L., *George Cruikshank: Life, Times and Art*, vol. 1 (London, 1982)

Pellew, George, *The Life and Correspondence of the Right Hon. Henry Addington, first Viscount Sidmouth* (3 vols., London, 1847)

Pemberton, W. Baring, *Lord North* (London, 1938)

Pembroke, *see* Herbert

Pendered, Mary Lucy, *The Fair Quaker, Hannah Lightfoot and her Relations with George III* (London, 1910)

Peters, M., *Pitt and Popularity: The Patriot Minister and London Opinion during the Seven Years War* (Oxford, 1980)

Phillimore, Sir Robert, *Memoirs and Correspondence of George, Lord Lyttelton, from 1734 to 1773* (2 vols., London 1845)

Plumb, J. H., *The American Experience*, The Collected Essays of J. H. Plumb, vol. 2 (Athens, Georgia, 1989)

—— *The First Four Georges* (London, 1956)

Plumb, J. H., and Wheldon, Huw, *Royal Heritage: The Story of Britain's Royal Builders and Collectors* (London, 1977)

Pocock Tom, *Horatio Nelson* (London, 1987)

—— *Sailor King: The Life of King William IV* (London, 1991)

Pole, J. R., ed., *The Revolution in America 1758–1788* (London, 1970)

Porter, Roy, *English Society in the Eighteenth Century* (London, 1982)

Postgate, Raymond, *That Devil Wilkes* (London, 1956)

Pote, Joseph, *The History and Antiquities of Windsor Castle* (London, 1749)

Pottle, Frederick A., *James Boswell: The Earlier Years, 1740–1769* (London, 1966)

Powys, Caroline, *Passages from the Diaries of Mrs Philip Lybbe Powys*, ed. E. J. Climenson (London, 1899)

Prochaska, Frank, *Royal Bounty: The Making of a Welfare Monarchy* (New Haven, 1995)

Pyne, William Henry, *The History of the Royal Palaces* (3 vols., London, 1819)

Quennell, Peter, *Caroline of England* (London, 1939)

Reid, Loren, *Charles James Fox: A Man for the People* (London, 1969)

Reitan, E. A., 'The Civil List in Eighteenth-Century Politics', *Historical Journal*, vol. 9 (1966), 318–37

Report from the Committee Appointed to Examine the Physicians who Attended His Majesty (London, 1788, 1789)

Rhodes, Raymond C., *Harlequin Sheridan* (Oxford, 1933)

Richardson, Joanna, *George IV: A Portrait* (London, 1966)

Ritcheson, C. R., *British Politics and the American Revolution* (London, 1954)

Roberts, Jane, 'Sir William Chambers and George III', in Harris and Snodin, eds., *Sir William Chambers* (q.v.)

Robinson, Nicholas K., *Edmund Burke: A Life in Caricature* (New Haven, 1996)

Rockingham, *see* Albemarle

Rodger, N. A. M., *The Insatiable Earl: A Life of John Montagu, fourth Earl of Sandwich* (London, 1993)

Rogers, Samuel, *Recollections of the Table Talk of Samuel Rogers*, ed. Morchard Bishop (London, 1952)

Romilly, Sir Samuel, *Memoirs of the Life of Sir Samuel Romilly Written by Himself* (4 vols., London, 1840)

Rose, George, *The Diaries and Correspondence of the Right Hon. George Rose*, ed. The Rev. Leveson Vernon Harcourt (2 vols., London, 1860)

—— *Observations respecting the Public Expenditure and the Influence of the Crown* (London, 1810)

Rose, J. H., *Life of William Pitt* (2 vols., London, 1911)

Rudé, G. F. E., *Hanoverian London, 1714–1808* (London, 1971)

—— *Wilkes and Liberty* (London, 1962)

Russell, F., 'King George III's Pictures Hang at Buckingham House', *Burlington Magazine*, CXXIX, 1987

Sandwich, John Montagu, Earl of, *The Private Papers of John, Earl of Sandwich, First Lord of the Admiralty 1771–82*, ed. G. R. Barnes and J. H. Owen (4 vols., London, 1932–8)

Savage, Nicholas, 'The "Viceroy" of the Academy: Sir William Chambers and the Royal Protection of the Arts', in Harris and Snodin, eds., *Sir William Chambers* (q.v.)

Scholes, Percy A., *The Great Dr Burney* (London, 1947)

Schweizer, K. R., ed., *Lord Bute: Essays in Re-interpretation* (Leicester, 1988)

Scott, James Renat, *Memorials of the Family of Scott of Scots Hall* (London, 1876)

Sedgwick, Romney, ed., *Letters from George III to Lord Bute, 1756–1766* (London, 1939)

———*see also* Hervey

Seward, William, *Anecdotes of Some Distinguished Persons* (4 vols., London, 1798)

Sheridan, Betsy, *The Journal of Betsy Sheridan*, ed. W. Le Fanu (London, 1960)

Sheridan, Richard Brinsley, *The Letters of Richard Brinsley Sheridan*, ed. Cecil Price (3 vols., Oxford, 1966)

Sherrard, O. A., *The Life of Lord Chatham* (3 vols., London, 1952–8)

Sichel, Walter S., *Bolingbroke and his Times* (London, new edn, 1968)

———*Sheridan* (2 vols., London, 1909)

Sidgwick, J. B., *William Herschel* (London, 1953)

Sime, James, *William Herschel and his Work* (London, 1900)

Smith, C. D., *The Early Career of Lord North, the Prime Minister* (London, 1979)

Smith, E., *Life of Sir Joseph Banks* (London, 1911)

Smith, E. A., *Lord Grey, 1764–1845* (Oxford, 1990)

Smith, H. C., *Buckingham Palace: Its Furniture, Decoration and History* (London, 1931)

Smith, Paul H., *English Defenders of American Freedom, 1774–78* (Washington, 1972)

Smith, R. A., *Late Georgian and Regency England, 1760–1837* (Cambridge, 1984)

Sobel, Dava, *Longitude* (London, 1996)

Stanhope, Philip Henry, fifth Earl, *Life of the Right Hon. William Pitt* (4 vols., London, 1861–2)

———*Notes of Conversations with the Duke of Wellington, 1831–1851* (London, 1888)

Stockmar, Christian Friedrich von Stockmar, Baron, ed., *Memoirs of Baron Stockmar* (2 vols., London, 1872)

Stone, Lawrence, *Road to Divorce: England 1530–1987* (Oxford, 1990)

Stone, Lawrence, and Stone, Jeanne C. Fawtier, *An Open Elite? England 1540–1880* (Oxford, 1984)

Stroud, Dorothy, *Henry Holland* (London, 1966)

Stuart, Dorothy Margaret, *The Daughters of George III* (London, 1939)

———*Life and Times of Lady Elizabeth Foster* (London, 1955)

Taylor, Sir Herbert, *The Taylor Papers: Being a Record of Certain Reminiscences, Letters and Journals in the Life of Lieut.-Gen. Sir Herbert Taylor*, ed. Ernest Taylor (London, 1913)

Taylor, Joseph, *Relics of Royalty or Remarks, Anecdotes and Amusements of George III* (London, 1820)

Temple, *see* Grenville

Thomas, Peter D. G., *British Politics and the Stamp Act Crisis* (Oxford, 1975)

———'George III and the American Revolution', *History*, vol. 70, no. 228 (Feb. 1985)

—— *The House of Commons in the Eighteenth Century* (London, 1971)
—— *John Wilkes: A Friend to Liberty* (London, 1996)
—— *Lord North* (London, 1976)
—— *Tea Party to Independence* (Oxford, 1991)
—— 'Thoughts on the British Constitution by George III in 1760', *Historical Research. The Bulletin of the Institute of Historical Research*, vol. 60, no. 143 (Oct. 1987)
—— *The Townshend Duties Crisis* (Oxford, 1987)
Thompson, F. M. L., ed., *The Cambridge Social History of Britain, 1750–1850* (Cambridge, 1990)
Thomson, M. A., *A Constitutional History of England, 1640–1801* (London, 1938)
'Thormanby' [Willmott Dixon], *Kings of the Hunting Field* (London, 1899)
Thrale, Hester, *Thraliana*, ed., Katherine Balderston (2 vols., Oxford, 2nd edn, 1951)
Tighe, Robert Richard, and Davis, James Edward, *Annals of Windsor, being a History of the Castle and Town* (London, 1858)
Tillyard, Stella, *Aristocrats: Caroline, Emily, Louisa and Sarah Lennox, 1740–1832* (London, 1994)
Tomalin, Claire, *Mrs Jordan's Profession: The Story of a Great Actress and a Future King* (London, 1994)
Trench, Charles Chenevix, *Portrait of a Patriot: A Biography of John Wilkes* (Edinburgh, 1962)
—— *George II* (London, 1973)
—— *The Royal Malady* (London, 1964)
Trevelyan, Sir George Otto, *The American Revolution* (3 vols., London, 1905)
—— *George III and Charles Fox* (2 vols., London, 1912–14)
Trimmer, Sarah, *Some Account of the Life and Writings of Mrs Trimmer* (2 vols., London, 1814)
Tucker, R. W., and Hendrickson, D. C., *The Fall of the First British Empire* (Baltimore, 1982)
Tunstall, W. C. B., *William Pitt, Earl of Chatham* (London, 1938)
Turberville, A. S., *The House of Lords in the 18th Century* (Oxford, 1927)
—— ed., *Johnson's England* (2 vols., Oxford, 1933)
Turner, E. S., *The Court of St James's* (London, 1959)
Twiss, Horace, *The Public and Private Life of Lord Chancellor Eldon* (3 vols., London, 1844)
Uglow, Jenny, *Hogarth: A Life and a World* (London, 1997)
Valentine, A. C., *Lord George Germain* (London, 1962)
—— *Lord North* (2 vols., Norman, 1967)
Van der Kiste, John, *King George II and Queen Caroline* (Far Thrupp, Stroud, 1997)

441

Van Tyne, Claud H., *Causes of the War of Independence* (Boston, Mass., 1922)

Von Erffa, H., and Staley, A., *The Paintings of Benjamin West* (New Haven and London, 1986)

Vulliamy, C. E., *Royal George* (London, 1937)

Waldegrave, James, second Earl, *The Memoirs and Speeches of James, second Earl Waldegrave, 1742–1763*, ed. and intro. J. C. D. Clark (Cambridge, 1989)

Walpole, Horace, *Last Journals*, ed. A. Francis Steuart (2 vols., London, 1910)

——*Letters*, ed. Mrs Paget Toynbee (19 vols., London, 1918–25)

——*Memoirs of the Last Ten Years of the Reign of George the Second*, ed. Lord Holland (2 vols., London, 1822)

——*Memoirs of the Reign of King George III*, ed. G. F. R. Barker (4 vols., London, 1894)

——*Memoirs of King George II*, ed. John Brooke (3 vols., New Haven, 1985)

——*Reminiscences Written by Horace Walpole in 1788*, ed. Paget Toynbee (Oxford, 1924)

——*Selected Letters of Horace Walpole*, ed. W. S. Lewis (New Haven, 1973)

——*Walpoliana*, ed. John Pinkerton (London, 1894)

——*The Yale Edition of Horace Walpole's Correspondence* (48 vols., New Haven, 1937–83)

Watson, J. S., *The Reign of George III, 1760–1815* (Oxford, 1960)

Weinreb, Ben, and Hibbert, Christopher, eds., *The London Encyclopaedia* (London, 2nd edn, 1993)

Wendorff, Richard, *Sir Joshua Reynolds: The Painter in Society* (London, 1996)

Wesley, John, *Selections from the Journal of John Wesley*, ed. Hugh Martin (London, 1955)

Wess, *see* Morton

White, R. J., *The Age of George III* (London, 1968)

Whiteley, Peter, *Lord North: The Prime Minister Who Lost America* (London, 1996)

Whitley, William T., *Thomas Gainsborough* (London, 1915)

Wickwire, Franklin, and Wickwire, Mary, *Cornwallis and the War of Independence* (London, 1970)

Wilkins, W. H., *Mrs Fitzherbert and George IV* (2 vols., London, 1905)

Willcox, William B., *Portrait of a General: Sir Henry Clinton in the War of Independence* (New York, 1964)

Williams, A. F. B., *The Life of William Pitt, Earl of Chatham* (2 vols., London, 1913)

Williams, Clare, *Sophie in London* (London, 1933)

Williams, E. N., ed., *The Eighteenth-Century Constitution: Documents and Commentary* (Cambridge, 1960)

Willis, G. M., *Ernest Augustus, Duke of Cumberland and King of Hanover* (London, 1954)

Wilson, B., *George III as Man, Monarch and Statesman* (London, 1907)

Windham, W., ed., *The Windham Papers* (2 vols., London, 1973)

Winstanley, D. A., *Lord Chatham and the Whig Opposition* (London, 1912)

——*Personal and Party Government in the Reign of George III* (London, 1910)

Wraxall, C. F. L., *Life and Times of Caroline Matilda* (London, 1864)

Wraxall, Sir N. W., *Historical Memoirs of My Own Time* (2 vols., London, 1815)

——*Posthumous Memoirs of His Own Time* (3 vols., London, 1836)

——*A Short Review of the Political State of Great Britain* (London, 1787)

Wrottesley, Hon. George, *The Life and Correspondence of Field Marshal Sir John Burgoyne, Bart.* (2 vols., London, 1873)

Wynn, Frances Williams, *Diaries of a Lady of Quality for 1797 to 1844*, ed. A. Hayward (London, 1864)

Wyvill, Christopher, *Political Papers* (6 vols., York, 1794–1802)

Yorke, P. C., *Life and Correspondence of Philip Yorke, Earl of Hardwicke* (3 vols., London, 1913)

Young, Sir George, *Poor Fred: The People's Prince* (Oxford, 1937)

Ziegler, Philip, *Addington: A Life of Henry Addington, first Viscount Sidmouth* (London, 1965)

——*William IV* (London, 1971)

INDEX

Before his accession George III is referred to as Prince George; after his accession as G.III. Queen Charlotte is referred to as Q.C. and their eldest son as P. of W.

Markham, William, Bishop of Chester, *later* Archbishop of York (1719–1807), 100–101, 223, 375

Marlborough, Duchess of (d. 1811), 377–8

Marlborough, George Spencer, 4th Duke of (1739–1817), 31, 188

Mary, Princess (1776–1857): and her Papa, 99; bored by Weymouth holidays, 379–80; marries, 384; and Princess Amelia, 394, 399; on Q.C, 402; proposals for comforting her parents, 402–3

Meadows, John, 397

Mecklenburg-Strelitz, Adolph Frederick IV, Duke of (b. 1738), 42, 96

Mecklenburg-Strelitz, Dowager Duchess of (d. 1761), 41

Medmenham Monks, 116, 117

Melbourne, Peniston Lamb, 1st Viscount (1748–1819), 328

Mercier, Philippe (1689–1760), 10

Miller, John, 194

Milliken, Michael, 98

Milman, Sir Francis (1746–1821), 340, 344

Minto, Earl of, *see* Elliot, Sir Gilbert

Moira, Francis Rawdon-Hastings, 2nd Earl of, *later* 1st Marquess of Hastings (1754–1826), 336

Molesworth, Lady (d. 1763), 211

Mongenêt, Thérèse-Bernardine, 364

Montagu, Lady Lucy (d. 1734), 138n

Montagu, the Hon. Mary (1746–1840), 79

Montagu, Lady Mary Wortley (1689–1762), 22

Moore, John, Archbishop of Canterbury (1730–1805), 197, 245, 328, 375

Moore, Sir John (1761–1809), 376, 389

More, Hannah (1745–1833), 276

Mozart, Wolfgang Amadeus (1756–91), 75

Mudge, Thomas (1717–94), 195

Münchausen, Philip Adolphus, Baron von, 36

Murray, Lady Augusta (c. 1762–1830), 370, 371–2

Murray, John, 59

Neale, Sir Harry (1765–1840), 319

Nelson, Horatio, *later* Viscount Nelson (1758–1805), 81–2, 361, 386

Nelson, William Nelson, 1st Earl (1757–1835), 386

Newbattle, William Kerr, Lord (1737–1815), 37–8

Newcastle, Thomas Pelham-Holles, Duke of (1693–1768): and Hayter, 16; and Stone, 16; personality, 27, 85; Prince George's opinion of, 27; and Prince George's request for military employment, 28; G.III and, 34, 85–6, 88, 124; First Lord of the Treasury, 35; and G.III's marriage, 41; his house, 57; resigns, 88; Cumberland and, 108; and Pitt, 110; Lord Privy Seal, 114; left out of Administration, 126; Wilkes riots, 132

Nicholson, Margaret, 226

Nollekens, Joseph (1737–1823), 196n

North, Francis North, 7th Baron, *later* 1st Earl of Guilford (1704–90), 12, 15, 159–60

North, Frederick, *later* 2nd Earl of Guilford, *better known as* Lord North (1732–92): Leader of the House, 138; appearance, 138; physical resemblance between G.III and, 138n; personality, 139, 156; and War of American Independence, 151, 156–7, 162; Fox condemns, 152; protests his inadequacy, 157–8; and Chatham, 158; G.III's generosity to, 159; financial affairs, 159–60; to remain in office, 160; tenders resignation, 163; resignation speech, 164; Royal Marriages Act, 173; Keppel riots, 215; and appeal against Catholic Relief Bill, 218; relations with G.III, 234; and Drummond's Bank debt, 234; and Fox–North coalition, 234–5; Secretary for Home and Colonial Affairs, 235; in Sayers's caricature, 244; and seals of office, 245; G.III on, 280 and n; G.III's compassion for, 286

North America (*see also* War of American Independence): Britain and administration of territories in, 122; violent opposition to Stamp Act, 123; clashes